D1606450

IN MIST APPARELLED

RELIGIOUS THEMES
IN PLUTARCH'S MORALIA AND LIVES

BY

FREDERICK E. BRENK, S.J.

LUGDUNI BATAVORUM E. J. BRILL MCMLXXVII

IN MIST APPARELLED

RELIGIOUS THEMES
IN PLUTARCH'S MORALIA AND LIVES

MNEMOSYNE

BIBLIOTHECA CLASSICA BATAVA

COLLEGERUNT

W. DEN BOER • W. J. VERDENIUS • R. E. H. WESTENDORP BOERMA

BIBLIOTHECAE FASCICULOS EDENDOS CURAVIT

W. J. VERDENIUS, HOMERUSLAAN 53, ZEIST

SUPPLEMENTUM QUADRAGESIMUM OCTAVUM

FREDERICK E. BRENK, S.J.

IN MIST APPARELLED

RELIGIOUS THEMES
IN PLUTARCH'S MORALIA AND LIVES

LUGDUNI BATAVORUM E. J. BRILL MCMLXXVII

IN MIST APPARELLED

RELIGIOUS THEMES
IN PLUTARCH'S MORALIA AND LIVES

BY

FREDERICK E. BRENK, S.J.

LUGDUNI BATAVORUM E. J. BRILL MCMLXXVII

PA
4383
.B9

ISBN   90 04 05241 0

FRANCISCO SANDBACH,

DOCTISSIMO VIRO,
OPTIMO MAGISTRO

MULIERIQUE MARIAE

TABLE OF CONTENTS

PREFACE

To write perfectly on Plutarch one should have a perfect knowledge of all Greek and Roman literature, philosophy, religion, and art up to his time—awesome if not impossible. The reader's indulgence is asked for many inadequacies. I have tried to approach the subject from the inner bond which ties his work together and from an understanding of his total contribution. Hopefully this study will shed light on Plutarch as a warm and intelligent religious and literary personage who deeply loved classical civilization and thought it more valuable to pass over its shortcomings than highlight its faults. He was a representative of a period in which men looked back with nostalgia on the remarkable changes which had taken place in preceding culture and history, without being aware of all the changes going on within themselves. This subtle shift of emphasis and conception, joined to a healthy eclecticism and broadmindedness, lends a certain elusiveness to his thought which has defied generations of scholars. A peculiar combination of originality and use of others' ideas makes him a most valuable, even if sometimes baffling, person with which to approach his age.

I am very much endebted to Professor F. H. Sandbach of Trinity College, Cambridge, who was my director at that university and has given me much encouragement and assistance since. Professor Robert Flacelière of the École Normale Supérieure at Paris kindly invited me to speak at the Budé Congrès at Paris during that time. I am greatly endebted to Professors Hubert Martin and John Scarborough of the University of Kentucky. In one way or another I am also endebted to Professors E. N. O'Neil of the University of California at Los Angeles, C. P. Jones of the University of Toronto, D. A. Russell of St. John's College, Oxford, Thomas Kraabel of the University of Minnesota, Heinrich Dörrie of Münster, Ernst Badian of Harvard, Heinz-Gerd Ingenkamp of Bonn, and John Dillon of the University of California at Berkeley. I am grateful to Professor Martin, Patricia Brannan, J. Patrick Donnelly, S. J., Thomas A. Caldwell, S.J., and Jacqueline Strand for work with the manuscript and proofs.

Marquette University
August 1976

REFERENCES TO THE *MORALIA* CITED IN THIS WORK

Ad princ. inerud.	=	Ad principem ineruditum
Adv. Col.	=	Adversus Colotem
Amat.	=	Amatorius
An sen.	=	An seni respublica gerenda sit
An virt. doc.	=	An virtus doceri possit
An vitios.	=	An vitiositas ad infelicitatem sufficiat
Ap. Lac.	=	Apophthegmata Laconica
Aqu. an ign.	=	Aquane an ignis sit utilior
Bell. an pac.	=	Bellone an pace clariores fuerint Athenienses
Brut. an.	=	Bruta animalia ratione uti, or Gryllus
Coniug. praec.	=	Coniugalia praecepta
Consol. ad Apoll.	=	Consolatio ad Apollonium
Consol. ad ux.	=	Consolatio ad uxorem
De Alex. fort.	=	De Alexandri magni fortuna aut virtute
De amor. prol.	=	De amore prolis
De an. procr.	=	De animae procreatione in Timaeo
De cohib. ir.	=	De cohibenda ira
De comm. not.	=	De communibus notitiis adversus Stoicos
De def.	=	De defectu oraculorum
De E.	=	De E apud Delphos
De es. carn.	=	De esu carnium
De exil.	=	De exilio
De fac.	=	De facie quae in orbe lunae apparet
De fort.	=	De fortuna
De fort. Rom.	=	De fortuna Romanorum
De frat. amor.	=	De fraterno amore
De garr.	=	De garrulitate
De gen. Soc.	=	De genio Socratis
De Her. malign.	=	De Herodoti malignitate
De invid. et od.	=	De invidia et odio
De Is.	=	De Iside et Osiride
De lat. viv.	=	De latenter vivendo
De mus.	=	De musica
De placit. phil.	=	De placitis philosophorum
De prim. frig.	=	De primo frigido
De Pyth.	=	De Pythiae oraculis
De se ips.	=	De se ipsum citra invidiam laudando
De ser. num.	=	De sera numinis vindicta
De soll. an.	=	De sollertia animalium
De Stoic. repugn.	=	De Stoicorum repugnantiis
De superst.	=	De superstitione
De tranq. an.	=	De tranquillitate animi
De tu. san.	=	De tuenda sanitate praecepta
De virt. et vit.	=	De virtute et vitio
De virt. mor.	=	De virtute morali
De vit. aer. al.	=	De vitando aere alieno
De vitios. pud.	=	De vitioso pudore
Fr.	=	Fragmenta

Inst. Lac.	=	Instituta Laconica
Lac. ap.	=	Lacaenarum apophthegmata
Max. cum. princip.	=	Maxime cum principibus philosopho esse disserendum
Mul. virt.	=	Mulierum virtutes
Non poss.	=	Non posse suaviter vivi secundum Epicurum
Par. Graec. et Rom.	=	Parallela Graeca et Romana
Praec. ger. reipub.	=	Praecepta gerendae reipublicae
Qu. conv.	=	Quaestiones convivales
Qu. Graec.	=	Quaestiones Graecae
Qu. nat.	=	Quaestiones naturales
Qu. Plat.	=	Quaestiones Platonicae
Qu. Rom.	=	Quaestiones Romanae
Quomod. adul.	=	Quomodo adulescens poetas audire debeat
Quomod. adulat.	=	Quomodo adulator ab amico internoscatur
Quomod. quis suos.	=	Quomodo quis suos in virtute sentiat profectus
Reg. et imper. ap.	=	Regum et imperatorum apophthegmata
Sept. sap. conv.	=	Septem sapientium convivium

REFERENCES TO THE *LIVES*

Aem.	=	Aemilius Paullus	Galb.	=	Galba
Ages.	=	Agesilaus	G. Gracch.	=	Gaius Gracchus
Ag.	=	Agis	T. Gracch.	=	Tiberius Gracchus
Alc.	=	Alcibiades	Luc.	=	Lucullus
Alex.	=	Alexander	Lyc.	=	Lycourgos
Ant.	=	Antony	Lys.	=	Lysander
Arat.	=	Aratos	Marc.	=	Marcellus
Arist.	=	Aristides	Mar.	=	Marius
Art.	=	Artaxerxes	Nic.	=	Nicias
Brut.	=	Brutus	Num.	=	Numa
Caes.	=	Caesar	Oth.	=	Otho
Cam.	=	Camillus	Pel.	=	Pelopidas
Cat. mai.	=	Cato the Elder	Per.	=	Pericles
Cat. min.	=	Cato the Younger	Philop.	=	Philopoimen
Cic.	=	Cicero	Phoc.	=	Phocion
Cim.	=	Cimon	Pomp.	=	Pompey
Cleom.	=	Cleomenes	Pop.	=	Poplicola
Cor.	=	Coriolanus	Pyr.	=	Pyrrhos
Crass.	=	Crassus	Rom.	=	Romulus
Demet.	=	Demetrios	Sert.	=	Sertorius
Demos.	=	Demosthenes	Sol.	=	Solon
Dion	=	Dion	Sul.	=	Sulla
Eum.	=	Eumenes	Them.	=	Themistocles
Fab.	=	Fabius Maximus	Thes.	=	Theseus
Flam.	=	Flamininus	Timol.	=	Timoleon

INTRODUCTION

Few people are aware of the vast range of Plutarch's writings, and even many classical scholars are not aware of the enormous diversity of the *Moralia*. The last years, however, have seen a great resurgence in Plutarchan studies. A testimony to this was the VIIIe Congrès de l'Association Guillaume Budé, which was dedicated to Plutarch, a meeting attended by scholars from around the world. But since then, there has been a constant flow of important books and articles on Plutarch. Each one relies in some way on the work of a predecessor, especially on the foundations laid by Konrat Ziegler and Robert Flacelière, tireless workers in this field. This work itself would be impossible without the many studies both on Plutarch's work in general and in particular aspects of it which have appeared in recent years.[1]

This work is primarily concerned with the development and nature of Plutarch's thought in so far as it touches upon religious problems, in the hope that it may give us a better understanding of the period in which he lived. Only one who has worked in the field for some time can realize how many challenges it offers. Many apparent or real contradictions appear in the vast Plutarchan corpus, which is greater than that surviving from any other classical author up to his time, and yet it is only a part of what he actually wrote. We are faced with the problem of sources, relative chronology, lost philosophy and history, religious developments, social customs, literature, and foreign influence, all of which can at times be both baffling and maddening. In short, Plutarch is an immense challenge

---

[1] An admirable survey of work up to that time on Plutarch was given by R. Flacelière as an introduction to the Budé Congrès volume on Plutarch, entitled, "L'état présent des études sur Plutarque," pp. 483-505. New editions of individual works which have appeared since then can be found in the beginning of the bibliography. The most important works outside these are C. P. Jones, *Plutarch and Rome* (Oxford: 1971), H. Ingenkamp, *Plutarchs Schriften über die Heilung der Seele* (Göttingen: 1971), H. Görgemanns, *Untersuchungen zu Plutarchs Dialog De facie in orbe lunae* (Heidelberg: 1972), B. Bucher-Isler, *Norm und Individualität in den Biographien Plutarchs* (Bern: 1972), D. A. Russell, *Plutarch* (London: 1973), A. E. Wardman, *Plutarch's Lives* (London: 1974), H. Adam, *Plutarchs Schrift Non Posse Suaviter Vivi Secundum Epicurum* (Amsterdam: 1974), and J. Dillon, *The Middle Platonists* (London: 1976), which contains a chapter on Plutarch.

to the classical scholar and has attracted people of quite different scholarly backgrounds.

At times an attempt has been made in this work to fill out an area otherwise only lightly touched upon by previous studies. At other times a whole new topic has been developed, such as Plutarch's use of dreams. The most controversial subject is that normally referred to as Plutarch's demonology. The word "daimonology" has used been throughout this work and *daimones* in place of "demons." Although one should coin words with reluctance, there are a number of good reasons for avoiding the very loaded term "demonology." First, modern classical scholars tend more and more to use words which most convey the meaning of the Greek originals, and when possible or necessary they prefer to use the ancient word. A modern reader sees a type of creature like Hieronymus Bosch's devils in the word "demon;" and, though at times a *daimon* is this sort of creature in Greek thought, a *daimon* may just as well be the divinity itself, a god, a minor god, a good spirit, fate or fortune, or the soul or the higher part of the soul. These meanings are often related, punned upon, or unclear in a particular passage. For this reason the word "demonology" seems woefully inadequate, whereas the word "daimonology" allows the ambiguity of the Greek to remain. Moreover, even when speaking of demons, such scholars as Guthrie prefer now to use the word *daimones*.

On the subject of the evil *daimones* I have taken a rather unorthodox stand—one jokingly described by Flacelière as *téméraire*—but I feel that it flows out of, rather than contradicts, the work of such great Plutarchists as Ziegler and Flacelière. My main point is that previous works have not given sufficient attention to the *personae* or nature of an essay when treating this topic, or taken into consideration all that Plutarch said on a particular subject, but rather have concentrated, in a misleading way, on an individual essay in the *Moralia*. Since the *Vitae* are usually totally or at least to a large extent neglected when treating Plutarch's attitude toward *daimones*, an attempt has been made to incorporate a large amount of material from the *Lives*. Coming as it does in Middle-Platonism, the daimonology has great bearing upon the development of ancient philosophy, and for our understanding of classical thought in this period. It is for this reason that it has so much interested scholars in the past, and it will be hoped that the reader will be indulgent for the amount of space devoted to this subject.

Before getting into some of the more particular problems in Plutarch's religion, a few words about some past trends in Plutarchan scholarship are in order. A few ghosts still flit around this house. First, something must be said about that great Gorgon, *Quellenforschung*. The 19th Century could almost be captioned, "the Quest for Quellen." The enormous influence of this method on biblical studies cannot be overlooked, and scholars were hopeful that the same results might be achieved in classical endeavors.[2] The reconstruction of Greek history and historians between Xenophon and Tacitus was there for the patient and ambitious soul—or so they believed. Unfortunately their hopes were largely shattered. Far less encouraging was the reconstruction of Greek philosophy for the same period. Here the results proved to be more illusory. For both studies Plutarch was the mainstay, and so the 19th Century bibliography is filled with source criticism of Plutarch, laboring under the belief that he must have lifted page by page from an author previously only known by name. The colossal failure by Reinhardt to reconstruct the philosophy of Poseidonios by this method [3] stands as a monument to the whole

---

[2] One of the first studies on Plutarch in the 19th Century looked to source criticism for salvation from the contradictions contained within his daimonological writings: G. Schömann, *Opuscula academica*, I, p. 371 ff. —described in F. Bock, *Untersuchungen zu Plutarchs Schrift De genio Socratis* (Munich: 1910), pp. 6-8. Wild impetus to the movement was given by R. Schmertosch, *De Plutarchi sententiarum quae ad divinationem spectant origine* (Leipzig: 1889) who found Xenocrates lurking behind two daimonological speeches. In *Xenokrates* (Leipzig: 1892), R. Heinze managed to distinguish the parts "lifted" from Xenocrates from those "lifted" from Poseidonios. R. Hirzel, *Der Dialog*, II (Leipzig: 1895), p. 157, was more ingenious: in the same speeches he discovered three Stoic sources, and Dicaiarchos! E. Norden, *Kommentar zum Sechsten Buch der Aeneis* (Leipzig: 1903), pp. 22-48, and M. Adler, *Quibus ex fontibus Plutarchus libellum "De facie in orbe lunae" hauserit*. (Diss. Vienna: 1910), p. 87 ff., settled on Poseidonios. H. von Arnim took a similar tack: the views were too diverse to have been thought out by Plutarch; and must, therefore, have been from an eclectic Platonist of the 1st Century; Plutarch himself did not realize that what he was putting together was irreconcilable, *Plutarch über Dämonen und Mantik* (Amsterdam: 1921), p. 42. No modern scholar today subscribes to such views.

[3] *Kosmos und Sympathie* (Munich: 1926) Reinhardt's views were based on Cumont's hypothesis that Poseidonios was the father of solar eschatology, an hypothesis shattered by R. Jones in "Posidonius and Solar Eschatology," *Class. Philol.*, 27 (1932), 113-31. P. Boyancé in a later study followed Jones in refuting Reinhardt and Cumont, *Études sur le Songe de Scipion* (Paris: 1936), pp. 78-104.

effort, which was largely the work of German scholars. Yet, even in the 1940's Guy Soury was looking for an immediate source for Plutarch's daimonology, hopefully a Semitic one.[4] By a quirk of fate the end result has been beneficial: it has pointed to the limits of credibility in the approach, and to the originality of Plutarch himself. The recent excellent studies by Stadter and Martin [5] point conclusively in this direction, and they have behind them the previous work of Jones [6] and Hamilton [7].

Another ghost of past Plutarchan scholarship is that of Plutarch's Stoic eclecticism. This ghost was largely laid to rest by R. Jones in his study of Plutarch's Platonism.[8] More recent efforts have studied

---

[4] *La Démonologie de Plutarque* (Paris: 1942). In general Soury looks for Pythagorean influence in the daimonological treatises, following G. Méautis, *Recherches sur le Pythagorisme* (Neuchatel: 1922), and P. Boyancé, "Les deux génies personnels dans l'antiquité grecque et latine," *Rev. de Philol.*, 79 (1935), 189-202. However, he was unable to shake off completely the traces of Cumont and Reinhardt.

[5] P. Stadter, *Plutarch's Historical Methods, an Analysis of Mulierum Virtutes* (Harvard: 1965); and H. Martin, Jr., "Plutarch's Citation of Empedocles at *Amatorius* 756D," *Greek, Roman, and Byzantine Studies*, 10 (1969), 57-70, and "*Amatorius*, 756 E-F: Plutarch's Citation of Parmenides and Hesiod," *AJP*, 90 (1969), 183-200. Both strongly object to the hypothesis of *Mittelquellen*, and firmly uphold Plutarch's originality. Among others who have been important in attacking the idea of *Mittelquellen* have been A. W. Gomme, *A Historical Commentary on Thucydides* I (Oxford: 1945), pp. 54-84; A. Dihle, *Studien zur Griechischen Biographie* (Göttingen: 1956); and H. Erbse, "Die Bedeutung der Synkrisis in den Parallelbiographien Plutarchs," *Hermes*, 84 (1956), 398-424; D. A. Russell, *Plutarch*, pp. 42-62; C. P. Jones, *Plutarch and Rome*, pp. 80-87; and Flacelière in his general introduction to the *Vies* and in the introduction to almost every *Life*. One can also consult Wardman, *Plutarch's Lives*, pp. 80-87, and finally Ziegler, *Plutarchos von Chaironeia* (Stuttgart: 1964), pp. 273-276. This is the standard reference work on Plutarch and can be consulted on almost every question which occurs on the general background of his works.

[6] *The Platonism of Plutarch* (Menasha: 1916). However, the earliest school of French and German scholars, e.g. Zeller and Gréard, looked upon Plutarch either as a Platonist or in Zeller's terms as a "Pythagoraisirende (sic) Platoniker." See Bock, pp. 6-18; O. Gréard, *De la Morale de Plutarque* (Paris: 1866), p. 336; Zeller, *Philosophie der Griechen* III, 2 (1852), pp. 193-94; G. Ettig, "Acheruntica," *Leipziger Studien*, 13 (1891), 329.

[7] W. Hamilton, "The Myth in Plutarch's De Facie," *CQ*, 28 (1934), 24-30 and "The Myth in Plutarch's De Genio," *CQ*, 28 (1934), 176-82. In an attempt to derive all Plutarch's inspiration from Plato, Hamilton—and to some extent Jones—put Plutarch's work slightly out of historical perspective.

[8] The studies by Hamilton, cited above, belong to this trend of thought. No one has questioned since that the myths owe their inspiration primarily and almost exclusively to Plato. Cf. H. Cherniss' introduction to *De facie*,

the nature of his Aristotelianism [9] and Stoicism and his reaction against one or the other, but at the same time they do not fail to emphasize Plutarch's creative cast of mind. Very important in this direction is the study of Plutarch's reaction to the Stoics, by Daniel Babut, who goes at great length through the whole Plutarchan corpus—and even some pseudo works found there—to show the extent of this influence.[10]

Much effort has been given to establish the relative chronology of Plutarch's works, and the recent work of C. P. Jones has put it on a sounder basis than ever before.[11] The effort has used every conceivable technique from metrics to internal evidence. Much has been achieved, but to be honest, for the development of Plutarch's religious thought, one is often reduced to sheer speculation. The lure of relative chronology has even seduced a few scholars to an overhasty reliance upon it in establishing an hypothesis. For instance, one of the most solid achievements of Jones' study was thought to be the dating of *De Iside et Osiride* through the character to whom it is dedicated. Yet, recently doubt has been cast upon this, on the basis of a possible case of mistaken identity.[12]

Loeb, *Mor.* XII (1957), pp. 2-33. But in a number of articles H. Dörrie has attempted to study the influences upon him. Of most importance is "Die Stellung Plutarchs im Platonismus seiner Zeit," *Philomathes* (Merlan Festschrift) R. Palmer, ed. (The Hague: 1971), pp. 36-56. In *Plutarch et le Stoïcisme* (Paris: 1969), D. Babut has attempted to relate him to Stoicism, and J. E. Whittaker, "Ammonius on the Delphic E," *CQ*, 19 (1969), pp. 185-192, suggests, in a stimulating article, links with Neopythagoreanism. See also my article, "From Mysticism to Mysticism; the Religious Development of Plutarch of Chaironeia," *Soc. of Bibl. Lit. Seminar Papers*,1 (1975), 193-198, and J. Dillon, *The Middle Platonists*, pp. 189-229, who also is intrigued by the influences of Neopythagoreanism and Alexandrian Platonism upon him.

[9] See G. Verbeke, "Plutarch and the Development of Aristotle," I. Düring and G.E.L. Owen eds., *Aristotle and Plato in the Mid-Fourth Century* (Göteborg: 1960), pp. 235-38. Verbeke is much impressed with Plutarch's understanding of Aristotle.

[10] *Plutarque et le Stoïcisme* (Paris: 1969). Babut—who follows some disappointing conclusions of Soury on Plutarch's daimonology—attempts to justify his belief of growing superstition in Plutarch's writings; but his study of Plutarch's reaction to Stoicism is extremely important for placing Plutarch in his own period.

[11] C. P. Jones, "Towards a Chronology of Plutarch's Works," *JRS*, 56 (1966), 61-74, and *Plutarch and Rome*, pp. 135-37.

[12] G. W. Bowersock, "Some Persons in Plutarch's Moralia," *CQ*, 15 (1965), 267-70, and Jones, pp. 71 and 73, thought that the Clea on two inscriptions was the same as the Clea to whom the treatise is dedicated, but now E. Kapetanopoulos, "Klea and Leontis, Two Ladies from Delphi," *Bull. de*

The relative chronology of the *Lives* still seems to be in hot dispute, due to the puzzling and contradictory cross-references contained within them. Here again, scholars have recently seen the need to question or modify previous theories.

Since much of the importance of this work depends upon the value of the investigation into Plutarch's daimonology, it seems well to explain why the whole affair has become so involved. In spite of a word of caution now and then from prominent scholars, it is often almost tacitly understood or taken without question that Plutarch believed ardently in evil *daimones* (to use the Greek term, *daimon*, which is more general and philosophically more significant than the English, demon,[13] French, *démon*, or German *Dämon*). The more loaded terms of the modern languages may in fact be responsible for some of the confusion in interpreting the Greek word in a context, since translators are often only too eager to translate "demon" where another possibility is left open by the Greek. Moreover, it is implied that Plutarch moved as a youth

---

Corr. Hell., 90 (1966), 119 ff. thinks that two women are involved. See Babut, p. 145 n. 3. However, Flacelière, *Budé Congrès*, p. 487, does not accept Kapetanopoulos' argument.

[13] Traditionally scholars have tended to systematize Plutarch's daimonology from the disparate treatises and characters of his dialogues, and to picture it as very close to Neoplatonism: so Zeller, III, 2, p. 193 ff.; Pohl, *Die Dämonologie des Plutarch* (Breslau: 1859)—the first monograph on the daimonology, but uncritical and largely a repetition of Zeller; Gréard, *De La Morale de Plutarque*, p. 336 ff.; R. Volkmann, *Leben, Schriften und Philosophie des Plutarch von Chaeronea* II (Berlin: 1896), pp. 247-323, esp. pp. 292-323; R. Hirzel, *Der Dialog*, II (Leipzig: 1895), who called it the "eigentlicher Mittelpunkt von Plutarchs religiösen Ansichten," p. 157; and M. Pohlenz, who described his daimonology as more Neoplatonic than that of Maximus of Tyre or Apuleius, *Vom Zorne Gottes* (Göttingen: 1909), pp. 136-37. The opposition is rather slight; R. Trench, *Plutarch* (London: 1873) did not mention the *daimones*; R. Fabricius, *Zur Religiösen Anschauungsweise des Plutarch* (Königsberg: 1879), only mentions the *daimon* of Caesar in *Caes.* 69—which he took to mean the divinity; Eisele sarcastically called the whole business "die imaginäre Dämonologie Plutarchs," and insisted that all the canons of Platonic scholarship were being violated in the case of Plutarch, "Zur Dämonologie des Plutarchs von Chäronea," *Arch. f. Gesch. d. Philos.*, 17 (1904), 43-50, but his overly restricted view of the *daimon* as "die besondere Kraft der enthusiastisch veranlagten Seele" and the real daimonic power as the evil precosmic soul, caused him to be ignored; Bock, p. 49, ridicules the comparison made between Plato's Ideas and Plutarch's demons as the basis of a philosophical system; and Jones, p. 39, speaks with reservation about Plutarch's commitment. However, B. Latzarus, *Les Idées Religieuses de Plutarque* (Paris: 1920); E. Seillière, "La religion de Plutarque," *Séances et Travaux de l'Académie des Sciences Morales*, 181 (1921), 422-34; and to a large extent Soury, return to the views

from rational scepticism to a restrained mysticism in later life.[14] Both these positions sometimes depend on gross clumsiness in handling the relative or assumed relative chronology of a dialogue, and in failing to appreciate the nature of the statements made in their context, or to take into consideration other essays or statements made by Plutarch on the same subject, or to assess the role of the speaker, or to note the ambiguity of a passage. It is the opinion of this author that Plutarch's belief in *daimones* is much more sceptical and more complicated than most scholars would lead one to believe, and that the descriptions of it in the histories of philosophy are often if not a pure fiction, at least downright misleading.[15]

---

of Zeller; as does J. Moellering, *Plutarch on Superstition* (Boston: 1963), pp. 156-57. H. Erbse, "Plutarchs Schrift *Peri Deisidaimonias*," *Hermes*, 70 (1952), 296-314, minimizes the supposed differences in the development of Plutarch's thought and attempts to make use of relative chronology; but he does not seem to escape from Zeller's presuppositions completely. The same can be said for Babut who seems to be looking for an uninterrupted move toward Neoplatonism in Plutarch's writings.

[14] For the difficulty of the problems involved, see the articles by Soury and Flacelière debating the relative importance and chronology of the daimonology: "Plutarque, Prêtre de Delphes, L'Inspiration prophétique," *REG*, 55 (1942), 50-69; "Plutarque et la Pythie," *REG*, 56 (1943), 72-111; and the commentary on their views by V. Goldschmidt, "Les thèmes du 'De Defectu Oraculorum' de Plutarque," *REG*, 61 (1948), 298-302—who in general supports Flacelière (anti-demonology) against Soury. Soury's disregard of chronology and *personae dialogi* is criticized by M. Pohlenz in his review of Soury's book, *Gnom.*, 21 (1949), 347-54. Ziegler takes a very moderate stand, limiting Plutarch's belief in *daimones* to that of Plato, and expressing scepticism over attempts to establish a relative chronology for the mature religious treatises, or to systematize the daimonology, p. 304. Pohlenz' views here are strikingly different from those in the much earlier *Vom Zorne Gottes*.

[15] M. Nilsson, before his description of Plutarch's daimonology, cautions the reader that he is giving opinions which appear in Plutarch's works, not necessarily those of Plutarch, *Geschichte der Griechischen Religion*, II (Munich: 1951, 2nd ed., 1961), p. 403; no such warning is given by P. Merlan, "The Later Academy and Platonism," in A. H. Armstrong (ed.), *The Cambridge History of Later Greek and Early Medieval Philosophy* (Cambridge: 1967), pp. 53-64. Moreover, some assertions are patently false, e.g. that the answers to the delay of divine justice and the metric form of the Pythia's verses at Delphi imply demons, p. 63, and other statements are misleading. More recently A. Corlu, *Plutarque, Le Démon de Socrate* (Paris: 1970), pp. 45-81, and J. G. Griffiths, *Plutarch, De Iside et Osiride* (Swansea: 1970), pp. 25-33, feel that the nature of the treatise he is writing is very important for understanding the demonology. D. A. Russell gives it a balanced picture in *Plutarch* (London: 1973), pp. 62-83, esp. pp. 79-81, and see my articles, "Le songe du Brutus," *Budé Congrès* (1968), 588-594, and "A Most Strange Doctrine: *Daimon* in Plutarch," *CJ* 69 (1973), 1-11 and "From Mysticism to Mysticism," 194.

A great amount of ground must be covered, such as is demanded by the enormous range of Plutarch's interests and the classical literature which was his heritage. It is hoped that through this study a better appreciation of Plutarch's thought, and that of the period in which he lived, may be the gain of such as we who live in a period encumbered by quite different, technological and technocratic, problems.

CHAPTER ONE

IN THE THROES OF SUPERSTITION:
SOME PRELIMINARIES ON THE
DEVELOPMENT OF PLUTARCH'S THOUGHT

In discussing Plutarch's religious ideas and the development of
his religious thought, almost all authors begin with an essay called
De superstitione.
The essay reminds one of Theophrastos' essay on the character
of the superstitious man, but gives a picture of greater depravity and
internal guilt, and goes beyond the taboos and magical ablutions of
folk belief to lay stress on the reliance upon dreams, the recourse to
seers and oracle-mongers, and the belief in punishment after death,
as described in Orphic terms.[1] The essay ends with an illustration
of the incredible depravity of the superstitious, their willingness to
sacrifice human beings, even their own beloved children, in the
hope of placating those deities in the fear of which they lead out
their wretched existence. Plutarch concludes by suggesting that
superstition *(deisidaimonia)* is a vice worse than atheism, but
that both extremes are to be avoided, and the mean, true devotion
(eulabeia) is to be desired.
The essay has puzzled scholars from the time it was first studied,
and a number of hypotheses have been proposed to account for
its seeming variance with the rest of the Plutarchan corpus.[2] Though

---

[1] E. R. Dodds' picture of Greek religion is one of continuing accumulation
of guilt feelings and anxiety over sin as the Hellenistic and Roman periods
went on, culminating in the Christian revolution. The contrast between
Theophrastos and Plutarch is therefore important for his thesis: "...
we can get some measure of the change by comparing the 'Superstitious
Man' of Theophrastus, who is hardly more than an old-fashioned observer
of traditional taboos, with Plutarch's idea of a superstitious man as one
who 'sits in a public place clad in sackcloth or filthy rags, or wallows naked
in the mire, proclaiming what he calls his sins'," *The Greeks and the Irrational,*
p. 253. Cf. also Dodds' *Pagan and Christian in an Age of Anxiety* (Cambridge:
1968). His thesis may be exaggerated since elsewhere Plutarch gives counter-
evidence, to the effect that men of his day were not really afraid of hell.
A corrective to Dodds' views can be found in R. Gordon, "Fear of Freedom,
Selective Continuity in Religion during the Hellenistic Period," *Didaskalos,*
4 (1972), 48-60.
[2] Gréard, *De la Morale de Plutarque,* p. 274, indicates that the essay
stirred up much controversy in Enlightenment and post-Enlightenment

this impression may be false or exaggerated, still it is true that
Plutarch elsewhere professes credence in oracles and omens—
especially in the *Lives*, where he departs from the canon of the
rationalist Thucydides—and his essays and dialogues on several
occasions contain, or conclude with, a sublime eschatological myth
similar to, and often going beyond those of Plato, which contain
the very phrases which Plutarch ridicules in *De superstitione* as
fantasy pictures of imaginary torments after death. The eschatological myths might be a literary convention, but—as Hirzel noticed—
unlike Plato, Plutarch tends to put the main philosophical content
of a treatise into the myth. Besides this he fills his *Lives* with
"true" and portentous dreams and elsewhere in the *Moralia*
treats them with enormous respect—almost as a stepping-stone
into a world of far greater value, truth, and reality than this
ever-changing and impermanent world of flux and multitudinous
half-entities.

How then can one explain the contradiction? In general, three
lines of thought have been taken in order to arrive at a solution.
However, behind all three lurks the presupposition that Plutarch in
later life was a full-fledged advocate of a kind of Neoplatonic
daimonology, one which saw good and evil spirits everywhere
interfering in the lives of men. The first of these explanations,
largely basing itself on source criticism, would see Plutarch as a
writer with little competence in Epicurean or Cynic philosophy
who constructed something resembling a scissors-and-paste collage,
without understanding that the result was inconsistent with the
rest of his philosophy. Even the modifications which are due to
his personal sentiment do not, in this view, conceal the basic
process.

The second approach stresses the influence of the rhetorical
schools. According to this interpretation *De superstitione* should
not be treated seriously, but should rather be understood as a one-

thought: "On a soupçonné Plutarque d'incliner secrètement à l'athéisme,
les uns s'en applaudissant, comme Bayle... dans ses *Pensées sur la Comète*...
les autres s'en affligeant, comme le bon Amyot (*Les Observations de Clavier*,
1819). Vivement attaqué Plutarque n'a pas été defendu avec moins de
zèle—citing Buddée, *Theses theologicae de atheismo et superstitione*, 1716;
Reimann, *Historia atheismi*, 1725; Cudworth, *Intellectual Systems*; and
Fabricius, *Bibilothèque grecque*— ... et parmi ses défenseurs, il faut compter
au premier rang, un des plus savants traducteurs du Traité, Tannequy,
Le Febvre, le père de madame Dacier (1666)." Gréard himself thought the
misunderstanding was due to rhetorical exaggeration in *De superstitione*.

sided debate or rhetorical piece in which Plutarch is making use of traditional anti-superstitious material. Presumably it is equivalent to one side of a debate in which the adversary is showered with contrary arguments and no attempt at balance is necessary. Given the opposite position, atheism, to defend, Plutarch would have written an equally damning account.

The third approach tries to make use of the gains in the study of Greek philosophy through an understanding of the relative chronology of various treatises [3] and the development of a philosopher's ideas. One can recall the great advances made in Platonic and Aristotelian studies through this method. According to this school of thought it is stupid to imagine that the thought of any intelligent thinker remains static, and such sterility should not be attributed to Plutarch any more than to Plato or Aristotle. The conclusion came in a flash of brilliant illumination: just as Plato (in this interpretation) and Goethe turned from youthful rationalism and immature scepticism to a heightened faith and mysticism in later life, so Plutarch must have grown in stages from the rationalism of the Academy he attended as a youth, to a deepened faith in the power of the supernatural as his life went on. *De superstitione* then would represent the heady cynicism of youth, while the religious treatises—which with their demons, prophecy, and punishments after death seem to contradict it, and the *Vitae*—with their terrifying dreams indicative of the course of future events, the oracles testifying to the foreknowledge of the divine, and the innumerable portents and prodigies—would represent the dazzling spectrum of Plutarch's mature thought, especially that of his latest years when he looked down upon the world from the lofty heights of Delphi.[4]

---

[3] Some success in determining the relative chronology of a treatise has been obtained through stylometry. Plutarch's mature treatises avoid hiatus and make use of certain rhythms. However, debate exists as to the extent of this avoidance of hiatus, and the restoration of faulty texts on the use of this principle. See Ziegler, pp. 297-98; J. R. Hamilton, *Plutarch: Alexander* (Oxford: 1969), pp. lxvi-lxix; A. J. Kronenberg, *Mnemos.*, 5 (1937), 311; F. H. Sandbach, *CQ*, 33 (1939), 197, and *CQ*, 34 (1940), 21, as well as D. A. Russell, *Proc. Camb. Philol. Soc.*, 12 (1966), 37 ff., and with extremely helpful common sense, Flacelière, *Budé Congrès* 498-99, points out that Plutarch himself (*De aud.* 42 d, *De glor. Athen.* 530e, *De vit. pud.* 534f.) spoke out against the avoidance of all hiatus. Ziegler's Teubner texts eliminate hiatus altogether.

[4] Volkmann, pp. 260 and 274, thought *De superstitione* early and inconsistent with Plutarch's later thought, concentrating upon the belief

The theory is very attractive, and with some modifications has been accepted by all modern scholars, and by most in the past, except Eisele—who rejected any belief by Plutarch in the power of evil spirits. The weakest part of the argument is the circularity with which it is sometimes applied. It is presumed that a treatise is late because it contains superstitious elements; then this is given as a proof that *De superstitione* is early. Another variation on this method is that of Babut who works off the hypothesis that Plutarch's writings are a gradual and continual approach toward the Neoplatonic daimonology, which in many respects is similar to the early Christian belief in devils and angels.

The circularity can be avoided by relating the essays to Plutarch's intellectual development in so far as we know it on external evidence.[5] As a young man he completed the course of

in evil demons. Hirzel, *Plutarch*, p. 10, and *Der Dialog*, p. 157, n. 2, followed Volkmann and claimed that Plutarch progressed from rationalism to "religiöser Tiefsinn und Hang zur Mystik," like Plato and Goethe, but also claimed the Cynic, Bion, as the source. Eisele, *Zur Dämonologie*, p. 50, rejected the whole idea of using the daimonology to date the essay. G. Abernetty, *De Plutarchi Qui Fertur de Superstitione Libello* (Regensberg: 1911) expanded on Hirzel's thesis. R. Jones seems to prefer the rhetorical explanation, p. 27; Ziegler, p. 190, takes the writing as early. Recently M. Smith, "De Superstitione, *Moralia* 164E-171F," in *Plutarch's Theological Writings and Early Christian Literature*, H. Betz, ed. (Leiden: 1975), pp. 1-8, questions the authenticity of the piece, but his arguments do not seem that cogent in the light of development and Plutarch's tendency to shape his thought to the theme discussed. See also, M. Codignola, "La Formazione Spirituale di Plutarco e la sua Personalità Filosophico-religiosa," *Civiltà Moderna*, (1934), 471-490; and H. Braun, "Plutarch's Critique of Superstition in the Light of the New Testament," *Occas. Papers of the Inst. for Antiquity and Christianity*, 5 (1972), 193-198. See also Russell, pp. 79-81, who gives a balanced account of it.

[5] Volkmann thought the essay could be dated through the reference to the Jews' refusal to fight on the sabbath, thereby losing their city through superstition; but this view was rejected by Abernetty, p. 46— followed by Ziegler, p. 189— on the basis that Josephus, *BI* 6.9 ff., Cassius Dio, 64.4, and Tacitus, *Hist.* 5.9 ff., describe this as a great struggle. Abernetty refers it to the siege in 320 B. C. under Ptolemy Lagos, which fits the description, and was used as an example of superstition by Agatharides (Josephus, *Contra Apionem*, 1.205) Babbitt, Loeb, *Mor.* II, p. 481, n. f, refers it to the siege either under Pompey in 63 B. C. or under Antony in 38 B. C. All these authors fail to mention Cassius Dio's description of Pompey's siege as fitting this description, 47.13. Dio here digresses on Jewish religion at this point—the invisible God, and sabbath. Though Plutarch's own knowledge of Judaism is abysmal (*Qu. Conv.* 4.5 and 6) and in the *Lives* including *Pompey* he shows a complete lack of interest in it, his silence in *Pompey* could suggest he is following Agatharides.

rhetoric, then entered the Academy which was renowned at the time for a moderate scepticism (*epoche*). It therefore seems justified to place the essay in his youth when he might have been over-influenced by his rhetorical training and the rationalism of the Academy, rather than in a later period when he would be moving toward, or already in possession of the Delphic priesthood. Moreover, the essay lacks a certain polish which one generally finds in the later essays, and contains a unique peculiarity, a first person reference to himself by name.[6] And, as is evident from the argument thus far, the essay is very rhetorical. It seems certain, then, that the essay does not belong to the latest period in his life when an attack on oracles and myths about the afterlife might be construed as an attack upon the Delphic religion which he expounds in the Pythian dialogues.

The difficulties with this position are not overwhelming, but it should be borne in mind that the dating for almost every dialogue or treatise of Plutarch is relatively uncertain, and for some of the religious treatises one can do no more than place them rather vaguely in Plutarch's mature period. Also, on occasions Ziegler has attempted to get out of a difficulty where an essay is known to be late, yet remains highly rhetorical, through recourse to the hypothesis that Plutarch composed an epideictic piece for the benefit of his students as an example of his former powers. A more modern objection is that the opinions expressed in *De superstitione* are really not all that different or contradictory from those in later essays on in the *Lives*. This has been the approach of H. Erbse in an article written in 1952 on *De superstitione*,[7] and it is evident

---

[6] ἐγὼ γοῦν ἂν ἐθέλοιμι μᾶλλον τοὺς ἀνθρώπους λέγειν περὶ ἐμοῦ μήτε γεγονέναι τὸ παράπαν μήτ' εἶναι Πλούταρχον ἢ λέγειν ὅτι Πλούταρχός ἐστιν ἄνθρωπος ἀβέβαιος ... (169f). Ziegler, *Plutarchos*, p. 190, thinks this passage is very striking. The source of the ideas he believes to be very complex; ultimately Theophrastos and Menander are behind them, but contributions were made by Cynic and other authors. Smith, p. 1, sees the mark of the forger in the passage cited.

[7] "Plutarch's Schrift *Peri Deisidaimonias*," *Hermes*, 70 (1952), 296-314. He instances *Non poss.* 1101d and *De Is.* 355c on superstition as an extreme, and as bad as atheism; *De ser. num. vind.* 552 a and *Marc.* 3 against human sacrifice; superstition as a wretched vice, *De virt. et vit.* 100 f., and *De ser.* 556b; science as a liberator from superstition, *Aem.-Tim.* 1, *Per.* 6, and *Tim.* 26; the apparent approval of "*pia fraus*" in *Sert.* 11, *Eum.* 13, and *Marc.* 6; the Jews' refusal to fight on the sabbath, *Absurd. poet. dic.* 1051e; and the anti-myth passages in *De lat. viv.* and *Non poss.* Erbse's theory, however, that *De superstitione* is a conflation of a Cynic and Aristotelian source would seem to be disproved by these parallels with Plutarch's later writing. Smith, p. 4, note 4, answers Erbse's arguments.

to anyone who approaches Plutarch's writing with an open mind that there are some striking similarities between what is said in *De superstitione* and in other works. Erbse indicated that previous scholars were exaggerating the differences, though he himself did not question the basic presupposition that Plutarch in later life endorsed a kind of Neoplatonic daimonology. Erbse also relied heavily on a questionable chronology for the *Lives* in order to reinforce the development hypothesis. However, in Erbse's view, Plutarch's statements on superstition, on human sacrifice, on the Jews' refusal to fight on the sabbath, and on punishment after death, can be paralleled by statements in writings regarded as late. One could add more examples to Erbse's list: Plutarch's statements on the true interpretation of myths, and the nature of the vices of superstition and atheism of which the virtue and mean is true devotion (*eulabeia*).[8]

There is, therefore, good reason to maintain that *De superstitione* is an early work of Plutarch, but it is probably not as important for the development of his thought as sometimes believed. At least many sentiments in his later writings which reflect those in *De superstitione*, suggest that there is often as much continuity as discontinuity between the later writings and *De superstitione*. At least, the sceptical, "atheistic" side of the essay has been exaggerated. Later, an attempt will be made to investigate another aspect of Plutarch's early thought, his interest and belief in Pythagoreanism, and the mysticism associated with this school; such

---

[8] E.g. *De Is.* 352b, 355d, 377d-378a, *Cam.* 6. Einarson-DeLacy in the Loeb give the following definition of superstition: " '*Deisidaimonia*' (superstition) is literally 'fear of demons'," *Mor.* XIV, p. 113. However, as Erbse points out, p. 289, Aristotle (*Pol.* 1315a) and Xenophon (*Ages.* 11.8, *Cyropaed.* 3.3.58) give it a good connotation—respectful reverence—a meaning which appears even in Theophrastos' time (Diod. 1.70.8, Heracl. *Qu. Hom.* 1). Theophrastos defines it as fear of the divinity (δειλία τις πρὸς τὸ δαι- μόνιον) *Char.* 16, and this is probably the meaning of Polybios when he says it kept the Romans united, 6.56.7. Erbse rightly concludes that it differs in degree rather than in essence from *eusebeia*, but fails to note that Plutarch has something of a double standard in his definition and actual application of the word. Smith, p. 4, notes that Plutarch never distinguishes between proper and improper fear of the gods, and following P. Koets, *Deisidaimonia* (Utrecht: 1929), p. 102, believes the Christians were the first ones to use it for the fear of demons. For the meaning of the Latin term, which underwent a similar transformation, see L. Janssens, "Die Bedeutungsentwicklung von superstitio/superstes," *Mn.* 28 (1975), 135-189, D. Grodzynski, "Superstitio," *REA*, 76 (1974), 36-60, and S. Calderone, "Superstitio," *ANRW* I, 2, (1972), pp. 377-96.

beliefs run counter to the generally accepted thesis that Plutarch turned from scepticism and rationalism in youth to mysticism and deep religious piety in later life. However, before we make this investigation, it will be advantageous, in the next chapter, to examine some of the major themes which appear in *De superstitione* and to determine whether they appear in the later writings, and in what form.

CHAPTER TWO

DREAMS AND THE TORTURES OF THE DAMNED

In *De superstitione* Plutarch makes particular fun of the superstitious—who in their contemptible belief in the power of dreams—rise in the morning only to rush to the nearest seer, charlatan, or magician, in the hope of averting those evils they saw foretold in their fantasies during the night. In line with the rhetorical style of the essay some interesting paradoxes are applied. Those who suffer from bodily disease or who are imprisoned can at least find some alleviation when night comes and sleep takes away their burdensome cares, but the superstitious deprive themselves of even this solace; for their sleep itself is a torture, filled as it is with horrifying visions and dreadful phantoms. Heracleitos, according to Plutarch, had said that dreamers do not share the same world as other men. Plutarch puts a twist on this: the superstitious do not even share the same world when awake. In Plutarch's view they imagine dangers and avert them by means which are incomprehensible to ordinary mortals.

The first impression one might get is that this is an all-out attack on the belief in the power of dreams and oneiromancy. However it must be noted that Plutarch is always thinking in terms of the superstitious, and never explicitly attacks the belief in dreams on general philosophical principles. No mention is made of the validity of dreams coming to normal, tranquil mortals. Yet, the general impression is that not much reliance should be put on dreams, that they are deceptive, that they do not reflect the course of future events, and that one should not have recourse to soothsayers—a fraudulent race of contemptible creatures—in order to find their meaning.

Such views seem to be quite at variance with the importance of frequent dreams in the *Vitae*, and a person who had only read the *Lives* would be astounded to find that the same author was responsible for the opinions of *De superstitione*. But it is not only in the *Vitae* that dreams have important significance for Plutarch.[1]

---

[1] There is no comprehensive study of dreams in antiquity since B. Büchsenschütz' *Traum und Traumdeutung im Altertum* (Berlin: 1868).

One can point to a work in the *Moralia* which exalts the power of dreaming to the skies, and incidentally gives us much of the theory for understanding the use of dreams in the *Vitae* and in other passages of the *Moralia*.

One of the finest and most interesting of Plutarch's treatises, and one which gives an excellent glimpse of the humanity of his nature and the character of his ethical principles is the *Amatorius* (*Erotikos*). One should remember that the Hellenistic age was profoundly influenced by the account of Eros given by Plato in his *Symposium*, and that the poetry and art of the entire period is dominated by allusions to the lustful god of love in whose person the deepest philosophical speculation could be combined. The work is one of those peculiar semi-dialogues of Plutarch in which one person introduces another, who introduces the speech of another, etc. Here a person named Flavian introduces Autoboulos, a son of Plutarch, who in turn gives an account of his father's part in a debate on love at the sanctuary of the Muses on Helicon, something which supposedly took place years before the literary date of the dialogue, shortly after Plutarch's marriage, and before his son's birth. It is—according to the son, who is the narrator of the piece—through his father's vivid recollection of the event that he is now able to communicate his father's thoughts to his friends.

The recital is motivated by a romantic upheaval in the sleepy town of Thespiai, where a young widow suddenly decides to marry, with some lavish inducements, a handsome young man several years her junior, thereby setting the town on its ear. The young man's male lovers and friends impetuously debate whether it is to his advantage to accept the offer, and this gives Plutarch an opportunity here as well as later at 756b-763f, and at 764b-e, and in the stories which form the conclusion, to propound one of his characteristic ideas, the nobility of married love and the worthiness of heterosexual love, in opposition to the vanity of boy-love.[2]

Most useful is Dodd's work in *The Greeks and the Irrational*, "Dream Pattern and Culture Pattern," pp. 102-34. A full bibliography is given in note 1 to chapter X.

[2] In his introduction to the *Amatorius* (Loeb, *Mor.* IX, p. 304) W. C. Helmbold claims that the Stoics had already advocated romantic married love, making use of Antipater (*SVF* III, p. 254); but one should note that Plutarch here stresses loyalty on the part of the wife, and one must be careful not to read modern ideas into either Plutarch or the Stoics.

It is in connection with one of the more important ideas in the dialogue, the analogy between Eros and the sun—which incorporates mythical and astronomical lore associated with this idea—that the power of dreams is first mentioned. As an illustration of how the soul of the lover is able to rise above the visible world to the beauty of the other world "the divine and blessed entity which is the real object of love" (765f) Plutarch claims that the experience of erotic exhilaration, or inspiration, is similar to that of dreaming: when we wake in the face of a brilliant light everything we see in our dreams vanishes; and such an experience is similar to the state of the soul when it is born upon the earth, and forgets that knowledge which it had acquired in its previous existence. In what appears as a startling antithesis to the deceptiveness of dreams insisted upon in De superstitione, we learn here that the soul's true period of consciousness is not in its waking moments, but rather is in "the other realm and life" (746f), and that since the arrival of the soul in this world, its only contact with the most beautiful and divine world it left behind, is in the joyful contact it can achieve with it while asleep and dreaming. Plutarch goes so far as to take a line originally meant to apply to the deceptiveness of dreams (ἀμφὶ δέ οἱ δολόεντα φιλόφρενα χεῦεν ὄνειρα. 764f, fr. anon. 381), and twists it around so it applies not to the dream world but to the waking world of the senses: dreams—i.e. the sights and pleasures of this world—surround and deceive the soul so that it imagines beauty and value are to be found in this life, and is only saved from this hopeless deception in which it is enmeshed by Eros who like a good mystagogue leads it back to Plato's "plain of truth" (764e-765a; cf. Phaedrus 248b, 254b).

On the surface at least, the whole tenor of the De superstitione passage has been reversed: the real world is the world of dreams; the world of deception and insubstantiality is the world men imagine to be real, not the fantasy world of the dreamer. However one should take into consideration that Plutarch is here working within the framework of Platonic conventions such as the dialogue, the praise of Eros, the contrast between Being and Becoming, the Ideal World, and the rise of the soul through inspiration to this world of higher reality.

Elsewhere, Plutarch is only too ready to warn against the deceptiveness of dreams, or to accept this liability as a necessary fact of human life. In one place he rejects the Epicurean theory of shapes (*eidola*) as the scientific explanation of the frequency of disturbing dreams in autumn,[3] and prefers an Aristotelian solution which depends upon a change in constitution (*krasis*) of the body to explain their deceptiveness, a theory which appears in *De defectu oraculorum*, and *De Iside et Osiride*.[4] In *Coriolanus* 38, *Brutus* 37 and *De sera numinis vindicta* 555a-b dreams and hallucinations are closely associated with disturbed psychological states and guilt feelings. In *De genio Socratis* (587a-c) the conspirators under Epaminondas debate at some length the meaning of the dreams which have been related to them.[5] It is an indication of the dubious interpretation of dreams even at a moment of profound significance for history. Likewise in the myth in *De sera*, the Sibyl tells Thespesios that there is an oracle held in common by Night and the Moon which has no outlet or any single place but roams everywhere throughout mankind in dreams and visions, being the source of dreams which disseminate the deceptive and subtle with the unadorned and true (566c).[6]

Another important principle concerning the power of dreams is stated in the *Moralia*. In *De defectu oraculorum* Lamprias, who almost certainly is speaking for Plutarch here, claims that "all

---

[3] *Qu. conv.* 8.10 (734d-736b). Since the bodies--from which the *eidola* rise--are not hot, the *eidola* are not as sharp as usual. Moreover, the roughness of the air at this time of year interrupts their smooth passage to the mind so that they leave indistinct impressions which manifest themselves confusedly in dreams.

[4] 437e-f, and 383e-384b. In *De Is.* 383e-384b, the drug *cyphi* is said to have been used by the Egyptians as a help toward correct dreaming, much as the lyre was used by the Pythagoreans before going to sleep. In Plutarch's view the drug produced a beneficial exhalation (*anathymiasis*). For the Pythagorean lyre cf. also Plato, *Tim.* 45d and Quint. 9.4.12. On the use of myrrh just before sleep, M. Marcovich has made a very good textual emendation, "Plutarch, *De Iside* 383D," *Hermes*, 102 (1974), 507-08.

[5] Two dreams are related, one that the host's house was in labor, another that Thebes was enveloped by fire but the Cadmeia only in smoke. Theocritos' benevolent interpretation of the dream is correct; but in similar circumstances, *Pyr.* 29, when Pyrrhos interprets the dream as propitious, he is led to ruin.

[6] The Greek reads: ἀπατηλῷ καὶ ποικίλῳ τὸ ἁπλοῦν καὶ ἀληθὲς παραλαμβάνοντες διασπείρουσι. Einarson and De Lacy, Loeb, *Mor.* VII, p. 289, translate ποίκιλος as colorful, and take τὸ ἁπλοῦν to mean white; but this may be less than the words suggest since the passages they cite in support, *Alc.* 23, and *Quomod. Adul.* 53d are not entirely exclusive. In LSJ ποίκιλος is used to describe a labyrinth (*Hdt.* 2. 148), an oracle (Id. 7. 111), a double entendre (S. *Ph.* 130 and Ar. *Eq.* 196). In Eur. *Med.* 300 it means intricate or subtle, and in Arist. *EN* 1101a 8, changeable or unstable.

3

souls possess the faculty of prophecy, but that it is revealed mostly in dreams and at the hour of death when the soul is purified and attains a disposition (*krasis*) suitable for releasing the rational faculties of the mind from the present world so that they may turn toward the irrational and visionary" (*to phantastikon*, 432c). It is perhaps important also that in the Thespesios myth of *De sera*, Thespesios hears the Sibyl prophesying his death in verse (566d), though she predicts nothing else for him. Some have thought that Plutarch himself was addicted to a superstitious belief in dreams. The evidence cited is a somewhat unclear passage in the *Symposiacs*, but he evidently abstained from eating eggs for a time due to a warning he believed he had received in a dream.[7]

The dreams of the *Lives* will be treated in greater detail in a following chapter, but a few brief points are in order here since they relate to *De superstitione*. On occasions Plutarch is anxious to indicate that the person who received the dream which he feels worthwhile relating, was not addicted to superstition.[8] Then there are two cases where the dreams seem to be encouraging the recipients to patently immoral behavior, namely human sacrifice, which the heroes refuse to condone.[9] Some dreams are falsely

---

[7] *Qu. conv.* 2.3 (635e-f). E. R. Dodds noticed the passage: "the Emperor Marcus Aurelius thanked the gods for medical advice vouchsafed him in sleep; Plutarch abstained from eating eggs because of certain dreams; Dio Cassius was inspired by a dream to write history," *The Greeks and the Irrational*, p. 121.

[8] Calpurnia, who dreams of her husband's impending murder, is said to have never revealed any feminine superstition (γυναικισμὸν ἐν δεισιδαιμονίᾳ *Caes.* 63); and a man who claims to have had a dream in which Jupiter revealed his wrath over a procession in which a slave was being beaten is described as quiet, modest, and free of *deisidaimonia* (*Cor.* 24), even though the phrase does not appear in the account as given in Liv. 2.36, Val. Max. 1.7.4, and Dion. Hal. 7.68-69.

[9] In *Pel.* 21 the daughters of Scedasos appear in a dream to Pelopidas before the battle of Leuctra and demand the sacrifice of a maiden—in reparation for the rape commited by the Spartans against them—if he wishes to be victorious in battle. Pelopidas refuses, sacrifices a filly instead, and wins a resounding victory. The story is told in the spurious *Amatoriae narrationes* (773b-774d) and fr. 77 of Ailian suggests a larger independent version. See H. D. Westlake, "The Sources of Plutarch's Pelopidas," *CQ*, 33 (1939), 11-22. In *Ages.* 6, Agesilaus, at Aulis before setting out for Asia, is commanded by a mysterious voice in a dream to sacrifice his daughter, as Agamemnon had done, if he wishes to be successful. Agesilaus refuses; but the sacrifices which he substitutes are stolen by the Boeotians, and he leaves with foreboding that he will accomplish nothing. Plutarch, however, covers over this theme, portraying him as victorious in 14, 19, and 20,

interpreted and lead to ruin.[10] He condemns Dionysios of Syracuse for putting Marsyas, one of his courtiers to death on the basis that having dreamed he had assassinated Dionysios, Marsyas must have intended it (*Dion* 9), and Plutarch mentions that the body of the "contemptible" Mithridates was found with oneiromantic books interpreting his own and his wives' dreams (*Pompey* 37). At the beginning of *Alexander* he relates the dreams associated with the Alexander legend; but he seems to discount them and gives a rationalistic explanation of their meaning.[11] Moreover, in accordance with the theory expounded by Lamprias in *De defectu oraculorum* 432c,[12] the dreams frequently come just before the death of the hero, and are predictions in very vivid form of that coming event. Plutarch would have felt that such an intimation of the future could be justified on the principles of Plato's philosophy and traditional religious belief in the prophetic and sacred nature of the hour of death.

Not quite so much attention need be given to Plutarch's idea of punishment in the afterlife, though his thought here is equally per-

and his failure in Asia as due to dissension at home, and the decline at Sparta under his rule as due to neglecting the Delphic command about the succession.

[10] E. g., Plutarch explains that the Magi interpreted Dareios' dream to please him and not κατὰ τὸ εἰκός (Dareios had dreamed of the Macedonian phalanx on fire, and Alexander in the robes Dareios formerly wore as a courtier): in Plutarch's own opinion the dream indicated Alexander would be victorious (*Alex.* 18). In *Pyr.* 29 Lysimachos rightly sees Pyrrhos' dream of lightning striking Sparta as a bad omen, but Pyrrhos, claiming that the only good omen is to fight for Pyrrhos, goes ahead, fails to capture Sparta, and barely escapes with his life. His words are a play on *Iliad* 12.248, Hector to Polydamas, substituting Πύρρου for πάτρης. Flacelière, *Vies* VI, p. 11, believes the scene is due to Plutarch's probable source, the melodramatic Phylarchos, who engaged in pathetic history.

[11] In a burst of rationalism Plutarch explains that the snake seen at the birth of Alexander, and which appeared in a dream, was a part of the accoutrements of Olympias, Alexander's mother, who was a passionate devotee of the rites of the Thracian Orpheus in which snakes were used. See Hamilton, *Alexander*, pp. 4-5, for more gullible authors, and for the link between the dreams and stories related in *Alex.* 1 and the divinity of Alexander in the Hellenistic tradition.

[12] Some mss. read τὰς τελετάς here, i.e. the mysteries, rather than τὰς τελευτάς the ends (of life). Soury, p. 106 prefers τελετάς, but Flacelière, *Sur la Dispar.*, p. 73, claims that the other reading was the general view of antiquity (Cic. *Div.* 1. 30; Plato, *Apol.* 39c), and he is supported by D. A. Russell, "Notes on Plutarch's *De Genio Socratis*," *CQ*, 48 (1954), 61-63, and F. H. Sandbach, "Three Notes on Plutarch's *Moralia*," *CQ*, 6 (1956), 87-88.

plexing and intriguing. Again it is probably a matter of apparent rather than real contradiction. In *De superstitione* 166f-167b Plutarch ridicules the fear of punishment after death. In doing so he repeats the phrases associated with such torments in the traditional literature, and especially that often called Orphic: here are rivers of fire, the Styx, fantastic shapes, judges, torturers, abysses, and chasms. The passage, however, is not apparently directed specifically against the Orphics, for whom the most individualistic characteristic of the underworld was the mud in which the uninitiated or unclean were forced to sit. In short the Greek equivalent of hell seems to be rejected, and the opening words in which this passage is introduced suggest the atheistic abandonment and idealism of the Epicureans: "death is the end of all" (πέρας ἐστὶ τοῦ βίου πᾶσιν ἀνθρώποις ὁ θάνατος.).[13]

Does this picture square with the rest of Plutarch's religious writing? The individual descriptions of his eschatological myths will be given in greater detail later, but one must recall that the religious treatises of the *Moralia* are quite memorable for these myths which go far beyond Plato in their description of infernal punishments, and describe them in exactly those phrases satirized in the *De superstitione* passage.

How can we account for this? Did Plutarch suddenly abandon his earlier principles and escape to the mad world of superstition condemned in youth, as many scholars believe, or are the myths just a clever tongue-in-cheek deception of the naive reader, or a bit of literary persiflage in imitation of Plato? The evidence does not reveal that the matter is simple at all, and there are some indications, not altogether enigmatic, even in Plutarch's later writings that corporal punishment is irreconcilable with the tenets of his philosophy, that Platonism which upheld at all costs the spirituality and immateriality of the soul.

In two of his anti-Epicurean tracts Plutarch suggests that the only real punishment of sinners after death is oblivion. The first carries the literal Latin translation of the long Greek title, *An recte dictum sit latenter esse vivendum*, but is usually referred to by the

---

[13] The quotation which introduces this section is not, however, from Epicuros. It is cited by Demosthenes, *De cor.* 97, and by Plutarch in another place, *De fort. Alex.* 333c—another work regarded as early. Babbitt, Loeb, *Mor.* IV, p. 420, n. a, thinks it has a Euripidean flavor, and would rearrange it in verse to read ὁ θάνατός ἐσθ' ἅπασιν ἀνθρώποις πέρας.

shorter Latin title, *De latenter vivendo*.[14] Here, Plutarch makes sport of the Epicurean maxim, "λάθε βιώσας", a term which the Loeb edition translates into English as "Live unknown." Plutarch— whose aim is to set the Epicurean argument on its head—argues that nothing is more ridiculous than this precept which negates both the aspirations of noble minds and the benefits they might shower upon humanity: man by his very nature seeks the light, desires to know and to be known (Epicurus himself dishonestly uttered the maxim since his own motive was the desire for fame). Plutarch ends with the *petitio principii* argument that those who have won fame for virtuous activity are rewarded after death whereas the oblivion that follows those who have accomplished nothing is their own punishment (1130c-e).

The final argument is heightened by the mythical and escha- tological language with which it is developed: a fragment of Pindar on the joys of the Elysian fields is quoted; this is developed in Plutarch's own language; then another enigmatic fragment from Pindar about the impious being carried forth on murky sluggish streams is cited, which streams—Plutarch adds—lead from the river Lethe to a pit of darkness where the souls are engulfed in obscurity and oblivion. In proof that oblivion is the punishment, poetic language is used to clothe the philosophical principle that the soul being immaterial cannot suffer other torments: neither vultures tear at the liver, nor do the souls carry heavy burdens for they have no remnant (ὑπόλειμμα) of the body, which has already been consumed by fire or rotted in the earth. In other words Plutarch sees here the immateriality of the soul as an obstacle to the traditional description of the underworld. In a somewhat cavalier attitude this punishment is not reserved for the wicked, as one would expect, but in accordance with the witty extravagance of the rhetorical tradition, is the fate of those "who

---

[14] Unfortunately much doubt exists as to the exact date of this treatise, but it does seem to fall into Plutarch's mature period. Ziegler, pp. 129-30, notes that the abrupt ending and relatively large number of unallowed hiatus leave the impression that the work is sketchy and unfinished; and he agrees with Pohlenz, Teubner, *Mor.* I, p. vii, that it is among those works published not by Plutarch himself but by his heirs. Objecting to G. Mameli-Lattanzi, "La composizione del De latenter vivendo," *Riv. di Filol.*, (1932), 336 ff., and Hirzel, *Der Dialog* II, p. 219 ff., he finds it im- possible to state the exact connection it has with the other anti-Epicurean works—five of which are lost—or to put it in Plutarch's "latest" period. He believes, however, that the anti-Epicurean works are after the anti-Stoic.

fail to serve or take action, and all that is inglorious or unknown," and the place to which they are led—"to a joyless river and from there to a bottomless and yawning ocean" (εἰς ἄβυσσον καὶ ἀχανὲς πέλαγος, 1130e)—suggests the immateriality of this punishment. Throughout, the punning on λάθε and Λήθη keeps the essay on a witty plane.

The second anti-Epicurean treatise attacks the Epicurean conception of the afterlife along similar lines, this time attempting to subvert the fundamental position of the school—that Epicurus had become one of the greatest benefactors of mankind in freeing men from the fear of punishment in the next life. Like the first, this also carries a long Latin title, *Non posse suaviter vivi secundum Epicurum*. It argues that the pleasures of the body are of little consequence, that those of the mind which the Epicureans propose are of even less substance, while they reject the contemplative life which contains the highest pleasures and no pain, and despise the active life which brings greater pleasure than the trivial activities the Epicureans carry on in their gardens (1089d-1100e). The final part of the dialogue turns to the Epicurean position on the afterlife and the survival of the soul. The argument is concerned not with the truth or falsity of any position on the afterlife, but rather with whether the Epicurean position does in fact give greater pleasure than the Stoic or Platonic, since the Epicureans must be slain with their own weapons.

It is at this point that Aristodemos claims that the Epicureans, who have destroyed the pleasures of religious belief and the hope of reward after death—which might give hope to an otherwise joyless existence—offer in return only the dismal prospect of complete annihilation (1100c-1104a). In the last chapters Aristodemos is replaced by Theon as Plutarch's principal speaker, who argues that it is advantageous for the wicked to believe in punishment after death for their vices, since it will turn them to a life of virtue, which will provide them with true pleasure, but that in fact mortals have more dread of extinction than they do of punishment after death, and if death is annihilation, that it is indeed then a fearful prospect we must face (1104a-1107c).

The supercilious attitude taken toward the reality of these punishments—almost as if the whole affair were a *pia fraus* on the part of the intellectuals in order to keep the masses under control— is to modern ears, used to the seriousness with which preachers throughout the course of Christianity have taken the concept of hell, most surprising.[15] But what is more unexpected—in view of the picture of Greek religion which has been given us by Murray and Dodds—is to find Theon claiming that hardly anyone believes in these torments anyway and that those who do lightly fancy they can escape through the performance of certain rites (1105a-b).

In another essay, *De virtute morali*, Plutarch not only questions the belief in hell but calls it insane. His intention is to illustrate varying degrees of psychological repulsion, and as an example states that some men have a mild repugnance to poverty, others a more serious one, and some when afflicted by it reach such a pitch of madness as to leap off a cliff. He argues that this is a form of insanity equal to that of people "so mad that they believe in torments under the earth" (450a). The statement is certainly perfectly consistent with *De superstitione*; and it is more surprising since it seems to include the general belief in punishment after death, not just the fears of the superstitious.

A similar statement of disbelief occurs in *De audiendis poetis* where Plutarch is interested in the correct interpretation of literature. He declares that the poets did sincerely believe in the gods sending *ate* to an individual for his destruction, but—after satirizing the afterlife account in the style of *De superstitione* —that neither Homer, Pindar, or Sophocles believed in the torments of the underworld (17c).

There is another suggestion that such torments are non-existent, in a fragment from Plutarch's *De anima*, which may have been modeled on Aristotle's *Protrepticos*. Here the principal speaker, Timon, seeks to allay the fear of the world to come by showing

---

[15] At 1101d-e Aristodemos holds that it is better for the masses to fear God than to wipe out superstition altogether. Theon, like Plato (*Phaedo* 89e-90a) divides men into the wicked, the majority, and the upright and intelligent. Though Ziegler gives only internal evidence, he regards *Non posse* as late ("die positiven Darlegungen, besonders in *Non posse*, tragen das Gepräge der Reife," p. 130).

For more on the dating of *Non posse*, see Jones, "Chronology", p. 72, and H. Adam, *Plutarchs Schrift, Non posse suaviter vivi secundum Epicurum* (Amsterdam: 1974), pp. 3-4, and 67-70. She discusses the apparent inconsistency between the treatment in *De superstitione* and *Non posse* compared to that in the myths and concludes that Plutarch believed in some sort of punishment after death, and that some men might be led to a better life—like Thespesios in the myth—if they had graphically portrayed for them the terrors of the damned. She cites Beck, *Mythopoiie des Plutarch* (Diss. Heidelberg, 1953).

that the etymology of the words for death symbolically indicate a glorious rebirth which is to be welcomed rather than feared.[16]

Finally in two of Plutarch's essays which are regarded as products of his mature period there are hints of disbelief in the horrors of the afterlife. The first, *De sera numinis vindicta*, is Plutarch's major contribution to that crime and punishment literature often to be found in the western world, and is based upon the maxim "the mills of the gods grind slow but sure," an expression he alludes to in the essay (549e). But was Plutarch really a hell-fire preacher? The first part of the treatise naively argues that all vices are punished in this life, though he must have recourse to the archaic theory that the sins of the parents are visited on their children. The final section which contains Plutarch's most unoriginal eschatological myth, illustrates the punishment of the wicked in the next life. Since the first section suggests that all evil is punished in this life, the myth does not seem to be entirely essential to the argument of the essay and may, therefore, have been added largely for literary reasons in imitation of Plato. In the myth the sinners are distinguished into three types. The milder ones are subject to a purgatory before they are reincarnated on earth; the last class are the incurables who are imprisoned "piteously and cruelly in the unspeakable and unseen" (τὸ ἄρρητον καὶ ἀόρητον, 564f), a description which fits the anti-Epicurean tracts.

Finally in *De E apud Delphos* another hint is given that the real torment of the wicked is not punishment of the gross sort described in the Orphic literature, but is a form of oblivion. The essay attempts to give a satisfactory philosophical and theological explanation for the mysterious letter Ei which was displayed in a prominent position at Delphi and which was thought to have important mystical significance. Here Ammonios, who was the master of Plutarch in the Academy and gives the principal and concluding speech in the dialogue, identifies the letter with the eternal existence of God, who is the Good, One, Beautiful, and Immutable, and is in reality Apollo, the image of which is the sun (391e-394c).

---

[16] Fr. 177, Sandbach; vi, 18-36, Bernardakis, The passage is taken from Stobaios, *Flor.* 120.28. The *De anima* contained several books and was introduced by the history of the suicide epidemic of the Milesian girls, an event also related in Plutarch's *Mulierum virtutes*. In fr. 177 γένεσις is interpreted as νεῦσις ἐπὶ γῆν; γενέθλιον= γενομένη ἄθλων; δέμας = δεδεμένη (παρὰ φύσιν); βίος= βία (by which we are bound on earth); later τελεῖσθαι and τελευτᾶν are identified (168).

Apollo is in turn opposed to the god of the underworld, *Plouton*, who is associated with darkness and silence (394a-b). In conclusion, Plutarch's attitude in *De superstitione* is not so far removed from that in the rest of his writings as has sometimes been thought. He objects to the overreliance upon dreams by the superstitious; but this is no more an attack on dreams in general than an attack on drunken driving today would be considered an attack on driving in general. Even in his *Lives* and *Moralia*, Plutarch frequently suggests caution in the interpretation of dreams. He certainly believed in the mantic power of dreams, but his words in *De defectu oraculorum* suggest that this is somewhat restricted to certain "daimonic" men, and that for others it may come about only at the hour of death. His attitude toward punishment after death reveals a similar pattern. The great versatility with which he concocts his myths in the *Moralia* in order to illustrate a particular point, and the sometimes contradictory divergencies among his myths, suggest that for Plutarch hell is symbolic rather than real in that literal sense in which Christians have understood it. He keeps to the archaic phraseology even after he has located the underworld on the moon as in *De facie in orbe lunae*.[17] Real punishment for the soul in the gross material descriptions of it—would be inconsistent with his ideas on the immateriality of the soul. If there is an eternal punishment, it would seem to be for Plutarch not torment of a physical kind, nor annihilation, but oblivion.

---

[17] Hamilton, "The Myth in Plutarch's De Facie," *CQ*, 27 (1934), 24-30, and "The Myth in Plutarch's De Genio," *CQ*, 27 (1934), 176-82, takes the literal words of the myths rather seriously; but Cherniss, Loeb. *Mor.* XII, p. 25, and Ziegler, *Plutarchos*, p. 217, rightly object. In Ziegler's words, they should be taken "nicht wörtlich, sondern nur symbolisch." For a summary of prominent views see Corlu, *Le Démon de Socrate*, pp. 60-80.

CHAPTER THREE

WAX GODS AND THE SHADOW OF THE MOON

Another impression of hostility toward traditional religious belief is given by the attitude of *De superstitione* toward the cult of images.[1] The hostile passage states that the superstitious stand in awe of those who fashion gods for them out of metal, stone, or wax in the likeness of human beings (ἀνθρωπόμορφα τῶν θεῶν τὰ εἴδη ποιοῦσιν) which they dress up and worship, but that they hold in contempt philosophers and statesmen, in whose person the highest virtues of God are best represented; thus the atheists are indifferent to their benefactors (the gods) while the superstitious fear what is most helpful to them (167e-f). This seems like bald iconoclasm, but it must be taken with a grain of salt, since both in this essay and elsewhere, Plutarch speaks of the great joys which come to men in the observance of religious festivals; and these, in Greek life, are often associated with the cult of a particular statue. One could think of his description of Alcibiades' return to Athens on the day when the Plynteria of the goddess Athena were being celebrated, "the day on which the Praxiergidai in strict secrecy removed the robes of the goddess and covered up her image" (*Alcibiades*, 34).

Views reflecting the ideas of the *De superstitione* passage appear elsewhere as one might expect, and as usual, with subtle variations. The opinion that a better likeness of God is to be found in the living ruler rather in inanimate wood or stone is found both in

---

[1] Plutarch's attitude was discussed at some length by C. Clerc, *Les Théories Relatives au Culte des Images* (Paris: 1915), pp. 110-14, also printed as "Plutarque et le culte des images," *Rev. Hist. Rel.*, 70 (1914), 8-114. Clerc, who was not aware that *De superstitione* might be early, gives a confused account: in the first part of his work Plutarch is hostile; in the second he is a moderate and conservative thinker who maintained a tenuous balance between his religious and philosophical views. A short, uncritical survey of the problem in antiquity is given as an appendix by Moellering, *Plutarch on Superstition*, pp. 165-173. Unfortunately, Moellering does not bring out the subtleties of the Christian iconoclasts, who based their distinctions on the dual nature of Christ; and, therefore, introduce more complexities into their opposition.

the *Vitae* and the *Moralia*. In Plutarch's very flattering biography of Pericles he explains that Pericles was called Olympian "because his pure and undefiled exercise of power was an image of the immortal gods," and that this representation was far superior to the literary conceptions of the poets who attributed the basest passions to them (*Pericles*, 39). Added to the *De superstitione* sentiment is the familiar Platonic criticism of the myths.

A similar critique is to be found in *Ad principem ineruditum*, a fragmentary essay, and one of the few surviving works of Plutarch which give political advice. This particular one is part of the genre which is directed to a young prince. Many of the ideas are stock Platonic thought, but there are a few touches characteristically Plutarchan such as the comparison between God and the sun. The gist of the essay is that rulers fear for their power but should rather concern themselves with the soundness of their inner self: the ruler should carry law (*nomos*) within himself in the image of Zeus who rules the entire universe; the untiring care for justice should be his greatest concern; freedom from responsibility keeps one from mistakes, but with power there is a great temptation to surrender to the passions; it does not conceal the vices of the soul but only makes them more evident. All this is a far cry from Machiavelli's prince, but in his exposition of his ideas in 780e Plutarch goes even farther: the ruler is the image of the divinity which rules the world, a being which needs no famous artists to represent it. Then in a vein similar to that of the theology contained in the religious treatises, *De E apud Delphos* and *De genio Socratis*, the passage states that just as the sun and the moon are the most beautiful images of God in the visible universe, so the ruler is the image of God in the polis. Plutarch expresses his disgust at the artistic representations of the ruler in the guise of Zeus as a symbol of power, which he regards as repugnant to the true nature of the divine which is rooted in *nomos* rather than force. Thus the iconoclast strain is revealed again, this time in his attack on the type of representation which is to be found, not in foreign, superstitious cults alone, but in classical Greek religion itself.

The same iconoclast tendency is thinly disguised in *Numa*. Here, laboring under the mistaken belief that the early Romans did not portray their gods in visible form because they had been forbidden to do so by Numa, and because he in turn had probably been so instructed by Pythagoras, Plutarch commends Numa for his attitude.[2] According to Plutarch—whose arguments somewhat resemble those of the Byzantine iconoclasts—Pythagoras maintained that the first principle of being was beyond sense or feeling, was invisible and uncreated, and discernible only by the mind, and in line with these principles the Romans for their first one hundred and seventy years made no statues for their shrines "convinced that it was impious to liken higher things to the lower, and that it was impossible to apprehend God except through the intellect" (*Numa*, 8). The same attitude is responsible for Plutarch's sympathetic treatment of animal worship in *De Iside et Osiride*, his treatise on Egyptian religion: since animate things reflect divinity equally as well, if not better than inanimate objects, the practice should not be despised; "for the divinity cannot be contained in lines or colors" (382a-b).

Another curious feature of Plutarch's religious interest is his concern over sweating or talking statues. Devotion to an image which was thought to have wept, sweated, talked, or in some other way acted mysteriously, apparently was widespread among the masses. Here Plutarch's interest is mainly reflected in the *Lives*, though the theoretical principles involved are also discussed in the *Moralia*. On a few memorable occasions in the *Lives* Plutarch

---

[2] The view that the Romans in the first 170 years of their history had no images comes from Varro: "antiquos Romanos plus annos centum et septuaginta (reckoned to the end of the reign of the first Tarquinius) deos sine simulacro coluisse" (Aug. *Civ. Dei*, 4.31). As K. Latte points out, *Römische Religionsgeschichte* (Munich: 1960), p. 150, n. 1, vs. L. R. Taylor, *Studies in Honor of J. C. Rolfe* (Philadelphia: 1931), p. 305, anthropomorphic cult images spread out from only a few centers in the Mediterranean. The date is important for ascertaining the time of the Etruscans' expulsion from Rome, but it is surprising that many historians put unlimited credence in Varro here. The Pythagorean interpretation is undoubtedly due to the Neopythagorean reinterpretation of Roman religion, which is handled by Latte under the title "Die Bücher Numas," pp. 268-70. In 181 B.C. two urns were discovered: one was empty and contained an inscription that it held the bones of King Numa, the other contained seven rolls in Latin and an equal number in Greek and concerned the Pontificate; but on the advice of the praetor that these contained undesirable matters for publication, the senate was persuaded to burn them (Cassius Hemina in Plin. *N.H.* 13.84 ff., Liv. 40.29.3 ff., Varro in Aug. *Civ. Dei*, 7.34). Latte points out that such apocryphal literature had already been prominent in the east in the 2nd Cent. However the whole affair is very mysterious, and our knowledge of Pythagoreanism in South Italy is scanty. Recently H. Wagenvoort, "Wesenzüge Altrömischer Religion," *ANRW* I,2, pp. 348-376, defends a modified form of dynamism against Dumézil who holds that the Romans inherited a well-developed religious system.

is faced with a choice of accepting a traditional account of a statue portent, or of rejecting it and thereby irritating his readers. Since this is particularly the case where he is treating rather sacrosanct Roman history and he is treading on delicate ground, this may account for his obvious circumspection. The view of scholars is usually that Plutarch was divided in his own mind or that he inclined toward superstition, but a close inspection of these passages suggests rather that he leaned toward scepticism. An example of this is his account of the talking statue at the capture of Veii in the biography of Camillus.[3] After sacking the city Camillus decides to transfer the Etruscan Juno to Rome, and as he is praying and sacrificing to her for this purpose, "the goddess spoke in a low tone that she was willing" (Camillus, 6). Plutarch then adds that Livy, on the other hand wrote that it was the bystanders who said that she was willing. Livy's scepticism is taken note of by Plutarch and it is important for our consideration of the passage that he does so. He does not, however, quote Livy exactly; in Livy's version not Camillus, but one of the Roman soldiers addressed the goddess; and the others claim she nodded, which leads Livy to conclude that the garbled version of this incident led men to include in the story that the goddess had spoken.[4] It is

---

[3] It is interesting how different authors have interpreted this passage. Gréard, p. 179, saw it as a reconciliation of Plutarch's religious and scientific beliefs; Volkmann, pp. 257-58, thought Plutarch concealed his position behind a number of possibilities with the daimones always ready as a last resort; J. Schroeter, Plutarchs Stellung zur Skepsis (Greifswald: 1911), p. 24, used it in proof that Plutarch was a complete sceptic in the style of Carneades; recently D. Babut, pp. 517-18, attempts to see the Camillus passage as more sceptical than the Coriolanus, thereby fitting it into his scheme of growing superstition in Plutarch, since the cross references indicate Camillus is earlier. See Stoltz, Zur Relativen Chronologie der Parallelbiographien Plutarchs (Lund: 1929), p. 135, and C. P. Jones, "Towards a Chronology of Plutarch's Works," JRS, 56 (1966), 61-74, who supports Stoltz on this point. As a matter of fact, however, the rationalistic critique seems to be stronger in Coriolanus, the later Life, rather than in Camillus; and, therefore—if the chronology is to be trusted—these passages do not really support Babut's thesis of growing superstition in Plutarch's writings.

[4] The Latin reads: Dein cum quidam seu spiritu divino tactus seu iuvenali ioco, "Visne Romam ire, Iuno?" dixisset, adnuisse ceteri deum conclamaverunt. Inde fabulae adiectum est vocem quoque dicentis velle auditam (5.22.5-6). R. M. Ogilvie, A Commentary on Livy, Books I-V (Oxford: 1954), p. 678, thinks it logical for Plutarch to attribute the address to Camillus; but he is inclined to think that Plutarch's memory failed him. He wisely rejects the idea of a variant text—as some scholars whom he cites have suggested—and of a variant source—as another scholar whom he mentions has held. However, it seems unnecessary to have recourse to the faulty memory theory here.

common for Plutarch where he does not have much biographical material to transfer common actions to the hero, and this would in itself account for the more important part played by Camillus in his version. He may have omitted the nodding head because he felt it too gross a superstition. Having omitted the story of the nodding head at first, it would have been clumsy for Plutarch to introduce the story at that point in the passage where he cites Livy for his scepticism about the supernaturalness of the occurrence of the talking statue. Moreover, if Plutarch's purpose is to discredit the story, the omission of the nodding head makes Livy seem even more rationalistic than he is; and Plutarch's Roman readers would less likely be offended if they realized that Plutarch's hesitancy to accept the account came not from Greek jealousy over Roman origins, but was based rather on the wisdom of the greatest of Roman historians. Plutarch's knowledge and use of Livy is a mystery to Plutarchists, and has involved countless discussions and problems; [5] yet, one must be careful not to bury

---

[5] In *Demos.* 2 Plutarch informs his readers that he had to learn Latin at a late period of his life, and that in reading he was able to understand it better by his prior knowledge of the events related than through the actual words themselves. He states, though, that it was a beautiful language, even if all the stylistic devices were not appreciated by a Greek, and that it was worth the effort learning for one who was younger or had more time.

Most scholars today believe Plutarch read Livy in the original Latin. The best discussion, after Ziegler, *Plutarchos*, pp. 289-90, is Flacelière's introduction to the Budé series. Others to treat it are C. Theander, *Plutarch und die Geschichte* (Lund: 1951), esp. pp. 37-82; R. E. Smith, "Plutarch's Biographical Sources in the Roman Lives," *CQ*, 34 (1940), 1-10; A. J. Gossage, "Plutarch," in *Latin Biography* (London: 1967), pp. 45-79; and—somewhat unreliably—R. H. Barrow, *Plutarch and His Times* (London: 1967), pp. 150 51, who alters the citation in presenting it, p. 191. Flacelière notes errors which he thinks Plutarch made in citing Livy, because of his incomplete knowledge of Latin. Ziegler is less ardent about Plutarch's knowledge of Latin, noting that outside of *Quaestiones Romanae* he only quotes Latin writers twice in the entire *Moralia*: Livy in *De fort. Rom.* 326a and Cicero in *An sen. resp.* 797d; and that he relates only one Latin anecdote, one from Seneca in *De coh. ir.* 461f. Ziegler thinks Plutarch had read Sulla's *Memoirs* but not Fabius Pictor, and that in general he relied on his Roman friends for information. The matter has never been adequately studied, but one might ask why Plutarch should not have insisted on having Livy near him. The absence of Latin quotations elsewhere might be explained by the Greek subjects and traditions behind the *Moralia*. Jones, *Plutarch and Rome*, pp. 80-87, feels he had a working knowledge of Latin. Russell, *Plutarch*, p. 54, is less confident, but gives him a good reading knowledge, with reliance on friends. He believes that he read Livy but was dismayed by his bulk. Wardman, *Plutarch's Lives*, pp. 159, 230, thinks his deficiencies in Latin hurt the Roman lives, while Polybios and

WAX GODS AND THE SHADOW OF THE MOON   33

oneself under the mountain created by this molehill. At least here, it would be rash to suppose that Plutarch's knowledge of Livy is defective or non-existent, and to conclude from this passage that he had no first-hand contact with the works of the Roman author.

At the end of the passage Plutarch offers an alternative argument to the pious: those who wished to believe in the event still, could perhaps have a case in the fortune (*tyche*) of the city which raised Rome from insignificance to greatness; but statues or images which sweat, groan, avert their faces, or close their eyes are a commonplace of history and conversation; eager credulity and excessive incredulity are alike dangerous "because of the weakness of our human nature which sets no limits and has no mastery over itself but is carried now into vain superstition (εἰς δεισιδαι-μονίαν καὶ τῦφον), now into contemptuous neglect (εἰς ὀλιγωρίαν τῶν θεῶν)." He ends with an appeal to caution (εὐλάβεια) and restraint (τὸ μηδὲν ἄγαν).

A similar but slightly different treatment is given in the account of the statue of the Fortuna Muliebris, erected in thanksgiving after the deliverance from the Volscian threat (*Coriolanus*, 37). As it was erected "it was said" to have thanked the women.[6] This time Plutarch devotes a whole chapter to a discussion of the event (38). He begins with words expressing disbelief (μυθολογοῦσιν, ἀγενήτοις ὅμοια καὶ χαλεπὰ πεισθῆναι) and gives the rationalistic explanation that wood or stone is often affected by atmospheric conditions which either cause moisture to collect or produce a change in color; similarly wood or stone, especially when splitting within, might give off a sound like a voice, though in either case it could remain a true sign from the gods. However, if such is not the case and the testimony is clear and sound, then an internal

---

Dionysios were not that conducive stylistically to him. Flacelière, *Vies* IX, p. 149, thinks the more frequent errors in *Caesar*, over *Alexander*, were due to his difficulty in reading Latin.

[6] Plutarch writes that the statue said: "Θεοφιλεῖ με θεσμῷ γυναῖκες δεδώκατε." The biography is based almost entirely on Dionysios of Halicarnassos who had used in his version "ὁσίῳ πόλεως νόμῳ γυναῖκες γαμεταί δεδώκατέ με" (8.56.2). In Plutarch's early *De fortuna Romanorum* he had used the Dionysian version. D. A. Russell, "Plutarch's Life of Coriolanus," *JRS*, 53 (1963), 21-29 thinks the alliteration, rhythm, the solemn θεσμῷ, and the avoidance of the clumsy γυναῖκες γαμεταί to translate *matronae* demonstrate Plutarch's originality in adapting Dionysios to the aims of biography.

sensation must have been produced in the imagination, leading the bystanders to believe they actually experienced an external sensation; such an experience is similar to that which one has in sleep.[7] He adds, though, that those who are unable to accept this answer could possibly defend themselves on the view that the nature and actions of God are incomprehensible to men, since his nature far exceeds theirs. Much depends on where one thinks the weight of this digression is. However, the fact that the digressions generally seek to offer a rationalistic solution, and that *De Pythiae oraculis* supports the anti-superstitious argument that inanimate objects cannot speak, should make us lean toward interpreting the digression not as support of the miracle, but rather as the opposite.

The argument in *De Pythiae oraculis* is intimately related to the central question of the dialogue, why the utterances of the Pythia are stylistically unworthy of the god whose words she is supposed to be reporting. The dialogue begins with a guided tour through the antiquities of the shrine, at which the participants marvel at the unusual patina on the bronze, and seek a cause for it in the air at Delphi. One of the speakers, then, Diogenianos, wonders why the verses of the oracle are stylistically and metrically so unpolished since they come from the poet-god of the muses; and pious poet Sarapion, against the cynical detractor, Boethos, attributes it to the present decline in taste. Theon, however, who seems to be Plutarch's representative in the dialogue, insists that the prophetical content alone comes from the god, the form is completely dependent upon the Pythia. A digression takes place in the form of an argument between Boethos and Sarapion over whether the oracle is mere humbug, with Sarapion citing some very exact prophecies in defense; and the dialogue is then interrupted by an interesting discussion of the antiquities at the shrine. When this is finished the participants return to the central theme. Theon insists that even in ancient days the priestess frequently spoke in prose; that those times were more suitable for verse, whereas in the present time such utterances are suspect due to the misuse of them by charlatans; that the world-shaking utterances of former days had to be clothed in obscurity since they were used by states and tyrants, while the ordinary, unimportant questions now asked

---

[7] The explanation seems to be based on Aristotle, *De somn.* 450-451, and is used again by Plutarch in *Brut.* 37.

deserve no such dramatic responses; and finally that the 3000 year history of the oracle should be enough to affirm its divine sanction. It is in a passage treating the portentous activity of statues that Theon's principle of instrumental causality is invoked; this is necessary for settling the larger question of the Pythia's responses. Philinos—in a position dangerously close to the pantheism of the Stoics—had claimed that the statues were filled with divinity (πεπλησθῆναι πάντα θειότητος) and moved in sympathy with divine providence. His viewpoint is in direct opposition to that of the Epicurean Boethos, for whom such occurrences are the result of chance (*tyche*) and the spontaneous (*to automaton*). The extreme position of the naive Philinos involves a difficulty which the others immediately grasp: it leads to degrading of the divine dignity (λιθῷ παντὶ καὶ χαλκῷ συμφύρσομεν αὐτόν, 397e).[8] Theon, who rejects the positions both of Philinos and Boethos—which are probably meant to represent the Stoic and Epicurean schools—introduces an alternate theory based upon efficient and instrumental causality. In his explanation, an object such as a cylinder cannot roll like a ball; similarly musical instruments cannot utter a sound different from that for which they were designed (404e-f). Since Theon's words are meant as a preliminary to the answer intended for the central problem of the dialogue—why the Pythia no longer speaks in verse—the point is extremely important in understanding Plutarch's thought both here and in the religious digression of *Coriolanus* 38. Theon clearly rejects—as Plutarch consistently does—the atheism of the Epicureans; at the same time Plutarch objects violently—if we are to take Theon as his representative—to making the god (or God) "transport himself and incorporate himself into a statue" (398c). Put in other words, a statue cannot really speak unless there is a god (or God) inside it; and this is something Plutarch cannot accept.

In accordance with Plutarch's timorous attitude toward statue

---

[8] Ziegler, *Plutarchos*, p. 45, notes that Philinos grew up with Plutarch in Chaironeia, traveled with him to Rome on his second journey, and possibly was on Plutarch's Egyptian trip (*Qu. conv.* 8.7, 4.1, and *De soll. an.* 976b). Something of his naïveté is revealed in his being impressed in Egypt with an old woman who slept with a crocodile. Philinos is portrayed as a vegetarian whose children are so well-trained when they go out to dinner that they do not reach for the sweets. Ziegler thinks he may represent the views of the youthful Plutarch. On his family see Jones, *Plutarch and Rome*, p. 10, and "A Leading Family of Roman Thespiae," *HSCP*, 74 (1970), 223-255.

portents, he exercises an unusual amount of restraint in the *Lives* when it comes to relating the miraculous occurrences associated with statues in Greek or Roman history. We have already seen that the cases of two statue portents which he found in early Roman history required digressions over the possibility either that they happened as related or that some internal sensation was produced so that it was believed they happened. Moreover, to one of these explanations an entire chapter was devoted. Elsewhere Plutarch seems to avoid relating a statue portent unless it has direct symbolic significance for the hero whose life he is concerned with. A few examples can be given where we can compare him with other classical authors. For instance, at the outbreak of the civil wars Appian (*BC* 1.9) relates a number of portents, some of them associated with statues, but Plutarch says not a word about them. Similarly, on the approach of Hannibal into Italy, Livy (22.1) mentions the statue of Mars on the Appian Way and the statues of the she-wolf in the city breaking out into sweat; Plutarch says nothing. Again, at the death of Cicero, the much later Cassius Dio (45.7) claims that the statue of Minerva Custos was shattered, and the statues of Vibius and Mater Deorum turned round on their pedestals. Here, Plutarch's silence is even more impressive, since Cicero himself had dedicated the statue, and presumably it would have had great symbolic meaning for his impending cruel murder.

Where Plutarch does relate statue portents they are symbolically of great value either for the hero or for the destiny of a city or state. This is obviously the case with the transference of the statue of Juno from Veii to Rome, and with the utterance of the Fortuna Muliebris. In regard to the latter, it should be kept in mind that both the *Lives* and the *Moralia* are filled with references to the amazing *fortuna* or *tyche* of the Romans, and one complete essay, *De fortuna Romanorum*, is dedicated precisely to this question. It is not unnatural then that the statue of Fortuna should have had deep overtones in the philosophy of history for Plutarch and that somehow he felt that the devotion to this *Tyche* may have aided the Romans in their conquest of the world. In his *Moralia* essay he offers as proof that the Romans were aware of the extraordinary benefits of *Tyche* to this one race, their devotion to the Fortuna Muliebris (318e-f).

For a similar reason he includes accounts about statues of

some famous heroes. He relates in *Caesar* 47, as does Valerius Maximus (1.6.12), that the statue of Caesar at Tralles was seen to have a palm tree grow around it during the battle of Pharsalos; at the same time Plutarch omits other statue portents which Valerius includes. Another example of this type of inclusion is the relation of statue portents which were reported during or before the battle of Actium. Here, (*Antony* 60) he mentions that the statue of Dionysos in the statuary group called the Battle of the Giants, at Athens (the dedication of Attalos I of Pergamon on the south wall of the Acropolis) was blown to the ground in a storm, and that the Heracleion at Patrai was destroyed through lightning. Since Plutarch has already prepared the ground well, by noting the special association these gods had with Antony, the reader easily comprehends what symbolic meaning the destruction of the statues of Antony's patrons must have for his own life.

Another example in which the symbolism is very evident appears in the conquest of Sicily by Timoleon. After his victory before Adranitai (*Timoleon* 12), as he is approaching the city, the priests rush out to tell him that during the battle the doors of the temple sprang open of their own accord, and the statue of the founder Adranos—who was honored as the founder hero-god by the city and whose temple this was—brandished his spear and his visage ran with sweat. Obviously Timoleon was well pleased with the omen; but Plutarch must have been even more delighted with the story since it suited his theme—how Timoleon's conquest of Sicily was pleasing to the gods—and the narrative of this favor could run through the *Life* not only consisting of events on the human level but also on the supernatural. At the same time, it is the priests who make the claim: Plutarch's intellectual and sceptical readers need not believe it. Similarly the other accounts of statue portents are invariably prefaced with such words of caution as ἱστορεῖται, λέγεται, τάδε γενέσθαι λέγεται. In fact so great is Plutarch's caution in relating statue portents that the only one which does not seem to be intimately connected with the characteristics of a person or city is that in *Sulla* 11 in which a statue of Nike carrying a wreath is being lowered over the head of Mithridates by a crane. The statue is shattered, as are Mithridates and the people; for the crown falls to the ground.

Nonetheless, there is a certain complexity in Plutarch's attitude toward statues and statue portents. He seemed to have abhorred the excesses of his time, and to have sought some painful compromise to extricate himself from the difficulty of being accused of irrational superstition or irreligious scepticism. His compromise would seem to be the following: statues and the portents connected with them should not be despised, but at the same time the divinity cannot be adequately represented in them; it is better to represent God altogether without recourse to icons, and to see the divinity in living men of high principle; perhaps portents take place, but if so this is probably some internal sensation produced by the divinity in the minds of the bystanders since the divinity does not constrain nature. Finally, though Plutarch takes more liberties in relating these statues in his *Lives* than in his *Moralia*, he is acting for the purpose of dramatic symbolism, so that such occurrences should be taken with a grain of salt, and even so he is careful to preface his accounts himself with a word of caution.

In contrast to the difficulty of interpretation which we have with the cult of images, Plutarch's attitude toward eclipses—especially that lunar eclipse, "the shadow of the moon"—is relatively consistent and untroubled with contradictions.[9] Throughout

---

[9] Plutarch's interest in astronomy crops up throughout his writings, such as in *Lys.* 12, where in conjunction with Anaxagoras' interpretation of the meteor which fell at Aigospotamoi he gives his own explanation; and in *Non poss.* 1093 d-e, where he extolls astronomy as one of the greatest pleasures given man; but he ridicules astrology in *Rom.* 12, satirizing one of Varro's friends who had tried to determine through mathematics and astrology the facts of Romulus' life, on the basis of the eclipse which took place at his birth. The most extensive treatment is the long and involved, but extremely interesting treatise, *De facie in orbe lunae*, in which lunar astronomy is discussed and debated at some length, while Plutarch's own position, basically sound, is represented by his brother Lamprias. The treatise concludes with an involved eschatological myth, which incorporates much pseudoscientific theory, in which the souls of the dead either are reincarnated on the earth after suffering purgation on the moon, or suffer a second death, the separation of *nous* from *psyche* out of love of the image of the good as reflected in the sun. The extent of Plutarch's knowledge on this question is adequately discussed by R. Flacelière, "Plutarque et les éclipses de la lune," *REG*, 53 (1951), 203 ff.; F. H. Sandbach, "The Date of the Eclipse in Plutarch's De Facie," *CQ*, 23 (1929), 15-16; K. Ziegler, *Plutarchos*, pp. 73-74; and H. Cherniss' introduction to *De facie* in the Loeb (*Mor.* XII, 1957). A very full recent account is H. Görgemanns, *Untersuchungen zu Plutarchs Dialog De facie in orbe lunae* (Heidelberg: 1970). In his favorable review of the work, *CR*, 33 (1973), 32-34, F. H. Sandbach notes Plutarch's heterodoxy in treating the moon's substance as earth, a doctrine not in vogue in the philosophic schools for centuries,

he holds that they should not be treated as portents and rather belong within the ambit of scientific study. The *Lives* offer some slight inconsistencies, but they can probably be explained away on the basis of the exigencies of the biographical treatment.

Once again in a display of rhetorical extravagance—at 169f in *De superstitione*—Plutarch writes that Anaxagoras was unjustly condemned for teaching that the sun was a stone whereas the worse impiety of superstition went unpunished. Plutarch takes his stand here unequivocally on the side of the suspect naturalist (*physikos*). No less praise is given to him in the *Lives*. In *Pericles* 6 his association with Pericles is given as a most important influence for that brilliance in the intellectual development of Pericles which kept him from superstition (*deisidaimonia*), defined here as a deranged amazement at celestial phenomena among those ignorant of their causes—a disease which natural science (ὁ φυσικὸς λόγος) can cure by replacing it with piety founded upon hope (εὐλάβεια [εὐσέβεια] μετ' ἐλπίδων ἀγαθῶν).

What truer reflection of *De superstitione* would one want? Yet, as the passage continues, the muddy waters of superstition begin to disturb that reflection, and we begin to wonder if Plutarch is in fact so innocent of the disease himself. Immediately following the definition of superstition—and quite inconsistently—he relates that a dispute occurred between Anaxagoras and a famous seer of the time, Lampon, over the significance of a ram which had recently been born with only one horn. Against the shrill cries of Lampon that it was a portent sent by the gods to show that of the two men in the city with power, Pericles and Thucydides, to only one would power in the future be given, Anaxagoras cooly dissected the skull to show that the brain had not filled the cavity properly but had drawn together "to a point like an egg, where the root of the horn began." [10] Plutarch comments that the crowd

---

but existing in certain non-scientific contexts, in the *mythoi* of the Pythagoraens and "space fiction", and not appearing in scientific or philosophical contexts after Plutarch. He describes him as on a lucky guess getting hold of a fruitful idea, but making mistakes a specialist would have avoided. On the structure of the piece see H. Martin, "Plutarch's *De facie*: the Recapitulations and the Lost Beginning," *GRBS*, 15 (1974), 73-88. Sandbach sees a close link between physical and spiritual cosmology.

[10] ὀξὺν ὥσπερ ᾠόν regarded as suspect by Hartman, but printed by Ziegler, and probably correct since it suggests what a mountain the superstitious were making out of this molehill. The story is also given in *Diog. Laert.* 2.7.

was impressed at that time with Anaxagoras but later with Lampon since Pericles achieved mastery of the city. Is this really a case of balance, though? What could be more obscure, even for Plutarch, than Lampon's banal prediction—which even refused to say who the sign was propitious for, and which used the *petitio principii* that "he would receive the power for whom the sign was propitious". The original version of the story, coming so close after the definition of superstition, was obviously meant as an example of how Anaxagoras combated superstition in the city. But Plutarch —who is always looking for supplementary material on the youth of a hero, and for predictions of future greatness—could not let this one pass by. We should not be too quick to suspect him of weakening in his anti-superstitious attitude here.

His attitude toward Anaxagoras does not change in the *Life*. In 4 his doctrine on mind (*nous*) is praised for its beneficial influence on Pericles; in 8 the brilliance of Pericles' rhetoric is attributed to the foundation of natural science supplied by Anaxagoras; in 16 the philosopher is praised again, and Pericles condemned for neglecting him in old age. In 35 another story about eclipses is related. Since this is labeled "from the schools of philosophy" (ἐν ταῖς σχολαῖς τῶν φιλοσόφων), it seems likely that the previous stories about Anaxagoras and Pericles came from the same source. Here Pericles is about to embark on an expedition during the height of the Athenian plague and stands on his trireme ready to sail, only to be met by an eclipse of the sun and a terrified pilot who refuses to stir. Casting his cloak over the man's head he asks him if that darkness is terrible; and when the poor man responds, "no," Pericles asks him then if the darkness of an eclipse is more dreadful than this though it is on a larger scale. Pericles fails on this expedition, and the next, the siege of "sacred Epidauros," but no attempt is made to link the failure of these attempts with the eclipse: rather the plague is responsible (ἀπέτυχε διὰ τὴν νόσον). Toward the end of the life (38) describing how Pericles himself fell victim to the plague, Plutarch recounts a story about the hero's degeneration into superstition which he has taken again from the philosophical literature (Theophrastos' *Ethics*). In the story Pericles is an exemplification of how misfortune (*tychai*)

Guthrie, *HGP* II, p. 267, notes its importance and cites it in his chapter on Anaxagoras. Παρ' ᾧ γένοιτο τὸ σημεῖον (16.2) probably means "to whom the portent referred."

can bend even a noble character: while suffering under the plague he had reached such a state of folly as to point out to one of his friends an amulet which the women had given him and which he was now wearing around his neck. Perhaps in the original story this was due to the absence of Anaxagoras, or to Pericles' neglect of him in old age.

A somewhat similar picture arises from the *Nicias*; and again we have richer, fuller, variations on the baldly rhetorical *De superstitione*. This incident is the eclipse of the moon before the disastrous defeat of the Athenians in the Sicilian campaign of 413 B.C. In the essay (169a), Nicias is condemned for his inactivity, through which the lives of 40,000 noble Athenians were lost due to his fear of the eclipse; Plutarch makes use of the witty *esprit* that the disappearance of light caused by the earth coming between the sun and the moon is not near as frightful as the darkness of superstition coming over the human mind.

A more balanced picture is given in the *Life of Nicias*. Nicias is here praised for his piety in chapters 3 and 4 on the occasion of his dedication of the Delian games, and similar praise is given the hero at the time of the peace named after him (9); in 17 it is suggested that *tyche* rather than any inglorious defects in the Athenians or Nicias was responsible for the disaster at Syracuse; and in his retreat (26) the general is described as a devout man who had been afflicted unworthily by an unjust *tyche*; in the comparison with Crassus—the victim of an equal disaster, but totally different in character from Nicias—the failure of Nicias' campaign is attributed to his illness at the time and the fact that there was internal dissension and jealousy at Athens (5). On the other hand, the superstitious crack in an otherwise noble edifice begins to loom as a tragic flaw in other passages of the hero's *Life*. In 4, while giving the ethical traits of his hero, as is customary in the early chapters of the *Bioi*, Plutarch puts Nicias' superstition in a rather extravagant way (σφόδρα γὰρ ἦν τῶν ἐκπεπληγμένων τὰ δαιμόνια καὶ θειασμῷ προσκείμενος).[11] He cites Thucydides (7.50.4) as his

---

[11] Compare this with the milder statement in Thucydides, 7.50.4, at the time of the eclipse: ἦν γάρ τι καὶ ἄγαν θειασμῷ τε καὶ τῷ τοιούτῳ προσκείμενος, the language of which, however, Plutarch has largely reproduced. Gomme, Andrewes, and Dover, *A Historical Commentary on Thucydides* IV (Oxford: 1970), p. 428, note how both classical and modern authors have been led astray in exaggerating Nicias' superstition. Some translators read the phrase as "excessively given to superstition" but these authors

42   WAX GODS AND THE SHADOW OF THE MOON

authority for this view, but if one is willing to take the trouble to look up this reference, one will find that this is a relatively banal, and perhaps exaggerated statement, made by Thucydides at the time of the eclipse when Nicias refused to stir. In the absence of other information—something common to the early chapters of Plutarch's *Lives*—Plutarch has projected Thucydides' comment at the time of the eclipse back into the earlier life of the hero. This attitude is reflected in the rather contradictory syncrisis: Plutarch seems troubled that Nicias perished by cultivating mantic, Crassus by ignoring it; but as usual, between the extremes of contempt and superstition he recommends cautious traditional religious piety (*eulabeia*) again.

The principal passage for our study is chapter 23 which discusses Nicias' conduct at the time of the eclipse and in which to some extent, in accordance with Plutarch's usual liberality toward his heroes, he attempts to excuse Nicias. More surprising, in view of the *De superstitione* passage, is Plutarch's comment that a good soothsayer would have saved Nicias independently of the scientific knowledge of eclipses. The passage meant to excuse Nicias is often cited; and since it gives such a delightful nutshell glimpse of the growth of Greek intellectual life, it seems worthwhile here to quote it in the most recent translation, that by Ian Scott-Kilvert. Plutarch has just explained that Nicias and his superstitious soldiers were terrified by the eclipse, since, though by this time even the uneducated understood that eclipses of the sun were caused by the shadow of the moon, they could not understand what crossed the path of the moon and caused it to give off so many different colors, and, therefore, they thought it a supernatural warning of calamity. Plutarch continues:

of the commentary regard the *LSJ* definition of θειασμός as superstition to be erroneous and on the basis of the verb which means to be in a frenzy or inspired, correctly define it as a human utterance about the divine in an inspired state. See also Flacelière *Vies* VII, pp. 132-39, and Wardman, *Plutarch's Lives*, pp. 154-57. Both use the *Nicias* as a study in use of sources. P. Stadter, "Thucydidean Orators in Plutarch," *The Speeches of Thucydides*, P. Stadter, ed. (Chapel Hill: 1973), pp. 109-23, notes how Plutarch, while not using Thucydides' speeches, was influenced by them in portraying character. In "Plutarch's Comparison of Pericles and Fabius Maximus," *GRBS* 16 (1975), 77-85, he shows how subtle deletion of unflattering material helps Pericles at the expense of Fabius. See also, L. Gil, "La semblanza de Nicias en Plutarco," *E. Clas.*, 6 (1962), 404-50.

The first man to attempt to explain in writing the illumination and eclipse of the moon was Anaxagoras, and his account was the boldest and the most lucid of all. But this was a recent theory, nor did it enjoy much repute: in fact, it was still treated as a secret, confined to a small circle and only communicated with great caution rather than with confidence. Public opionin was instinctively hostile towards natural philosophers and visionaries, as they were called, since it was generally believed that they belittled the power of the gods by explaining it away as nothing more than the operation of irrational causes and blind forces working by necessity. For this reason even Protagoras was driven into exile, and Anaxagoras imprisoned, till Pericles managed to rescue him with great difficulty, while Socrates, although he had nothing to do whatever with this kind of speculation, was nevertheless put to death for his connection with philosophy. It was not until later that the glorious fame of Plato shone forth, and served, not only through the example of his life, but also through his teaching that the forces of nature are subject to a higher principle, to dispel the odium which had attached itself to such theories, thereby enabling them to circulate freely. At any rate, Plato's friend Dion remained unperturbed although an eclipse of the moon took place at the time when he was to embark at Zacynthus for his conspiracy against Dionysius, and he continued his voyage to Syracuse, landed there, and drove out the tyrant.[12]

At the end of this passage Plutarch gives the impression of reneging on his principles—in another one of those amazing concessions to contemporary superstition—but as in the case of the passages previously examined where this characteristic appears, the turn toward superstition is not necessarily as dreadful as it

---

[12] *The Rise and Fall of Athens* (London: 1960), pp. 236-37. "The natural philosophers and visionaries" are τοὺς φυσικοὺς καὶ μετεορολέσχας. In Plutarch's consolatory essay, *De exilio*, Anaxagoras is described as busy in prison squaring the circle, and Socrates happy in discussing philosophy, but Protagoras does not appear (607e-f): apparently he accomplished nothing in his exile. D. A. O'Brien, "The Relation of Anaxagoras and Empedocles," *JHS*, 88 (1968), 93-114, and "Derived Light and Eclipses, in the 4th Century," *JHS*, 88 (1968), 114-28, claims that the *Nic.* 23 passage indicates that Parmenides did not think that the moon was illuminated by reflected light—as scholars have often imagined—but rather that the philosophers held that the moon was kindled from the sun. The reason O'Brien gives is that Parmenides is here not stated as the first to give the correct theory. In support of his argument O'Brien cites another passage in Plutarch, *Adv. Col.* 1116a in which Parmenides says that the moon is lit by the sun, but he apparently forgot to add what follows immediately, the comparison of the moon to a lump of hot iron, a comparison which would certainly seem to support O'Brien's claim.

seems at first. Plutarch goes on to mention that the trusted companion of Nicias, the soothsayer Stilbides, who had up to this time kept Nicias' superstition under control, had recently died. Plutarch then gives the views of two obscure writers in support of his suggestion that Stilbides, if he had lived, would have given Nicias good divinatory advice. The first of these is Philochoros, who wrote that in any case the eclipse was a good sign since darkness would have covered the movements of a retreating army; and the second is Autocleides, who in a book which was apparently devoted to soothsaying (ἐν τοῖς ἐξηγητικοῖς), had recommended only a three days' wait at the time of an eclipse. Nicias in fact had delayed a whole month, and this was the ultimate cause of the disaster.

Did Plutarch intend the mantic explanation of the eclipse at Syracuse to have equal weight with the scientific exclusion of eclipses from the mantic category? This would be difficult to believe. The scientific explanation is too often mentioned in the *Moralia* and *Lives* to be put on a par with this side remark in *Nicias* 23. Rather, the long digression on the nature of eclipses and the philosophical history behind that discovery—which Plutarch finds so important to introduce at this point—can only have been introduced at this critical point in the narration because Plutarch believed that Nicias failed through superstition. This is the interpretation of *De superstitione* and perhaps of the rhetorical and philosophical schools. It is not the interpretation of Thucydides. In the account given by Thucydides (7.48-50) the eclipse plays a relatively minor part; and the sceptical reader could easily interpret the delay because of it as a pretext employed by Nicias in order to avoid prosecution at Athens if he should fail to achieve the purpose of the expedition. On three occasions—as though countering a false impression which may have gained credence at Athens after the war—Thucydides argues that Nicias had much in favor of his decision to wait: the enemy were weaker than they appeared; they were short of money; and they were equipped with an inferior fleet dependent upon mercenaries. In the first two instances the argument is put in the mouth of Nicias; but the last time it appears to be Thucydides' own judgment. The passage is punctuated with "Nicias stuck to his point because he had accurate information on the state of affairs in Sicily," and we are told that a peace party at Syracuse was urging him to continue the siege. The eclipse in Thucydides' account comes only at the final stage, and perhaps when the situation was out of control. Even so Nicias by this time is inclined to withdrawal. When the eclipse does take place it is not Nicias, but "most of the Athenians" who demand staying (7.50.4). It is then that Nicias refuses to hear of withdrawal until three times the nine days required by the soothsayers is spent, and only here that he is described as being a man "excessively given to divination and such things." Previously Nicias has said that he is afraid the soldiers now clamoring for withdrawal would change their minds once back at Athens (7.48. 3-4). In Thucydides' account then, Nicias' prime considerations are Athenian public opinion, and a possible disintegration of the Syracusans' morale rather than any warning from the eclipse; and outside of one sentence there is nothing describing him as superstitious. The extent of Plutarch's distortion of the Thucydidean account is exemplified in the travesty of history which begins chapter 24, "Abandoning almost everything else, Nicias lay there sacrificing and dividing until the enemy came up against him." Basically Plutarch's whole interpretation of Nicias is biased by the ideas of *De superstitione*.

In the account of the battle of Pydna at which Aemilius Paullus defeated the Macedonian king Perseus, Plutarch again crusades for the understanding of eclipses as non-portentous (*Aemilius Paullus*, 17). Just before the battle a lunar eclipse takes place, and Plutarch registers the superstition of the masses: the Romans beat their utensils together and hold up torches to bring back the light; the more philosophical Macedonians, in terror, see the extinction of their monarchy. Aemilius himself must have been dreadfully frightened at the time since he offers rather impressive sacrifices (eleven heifers to the moon, and twenty-one oxen to Hercules), until he gets a propitious omen—and about the weakest possible at that, interpreted as a promise of victory if he stays on the defensive! But Plutarch covers over Aemilius' superstition, saying that he did it "out of piety, a love of sacrifice, and a spirit given to divination," and that he was "not completely ignorant of the nature of eclipses"—which Plutarch has just correctly described for the benefit of the reader. He makes nothing of the fact that the eclipse did apparently portend the eclipse of Perseus.

In *Agesilaus* 7 Plutarch has fewer problems. An eclipse takes place before the battle of Coroneia, just after Agesilaus has learned of Peisander's defeat. Here Plutarch approves of the way in which Agesilaus disguises the defeat and disregards the eclipse. The passage on Dion's departure from Zakynthos, which was alluded to in *Nicias* 23, is related in *Dion* 24. As in *Nicias* 23, Plutarch is quick to confirm that the true nature of the lunar eclipse was known to Dion's circle; but he goes on to give the true explanation anyway. Curiously though, Plutarch relates that a soothsayer was sent down—probably in accordance with the theory of *pia fraus*—to inform the terrified soldiers that the omen was indeed propitious for them since "*to daimonion* was signifying the eclipse of one of the resplendent ones." Plutarch's attitude here is interesting because the explanation of the seer, Miltas, is separated from the account of the prodigies which foretold Dion's victory.[13] However, the line which separates them is very narrow indeed. The eclipse before the battle of Gaugamela is not even separated by such a narrow line (*Alexander* 31); but it would probably have been almost irresistible for Plutarch—considering the eclipse of the Persians, and their sun god, Ahura Mazda, which was about to take place—to omit putting this in a portentous context.[14]

But even when ignoring an eclipse means disaster for those involved, Plutarch sticks to his guns. Before the battle of Cynoscephalai an eclipse of the sun took place; but in opposition to the seers and most of his own men, Pelopidas led out a band of volunteers who had remained undaunted. The result was disastrous; but Plutarch blames the impetuosity of Pelopidas—for which he is paralleled with Marcellus, and not his contempt for an eclipse (*Pelopides* 31). He may even have expected the more intelligent reader to deduce from this event how a terrible superstition broke the back of a noble state.

In these days of women's liberation it seems appropriate to finish with an interesting comment Plutarch makes about the education of women. Plutarch wrote a short treatise for some of his

---

[13] In an earlier chapter of the life (19) Helicon of Cyzicos is said to have been admired at the Sicilian court for his prediction of an eclipse for Dionysios. Helicon was another member of Plato's circle.

[14] Plutarch's attitude, however, is superior to that of other ancient writers. Curtius, 4.10, claims that the Egyptians—who really knew how an eclipse was caused—interpreted the sun to be the Greeks and the moon to be the Persians. Pliny, *NH* 2.180 is not loath to regard it as a genuine portent; as does Quintus in *De div.* 1.121, who goes so far as to attempt to prove the validity of divination from it. For more on the eclipse here see Hamilton, *Alexander*, p. 81, n. 8.

friends, a young married couple, a book of advice on how to insure conjugal happiness, *Coniugalia praecepta*. The basis of it is that true peace and happiness must be based on the equality of the partners, which pertains to education, fidelity, and finance.[15] In the course of it Plutarch relates that Aglaonice, a woman of Thessaly—a country noted for its witches—had gained a knowledge of astronomy and duped the women into believing she could bring down the moon, a story which appears as well in *De defectu oraculorum* (416f-417a). Plutarch adds that women should be educated, since the study of philosophy (Plato and Xenophon) will go far to eradicate the superstitious beliefs of women in his day (145c-d).

In conclusion, a remarkable consistency can be observed between the statements in *De superstitione* on the cult of images and those made in the *Lives* and elsewhere in the *Moralia* on the same subject. Throughout his works Plutarch remains a reluctant iconodulist, something of a pious free-thinker at odds with the religious excesses of his times. He even seems indulgent to the Egyptian animal worship as something preferable to the Greek representations of Zeus as the symbol of power incarnate. Plutarch's attitude toward eclipses reveals another facet of his consistency. Everyone is entitled to interpret superstition on his own terms, and Plutarch's attitude does seem a bit weird to us. We wonder why he should have given credence to every nonsensical portent reported in his time, or at least to have been unwilling to dispense with them altogether, whereas at the same time he consistently preens himself on regarding eclipses as purely scientific phenomena. As far as the development of Plutarch's thought goes we must be careful to avoid the excesses of those frogs of Aesop who sat on the log and were devoured by the snake, thus illustrating the moral that one should act: he who hesitates is lost—that is, to refuse to see any development in Plutarch—, and those who leaped into the fish's mouth, thus illustrating that one should look before he leaps—that is, being too ready to see a complete shift in Plutarch's views. Plutarch's thought obviously developed, but it did not develop in such a way as to annihilate the statements of *De superstitione*. There is a difference between the exaggerated rhetoric

---

[15] The Lamprias catalogue contains an entry on women's education, ὅτι καὶ γυναῖκα παιδευτέον, fragments of which are contained in Stob.' *Flor.* 18.28ff., but the many hiatus lead Ziegler, p. 155, to think it spurious.

of *De superstitione,* and exaggerated biographical flourishes of the *Lives,* or the religious themes of the *Moralia.* It is wrong to deduce from them that Plutarch drifted madly toward superstition in his later writings. The theme of each treatise or work strongly affects his material. The dramatic, almost theatrical approach to moulding history into biography affected his use of such supposedly scientific facts as eclipses. Whether he believed in them or not, he certainly found them most useful in expressing the psychology of those who did believe in them as religious portents, and in making the *Lives* a product of that flamboyant "baroque" age in which he lived.

CHAPTER FOUR

NOT A TEAR:
EARLY DAIMONES AND HUMAN SACRIFICE

Having considered Plutarch's attitude toward dreams, myths, afterlife punishments, the cult of images, and eclipses, we can now turn to another subject swept up in the winds of hot debate, his attitude toward evil demons—or more appropriately, *daimones*—a subject which leads in turn to the problem of the religious conceptions of the youthful Plutarch. The question of *daimones* is significant since some scholars have contended that in *De superstitione* Plutarch reveals no awareness of the daimonological conceptions, which in the view of these scholars, were his preoccupation in later life.[1] We must, then, set our sights on the *daimones* of *De superstitione*, see if there are significant traces of daimonology in the other supposedly early works of Plutarch, and then attempt to reconstruct his thought in the early period of his life. If no other picture emerges than that which one gains from *De superstitione*, then we will perhaps have to resign ourselves humbly to the traditional view of the sceptical youth turning toward ever greater superstition and mysticism as he climbed the ascent to Delphi. If, however, a different portrait can be recovered from

---

[1] Volkmann, *Leben, Schriften und Philosophie des Plutarch*, p. 294, noticed the contradictions between the statements about *daimones* in *De superstitione* and those of the later writings; but he ignored the possibility of relative chronology and the development of thought. Hirzel, *Der Dialog* II, p. 157, was the first to claim that in later life Plutarch distinguished between gods and *daimones*. Bock, *Untersuchungen zu De genio Socratis*, p. 46, follows Hirzel in developing the theory of relative chronology; as does Abernetty, *De Plutarchi qui fertur de superstitione libello*, p. 77; Andres, "Daimon", *RE* suppl. III, p. 301 ff.; and Soury, *La Démonologie de Plutarque*, p. 15, though Soury believes the differences are relatively minor and due more to the differences in sources and the *personae dialogi*. Ziegler, *Plutarchos*, p. 189, and Erbse, "Plutarchs Schrift *Peri Deisidaimonias*," *Hermes*, 70 (1952), 296-314, also lay stress on relative chronology and accept the view that no distinction is made between gods and *daimones* in *De superstitione*. This theory was first elucidated by F. Kraus, *Die Rhetorischen Schriften Plutarchs und ihre Stellung im Plutarchischen Schriftenkorpus* (Munich: 1912). Abernetty, p. 5, puts his own unusual twist on this theory: the superstitious treat the gods like *daimones*.

the dusty corpus of this voluminous writer, then a revolutionary approach is needed in studying his religious development.

Daimon is a word which has many shades of meaning in Greek thought. So far, the history of this concept has received no adequate treatment, and the answer to this is simple: the subject is so complex, it involves so much knowledge of Greek philosophy, and it is so difficult to determine the exact meaning in a context, that any study is bound to be unsatisfactory to the critical, and an appalling mountain to climb for those who set their eyes upon it: fools rush not in where *daimones* tread. For the sake of simplicity only the Liddell, Scott, Jones treatment of the word will be discussed, though a fuller treatment can be found in the old article of Andres for Pauly, in Nilsson's *Geschichte der Griechischen Religion*, and more recently by J. ter Vrugt-Lentz for the pre-Hellenistic period, and C. Zintzen for the Hellenistic and Imperial period in the *Reallexikon für Antike und Christentum*.[2]

The first meaning in *LSJ* is "a god or goddess" (Theocritos, 2.11; *Iliad* 1.222, 3.420 etc.; Empedocles, 59.1), but the entry also notes that the word frequently indicates the divine power or the deity, while *theos* denotes a god in person: thus πρὸς δαίμονα means "against the divine." The entry possibly should be reversed; the original meaning of the word may have been the impersonal divine force, the *numen* or *mana*. O. Jørgensen, a Danish scholar of the early 20th Century long ago noticed how Homer, when referring to a divine action, introduces the Olympian gods, while the characters themselves in their own speech sometimes refer

---

[2] Andres' work (*RE*, Suppl. III (1918), pp. 267-321) treats the matter by period, author, and different concepts in the author. Though largely descriptive it contains an enormous amount of information and a bibliography—now out of date—and exact references to texts. Nilsson's *Geschichte*, I, pp. 216-28, and II, pp. 210-18 offers a shorter, but perhaps more intelligible treatment since the concept of *daimon* is better related to the more general religious developments. J. ter Vrugt-Lentz, "Geister (Dämonen) II Vorhellenistisches Griechenland," *Reallexikon für Antike und Christentum* 68 (1974), pp. 598-615, sees a movement from dynamism (the spontaneous intrusion of an unseen and unpredictable power) to a personal guardian or evil spirit, with at the same time a movement toward identifying *daimon* with *tyche*. C. Zintzen, "III c Hellenistische u. kaiserzeitliche Philosophie," 68-69 (1975), pp. 640-668, sees Xenocrates as a key factor in interpreting Plato's speech in the *Symposium*, the essentials of which are given in Plutarch's *De defectu oraculorum*.

vaguely to a *daimon*[3]. By the time of Herodotos a new meaning has emerged, not entirely absent in the early literature: *daimon* seems to be equal to *tyche*. Thus κατὰ δαίμονα means the same as τύχη "by chance." Already in Homer *daimon* had the meaning of "fate" (*Iliad* 8.166, *Odyssey* 5.396). By the Hellenistic period this concept of *tyche* assumes incredible proportions and is used indiscriminately with *daimon*; but also the idea of the *daimon* as a good protective spirit or an evil destructive spirit has become prominent (e.g. Plato, *Phaedo* 107d; *Papyrus Magicus*, British Museum 121.505; Iambilichos, *De mysteriis* 9.1).

Another concept of *daimon*, which appears throughout Greek literature, is that of a departed soul, a meaning which is found as early as Hesiod (*Opera* 122). Also included in the *LSJ* definition is a concept which is extremely important for this study. Such is the well-defined idea of a *daimon* as an intermediate being between men and the gods (or God). This meaning, which figures prominently in Plutarch's daimonological passages, seems to have received a great impetus from Xenocrates, who—if we are to judge from the few fragments we have his philosophy—was interested in filling out the chain of being along the lines of tripartite division. Xenocrates' concept would seem to have included both good and evil *daimones*. Thus his scheme was extremely close to that which Christians are raised on, the existence of spirits above men and below God, namely angels and devils. The difference, however, between these Greek *daimones* and the Christian demons and angels is that the Greek *daimones* move with a considerable amount of fluidity from good to bad, and that it is never entirely clear that they are not human souls or at least capable of being incarnated in human bodies. The whole concept was so hopelessly muddled that no classical author seems even to have attempted to straighten out the mess. One should also mention a friendly *daimon*, a rather general protective spirit called the Agathos Daimon, who was often toasted at dinner parties, and who was thought to go about in the form of a snake. To the end of Greek literature, then, no one meaning was ever abandoned completely in favor of another;

---

[3] O. Jørgensen, "Das Auftreten der Götter in den Büchern der Odysee," *Hermes*, 39 (1904), 357 ff. His ideas were later developed in a thesis by E. Heden, *Homerische Götterstudien* (Uppsala: 1912). Earlier P. Regnaud, "Le *daimon*, histoire d'une idée," *Rev. Hist. Rel.*, 15 (1887), 156 ff., noticed that Homer rarely used the word *daimon* in the plural.

and this is what is so maddening for the ambitious daimonologist anxious to determine an exact meaning. Plutarch, with his innumerable treatises on different subjects and themes, probably adds more smoke to the fire than he clears away.

We can now attempt to determine the meaning which Plutarch gives to *daimon* in *De superstitione*. It does in fact appear seldom in the treatise: twice at 168c, and once at 171c.[4] In the first passage where Plutarch is contrasting the atheist with the superstitious man (ὁ δεισιδαίμων) — a word which suggests numerous puns in Greek — he states that the self-reliant atheist, when sick, looks to his regimen, in political troubles makes a self-examination or takes a good look at his friends and enemies, but the superstitious man regards all things as blows of God or a god, and attacks of the *daimon* — or a *daimon* (πληγαὶ θεοῦ καὶ προσβολαὶ δαίμονος). The phrase is prejudged by Babbitt in the Loeb, who translates it as "afflictions of God and attacks of the evil spirit."[5] Plutarch continues, "the superstitious man closes his door on the philosopher who has come to help him, showering the sage with such words as 'Leave me to pay my penalty, impious man that I am, hated by the gods and *daimones*' (τὸν θεοῖς καὶ δαίμοσι μεμισημένον). This time Babbitt is probably right in his translation, ("hateful to the gods and all the heavenly hosts" — an expression which he thinks is a reflection of Oedipus' complaint against heaven in *Oedipus Tyrannus* 1340).

---

[4] At 168d the superstitious accuses himself of having followed a route which was not allowed by *to daimonion* (ὁδὸν ὃν οὐκ εἴα τὸ δαιμόνιον). Soury, p. 49, quite unjustifiably claims that this clearly distinguishes the gods from the demons—"et si les mot grecs que nous venons de citer ne suffisaient pas allé prouver"—and claims we have here the same *daimon* as "le démon de Socrate." Erbse—who begs the question, p. 298 n. 2—claims *to daimonion* here is equal to *daimon*, which is in all cases completely parallel with *theos*. Babbitt in the Loeb. *Mor.* II, p. 475, oddly translates *to daimonion* in the phrase as "his conscience".

[5] *Mor.* II, p. 474. Soury also goes overboard here: "Ses malheurs, l'infortuné les donne pour des coups du dieu, pour des attaques du démon—de son démon, peut-on traduire. . ." p. 49. *Daimon* is rarely used for *theos* in Plutarch but it seems to be used this way in *Mul. virt.* 260a, perhaps *Cic.* 17, and almost certainly *Luc.* 19, *Demos.* 3, *Brut. comp.* 2, *Sul.* 28, and *Sol.* 27. The cases are interesting. In *Sol.* 27 he is following the vocabulary of Herodotos (1.30). *Demos.* 3, the *daimon* put many similarities into the nature of Cicero and Demosthenes. (Here he might mean it in the sense of fate or fortune.) The other examples are from Roman sources, perhaps translating *numen*, apparently citing ultimately Lucullus' memoirs, Catiline, and Sulla's *Memoirs. Brut. comp.* 2 is strange: Caesar was sent by the *daimon* like a good physician; it may reflect a Caesarian source.

In both instances evil spirits are probably not envisaged. At least the balanced expressions used here fit in with the balanced antitheses of the previous section about the atheist: ἀέρων ... καὶ τόπων, προσκρούσας ἐν πολιτείαις καὶ περιπέσων ἀδοξίαις καὶ διαβολαῖς (168b). Especially in the latter phrase θεοὶ καὶ δαίμονες is a very common expression used to include the whole heavenly panoply. However, since we are in a period verging on Neoplatonism the expression προσβολαὶ δαίμονος justifiably makes one suspicious that it is being used for an evil spirit, especially when put in the mouth of a superstitious person, the δεισιδαίμων, whose appelation literally means fearing the *daimon*. Certainly many of Plutarch's readers would have understood the phrase to mean the attack of an evil *daimon*, i.e., an evil spirit. And as a matter of fact, in the introduction to the lives of Dion and Brutus, Plutarch himself reveals that a play on *daimon* in *deisidaimonia* was a commonplace: καίτοι λόγος τίς ἐστι τῶν ἀναιρούντων τὰ τοιαῦτα, μηδενὶ ἂν νοῦν ἔχοντι προσπεσεῖν φάντασμα δαίμονος μηδ' εἴδωλον, ἀλλὰ παιδάρια καὶ γύναια καὶ παραφόρους δι' ἀσθένειαν ἀνθρώπους ἔν τινι πλάνῳ ψυχῆς ἢ δυσκρασίᾳ σώματος γενομένους δόξας ἐφέλκεσθαι κενὰς καὶ ἀλλοκότους, δαίμονα πονηρὸν ἐν αὐτοῖς τὴν δεισιδαιμονίαν ἔχοντας. (2)

The last instance of the word's use in the essay is even more strongly suggestive of an evil spirit and cannot be dismissed as cavalierly as the previous phrases. Intending to end the essay with the most horrible example of superstition, Plutarch enters into a treatment of one of the most terrible abominations, the sacrifice of innocent children in order to propitiate barbarous divinities who supposedly are placated by such things. In an extremely biting piece of satire he exclaims that it would be "better for the savages (Gauls and Scythians) to be atheists than to believe in the existence of gods who take delight in human sacrifice, and better for the Carthaginians to have taken Critias and Diagoras (famous atheists of antiquity) for their lawgivers and to acknowledge no *daimon* or god (μήτε τινὰ δαιμόνων μήτε τινὰ θεῶν νομίζειν) than to sacrifice to Cronos" (i.e. the Phoenician Baal).[6] In melodramatic

---

[6] Babbitt in the Loeb, *Mor.* II, p. 493, wrongly gives the Phoenician equivalent as El, though correctly giving the Hebrew for it as Moloch or Baal. The name of the god was Baal Hammon (Lord of the Incense), a derivative of the god El of the Ras Shamra tablets. Later his position was somewhat usurped by the female goddess Tanit in whose "sanctuary" the archaeologists have discovered thousands of urns containing the burned bones of children, thus confirming the horror of ancient writers. Diodoros

EARLY DAIMONES AND HUMAN SACRIFICE

style he describes the slaughter of the innocents: parents bring
up their own children before the altar, while those with none
buy them from the poor in order "to cut their throats as if they
were so many lambs or young birds, while drums beat and flutes
play to drown out the screams; and the mother of the poor child
stands by as the throat is cut with not a tear to wet her cheek."
Then he exclaims in feigned astonishment "If Typhons of Giants
were ruling the world after expelling the gods with what sort of
sacrifice would they be pleased or what other rites would they
require?" Added to this are examples of barbarian sacrifice, among
them the human sacrifice made by Xerxes' wife to the god Hades,
and the remark of Xenophanes to some Egyptians who were carrying
out a ritual lament for their gods, that if these were gods the Egyptians should not weep for them as though they were men, and
that if they were men, it was ridiculous to sacrifice to them as
to the gods (171d).

There are a number of grounds for suspecting that this last
phrase in *De superstitione* is aimed against the belief in evil *daimones*
and does make a distinction between them and the gods. First of all,
there is a peculiar inversion in the expression so that we do not read
down the hierarchy as normal (θεοὶ καὶ δαίμονες), but the reverse
(δαίμονες καὶ θεοί). Next, in the daimonological passages of the
later writings one of the first things which comes to mind is human
sacrifice. Thus, in Cleombrotos' speech about the *daimones*, in
De defectu oraculorum, he says fasting, beating of breasts, and
scurrilous language at the shrines is not meant for any god but
as apotropaic rites for the *daimones*, and continues by linking them
to human sacrifice in a manner similar to that of *De superstitione*:
it is not credible that in ancient times the gods demanded human
sacrifice, nor would the kings and generals of old have endured
giving over their children and submitting them to slaughter
(Plutarch stresses the idea of cutting their throats, as in *De super-*

Siculos, 20.14, records the sacrifice of 500 aristocratic children to Cronos
(sic) in 310 B.C. See B. H. Warmington, *Carthage* (London: 1960, Pelican
rpt. 1964), pp. 155-60. Cronos is frequently associated with *daimones* or
described as a *daimon* himself in Plutarch's writings: so *De def.* 419f, 421d;
De Is. 356a, 360f, 363e, 364a; and *De fac.* 942a and 944d-e. Only in the last
is the god of Carthage meant. However in *De ser.* 552 a-b and *Reg. et Imper.*
175a the sacrifice of Carthaginian children to Cronos is mentioned. The
idea that sacrifice is offered to *daimones* appears also in *Qu. Rom.* 284c
where it is described as offered to ἀλλοκότοις τισὶ δαίμοσι καὶ ξένους.

stitione) unless they felt that they were propitiating evil *daimones* (which Plutarch describes as acting "either as avengers or out of lust or some other base passion," (417d).

A similar link between human sacrifice and *daimones* is evident from a passage in the *Life of Pelopidas* (21). In a dream before the battle of Leuctra, the Theban general Pelopidas sees the daughters of Scedasos—native girls who had been raped by some Spartan strangers and after their death buried in a prominent tomb at Leuctra—who appear with their father to demand that the sacrifice of a maiden with auburn hair be made to them in reparation for the outrage committed against them by the Spartans, if the Thebans wish to be victorious. In the morning when Pelopidas relates the dream to his friends, a debate ensues: some of the speakers, among whom are the seers, demand that the sacrifice— which Plutarch calls "dire and unlawful"—be carried out; and they claim that such sacrifice in the past has had propitious results, among these, the sacrifice of Agamemnon of his daughter before setting out for Troy, and the sacrifice by Themistocles of some prisoners to Dionysos Omestes (the Devourer) before the battle of Salamis; and they further allege that Agesilaus' failure to sacrifice his daughter before setting out for Asia from Aulis was responsible for his expedition ending ingloriously and incomplete.[7]

---

[7] Plutarch's attitude toward Agesilaus' sacrifice is somewhat ambigious in *Ages*. (6), but his intentions can probably be deduced from the *Pelopidas* passage; the impression of divine wrath for ignoring the dream commanding the hero to sacrifice his daughter probably is due to the source of Agesilaus. He leaves "full of ill-boding on account of the omen and convinced his expedition will come to naught," after the sacrifices are stolen by the Boiotians. However, in chapters 14, 15, 19, 20, and the syncrisis Plutarch dispells this impression with descriptions of Agesilaus' triumphs. If there is a divine sanction, it is over the neglect of the Delphic oracle about the lame king. Cf. the syncrisis, ch. 3, *Lys.* 22, and *Alc.* 23. The interruption of the sacrifice but not the dream is related in Xenophon, *Hell.* 3.3.3, and Pausanias 3.9.1; Diodoros omits both. In *Popl.* 6 the ancient Brutus is condemned as brutish and godless for putting his sons to death; in *Cic.* 10 Catiline is accused of offering human sacrifice and eating flesh (cf. Cass. Dio, 37.30.3); in *Themistocles* Plutarch omits the story of the human sacrifice before Salamis; in *Theseus* he omits a story, found in Apollodoros 3.15.8, that in obedience to an ancient oracle the Athenians sacrificed the daughters of Hyacinth on the grave of Geraistos the Cyclops.

On the subject in general see the interesting treatment by W. Burkert, *Homo Necans* (Berlin: 1972), pp. 70-85, who sees sexual overtones here, in which the sacrifice seems to have a close relationship to ritual: "Zerstücke-lung der geschändeten Frau als Aufgebot zum Krieg." He notes that the places where it takes place seem to be famous ritual shrines. Among the

The others in this debate argue that such a "barbarous and un-lawful sacrifice" could be pleasing to none of the superior beings, since Typhons and Giants do not rule the world—but the father of men and gods—and that it is ridiculous to believe there are *dai-mones* who believe in human sacrifice, but if there are such, "they should be regarded as powerless since such strange and difficult desires could only originate in and remain in a being through weakness and perversity of soul." [8] The fact that moral weakness is weakness of soul (*psyche*) in a being which is nothing but soul is a highly sophisticated piece of daimonological reasoning, and would seem to depend upon the daimonology worked out in *De defectu oraculorum*. As such it seems to be a legitimate improvement upon the *De superstitione* passage, but there is no reason to believe that in both essays Plutarch should not have envisaged the same sort of *daimon*. The verbal parallels are so striking that they should be noted here:

De superstitione 171d-e	*Pelopidas* 21
εἰ δὲ Τυφῶνές τινες	οὐ γὰρ τοὺς Τυφῶνας ἐκείνους
ἢ Γίγαντες ἦρχον ἡμῶν	οὐδὲ τοὺς Γίγαντας ἀρχεῖν
τοὺς θεοὺς ἐκβαλόντες	ἀλλὰ τὸν πάντων πατέρα
ποιαῖς ἂν ἥδοντο θυσίαις	θεῶν καὶ ἀνθρώπων
ἢ τίνας ἄλλας ἱερουγίας	δαίμονας δὲ χαίροντας
ἀπῇτουν.	ἀνθρώπων αἵματι καὶ φόνῳ . . .

---

girls listed by him (p. 77, note 30), besides those in *Agesilaus* and *Pelopidas* are Macaria (Eur. *Heracl.* 408-601), the Theban maidens (Paus. 9.17.1), and the girls in the Messenian War (Paus. 4.9.4.).

[8] The story of the daughters of Scedasos is related briefly by Xenophon, *Hell.* 6.4.7, and Diodoros, 15.54.2-3, and in Ps. Plutarch *Amatoriae narra-tiones* (*Mor.* 773b-774d). A fragment of Ailian (77) suggests another in-dependent version, and it probably was related in Plutarch's lost *Epa-meinondas*. See H. D. Westlake, "The Sources of Plutarch's *Pelopidas*," *CQ*, 33 (1939), 11-12. Westlake, however, p. 13, fails to note how Plutarchan the sentiments are, and rather attributes the objection to Epicurean in-fluence. The language does reflect Kyria doxa 1 (D.L. 10.399): τὸ μακάριον καὶ ἄφθαρτον οὔτε αὐτὸ πράγματα ἔχει οὔτε ἄλλῳ παρέχει ὥστε οὔτε ὀργαῖς οὔτε χάρισι συνέχεται. ἐν ἀσθενεῖ γὰρ πᾶν τὸ τοιοῦτον. But surely this is a coin-cidence: Plutarch's thought here is founded on the essence of the Platonic concept of the deity which regards the gods of the myths as a perversion of true divinity which manifests itself in beauty, goodness, and justice (cf. *Rep.* 4 and 10, *Laws* 10; but it is an idea found throughout Plato's works).

Virtue triumphs in the *Pelopidas* passage; a filly fitting the color demanded by Scedasos appears and is sacrificed; the Thebans win the battle; and apparently the anti-superstitious triumph.

However, it is not necessary to prove from *De superstitione* alone that Plutarch at an early period of his life was acquainted with the daimonological literature. There is another work which is also considered early and in which he shows himself profoundly impressed with certain strains of Greek daimonology. This is *De esu carnium* a work in two parts, both badly mutilated, which contain the exaggerated rhetoric and naïveté associated with Plutarch's youthful works, even if the state of the text may be responsible for some literary deficiencies.[9] The treatise which strongly argues for vegetarianism in emotional phrases similar to those in *De superstitione*, such as "of the slaughter when for the first time throats were slit and hides flayed and limb torn from limb" (993b) regards all the arguments of the opposition as based on utility or self-defense; and these are brushed aside as hypocritical, while the practice of eating meat itself is condemned as unnatural and degrading to both mind and body. At the end of the first part he hesitantly indicates that the doctrine rests on lofty philosophical principles, the transmigration of the soul, which he treats as something novel and unheard of before, and which he links to the Empedoclean doctrine of the fall of the *daimon* for eating flesh, and the Orphic legend of the dismemberment and slaughter of Dionysos by the Titans, which Plutarch describes as an account of "rebirth and punishment" (996b). It is at this point that our text breaks off.

The resumption of the themes in the second part of the essay continues with the progressive degeneration of man through the slaughter of animals, who are treated as defending their lives, like prisoners before the slaughter. Like the first part, it ends with allusions to the doctrine of palingenesis stated not as absolutely certain, but with the wish that it would be proved so that the slaughter of animals would cease, Plutarch adds the arguments

---

[9] Looking at the Pythagorean doctrine and number mysticism to which Plutarch says he was addicted in his youth (*De E*, 387f) and the rhetorical style, Ziegler, p. 98, dates the essay as early and as among those writings probably published by Plutarch's heirs. The excerptor responsible for the jumbled text introduced two stupid interpolations, and even an extract from an entirely different work (994 b-d). See Helmbold, Loeb, *Mor.* XII, pp. 537-39.

that even if palingenesis is not demonstrable, it is better to suffer
the ridicule of non-vegetarians than to run the risk of slicing up
our ancestors, relatives, and friends whose souls may have found a
new abode in some animal frame, and that in any case it is only
one step from the slaughter of animals to the slaughter of human
beings.

It is at the end of the first essay (996b-c) that we find those mysterious lines about the Titans, Dionysos, *daimones*, and rebirth
which have been such a puzzle to scholars. Plutarch begins by
alluding to Plato's *Phaedrus* (245c) on reincarnation, then to
Empedocles—which must surely be the *Purifications* passage
on the fall of the *daimones* [10] though the text is lost here—and
continues with the imprisonment of the *daimon* in flesh after the
primal sin of cannibalism. Plutarch once more alleges that Empedocles enigmatically meant by these lines that human souls
are imprisoned in mortal bodies as a punishment for eating animal
flesh, and he again relates this to the Orphic legend of Dionysos
and the Titans: "since the irrational and violent elements of
human nature are described by ancient authors as not the divine
but the daimonic in us" (τὸ γὰρ ἐν ἡμῖν ἄλογον καὶ ἄτακτον καὶ
βίαιον, οὐ θεῖον ἀλλὰ δαιμονικόν).[11] Plutarch's treatment of the
Titans, and even to some extent the *daimones*, seems to be allegorical here, though in Empedocles at least some of the *daimones*
are very real. It is probably Plutarch's strained incorporation
of the Orphic legend into Empedocles' teaching which results
in the final allegory. [12] At any rate, here as in *De superstitione* and

---

[10] Probably σαρκῶν ἀλλογνῶτι περιστέλλουσα χιτῶνι fr. 126, which is repeated
at 998c.

[11] The line continues: οἱ παλαιοὶ Τιτᾶνας ὠνόμασαν καὶ τοῦτ᾽ ἐστιν κολαζό-
μενοι καὶ δίκην διδόντες. I. E. Linforth, *The Arts of Orpheus* (Berkeley: 1941)
p. 338, on rather slender grounds, used this text along with Olympiodoros
p. 84 (=fr. 20) to argue that for Xenocrates the Titans were imprisoned in
human bodies, not that men were born from them. Anything connected
with the Orphics tends to get cloudy, and recently, J. Strachan, "Who
Did Forbid Suicide at Phaedo 62b," *CQ*, 20 (1970, 216-20), points out that
Olympiodoros' statement on p. 84 is inconsistent with what he says on
p. 85 in which both the Dionysiac and Titanic natures are to be found in
the soul, not in the body: τίς ἡ τις φρουρὰ ὡς μεν τὸ φρουροῦν, αὐτὸς ὁ Διό-
νυσος . . . οὗτος γάρ ἐστι ὁ λύων τὸν δεσμόν . . . Thus, imprisonment is something from which only Dionysos can release us, and we are there because
of inherited guilt from the Titans or because our nature is Titanic.

[12] In connection with his argument Linforth cites fr. 100 of Xenocrates
in Clement where Xenocrates is said to have written a περὶ σαρκοφαγίας
in which he argued that the flesh of irrational animals is affected by their

Pelopidas, the Titans are treated rather light-heartedly, or as non-existent; the legend is an "allegory" about rebirth, as he says at the end of *De esu carnium.*[13] Perhaps it is a *jeu d' esprit* that he refuses to let those Titans, who once tore the little Dionysos to bits, now devour the maiden at Leuctra or Agesilaus' daughter.

We must now turn to that other issue which plagues the treatment of *De superstitione:* does *deisidaimonia* here exclude the fear of *daimones?* Erbse said yes, and attempted to absolve Plutarch from theological contradictions this way since if Plutarch feared the *daimones* later, as Erbse believes, then Plutarch would be practicing the very superstitions which he had condemned in an earlier essay. Erbse's argument is literally and etymologically correct, but if pushed too far makes practical nonsense. Both in *De superstitione* and elsewhere—notably in *De Iside et Osiride—deisidaimonia* is defined as fear of the divinity or of the gods; but in practice, like Theophrastos, Plutarch uses the term to cover a great variety of superstitious practices: credulity in dreams, fear of punishment in the afterlife, taboos and magic rites, abandoning oneself to conjurors, magicians, and old crones, magical purification, prostrations, mumbo-jumbo in addressing the gods, penitential exercises, confession of sin, dietary taboos, refusal to fight on the sabbath, magic charms and spells, ascetical exhibitionism, human sacrifice, and lamentations for the gods (in that order).[14]

Plutarch is hounding the traces of Theophrastos, who after defining *deisidaimonia,* like Plutarch, as fear of the divinity,

---

irrational soul and therefore harmful to the rational soul of man. If this is so, then Xenocrates' vegetarianism would seem to have little to do with palingenesis, and rather oppose than support Linforth's case. In *De esu* 996a, Xenocrates is mentioned in a humanitarian passage (being kind to animals leads to kindness to men), not in a palingenesis passage.

[13] In random passages Plutarch does make the Titans out to be *daimones* and elsewhere reincarnates *daimones* in his myths as punishment for their sins (on earth, and possibly as *daimones*), but there is no basis for thinking he seriously imagined that men were Titans imprisoned in mortal bodies. In the *De facie* myth, 945b, the Titans are--perhaps humorously--mind (*nous*)-less souls which on the analogy of his precosmic soul in *De animae procreatione in Timaeo,* wander about aimlessly until they have been charmed back to the moon from which they escaped.

[14] Erbse, p. 298. *Deisidaimonia* is fear of the gods in *De superst.* 164e, 165b, d, e, 166f, 167a, 168b, 170c, e, f. The other items are superstition in the following order: 165e-f, 168f; 165e, 169a, e; 166f-167a; 166a-166b; 166e; 168d; 169c.

immediately gives a list of a number of superstitious practices dissimilar to a kind of Calvinistic or Jansenistic fear of God we might think at first he is aiming at.[15] Theophrastos' list differs from Plutarch's in that it consists largely of more ancient taboos unconnected with guilt: washing one's hands, sprinkling oneself, putting bay leaves in the mouth, avoiding cats crossing one's path, not allowing red snakes in the house, avoiding various things (smooth stones at cross-roads, mice gnawing at bags, women in childbirth, the fourth and seventh days of the month when mulling wine), and spitting in one's bosom if a madman or epileptic is seen. However, Theophrastos' list is not entirely free of those guilt-ridden obsessions which supposedly only plagued the later religious world: the use of frankincense is ridiculed (Plutarch's "with trembling hand he sprinkles incense," 169e), and more important, frequent visitations to the priests before initiation into the Orphic rite. This is very close to Plutarch's ridicule of the fear of the afterlife since it is the Orphics who preached the fallen nature of man, the need for purification, and the impending horrors of the underworld for the unrepentent and uninitiated.

Elsewhere in the *Moralia* the definition of *deisidaimonia* is likewise ignored in order that Plutarch may concentrate his satire on superstitious practices. In *De Iside* (352b and 355d) and in *Non Posse* (1092c, 1110f, 1101c, 1101e, 1102c) the idea of *deisidaimonia* as an unreasonable fear of the divinity is given fair time; but then the concept is used to describe various practices. Particularly in *De Iside*, it is used to describe deviations from the "true worship of the gods" such as the improper worship of animals (379f-380b). Elsewhere we find the following things condemned

---

[15] Theophrastos defines *deisidaimonia* in the following way: ἡ δεισι-δαιμονία δόξειεν ἄν εἶναι δειλία τις πρὸς τὸ δαιμόνιον. *Char.* 6. E. R. Dodds, *The Greeks and The Irrational*, p. 253 and p. 267, n. 99, uses the passages from Theophrastos and Plutarch to contrast a naive folk superstition with an intense, personal, guilt-filled superstition ("Plutarch's neurosis"). One suspects that his picture is somewhat overexaggerated. The subject of earlier superstition is well treated in Nilsson, I, pp. 795-99, and in P. J. Koets, *Deisidaimonia* (Utrecht: 1929), which reviews statements in authors throughout Greek literature. Theophrastos' ideas are treated in H. Bolkestein, "Theophrastos' Character der Deisidaimonia," *RGGV* 21, (1929), 3ff. As Erbse points out, p. 289, Aristotle (*Pol.* 1315a) and Xenophon (*Ages.* 11.8, *Cyrop.* 3.3.58) give the word a good connotation, "respectful reverence," a meaning which appears well into Theophrastos' time (Diod. 1.70.8, Heracl. *Qu. Hom.* 1), and which Erbse sees behind Polybios' statement that *deisidaimonia* kept the Romans united, 6.56.7.

as superstition: fear of sacrificing without the wild playing of
flutes (*Quaestiones Romanae* 277f), excessive credulity in dreams
and visions (*De genio Socratis* 579f), practices connected with
the worship of certain Attises, and Adonises, in which "hermaph-
rodites" and women are involved (*Amatorius* 756c), the avoidance of the shrine Vicus Paternus by the Roman males (*Quaestiones
Romanae* 264c), burial taboos (*Quaestiones Romanae* 264f, 268f,
and *Instituta Laconica* 238d, cf. *Lycourgos* 27), throwing human
images into a river (*Quaestiones Romanae* 272b), fear of punishment
after death (*Non posse suaviter vivi secundum Epicurum* 1104b),
certain dietary taboos (*De Iside et Osiride* 353e); close to superstition are the worship of trees (*Quaestiones convivales* 703d),
and the apparatus of seers and sacrificers (*Regum et imperatorum
apophthegmata* 201b), while fear of the afterlife is considered by
Theon, a respectable speaker in one dialogue "a childish terror." [16]
    The same use of the term *deisidaimonia* to describe superstitious
practices in preference to limiting it to the more abstract fear of God,
is evident in the *Lives*. A number of taboos are classified as *desi-
daimonia*, some of them having to do with not sanctifying gates
(*Lycourgos* 27, *Aratos* 53, *Sulla* 35); then there is the fear of celestial
phenomena (*Pericles* 6, *Nicias* 23); excessive credulity toward omens
(*Sulla* 12, *Sertorius* 11, *Marcellus* 5 and 6, *Timoleon* 26, *Brutus* 39),
fear of natural phenomena as the indication of divine wrath
(*Romulus* 24, *Poplicola* 21, *Solon* 12), fear of leaving the Vestal
state (*Numa* 10), excessive credulity in dreams (*Caesar* 63, *Coriolanus* 24), fear of curses (*Crassus* 16), unlucky days (*Camillus*
19), and fear of a snake around a corpse (*Cleomenes* 39).
    Indirectly one can argue that *deisidaimonia* includes fear of the
daimones, since so many rites and practices which are associated
with *daimones* are condemned as expressions of *deisidaimonia*.
There is also an ambiguity in the word *daimonion*, which forms
part of the concept *deisidaimonia*, since *daimonion* is sometimes

---

[16] Some of the examples are interesting. In *Qu. Rom.* 264f, a man named
Aristinos had been buried by his too-hasty friends, but Delphi came to
his rescue and told him that he would pollute no one if he had himself
washed by the women "like a new-born babe." In Plutarch's view, 268f,
the Vestal Virgins were buried alive, not executed in another way, because
of superstition. In *Inst. Lac.* 238d Lycourgos is said to have done away
with superstition by allowing burial within the city. In *Qu. Rom.* 272b it
is said that Heracles substituted images for men once thrown by the Romans
into the Tiber. For the interesting mystery of the *Ageerfrage* see K. Latte,
Römische Religion, pp. 412-14.

used for *daimon* in indicating a good or evil spirit. Plutarch himself, with few exceptions, restricts himself to the word *daimon*; and where he does use another term, *daimonion*, he may be influenced by his source. Yet, a Greek reader would be familiar with either term to describe the spirits. Thus there is something linguistically very apt in labelling apotropaic rites as *deisidaimonia*, not only in *De superstitione* 171c-d, but also in *Romulus* 24—where strictly speaking it is purification, *Poplicola* 21, and possibly *Solon* 12; and in *Pelopidas* 21 and *De superstitione* 171c-d we have seen human sacrifice particularly linked to the *daimones*.

In two instances, *Numa* 8 and the introduction to *Dion-Brutus* (2), *deisidaimonia* is applied directly to the belief in evil *daimones*. Numa is portrayed as a primitive lawgiver struggling to bring a savage and unrestrained people under the sway of law and custom. Accordingly he makes use of the *pia fraus*, which his mentor, Pythagoras—who appears here as something of a charlatan—has apparently suggested to him. Therefore, Numa trains the Romans in the practice of religious processions and the like; but he also at times frightens them by reporting supernatural threats, strange apparitions of *daimones* (φάσματα δαιμόνων ἀλλόκοτα), and terrifying voices "in order to subject their minds through *deisidaimonia.*" In this passage, much as in the speech of the anti-superstitious Galaxidoros in *De genio Socratis* (579f), superstition is thought of primarily as the belief in visions and apparitions.

We have now seen that the term *deisidaimonia* was not only used to describe a number of practices associated with *daimones*, but also that on a few occasions the belief in *daimones* was directly called a form of superstition by Plutarch. A most conclusive passage is the use of *deisidaimonia* in the introduction to the parallel *Lives* of Dion and Brutus to describe the belief in *daimones*. What is peculiar here is that Plutarch's attitude in the introduction appears so ambiguous that most commentators regard him as indicating his belief in the visions of those *daimones* which are to be described later in the *Lives*.

Plutarch explains that one of the similarities in the lives of the two heroes was that each received a vision of their impending death. Later we learn that the vision to Dion was that of a huge Erinys sweeping his halls; that to Brutus, as he was setting out from Abydos for Greece, was a huge figure which tells Brutus that he is his evil *daimon*. Plutarch explains to the reader that he is inclined to accept these visions as true since both men had philosophical training but thought the events worthy of narration to their friends. Still he states before this—in an amazingly witty and piercing style for a gullible believer in these tales—that those who do not believe in such things claim that a vision of a *daimon* or a ghost-(φάσματα δαίμονος μήδ' εἴδωλον) is not the product of a sound mind, but that such are reported rather by women, children, and the sick in a moment of mental derangement (ἐν πλάνῳ ψυχῆς) or in some distemper of body (ἐν τινι δυσκρασίᾳ σώματος). Such "drag along empty and strange opinions, having in themselves the *daimon* of superstition" (δαίμονα πονηρὸν ἐν αὐτοῖς δεισιδαιμονίαν ἔχοντας).[17] Whatever Plutarch believed himself, the words of the passage suggest that *deisidaimonia* was a term frequently played upon in puns to suggest a belief in *daimones*.

Two scholarly reconstructions now seem to collapse over the insubstantial ground upon which they were erected: it seems unjustified and wildly hypothetical to maintain either that *deisidaimonia* was used so exclusively by Plutarch that only the fear of the gods was included in the meaning of the term and that it had nothing in the least to do with *daimones*, or that in *De superstitione* Plutarch was completely unaware of the distinction between gods and *daimones* which is found in the later writings. One might ask, indeed, why he should be unaware of this distinction when he wrote *De superstitione*. If he wrote the essay after being through the Academy it would be surprising that he had not read the works of one of the Academy's most ingenious masters, Xenocrates; and it is Xenocrates who most of all fostered the idea that there was indeed a distinction between *daimones* and gods. Moreover, the condemnation of superstition is a theme which belongs to the philosophic school. Even so the discussion

---

[17] He uses the words δόξας ἐφέλκεσθαι κενὰς καὶ ἀλλοκότους. The phrases suggest some others: in *De aud.* 15b eating the cuttlefish is supposed to be responsible for wild dreams (φαντασίας ταραχώδεις καὶ ἀλλοκότους); in *Qu. Rom.* 284c the Romans on the approach of Hannibal are commanded by the Sibylline books to sacrifice two Greeks and two Gauls to some strange and foreign *daimones* (ἀλλοκότοις τισὶ δαίμοσι καὶ ξένοις ἀποτροπῆς ἕνεκα). Thus, even the phrase used about the opinions of the superstitious seems to be a play on the belief in *daimones*: their *daimones* are nothing more than their own empty opinions. One could also add Numa's reports of celestial terror described as φάσματα δαιμόνων ἀλλόκοτα (*Num.* 8). On Numa see J. Poncet, "Les Sabins aux origines de Rome," *ANRW*, I, 1 (1972), pp. 48-135.

on human sacrifice in *De superstitione* is so closely paralleled by others in Plutarch's writings which collar the *daimones* responsible for all this mischief of human sacrifice, that one must sadly wonder why it should occur to scholars to omit these creatures from the *De superstitione* passage. As far as *deisidaimonia*, as a term to describe fear of *daimones* is concerned, one can only say that the human sacrifice passage, the loose use of *deisidaimonia* throughout Plutarch's writing, and the actual application of the term in several passages, should be sufficient inducement for us to give Plutarch a little more credit for intelligence than has sometimes been given in the past. On the other hand, flagrantly terroristic and delightfully sadistic in the eschatological myths of the *Moralia*, and flamboyantly exhibitionistic in his use of portents and dreams, in the *Lives*, including that sacred cow, eclipses, he reveals a different spirit, the "mature" which we can truly call Plutarchan. How dreadful for literature and religious psychology, even for revealing the spirit of his times, if he had restricted himself to the dull, even if true strictures of *De superstitione*.

CHAPTER FIVE

LIMB TORN FROM LIMB: MYSTICISM
AND THE YOUNG PLUTARCH

We can now turn to a subject which has broader implications for
the general flow of Plutarch's philosophical and religious conceptions. This is the nature of his early religious ideas and of the
surroundings in which they originated. The general view prevalent
today is that Plutarch was influenced by the Academy to accept
a rather thoroughgoing scepticism and rationalism, but that in
later life he rejected this in order to defend many traditional
religious practices and beliefs which we would today regard as
superstitious. In this view, by the time he became a priest of
Delphi he had virtually reversed all his earlier positions, thus
adopting a mentality inconsistent with his earlier ideas and earlier
Weltanschauung, a *Weltanschauung* irrecognizable in his later
works.[1] In contrast to this view, it will be argued here that the
young Plutarch was something quite different: idealistic, altruistic,
contemptuous of cold logic, leaning toward the softer mentality
of the philosophical mysticism to be found in Greek culture—
Empedoclean, Pythagorean, Orphic, and Platonic—rather than
to the harder thinking of scientific discussion for which the *physikoi*
were noted. This view is not entirely original since it is hinted at
by Ziegler on one occasion, and by Helmbold in his introduction
to the *De esu carnium*, but it has never been developed as one of
the indispensable elements in understanding the growth of Plutarch's

---

[1] Hirzel, *Plutarch*, pp. 8-10, and Flacelière, especially, "Plutarque et la
Pythie," *REG*, 56 (1943), 72-111, are primarily responsible for the promul-
gation of this view. For Hirzel there were two focal points in Plutarch's
life: at Athens he learned scepticism; at Delphi "religiöser Tiefsinn und
Hang zur Mystik." Flacelière goes so far as to make Plutarch a sort of
Thomas Aquinas: "il en vint à sentir plus 'théologien' encore que 'philosophe'
et sans renier à la philosophie à ne plus voir en elle que l'humble servante
de la théologie, *ancilla theologiae*" (p. 111). Flacelière is here referring to a
phrase which appears in a description of Cleombrotos in *De defectu oraculorum*.
This seems particularly inapt, since Cleombrotos is immediately ridiculed
(410b), and Flacelière puts this particular dialogue in Plutarch's philosophical
rather than theological period. For Plutarch's youth see Jones, *Plutarch
and Rome*, pp. 1-64.

religious philosophy. On the other hand, a very simplistic hypothesis has been unquestionably accepted, with not a voice raised in protest against it.

The school that maintains a rationalistic, sceptical, anti-superstitious Plutarch in youth stakes everything on *De superstitione*. Yet, it should be pointed out that even here he is no friend of atheism or Epicureanism. Atheism is constantly condemned as a vice, equal to that of superstition, and at the beginning of the essay he claims that the atomicatic theory of the universe (ἀτόμους τις οἴεται καὶ κενὸν ἀρχὰς εἶναι τῶν ὅλων) is a "false hypothesis," the only good of it being that it does not cause the same sort of "throbbing pain" as superstition (164f). But is this the only essay we have written by the young Plutarch? Why has this essay alone been chosen to represent his youthful views and all the others neglected? The answer is that it supported the dominant assumptions of 19th Century German scholars who were interested in the new theory of development, and like many an old ship, it has been kept in service long past its time of usefulness.

There is another picture of the young Plutarch which has been largely suppressed. We can begin with the vignette he gives of himself in *De E apud Delphos* where he describes himself as an ardent youth about to enter the Academy, which was then under the direction of Ammonios, and in which he gives a fairly long speech as one of the characters of the dialogue.[2] He describes

---

[2] In his article for the *Budé Congrès*, "Le platonisme de Plutarque," pp. 519-30, H. Dörrie argued that Plutarch's Platonism is a deviate Platonism out of the mainstream of Middle Platonism, that he never belonged to the Academy—though he probably received his philosophical formation there and then left immediately after, and that it is possible that neither he nor Ammonios were ever members of the Academy. Dörrie's heretical view was sharply opposed by two Plutarchists present, Flacelière and Cuvigny, pp. 529-30, who question whether Middle Platonism ever demanded such orthodoxy as Dörrie suggests. Besides Plutarch's testimony in *De E* about his entrance into the Academy, at the end of *Themistocles* he records that the town of Magnesia set up benefices for the descendants of Themistocles, and that a recipient of these was Themistocles of Athens, "an intimate and friend of mine in the school of Ammonios the philosopher." Our knowledge about Ammonios is excellently treated by C. P. Jones, "The Teacher of Plutarch," *Harv. Stud.*, 71 (1966), pp. 205-13, who regards Ammonios as an Alexandrian—something which seems mysterious due to his holding of the post of *strategos* at Athens. It seems inconceivable that Plutarch should have claimed either that he or Ammonios were in the Academy if in fact they were not, and certainly no ancient authority queried their

himself as passionately devoted to mathematics at the time, but his idea of devotion to mathematics, slightly lacking the sophistication of an Einstein or Russell, means that he has accepted the theory of mystical numbers by which the different types of being, the meaning of the myths and the gods in them, and the interrelationships between different aspects of reality can be reduced to numbers, to combinations of numbers, or to manipulations of numbers which give a deep insight into the realities they describe. If Plutarch did believe in these ideas at the time, he must later have discarded some of them, such as the identification of Apollo and Dionysos as different aspects of the same god (389a), or the idea that the cycles of the Dionysiac rite are signified through the dithyramb since the dithyramb expresses the ratio of 3 to 1, the relation of creation to conflagration (389b). Another use of the mystical number theory by the young Plutarch is the attribution of the pempad to the god Apollo-Dionysos, because the pempad "at times creates itself of itself, like fire, or at other times creates the decad out of itself" (389c-d). Later in the speech, more along the lines of traditional Platonism, the pempad is applied to the Good, which displays itself under five categories which Plutarch goes on to describe (391a).

A knowledge of Platonism and Aristotelianism is displayed in the essay, beyond that of a non-Academician. The conclusion seems inevitable: this is not an entirely accurate representation of Plutarch's youthful thought.[3] However, the essay is meant to

membership. J. E. Whittaker, "Ammonius on the Delphic E," *CQ*, 19 (1969), 185-92, takes the speech to be heavily influenced by Alexandrian Platonism and contemporary Neopythagoreanism, and as foreshadowing Neoplatonic developments. Both he and Dörrie are intrigued with the link which might exist between Plutarch and Eudoros of Alexandria, possibly mediated by Ammonios. See Dörrie's "Der Platoniker Eudoros von Alexandreia," *Hermes*, 79 (1944), 25-38, "Le renouveau du platonisme à l' époque de Cicéron," *Rev. de Théol. et de Philos.*, 24 (1974), 1-29, "Die Stellung Plutarchs im Platonismus seiner Zeit," (Merlan Festschrift), pp. 36-56, and J. Dillon, *The Middle Platonists*, pp. 189-191. Dörrie and Dillon differ over Plutarch's "orthodoxy". Dörrie sees him as unorthodox and has doubts about both him and Ammonios actually being in the Academy. Dillon sees him as original and independent at times, but very much in the Platonic trend of the time.

[3] For example he divides the soul into five parts (θρεπτικόν, αἰσθητικόν, ἐπιθυμητικόν, θυμοειδές, λογιστικόν, 390f) rather than into Plato's three parts (Cf. *Rep.* 4 and 10), the same division he uses in his *De virtute morali* where he adds Aristotle's αἰσθητικόν and θρεπτικόν to the Platonic tripartite

be a rather complete exposition of the meanings of the E; and it would be quite logical to let the youthful Plutarch of the speech say a bit more than he would have been capable of at the time, without, however, turning him upside down. After Plutarch finishes, Ammonios demolishes his arguments by pointing out numbers which are just as useful as those Plutarch has proposed. The passage, then, probably is something of a reflection of Plutarch's activity within, rather than before entering the Academy, though for our purposes this does not make much difference. Very significant is the fact that the young Plutarch ends his speech with an Orphic verse he has gleaned from Plato's *Philebus* (66a-c) though the verse is rather meaningless in itself (ἕκτῃ δ' ἐν γενεῇ κατα-παύσατε θεσμὸν ἀοιδῆς, 391d). Whether in or out of the Academy, Plutarch wishes to present himself as influenced by number mysticism and Orphism. It is not altogether impossible also that he was able to read Plato and perhaps some Aristotle before entering, or to have picked up their ideas from his brothers or friends.

The *De esu carnium* has already been described as a youthful writing; and we have already seen the preoccupation with Dionysiac legend and reincarnation which is the basis of the vegetarianism in it. As proof of the youthful style of the piece the opening paragraph is given here in Helmbold's translation (Loeb. *Mor.* XII, p. 541).

> Can you really ask what reason Pythagoras had for abstaining from flesh? For my part I rather wonder both by what accident and in what state of soul or mind the first man who did so, touched his mouth to gore and brought his lips to the flesh of a dead creature, he who set forth tables of dead, stale bodies and ventured to call food and nourishment the parts that had a little before bellowed and cried, moved and lived. How could his eyes endure the slaughter when throats were slit and hides flayed and limbs torn from limb? How could his nose endure the stench? How was it that the pollution did not turn away his taste, which made contact with the sores of others and sucked juices and serums from mortal wounds? (993 b-c).

One might almost think he were describing the innocent children slaughtered in sacrifice by the Carthaginians, who in the *De*

---

division (442b). Moreover, in the *De E* speech he omits the characteristic Pythagorean interpretation of the soul as a harmony of five elements (See *HGP* I, pp. 306-19, esp. p. 315).

superstitione passage are in fact butchered "like so many lambs or young birds" (171d).

More tenets of the essay which give something of the flavor of his mind at this time are:

Men originally refrained from flesh while they wallowed in vice and luxury, and only in a later period when they were hungry and were forced to eat mud and bark did they turn to flesh (993 e-f).

We do not eat wild animals like lions or wolves, but rather tame domestic animals who are our friends (994b).

Men pretend that animals crying out at the slaughter are inarticulate, whereas in reality they are crying out for justice (994e).

The viands on the table are corpses about to be eaten (994f).

Man's anatomy shows that he is not naturally carnivorous (994f).

The eating of flesh debilitates the soul (995e) (conceived here in a material sense— (τὰς ψυχὰς παχύνουσιν).

The philosophers who tell us to eat our children, friends, fathers, and wives after death are not as humanizing as Pythagoras or Empedocles (997e).

As tyrants begin the slaughter with the worst sycophants, so by beginning with harmful animals we turn to the humble and innocent (998b).

Even if the doctrine of transmigration is not proved, there is at least enough doubt to make us cautious (998d).

Both the fact that many of these views either were repudiated or not defended in the mature writings, and the fact that they are presented in *De esu carnium* in a rhetorical unrestrained way— which we like to think is characteristic of youth—seems sufficient proof that *De esu carnium* is indeed a youthful writing, and that the views presented in it were seriously held by its author. The strange rhetorical attitude which we meet with in the essay is particularly reflected in the passage at 996c on the doctrine of reincarnation, which is introduced by some lines from Empedocles. This passage, which is later alluded to again at 998c, refers to the fall of the *daimon*, the primal sin of flesh eating, and the myth of the dismemberment of Dionysos.[4] The Platonic myth of the

---

[4] The only article on Orphism in Plutarch is G. Méautis, "Plutarque et l'Orphisme," *Mélanges Glotz* I (Paris: 1932), p. 579 ff., a far-fetched attempt to prove that there was a pure Orphic sect existing in Plutarch's time. He took *Consol. ad uxor.* 611d-e where Apollo is identified with the sun, and linked it to a passage from Heracleides Ponticos (*Qu. Hom.* 6.10=Kern fr. 88) in an attempt to prove that the identification of the sun with Apollo was an Orphic idea that had been stolen from the sect by the Stoic Cleanthes, and that the doctrine could be found in the passage in Plutarch, in which

ascent and descent of the soul is introduced by citing the words of the *Phaedrus* that this is "great, mysterious, and above mortal thoughts," (τὴν δὲ μεγάλην καὶ μυστηριώδη καὶ ἄπιστον ἀνδρᾶσι δεινοῖς (δειλοῖς), 996b). In view of Plutarch's later myths where he takes reincarnation for granted, the gingerliness with which the doctrine is introduced here seems very surprising. Moreover, he seems to take the doctrine very seriously, without a stitch of humor, whereas in his later myths we often have our doubts as to how serious he actually is; and at least in one place he makes something of a joke out of the whole belief, managing to reincarnate the Emperor Nero as a frog, ready to croak his way through many a pond and puddle.[5]

Youthful sincerity and idealism and the appeal of the heart over the head are reflected throughout the essay. The young Plutarch is not too far removed from the youth communes of today, the flower children, and the hippies, at least insofar as these are concerned with a more natural and more primitive way of life which makes fewer incursions upon nature and its animals. At least it is pleasant to believe that something in common between the young Boeotian and the youth of today can be found. Particularly today when there exists a youthful protest against the destruction of many natural species, and when many young people have turned to eastern philosophies which they think are more respectful of nature, it is easy to see Plutarch's vegetarianism as a kind of

---

the soul is described as being in prison in the same way as a bird in a cage. Anyone acquainted with Plutarch's thought should be able to see through the absurdity of this type of text manipulation as a method of working with his philosophy.

[5] In the myth of *De sera numinis vindicta* (567e-568a), Nero is about to be reincarnated as a snake when a voice intervenes and he is permitted to be reincarnated as a frog; the favor is given him because of the emperor's benefactions to Greece. The subject has been treated in an interesting article—which investigates very carefully numerous parallels including every possible point of comparison between the myths of Plato and Plutarch, no matter how trivial—"Le châtiment de Néron dans le mythe de Thespésios," *Budé Congrès*, pp. 552-60, by J. Dumortier. He notes that Plutarch, who was twenty years old at the time of Nero's proclamation of liberty to Greece, and who may have been present at Corinth for the proclamation, possibly portrayed the spirit of the event while describing with exuberance the similar proclamation of Greek liberty made by Flamininus (*Flam.* 10 and 11). Dumortier—relying on Flacelière, *La Sagesse de Plutarque*, p. 146—uses a poor textual reading in connection with the description of Nero's mother as a snake. The matter is put correctly by Einarson and De Lacy (Loeb *Mor.* VII, p. 299).

youthful empathy with the natural world. But he certainly did not give up all these ideas in later life: his sympathy toward animals and the natural world is reflected throughout the *Moralia*, and to some extent is even found in the *Lives*.

There is one tantalizing work which is closely related to *De esu carnium*, though the satirical treatment suggests that the metempsychosis doctrine of that essay is no longer held so firmly. The essay has the long Latin title, *Bruta animalia ratione uti*, but is often referred to by the shorter title *Gryllus*, since Odysseus' companion, Gryllos, is the principal speaker. He has been transformed into a pig by Circe and in this form lectures the Greek wanderer, Odysseus, on the superiority of animals to men. The date, authorship, and sources have been much debated, but many of the ideas seem so thoroughly Plutarchan that one would have to be quite out of his mind to deny that Plutarch wrote the piece. Among some very characteristic touches are the inhumanity of man—which runs throughout the essay, the glorification of feminine courage (987f), the similarity in the age of a crow here (989a) with that in *De defectu oraculorum* (415c), the condemnation of man's insatiable and luxurious appetite, of deceit in women, and of homosexuality (990c-d), and the opinion that the eating of meat is not caused by hunger but rather by gluttony (991c-d). Gryllos' words on the courage of women are somewhat different from those we find elsewhere in the *Moralia*. In *Mulierum Virtutes* and *Amatorius* the courage of women is equal to that of men; but in *Gryllus*, the pig claims that among animals the female is equal to the male in courage, but not so among humans. Possibly Plutarch changed his mind in later life; but it is also true that in a burst of exuberance for the greater virtue of the bestial world, Gryllos may be guilty of some exaggeration.

The dialogue is cleverly conceived. Odysseus comes to Circe to reclaim his men who have been transformed by her charms, and he is quite surprised when she questions whether they will want to return to human form. Through Circe's magical powers Gryllos is enabled to talk —a pun on the title itself (*Do Beasts have Reason?*)—and in a topsyturvy state of inebriated enthusiasm for his newly discovered animal culture and morality, he scathingly attacks the human race and demonstrates to the famous cheat that animals are not only more just, virtuous, intelligent, chaste, and courageous, but also more cultured and naturally gifted in

almost every way than man. Odysseus has just thrown in the
red herring "But do they believe in God?" as our manuscript
breaks off. I suppose Gryllos would have replied that not only
do they believe in the gods, but they communicate their desires
to men who very often ignore them. Obviously Plutarch's sympathies are completely with the pig, which perhaps like Plutarch
is Boeotian, a race supposedly noted for its stupidity.

There is another dialogue, considered late and not beset by the
quibbling difficulties over authorship and date as is the *Gryllus*,
which enables us to make some interesting comparisons with *De
esu carnium*. This is *De sollertia animalium*, a title which does not
reflect the bifurcation of the Greek, πότερα τῶν ζῴων φρονιμώτερα
τὰ χερσαῖα ἢ τὰ ἔνυδρα.[6] The main point of the essay is that animals
are endowed with intelligence, an attribute which is not limited to
men. In the first part Autoboulos, Plutarch's father, criticizes
the Stoics for contradicting themselves in denying rationality to
animals; in the second he demonstrates that animals of all kinds
are rational. However, the actual framework is that of a debate
over whether land or water animals are more intelligent. The
essay rests upon sources apparently used by Pliny and Aelian
for their natural histories; but Plutarch makes use of them with
far more selectivity than these authors did.

The dialogue begins as a continuation of a meeting on the
previous day at which time a book in praise of hunting had been
read. It is possible that Plutarch wrote this book himself; but
it would seem strange if he actually had since its contents apparently
contradicted all the tenets of his vegetarian treatises. Autoboulos
admits that the reading of the book has stirred in him a fever
for the hunt; but when a friend, Soclaros, comments on how wonder-
ful it is to see—instead of the gladiatorial contests in which man
is pitted against man—the hunt in which intelligence and courage

---

[6] Ziegler, p. 103, thinks that Plutarch wrote the work as a piece of rhetorical ostentation for his pupils' benefit, but that it is a mature work; and he
cites several scholars who support this opinion. It is somewhat disturbing
the way the "rhetorical" argument for relative chronology is twisted around
by Ziegler: surely the "rhetoric" here is not that of *De superstitione* or
De esu carnium. In Ziegler's view, moreover, p. 9—though the picture of
Plutarch's father is an *Idealporträt*, and not *dokumentarisch*—his Pythagorean
and vegetarian tendencies cannot be a mere fiction. He also attributes
Plutarch's own tendencies in this direction to the father (*väterliches Erbe ist*).
We must be cautious here but the opinion of the greatest German Plu-
tarchist must be given consideration.

are pitted against brute force, Autoboulos can take no more; he exclaims that this is precisely where the trouble lies, and that this is the very source of insensibility spreading among men. He goes on to repeat the account, familiar to readers of Plutarch, of the growing thirst of the tyrants for blood at Athens, which appeared in *De esu carnium*; and he gives a similar short history of the growing barbarity of man as he slaughters ever more species of animals (959d-f).

Unfortunately Autoboulos ends here, saying he has already strayed too far from the subject of the dialogue, so we will never know whether Plutarch's father was truly a Pythagorean. However, even if he were not a Pythagorean, he is at least sympathetic to their doctrine, and he acknowledges the debt. Again we are faced with the difficulty of determining how much is Plutarch and not the personal idiosyncracies of the speaker, and at what stage in the development of Plutarch's thought we are. It may be significant that Autoboulos does not go on to say a few words about reincarnation. But then why should he? As he mentions himself, it is not the principal theme of this dialogue; and Plutarch may have felt that he had said enough about this subject in connection with vegetarianism.

In the course of the dialogue Autoboulos goes on to mention that animals—like all things endowed with soul—have perception, imagination, and intelligence. But the word he used for intelligence is *synesis* (960d), not *nous* or *logos* as we might have expected if under the animal shape a human form is imprisoned. In *De animae procreatione in Timaeo*, and throughout his works, Plutarch is often careful to separate soul from intelligence, given as *logos*, *dianoia*, or *nous*. One wonders how he could have reconciled the idea of intelligence in animals with the conceptions of his later treatises on the soul. However, *synesis* is rather ambiguous and could easily be used for what we would call the instinctive sagacity of animals. At any rate, Autoboulos must have had some inclination toward the doctrine in question, the affinity of the animal and rational world, since Plutarch is not in the habit of putting characters into his dialogues unless they satisfy the minimum demands for credibility. Thus Epicureans are selected for Epicurean parts, Stoics for Stoic, poets and critics for literary parts.

Another possibility suggests itself, that *De sollertia animalium* represents a stage of Plutarch's thought between *De esu carnium* and his later writings, where he does not advocate vegetarianism. In this case *De sollertia*'s restraint and silence over reincarnation would be significant, but one would have to propose this view with great caution since Plutarch is loath to repeat in one dialogue views which he has thoroughly discussed in another. Moreover, Autoboulos declines to enter further into the matter on just these grounds—that this is not the subject of the present work—which may be another way for Plutarch to gently inform the reader that he should consult *De esu carnium* if he wishes to learn more about reincarnation in animal form.

The spectre of vegetarian horror over the slaughter of animals did not seem to leave his conscience entirely untroubled in later life—if we are to judge by two of his *Symposiacs*. In the first, 8.8 (728d-730d), he apparently felt that some sort of divine sanction had to be called into play in order to justify the eating of meat, since he claims that an oracle from Delphi was responsible for removing the ancient prohibition against eating flesh. Up to this time supposedly the prohibition was universal; but in Plutarch's imaginary history, the animals so began to threaten crops that the gods came to man's rescue, and through the oracle permitted them to eat the flesh of animals. Even so his conscience is not entirely satisfied, and he finds it difficult to justify the eating of fish, a species which he regards as harmless to man and a luxurious food. It seems safe then to presume that in later life he either abstained from fish or ate it with great reluctance.

In view of Plutarch's earlier vegetarian superstitions, another *Symposiac*, 2.3 (635e-638a), takes on considerable meaning as a reflection of the guilt of the subconscious making its way to the surface (at least for those who like to substitute the Freudian myths of the modern world for the ancient ones which have wilted away). The title of this *Symposiac* is whether the chicken or the egg came first, or—to quote the Greek more precisely—whether the bird or the egg came first. The question strikes us as rather silly; but in the way in which it is developed in the dialogue it is not at all ridiculous and brings in a number of paleontological considerations, which unfortunately were not pursued in the ancient world. Since the classical mentality is admirably revealed in the short essay, it is worthwhile giving the gist of it. The first speaker, a friend of Plutarch named Sulla, who plays a large role in Plutarch's *De facie in orbe lunae*, argues that the egg came first on the basis that "incohate things, the indeterminate, must come before the determinate." As an example he cites the life of a butterfly, which must first exist in the caterpillar state before it burst forth in wings; and he adds that all things in the present time come from eggs. Only at the end of his argument does he briefly introduce the Orphic cosmogony, which attributed the origin of all things to a primal egg; and this he does in a humorous way (ἔφη γελάσας).

The second, and final speaker, is Sossius Senecio, a trusted friend of Trajan and consul in 99, 102, and 107 A.D. He is the host in the present *Symposiac*, the person to whom all the *Symposiacs* are dedicated, and is probably the person to whom the *Lives* were dedicated since his name appears several times in them: presumably the lost *Epaminondas-Scipio*, which began the series of *Lives*, contained a dedication to Senecio. His speech depends upon the characteristic Aristotelian-Platonic philosophical mish-mash we find throughout Plutarch's *Moralia*, including one very Plutarchan touch, the spontaneous generation of living creatures from dead bodies.[7] It seems safe then to deduce that the conclusion of this *Symposiac* adequately represents Plutarch's personal opinions and that the views were merely put into the mouth of Senecio as a tribute to him. Basically the argument used is that determinate things must precede indeterminate (καὶ λόγον ἔχει τοῦ ἀτελοῦς φύσει πρότερον εἶναι τὸ τέλειον, 636f), the reverse of the previous position. The argument is based upon the observation that no egg has arisen from spontaneous generation, whereas this is frequently the case with fully-formed animals from corpses. As an example he mentions the time of the slave revolt in Sicily when numerous corpses were on the ground and large numbers of locusts came from them. He argues, on the other hand, that the egg is the product of intercourse between two fully developed organisms

---

[7] At the end of *Cleomenes* (39), Plutarch relates that Ptolemy had cruelly murdered the Spartan general and had ordered his body to be hung up and flayed, but that a snake coiled around the hero's head, in such a way as to ward off the birds of prey, then the king in superstitious terror permitted the Alexandrians to perform purificatory sacrifices and to worship the dead Cleomenes as a hero (θεόφιλος καὶ κρείττων τὴν φύσιν). Plutarch then puts his own thoughts on spontaneous generation into certain "wiser men's" mouths. Supposedly these wiser men explained that bees generate spontaneously from oxen, beatles from asses, and snakes from human corpses; "thus they removed the superstitious fears of the people." Plutarch concludes that it is because of the spontaneous generation of snakes from human cadavers that these creatures are associated with the hero cult.

(636f-638a). The question is therefore not so ridiculous as it sounds, and recalls some of the 5th Century speculation associated with the Sophists over a progressive or degressive world.

However, the introduction is what concerns us, not the scientific or pseudo-scientific body of the question. Wishing to introduce the dialogue in a catching way, Plutarch relates that he was suffering from a dream which kept coming to him clearly (ἐναργῶς—an important word for the validity of dreams in oneiromancy), and, therefore, decided that he should abstain from eggs "in the hope that they might be the cause." His statement is somewhat mystifying to us, and his abstinence was even more mystifying to his friends. They suspected that he was abstaining from eggs on religious grounds (ἀφοσιοῦσθαι). The reason was, as Plutarch explains, that "the Orphics or Pythagoreans hold that the egg was the first principle of generation and therefore taboo, just as for some it is unlawful to eat the heart or brain." Plutarch adds that an Epicurean friend Alexandros, who was present at the dinner, teasingly recited a verse "Now eating beans is much like eating parents' heads" (ἶσόν τοι κυάμους ἔσθειν κεφαλὰς τε τοκήων); and he explains that those who believed in the words of the verse— who must certainly be Pythagoreans, not Orphics—saw mystical significance in the similarity between the words for bean (κύαμοι) and conception (κύησις).[8]

It is difficult to tell what happened in reality at this dinner party, if it did happen at all and is not just a clever *esprit* to begin a discussion on generation. Perhaps, we are underestimating Plutarch's genius in not taking the whole thing with a bit more salt than is sometimes done. Nonetheless, many elements in the account are very plausible. He feels that he would be ridiculed by the Epicurean if he told him the real cause of his abstinence; and the fact that he was simply experimenting—"as on a Carian,"

---

[8] The passage at 635e is Kern *Orp. fr.* 291. However, Linforth, *The Arts of Orpheus*, p. 286, rightly refuses to accept abstinence from eggs as Orphic doctrine, on the basis that this would be the only instance in extant literature where it is so attributed. In Linforth's view Plutarch has combined two strains of thought, the Pythagorean abstinence from eggs, and the Orphic cosmogony in which a primal egg plays a significant role. The two views have nothing in common. The fact that Boethos' verse is about beans rather than eggs, suggests that the people he is talking about are Pythagoreans not Orphics. The Pythagoreans did in fact abstain from eggs (Aristotle, DK 581b la). See also Guthrie, *HGP* I, p. 188 for a discussion of Pythagorean abstinence, including that from eggs.

as Plutarch puts it—to see if eggs really were the reason for the dream, would be sufficient to absolve him from the charge of gross superstition in the eyes of his readers.[9] The fact that he here seems to separate himself completely from Orphic or Pythagorean belief—in that his reason for abstinence is the dream and not any religious tenets of these schools—is significant for the development of his thought. At the same time, as Dodds and Ziegler have pointed out, the dream may very well reflect a real state of guilt or uneasiness in Plutarch's mind over having abandoned his previous stand of idealistic and humanitarian vegetarianism.[10]

There is one *Symposiac* which does not give us any doctrine held by Plutarch, which in itself might illuminate his youthful character. Nonetheless, because the essay underlines some relationships in his early life, it may add to our picture of his character as a young man. It may be far-fetched to draw any extensive conclusions from this essay, and no one seems to have used the essay so far in order to determine Plutarch's youthful aspirations. However, the passage may be important in lieu of the scanty biographical information we have on him. The title of this *Quaestio convivalis* (1.2) (615d-619b)

---

[9] Plutarch's attitude toward the dream and his experiments upon it, raise questions of his competence in and view of ancient medicine. The subject has been treated recently by J. Scarborough, *Roman Medicine* (Ithaca: 1969), p. 137 ff. Scarborough notes *De superst.* 168c, where Plutarch condemns the superstitious man for rejecting the aid of medical science, as symptomatic of his high regard for medicine. However, Scarborough notes important differences between Plutarch's attitude toward medicine and that of a modern intellectual: for Plutarch it was part of the classical heritage, a product of reason; the individual, enlightened man was himself largely responsible for his own physical health, for knowing what best suited him, and for ministering to his own ailments (Cf. *De tuend. san.* 136e-f, 137a).

[10] E. R. Dodds, *The Greeks and the Irrational*, p. 121, compares Plutarch, on the basis of this passage, to Dio Cassius, who began writing history because of a dream (72.23), and Galen, who once performed an operation because of one (17.219 ff.). In the view of Dodds—who is ever trying to condemn the Roman period of massive anxiety which thrust it into the arms of Christianity—the patronage of the Stoics was responsible for keeping alive what was in Cicero's words "a superstition whose only effect was to increase the burden of men's fears and anxieties" (*De div.* 2. 150). Dodds may be a bit taken in by the words of his classical authorities, especially if the others went about investigating the contents of their dream as coolly as Plutarch. Ziegler, *Plutarchos*, p. 98, thinks that this *Symposiac* is an indication that Plutarch never outgrew the vegetarian beliefs of *De esu carnium*.

reads like something out of Emily Post—"Whether the host should arrange the placing of his guests or leave it to the guests themselves?" Again we have a title which seems trivial, but the actual discussion reveals much about Greek society at the time. The father represents an older autocratic view which lays great stress on titles; the sons defend a newer "democratic" view in which social relationship should remain free and interesting.

The essay, then, represents a father-sons debate over some deep seated tensions in all society. The principal characters are Plutarch's two brothers, Timon and Lamprias, his father Autoboulos, and himself. In the real or fictional *cause célèbre* of this little vignette Timon has just given a party at which the guests were arranged according to their own likes rather than according to rank. As a result one of those invited—a wealthy and pompous bore, but an influential person in the town—felt insulted when he did not receive the best place and walked out to the brothers' "good riddance." The father is highly incensed at his son's conduct—which is supported wholeheartedly by his brother Lamprias—and claims that he has disgraced the family, which forever after will be accused of lacking order (*taxis*) (615e-616b). Perhaps an American would not feel the full effect of the father's words, but certainly many Germans, with an instinctive feeling for *Ordnung* would immediately grasp his point.

The family is now accused of disorder (*ataxia*, in the words of the father), something which would never have happened if his advice on seating the guests in order of rank had been followed in the first place. In support of his position he appeals to the good example of Aemilius Paullus, Homer, and the Creator, who—in Autoboulos' understanding—put order into the world. The little vignette, then, gives us an interesting glimpse into the workings of an upper-class Greek family of the 2nd Century, in which the father attempts to impose the traditional rigidity and aristocratic values which he finds important for the survival of the family's prestige, while the sons, apparently influenced by more casual and democratic values, resist almost in a spirit of contempt. Plutarch even describes his brother Lamprias as "reclining on the couch and speaking in his customary loud voice" telling his father he has never heard such nonsense (617f).

One might ask why the Greek father cites the example of Aemilius Paullus, the Roman general. The peculiar blending of Greek and

Roman, whether in real life or in the literary pages of the *Moralia* was a very marked facet of his society, one admirably brought out by Jones in *Plutarch and Rome*. One also wonders whether Plutarch may have been working on Aemilius at this time, with its speeches so close to those of Livy. The general is treated with respect in the *Life*, but the reader can see through the laudatory passages to a paternalistic busybody whose junior officers must have been bored by his frequent discourses on the duties and cares of a commander, and Plutarch himself may have become a little impatient with him, seeing in him his own father.

Plutarch puts his father in a similar role of giving advice on government to younger men in *Praecepta gerendae reipublicae*. In another *Symposiac*, 8.2 (718c-720c) which has as its subject "What was meant by saying God is always doing geometry?", as we might expect, the first thing that comes to Autoboulos' mind is that God is putting *taxis* into things. Whatever Autoboulos was in real life, the picture we get of him in the *Symposiacs* is that of a rather stern father who is somewhat unbending in his rigid attitude toward tradition and good management, which he describes as order. Moreover, of the three sons in the table etiquette discussion, Plutarch is the only one who is not only hostile but even almost contemptuous of the father. Is it unreasonable to suspect that the father's character was one which inclined him to the asceticism and vegetarianism of the Pythagoreans, and that of all his sons Plutarch may have been the most inclined to follow in his footsteps? We can add to this that one of his lifelong friends, who grew up with him in Chaironeia, traveled with him to Rome on his second journey, and possibly was on his Egyptian tour, Philinos, was a vegetarian, and brought up his children in this manner (*Quaestiones convivales* 728b).

Plutarch's early writings, then, reveal an acquaintance with at least one strain of Greek religious mysticism, the fall of the soul for a primal sin and its reincarnation in human or other bodies. The doctrine is regarded by Plutarch as Pythagorean, and it is in Pythagoreanism that we meet many of the most characteristic elements of Greek religious philosophy, including the belief in good and evil *daimones*. It is absurd to hold that *De esu carnium* is a youthful work, and then to deny that the youthful Plutarch was influenced by mysticism and exaggerated tendencies in the direction of superstition. There is also some reason to believe from his picture of his relationship to his father, that he would have at an early age become acquainted with Pythagoreanism through him. Moreover, of all Autoboulos' sons, he seems to have been the most docile and conservative in outlook. It is possible then that scholars have given too much attention to *De superstitione* as a portrait of his early religious views, and utterly neglected the vegetarian, mystical treatises which were also written in his youthful period. The real development of Plutarch's religious thought seems not to have been a conservative, mystical reaction against early scepticism. Rather the course seems to have been a movement from religious belief in the reincarnation of the soul and related matters, to a mysticism grounded more in Middle Platonism with a strong religious bent such as that we find in Ammonios' speech at the end of *De E apud Delphos* in which Plutarch identifies Apollo with eternal being—itself described in terms of Plato's highest Forms—of which the sun is the visible image.

The whole problem of Plutarch's vegetarianism gives us an interesting view of the difference between classical and modern attitudes toward superstition. In treating some topics which rose out of *De superstitione*, in the early chapters of this work, we saw some striking differences between his concept of the superstitious man and our own. He is willing to accept the mantic power of dreams, the belief in portents, and miracles and apparitions. He probably did not believe in evil *daimones*, in the sense of devils. In his youth he seems to have accepted the doctrine of transmigration into animal bodies, or at least believed that there was a strong possibility that this was so. On the other hand, human sacrifice is superstition; so is the belief in eclipses as portents, the use of penitential rites and the confession of guilt. At times he attempts to seek a scientific explanation for something like the evil eye. Yet he would be shocked if told he were superstitious.

Some historical perspective may help us here. Thomas Aquinas, the medieval schoolman and most learned man of his age regarded himself as not superstitious; yet, he did not think that the question of the possibility that angels might occupy space was absurd; nor did he attempt to combat the belief in devils. Similarly the Renaissance and Reformation were supposed to inaugurate a new era of rationalism. They, however, introduced the greatest witch hunts in history, not because men disbelieved in the power of witches but because they had a deathly fear that a witch conspiracy would take over the world. Perhaps a classical personage like Plutarch would have been astonished at certain superstitions among us. What would he think of our deathly fear of germs? Apparently some scholars would agree with him that the modern world is filled with illusory myths.[11]

Vegetarianism for Plutarch fell into the no-man's-land between crass superstition and the cultivation of one's philosophical heritage. For this reason, in later life he was probably able to look back upon it as a youthful superstition. Still, like all superstitions once embraced, the hook is difficult to remove in its entirety. Thus, he may actually have been bothered sufficiently to reexamine the whole question of abstinence from meat. Apparently the dream subsided for we hear no more of his being a vegetarian.

So far little has been said about an even more complicated issue, the relationship of the advances in philosophy—including natural science—to an increase in superstition. Plutarch presumes—as do many modern scholars—that education, and the study of natural science in particular, are the greatest means at man's disposal to wipe out the last vestiges of Neanderthal superstition. However, in the very breath with which Plutarch claims that the education of women will eradicate the superstition which is so prevalent among them, he lets slip the damning fact that Aglaonice of Thessaly became famous as a witch and deceived many women "because of her knowledge of astronomy." [12] It is well known that

---

[11] For one scholar's view on modern myths see Mircea Eliade, "The Myths of the Modern World," in *Myths, Dreams, and Mysteries*, (London: 1968), pp. 23-38. Eliade—basing himself on Malinowski—conceives myth as an "exemplary model and justification of human conduct." His view is now questioned by modern scholars who see myth as a more complex entity, and as a matter of fact in an article for the *Encyclopaedia Britannica* (15th ed. 1969) entitled "Myth," Eliade himself treated myth as more complex than in his earlier works. For the newer concept of myth, see G. S. Kirk, *Myth, Its Meaning and Function in Ancient and Other Cultures* (Cambridge: 1970), p. 7, and an article cited by Kirk, P.S. Cohen, "Theories of Myth," *Man*, 4 (1969), 337-53, especially p. 351.

[12] In *De def.* 417a and *Conj. praec.* 145d he refers to Aglaonice. In the first he says that the women of Thessaly gained the repute of being able to draw down the moon and that "the cunning deceit" gained credence when the daughter of Hegetor, Aglaonice "who was skilled in astronomy pretended at the time of an eclipse of the moon that she was bewitching it down and bringing it down (ἀστρολογικῆς γυναικὸς ἐν ἐκλείψει σελήνης ἀεὶ προσποιουμένης καὶ γοητεύειν καὶ καθαιρεῖν αὐτήν.) In the second instance, Plutarch describes Aglaonice as being acquainted with the periods of the moon and thus able

the whole astrology business of the Hellenistic period is a bastard offspring of the new astronomy. In a new book on Roman medicine, J. Scarborough has noted the close interrelationship between a rational pragmatism and magic in early Roman medicine. The recent studies of A. A. Barb on the later Roman period and D. Nugent on the Reformation, reveal that magic and witchcraft are not the remnants of previous superstition which has tenaciously refused to surrender to the new learning, but is a product of the new "enlightenment" itself.[13] In short, recent scholars have turned the evolutionist thesis on its head.

This new interpretation of the interrelationship between science and superstition can be clearly seen in the development of Plutarch's thought. A philosophical system, Pythagoreanism—not the crazed mutterings of a wild-eyed troll—was responsible for his early belief that killing fish or animals was equal to cannibalism, or at least that it might be; and perhaps because of this belief he speaks at times as though animals had human intelligence and feelings. Moreover, because of these philosophical beliefs—including the immortality of the soul and its capability of reincarnation—he leans to the view that guilt has been inherited from a previous

to predict a coming eclipse, convincing others that she was drawing it down; Plutarch is convinced that if women will learn philosophy they will laugh at creatures like Aglaonice.

[13] For astrology and the new belief in reward and punishment after death in a celestial heaven or hell, see M. Nilsson *Geschichte der Griechischen Religion* II, especially pp. 486-519, "Astrologie und Sonnenreligion: Astrologie und Weltbild," and pp. 543-559, "Der Toten- und Unterweltsglaube." Nilsson thinks that the fires of hell are dependent upon the philosophical Stoic conception of the fiery cataclysm, the *ekpyrosis*, which originally had nothing to do with religion. Cf. J. Scarborough, *Roman Medicine* (Ithaca: 1969), p. 17. Here Scarborough uses the term "magical-rational" to describe the instinctive medicine developed in primitive societies. A. A. Barb, "The Survival of the Magic Arts," in A. Momigliano, ed. *The Conflict Between Paganism and Christianity in the Fourth Century* (Oxford: 1963), pp. 100-125, emphasizes the distinction between magic and religion (magic attempts to force the supernatural to accomplish the magician's desires: religion says "thy will be done"); but he denies that magic is a step below religion in the progress of man. Rather he reverses the evolutionist theory to make magic dependent upon religion. D. Nugent, "The Renaissance and/of Witchcraft," *Church History*, 30 (1971), 1-10 attacks the view that the predominance of witchcraft in the Renaissance and Reformation was simply a remnant of beliefs which survived the Middle Ages or was merely created by the witchhunts. Rather he sees witchcraft and magic as a direct product of the new humanistic learning, which not only recreated the ancient astronomical world, but also resurrected those pseudo-sciences in the seamier side of ancient culture.

state and we are incarnated into a kind of terrestial purgatory. Plutarch seems to have outgrown these views, but he only escapes from the frying pan to leap into the fire. His sublime idea of the divine results in a monotheism which asserts the immateriality of God, His sublime power and goodness, as well as His infinite justice and benevolent providence. "Well and good," one might say. But these lofty conceptions bring in their train a whole nursery of illegitimate offspring: a reaffirmation of the belief in miracles, portents, omens, oracles, seers, divine retribution in this life, inherited punishment for the sins of parents —all of which Thucydides thought he had buried for good.[14] The older beliefs in animism and mana have reappeared in sophisticated form.

One could take a few instances and examine them in greater detail. His belief in the omnipotence of God, the immortality of the soul, and the new astronomy, leads him to create scenes of sadistic terror in the afterlife such as had never existed in literature before his time, and which still remain with us. Even if he himself did not take his descriptions seriously, posterity certainly did, and they could not have done so unless there was a philosophical and scientific grounding for the new *deisidaimonia*. Similarly Xenocrates, a philosopher, attempted to construct a rationalistic explanation of the universe. In doing so he filled in the chain of being with a race of *daimones*. What was up to that time a folk superstition to be indulgently smiled at by the intelligent, had now received a philosophical justification; it is no wonder that in his

---

[14] Note Plutarch's comment at the end of *Cor.* 38, after giving philosophical reasons why the Fortuna Muliebris could not have spoken:

> However, those who possess a deep reverence for the divine and cherish religion so strongly that they cannot disbelieve or reject phenomena of this sort, find a powerful support for their faith in the miraculous nature of the divine power and the fact that its ways are not ours. Yet the divine bears no resemblance to the human either in its nature or the scope of its activity or the skill or strength of its operations, nor is there anything incompatible with reason in the fact that it could achieve what is beyond our power or execute what is impracticable for us: on the contrary, since it differs from us in every respect, it is in its works above all that it is unlike and remote from us. However, as Heraclitus remarks, most of the attributes of the divine escape our understanding through lack of faith. (Ian Scott-Kilvert, *Makers of Rome*, p. 51).

Not only the rationalistic rejection of the belief in the speaking statue, but also the superstitious belief in it is grounded in the most legitimate philosophical speculation.

7

later works Plutarch seriously considers the role of *daimones* in almost every aspect of the supernatural. His belief in the immortality and spirituality of the soul, a product of his deep understanding of Platonism, leads him to reaffirm the prophetic nature of the soul and to seek elaborate justification to foster the otherwise dying oracle at Delphi. This in itself is based not only on the Platonic exposition of the mantic power of every soul, but on Platonic-Aristotelian "scientific" explanations of *aporroiai* and *pneuma*. The evil eye is still with him, but he has found a scientific basis for it.

In treating the development of Plutarch's religious thought, then, there are serious considerations to be kept in mind which have up to now escaped those scholars who see his development as a simple rationalism-mysticism antithesis. In the following chapters the intertwining of rationalistic, philosophic principles with folk belief, may give a better idea of the confusion which existed in the Imperial period. One could hardly pick any better author since he was no madman or eccentric, but judged by all his contemporaries as a magnificent intellectual representative of his age, one who traveled in the highest circles, and who constantly strove for balance, moderation, and the logical and rational interpretation of reality. Yet, it is in this very figure that we discover some of the wildest superstitious aberrations—no matter how disguised in a dignified robe.

CHAPTER SIX

NOT FOR ANY GOD BUT TO AVERT EVIL SPIRITS: CLEOMBROTOS' DAIMONES

A great amount of systematization of Plutarch's daimonology has been done in the past in order to present it as an intelligible transition to Neoplatonism. However, this has been done at a high cost. Ideas have been torn from the web of treatises built on different conceptions, different periods of the author's life, and different *personae dialogi*—even though in a dialogue they may oppose one another, and a contradictory position may be taken in another passage.[1] Both for the history of philosophy and for an understanding of Plutarch's own thought, this is fundamentally wrong. Unlike some philosophers, Plutarch records through the masks of various *personae* the many strands of philosophical and religious speculation in his day, often without clearly revealing his own position. Moreover, he introduces important parts of his thought into myths about the world after death, which were never taken with complete seriousness by his world, and always allowed great private ingenuity. With a delightful avoidance of pontification, he rarely introduces himself into a major treatise, and sometimes where he does, we cannot be sure that the opinion put in his own mouth is the one most acceptable to him.

All this makes the task of a Plutarchist difficult, but not impossible. Fortunately, he wrote an enormous amount so that we have a basis of comparison. Moreover, the final word in a dialogue usually represents the most satisfactory solution to a difficulty, and he generally gives us an inkling as to which speakers in the dialogue can be trusted. He has his own favorite representatives it would seem: his brother Lamprias, friend Theon, former teacher Ammonios.

The dialogue which has caused the most trouble and incited many

---

[1] On this see Introduction, note 13. Among those who largely systematize Plutarch's demonology from Cleombrotos' speech are Zeller, Pohl, Volkmann, Hirzel, Latzarus, Soury, Seillière, Merlan, and to some extent Babut and Griffiths. Eisele objected to it, and Russell is sensitive to the nature of the speaker here.

knotty discussions in the assessment of Plutarch's daimonology, and the one which is inevitable as a base to start such a discussion is *De defectu oraculorum*, a title usually translated into English as "On the Decline of the Oracles," though the Greek itself (Περὶ τῶν ἐκλελοιπότων χρηστηρίων) suggests better the idea of abandonment. It causes difficulty because it cannot be approached with an open mind. Rather it must be pursued on the heels of the 19th Century German scholars who in their exploratory exuberance— like that of the contemporary archaeologists—sometimes left a site in worse condition than when they found it. At any rate these scholars had a tendency to see Plutarch either uncritically endorsing every idea spoken by one of his characters, no matter how outlandish, or sitting like some philosophical crank, making a scissors-and-paste collage of his philosophical heritage, and covering over with transparent transitions, opinions which he was too ignorant to see as contradictory.

First, something should be said about the nature of the Pythian dialogues, of which *De defectu oraculorum* is a part. All three are written in answer to certain questions about the oracle of Delphi, and apparently were published at roughly the same time, though the exact interrelationship of one to another and the order of composition remain a mystery.[2] The first of the dialogues in the traditional order is *De E apud Delphos*. This is a discussion of various meanings of the mysterious letter E or Ei, which was displayed in a prominent position at Delphi, but of which the origin was no longer known. At the end of the dialogue, Plutarch's master in the Academy, Ammonios, identifies the E with the eternal being of God, taking Ei to mean "Thou art." At the same time this god is said to be Apollo who is eternal and immutable and

---

[2] Three historical allusions give a *terminus post quem*: the eruption of Vesuvius in 79 A.D., mentioned in *De Pyth.* 398e; Nero's visit to Greece at the time of the *De E* discussion; and the Pythian year of Callistratos, 83-84 A.D., shortly before the discussion in *De defectu*. The relationship of the Pythian to the other dialogues is also a matter of dispute. Hirzel, *Der Dialog* II, p. 196, and Adler, *Quibus ex fontibus*, p. 115-16, believed *De facie* came first; H. von Arnim, *Plutarch über Dämonen und Mantik* (Amsterdam: 1921), p. 42, argued that *De defectu* was first. As Hamilton ("The Myth in Plutarch's De facie," p. 28), Cherniss (Loeb, *Mor.* IX, p. 13), and Einarson and De Lacy (Loeb *Mor.* VII, p. 370) point out, it is impossible to prove dependance one way or the other. The more developed eschatology in *De facie*, however, suggests to me that this is later than the Pythian dialogues.

identical with Plato's highest Forms, and the visible image of which is the sun. It is probable that this dialogue was put first in the traditional order because it contains a dedication (to Sarapion who is a speaker in the next dialogue), because Plutarch figures as a youth in the piece, and possibly because the introduction speaks of it as an offering of certain Pythian *logoi*. The second dialogue in the series, *De Pythiae oraculis*, attempts to answer the difficulty posed by the Pythia no longer speaking in verse. The final solution to this difficulty is given by a person named Theon, who—speaking undoubtedly for Plutarch—answers that the Pythia is in reality a peasant girl who is used by the god very much the way an instrument is used by a craftsman or musician; the response—he argues—is that of the god, but the form is that of the Pythia. He adds that in times past a more primitive society delighted in poetry and that the enigmatic responses were more suitable for the world-shaking events entrusted to the Pythia at the time, but that now such responses were out of keeping in a better educated age, and when, moreover, only trivial questions are asked of the priestess. The dialogue is interesting also for the tour of the shrine by the local guides, whose banal explanations—which are continually interrupted by the scholarly company they are conducting round the place—reveal that the *genus* has not changed much in 2000 years.

The final dialogue in the traditional order is *De defectu oraculorum*, meant to answer why the oracle had declined both in the number of responses given and in its prestige throughout the civilized world.[3] The dialogue actually tries to kill two birds with one stone.

---

[3] The relative chronology of the Pythian dialogues and their relationship to one another is a mystery. *De E* contains a dedication to Sarapion, a poet living at Athens in Plutarch's day (see *Mor.* 396d and 628a); *De defectu* is dedicted to Terentius Priscus, a Roman friend of Plutarch. Ammonios and Lamprias take part in the first and last, Theon in the first and second dialogues. Ziegler, *Plutarchos*, p. 194, and R. Del Re *Il Dialogo*, and *De E Delphico*, introds., prefer the Stephanus order and insist on a relatively short time between the works. Flacelière, "Plutarque et la Pythie," 72 ff., thinks the *De Pythiae* was written much later, since it is based on a different inspiration theory. There seems to be good logic in Hirzel's view. *Der Dialog* II, p. 196, that the order of composition is *De defectu, De E, De Pythiae oraculis*, in spite of Ziegler. Recently R. M. Ogilvie, "The Date of De Defectu Oraculorum," *Phoenix*, 21 (1967), 108-119, has shown that there must be a difference in dramatic date of at least seven years between *De defectu* (83, 87, or 79 A.D.) and *De Pythiae oraculis* and *De E* (95) since Plutarch's son and a friend of his son are grown men in the latter two.

On the suggestion that the *daimones* who are responsible for the
prophecy at the shrine have fled to another world, there is a
long digression on how many worlds there are—if there are indeed
more than one. Therefore, besides the religious part, there is a
long astronomical or cosmological section, which is somewhat
different in tone from the discussion about the decline of the oracle.
Although Plutarch is fond of digressions, the length of this one
is quite surprising. His more usual method is to tag one discussion
onto another; for example, in *De facie in orbe lunae*, after a long
cosmological discussion, there is an eschatological myth about
the fate of the soul after death. The weakness of the link between
the two parts of *De defectu oraculorum* is evident: one only has to
ask why the *daimones* must go to another world and not just to
another planet. However, this question is never asked and so we
may reasonably conclude that the dialogue has been so devised
that the discussion on the flight of the *daimones* is largely designed
to introduce a cosmological discussion on the number of worlds.

The various answers given to the decline of the oracle suggest
that human nature has not changed much. A Cynic claims that the
degeneracy of contemporary civilization has made men unworthy
of the god's favor. Ammonios claims that the decline in population
(a statement hastily seized upon by Greek demographers) is
responsible for making the oracle redundant. These solutions
take little time to present. The final two take up almost the whole
discussion of the shrine. The most sensational of these is that of
Cleombrotos.[4] He argues that the oracle is dependent upon *dai-*

The best solution seems to be that they were written fairly close together
(since the *personae* are similar) but that *De Pythiae oraculis* may be somewhat later than the others; however it is unnecessary to make it as late as
Flacelière suggests. On the chronology see Jones, *Plutarch and Rome*, p. 136.
More recently in *Plutarque, Oeuvres Morales, VI, Dialogues Pythiques*
(Paris: 1974), p. 40, Flacelière puts the *De Pythiae oraculis* at a very late
date (125 A.D.), and, pp. 85-86, repeats his earlier view that *De defectu*
is the first, and a tentative statement, *De Pythiae oraculis* his final statement on inspiration there.
    [4] Eisele, *Zur Dämonologie*, pp. 40-42, sees Cleombrotos as satirized here.
R. Jones, *The Platonism of Plutarch*, p. 38, and G. Soury, "Plutarque Prêtre,"
pp. 50-69, as well as *La Démonologie*, p. 22off., take him very seriously.
Muhl, *Plutarchische Studien*, p. 69; Flacelière, "Plutarque et la Pythie,"
p. 72, and *Sur la Disparition*, pp. 22, 52-53, and 62-63; V. Goldschmidt,
"Les thèmes du De defectu oraculorum," 298-302; and Ziegler in the ad-
ditions to *Plutarchos*, p. 327, take a moderate position which gives some
weight to his views without taking him in all seriousness. Flacelière, *Sur
la Disparition*, p. 23, notes that he is a Spartan "et que ses compatriotes

mones to transmit the divine intentions, these abandon a shrine periodically to migrate to another world, and when this happens the place becomes desolate. The solution, which takes overwhelmingly the longest time to present, and which concludes the dialogue, is that of Lamprias, Plutarch's brother. He argues that the prophetic nature of the shrine is due to an exhalation or spirit (*pneuma*) which, though invisible and undetectable by ordinary means, is material and eventually dissipates itself, leaving the oracle without the prophetic power it once enjoyed. A modern reader might find both solutions to the problem rather insufficient, at the least. One might object to Cleombrotos' solution that if the oracles have been abandoned by the *daimones*, how do they still manage to function, even if in a rather trivial way. Lamprias' position helps to explain why there was a steady decline at the oracle, but the difficulty with it for the ancients would have been the lack of tradition for a *pneuma* at Delphi. However, both theories would have been interesting to Plutarch, particularly the latter, and they reflect two of his interests which have attracted the attention of posterity.

In this chapter an examination will be made of the statements which the first principal speaker in the dialogue, Cleombrotos, utters, and an attempt will be made to estimate how well these statements harmonize with the thought of Plutarch as we know it from other passages in his works. That is, just how representative is Cleombrotos of Plutarch's thought? In the following chapter the speech of Lamprias, which advocates a prophetic *pneuma* in opposition to the *daimones* theory of Cleombrotos will be analyzed.

As Cleombrotos enters the dialogue he receives one of those gently satirical introductions like those we are accustomed to from Plato when he has a colorful or eccentric personality to bring to our attention. Cleombrotos and his friend, Demetrios, are said to have come from opposite ends of the earth—staggeringly

en général ne passaient pas pour des intellectuels bien subtils;'' but the others are mostly Boiotians, also considered a stupid race. In *Dialogues Pythiques*, p. 88, Flacelière repeats his assertions about Cleombrotos' portrayal in the dialogue: "Au début du dialogue, il est qualifié comme Demetrios, d' 'homme divin' (ἱερός), mais l'entretien fait apparaître ses insuffisances, qui sont celles d'un amateur et d'un esprit superficiel, quelque peu obscurci par ses tendances mystiques. Mais naturellement le ton de Plutarque à son égard reste parfaitement courtois, si l'ironie est sous-jacente.''

opposite for the ancient world—from the Persian Gulf and from Britain in order to meet at Delphi. This meeting recalls a legend that at one time two swans or eagles flew from opposite ends of the earth and met at Delphi, thus proving that Delphi was in fact the center of the earth (409e-f). Lamprias, who is the principal speaker in the dialogue and who begins by relating this section, continues with the story that Epimenides of Phaistos once asked the oracle if the legend were true, and whether the *omphalos* were in fact the center of the earth. Living up to her reputation, the priestess replied in true oracular fashion that she did not know if there were a center to the world, but if there were one, it was known to the gods but hidden from men. Thus, in Lamprias' words, "Epimenides was repulsed for attempting to test an ancient myth as though it were a painting to be touched." The oracle's fear of *Entmythologizierung* is probably in a more humorous vein than some scholars would take it.[5] At any rate, after this introduction the dialogue moves quickly.

Both Demetrios and Cleombrotos are described as devout men, but outside of insignificant details of their life which are given in the dialogue—the fact that both are travellers, Demetrios a grammarian who had been in Britain, and Cleombrotos interested in theology—little is known about them. Demetrios was probably an actual historical personage.[6] Cleombrotos is mysterious. He

---

[5] Ziegler, pp. 200-10, makes far too much of this, comparing Epimenides to the doubting Thomas of the gospels, and finding religious scepticism to be the *Leitmotiv* of the dialogue. For different reasons—to show the superiority of *De Pythiae oraculis*—Flacelière, *REG* 56 (1943), 72 ff., also overemphasizes the scepticism.

[6] A Demetrius is mentioned on two dedications on small bronze tablets found at York in 1860, and there is a possibility this is the same Demetrios. See Ziegler, p. 36. Flacelière, *Dialogues Pythiques* on the basis that the English plaque does not contain the ethnic name remains sceptical about the identification with this Demetrios (p. 88, note 3), unlike Ziegler. Flacelière, *Sur la Disparition*, pp. 24-25, thought Cleombrotos was a real person, and that this accounted for the flattering introduction, though he makes no comment on this in *Dialogues Pythiques*. Jones, *Plutarch and Rome*, pp. 39-64, regards Cleombrotos as a real person (p. 42). But his views obviously are not so much his as that of previous philosophers, and his comments on the Red Sea might point to an Alexandrian source such as Eudoros who had Platonic-Pythagorean leanings and wrote on geography (e.g. the Nile). See Martini, *RE* VI (1909), col. 91-96, "Eudoros"; and such sources could have been taught to Plutarch by his teacher Ammonios from Egypt. See Whittaker, "Ammonios on the Delphic E," 191-192; Dörrie, "Der Platoniker Eudoros von Alexandreia," 297-300, and "Die Stellung Plutarchs im Platonismus seiner Zeit," 36-40.

CLEOMBROTOS' DAIMONES 91

appears in no other dialogue; there is no other historical record of him. It seems possible that he is a fictional character whose travels enable him to present doctrines from far and wide, the Persian Gulf, Egypt, and Greece. Neither is philosophically gifted, though Cleombrotos is described—in peculiar terms—as putting together studies that would serve theology (καὶ συνῆγεν ἱστορίαν οἷον ὕλην φιλοσοφίας θεολογίαν τέλος ἐχούσης, 410b),[7] for the purpose of which he visited the Troglodytes near the Persian Gulf and the priests of Egypt. At the shrine of Zeus Ammon he swallowed a story of the priests that the years were getting progressively shorter since the lamp consumed less oil each year. His friends point out that this is unacceptable in view of its catastrophic effect on the scientific conclusions of mathematics and astronomy, and Ammonios quickly explains how atmospheric conditions might be responsible for the varying consumption of oil. At any rate Cleombrotos is accused of making a mountain out of a molehill ("painting the lion from a single claw", 410c). Brushing aside this point the group inquire whether he has any useful information about the Egyptian shrine, why for example it has declined. Apparently stung by the previous criticism or his own inadequacy, "he looks down and does not reply" (411e).

Though Cleombrotos' silence does indicate his inadequacy—and if a fictional character, that of the solution he will propose—his silence enables Demetrios to give a short history of the decline of the oracle at Delphi. The digression here also enables Plutarch to present two alternate solutions which should be mentioned, but which really do not contribute to the dialogue's originality. The first is that of a Cynic named Didymos, with the nickname Planetiades, which is left unexplained but is perhaps self-evident. Claiming that the providence of the gods has abandoned mankind because of its wickedness and the contemptible way in which men approach the shrines, he is amazed in fact that the Delphic oracle still functions. However, Plutarch, apparently with a more optimistic view of human nature, has Heracleon seize the Cynic by

[7] J. Hartman, *De Plutarco Scriptore et Philosopho* (Leiden: 1916), pp. 188-89 and R. Flacelière, "Plutarque et la Pythie," pp. 109-11, imagine that Plutarch meant the statement to be a manifesto of his own philosophy of life. R. Hirzel, *Plutarch*, pp. 11-12, V. Goldschmidt, "Sur les Thèmes," pp. 298-302, and R. Del Re, *Il Dialogo*, pp. 54-55, disagree. Even if this were Plutarch's manifesto in some way, it seems incredible that he would introduce it at a moment where Cleombrotos is subjected to so much ridicule.

the cloak for accusing the gods of what we would call Indian giving: God—according to Heracleon—is of a good and gentle nature; if he gives birth and existence to men, and watches over men in every other respect, there is no reason for him to deny this one gift of prophecy. Ammonios' argument that the oracles have ceased because of a decline of population in Greece is presented with some fullness (413d-414c). It does not, however, satisfy Lamprias who is looking for a philosophical, that is, a scientific cause. God, for Lamprias, is not "some sort of ventriloquist who disappears at will." The solution for Lamprias is, then, to be discovered in some sort of material cause, and this quest for the type of matter which must decompose and bring on privation is the principal theme of the dialogue (414d-f).

It is at this point that Cleombrotos introduces his complicated daimonology, which involves elements from many Greek philosophers. It has been most interesting for historians of Greek philosophy in that it is almost the sole source for the daimonology of Xenocrates and the reconstruction of much of his thought. Cleombrotos objects to the traditional Platonic application of nature and matter (*physis* and *hyle*) to escape from the difficulty of the decline of the oracle, and thinks that "the schools of philosophy which envisage the activities of a third race between men and the gods, the race of *daimones*, offer more fruitful answers to the problem." Since Cleombrotos' history resembles a handbook, it will be reduced back into handbook language, though left largely in his own phrases.

1. The origin of daimonology is uncertain: it may be either Persian in origin (Zoroaster), Thracian (Orpheus),[8] Egyptian, or Phrygian.
2. Among Greek literary accounts we find that Homer uses the word *daimon* and *theos* indiscriminately, but Hesiod distinguishes four classes of rational being, gods, *daimones*, heroes, and men—the golden race being transformed into *daimones* and the demigods (ἡμίθεοι) into heroes.

---

[8] R. Heinze, *Xenokrates* (Leipzig: 1892), p. 85, thought this demonology was incompatible with Orphic teaching in which—as he saw it—souls were punished until they received new bodies; but Nilsson, *Geschichte*, I, p. 684, disagrees, as does Guthrie, *HGP* I, p. 478, who notes Orphic texts which support the opposite view.

3. Others claim that the *daimones* are really human souls which undergo a transformation similar to that which we see taking place in the generation of water from earth, air from water, and fire from air; in the course of time virtuous souls—who may have had to undergo a purgatory—come to share completely in divinity; others which yield to temptation must be reincarnated and lead once more a dismal mortal life (ἀλαμπῆ καὶ ἀμυδρὰν ζωὴν ὥσπερ ἀναθυμίασιν ἴσχειν, 415a-c).[9]

The greatest difficulty in this short passage, which is so important for our understanding of Greek daimonology as a whole, is its fuzziness over the distinction between *daimones* which are nothing more than human souls, and another type, those which are larger and more powerful than men. One would think that the existence of these two types arises from different modes of thought. At least in the words of Xenocrates, who is cited for the second type, an attempt is being made to fill in the chain of being in much the same way as the medieval scholastics found it necessary to posit a race of spirits between men and God. One might ask, in the passage in question, whether the doctrine of the "others" is parenthetical to Xenocrates' theory of the superior race, *daimones*, or whether it is meant to fill out this line of thought.

---

[9] Heinze, *Xenokrates*, p. 83—attributing perhaps more of the section to Xenocrates than is necessary—believed that for him *daimones* were former souls since at 417b they preserve a "remnant" of the passionate (λείψανον ὥσπερ περίττωμα). In the most recent article on Xenocrates, H. Dörrie, "Xenokrates," *RE* IX, a 2 (1967), pp. 1512-28, reconstructs his philosophy as one of triplet division in which his independent race of *daimones* is an example. Dörrie is, therefore, puzzled by the fragments which suggest the soul is a *daimon*: Arist. *Top.* 2.6.112a, 32, repeated in less specific form at 7.1.152a, 5: ὁμοίως δὲ καὶ εὐδαίμονα οὗ ἂν ὁ δαίμων ᾖ σπουδαῖος καθάπερ Ξενοκράτης φησὶν εὐδαίμονα εἶναι τὸν τὴν ψυχὴν ἔχοντα σπουδαίαν, ταύτην γὰρ ἑκάστου εἶναι δαίμονα and alluded to in Alex. Aphrod. *St.* 176.13, and Apul. *De deo Soc.* 15 and in a more explicit passage from the *Suda* 443.32, noticed recently by M. Detienne, *La Notion de Daïmon dans le Pythagorisme Ancien* (Paris: 1963), p. 65, n. 4: εἰ δὴ δαίμων ἑκάστου ἡ ψυχὴ καθὰ Ξενοκράτει, δόκει, εἴη ἂν εὐδαίμων ὁ εὖ τὴν ψυχὴν ἔχων ... It seems reasonable, however, that Xenocrates is not quoted as far down in the *De defectu* passage as Heinze thought, and that the "soul" passages are really a comment on Plato *Tim.* 90c: τὸ θεῖον ἔχοντα τε αὐτὸν εὖ κεκοσμημένον τὸν δαίμονα σύνοικον ἑαυτῷ διαφερόντως εὐδαίμονα εἶναι. The fragments from Xenocrates are puzzling, but two solutions suggest a way out of the difficulty. It is possible that Xenocrates, probably commenting on the *Timaeus*, did not take into account the contradiction involved in making the *daimon* a human soul in one passage, and a superior being in another. More likely, the conception of the *daimon* as a superior being belongs to a later work of Xenocrates.

The comparison of the human soul to mist or vapor suggests the pantheism and materialism of the Stoics. We will see that the materialism of this conception plays a prominent role in the eschatological myths of Plutarch. In them the vapor quality of the soul permits it to rise to the moon but no farther. However, in other places Plutarch speaks of the immortality and spirituality of the soul, and it is quite possible that he uses this Stoic-type materialism in a symbolic way to express the attraction of the soul for earthly things much the way that Plato does in his myths. Plutarch's innovation is to use the Stoic terminology and doctrine to express—with a different meaning—Platonic psychology and eschatology. The physical nature of the *psyche* both in *De defectu oraculorum*, and in the myths, also allows a second death, the separation of *nous* from *psyche*, something which is another important consideration for the myths. The digression on the death of the nymphs in the *De defectu* passage here is also confusing. It may be meant as an academic footnote to Hesiod's daimonology. At any rate it allows some discussion over whether the Stoic *ekpyrosis* is to be envisaged in such poetry and in the philosophy of Heracleitos.

After this interruption we come to the fourth point:

4. Xenocrates used triangles to describe the different orders of being: the equilateral triangle (equal in all its lines) is similar to the nature of God; the isosceles (partly equal and partly unequal) is similar to the nature of the *daimones*; the scalene (unequal in all its lines) is similar to the nature of man.

   Xenocrates also compares these orders of rational being to the heavenly bodies: the sun and stars are visible images and likenesses of the gods; the moon which is of mixed nature, is an imitation of the daimonic nature (μίμημα δαιμόνιον); beams of light and comets are images of man.

5. The following characteristics of the *daimones* can be noted (it is not at all clear whether this comes from Xenocrates):

   a. They are Plato's interpretative and ministering nature (*Republic* 260d, *Symposium* 202e).

   b. They are guardians of the sacred rites and prompters (ὀργιασταί) at the mysteries.

   c. They vary as to their degree of virtue, and some carry with them a dim remnant of the emotional and irrational (ἀσθενὲς καὶ ἀμαυρὸν ἔτι λείψανον ὥσπερ περίττωμα, 417b).

d. The clearest reflection of the truth about the *daimones* is in the mysteries, but, as Herodotos says (2.171), "let our lips be sealed."

e. Ill-omened days, and obscene and vulgar rites are meant to placate *daimones*; kings and generals in the past would not have offered up their children unless they thought they were placating the insane and imperious passions of *daimones* who either were unable or unwilling to have physical intercourse (σωμᾶσιν διὰ σωμάτων ὁμιλεῖν, 416f-418d).[10]

f. The tales of the myths are not the records of gods but rather of *daimones*: this includes the legend of Apollo's slaughter of the Python at Delphi and his banishment from the shrine.

When Cleombrotos finishes, Heracleon finds the whole thing an "extraordinary and presumptuous hypothesis" (ἀτόπους ὑποθέσεις καὶ μεγάλας τῷ λόγῳ διδόντες, 418d). Already the historian Philippos had objected to the daimonological interpretation to explain the abandonment of the oracles (418d). Now Cleombrotos applies it to the Delphic legend, claiming that the Delphic theologians had degraded Apollo by holding on to the myths as actual representations of his activities, though it foists immorality upon a god.

It is at this point that Philippos throws in a red herring by suggesting that Democritos' *eidola* either are the same as *daimones* or at least that Democritos recognized that there were both good and bad *eidola* since he prayed that he would only receive benevolent ones, "thus indicating that there was another class which had evil desires and impulses" (DK 166, *Aem.-Tim.* 1). Having finished

---

[10] The passage contains a somewhat ambiguous line to the effect that a person named Molos raped a νυμφή; and his body was later found decapitated; thus proving the *daimones* sometimes work on the side of law and order. Since νυμφή in Greek can mean either a nymph or a girl, the line has received different interpretations by scholars. Heinze, *Xenokrates*, p. 81, n. 1, made the slip of taking Molos to be a *daimon* who raped a girl. He was corrected by Bock, *Untersuchungen*, p. 11, who took Molos to be the victim of a *daimon*'s rage at his raping a nymph. Babbitt, Loeb, *Mor.* V, p. 393, had Molos rape a girl. The legendary Molos appears in *Il.* 10.269-70 and Diod. Sic. 5.79. Since the talk in this passage involves the appearance of nymphs as *daimones*, Bock, Flacelière, *Sur la Disparition*, p. 138, and Soury, *La Démonologie*, p. 60, are probably right in seeing Molos' illusions of grandeur punished by the loss of his head. In *Dialogues Pythiques*, p. 187, Flacelière notes that Molos was the father of Merion, the Cretan chief in the *Iliad* and gives, p. 118, "après avoir violé une nymphe." But see *LXX* Tob. 7.

with Democritos, Philippos comes to the aid of Cleombrotos with a story about the death of the Great Pan, which we might have expected to follow the earlier discussion of the *daimones'* life-span and death. Apparently Plutarch wanted to interrupt the heaviness of the philosophical discussion with a narrative digression.

At any rate Philippos relates an ancient mariner's tale in support of the hypothesis that *daimones* die. The tale has been midwife to the sometimes still-born brain children of several scholars, and probably will continue to be so for many years.[11] An Egyptian pilot named Thamous as he sails by the island of Paxi is addressed by a mysterious voice which orders him to announce the death of the Great Pan when he is opposite Palodes (ὅτι Πὰν ὁ μέγας τέθνηκεν, 419c). Thamous obediently did as told, and no sooner had he made the proclamation than a great cry of lamentation arose from an unseen multitude so that the report reached the ears of the emperor Tiberius; he, being convinced of its truth—in modern fashion—set his research scholars to glean information on Pan.

Demetrios will not be outdone. He relates a similar story from the coast of Britain which he has just visited. Here not one, but many great *daimones*, "the mightier ones" (οἱ κρείττονες) live on an island off the west coast. The inhabitants say the *daimones'* coming into life is gentle but on their passing from it, great tumults, lightning, thunder and other portents proclaim their death. Here lies Cronos bound in sleep where he is watched by Briareus while round about are many *daimones*, his attendants and servants.

These stories are somewhat inconsequential, even if interesting. Moreover, they are difficult to reconcile with Plutarch's eschatological myths. In these he describes the passing away of the *daimones* as a gentle second-death separation of *psyche* and *nous*, and this separation takes place on the moon. The central discussion

[11] S. Reinach, *BCH*, 31 (1907), 5-19, repeated in *Cultes, Mythes, et Religions* III (Paris: 1908), p. 1 ff., and *Orpheus* (Paris: 1909), p. 61, originated the view that the Syrian Adonis, known as Thamuz or Tammuz, was being lamented and that this was responsible for the mysterious cry. J. Hani, "Le mort du Grand Pan," *Budé Congrès*, pp. 511-19, has developed an even more plausible theory for those who like to deny the mysterious in life: the pilot—whose name is genuinely Egyptian though Syrian in origin—heard a combined lamentation from several points of the coast for a syncretist Pan (Egyptian Khnum or Shu)-Adonis-Osiris. Plutarch's friends, perhaps wisely, prefer to take the occurrence as something romantic, extraordinary, and inexplicable. For a summary of views see Flacelière, *Dialogues Pythiques*, pp. 92-95.

of the flight of the *daimones* to another world is resumed when Cleombrotos brings his witness into the argument. It is hard to believe that Plutarch is doing anything but spoofing here. At any rate Cleombrotos claims that this theory is backed up by a mystic he managed to meet near the Red Sea "only after an enormous trip to find him and after paying a large amount of money." Cleombrotos attempts to bamboozle his friends with tales of the mystic's accomplishments: he is the handsomest man Cleombrotos has ever seen, he never suffers from disease, spoke a Doric which was like music, and when he spoke perfume issued from his mouth.[12] Once a year, according to Cleombrotos, he held a conference "for kings and potentates," but most important of all, he "referred all his prophecy to the *daimones*." The rest of his time he spent with "roaming nymphs and *daimones*" (421a-c).

The mystic's tale turns out to be the anticipated interpretation of Delphic theology along daimonological lines. In the mystic's account a *daimon* slew the Python and was thereupon exiled to another world for eight cycles of the great year. On his return he was truly the radiant and pure one (*Phoibos*) and took over the oracle. Does this mean that the *daimon* turned into a god? Such would seem to be the meaning of the name *Phoibos*. On the other hand, if it is a god who is responsible for the oracle, the *daimon* theory of the oracles falls to pieces. The mystic adds that the myths of the Typhons, Titans, and Cronos are those of *daimones*, and he ends the account with a mini-eschatological myth. There are 183 worlds arranged in the form of a triangle each side having 60 worlds, with the 3 left over revolving around the angles; the inner area is the "common hearth" and the "plain of truth" (τὸ πεδίον ἀληθείας) in which are the "accounts, the forms and the patterns" (οἱ λόγοι, τὰ εἴδη, καὶ τὰ παραδείγματα, 422b). About them lies eternity from which the river of time like an ever-flowing stream is conveyed to the worlds. Once in ten thousand years the souls who have lived virtuous lives are permitted to see these things which in their sublimity leave the highest rites of the mysteries as a pale reflection.[13]

---

[12] Plutarch may not be spoofing here but he at least had a rationalistic explanation in the back of his mind. In *De facie* 938a and 939c Troglodytes are mentioned and perfume comes from the Isle of Cronos, but in *Alex*. 4— accepting a far-fetched claim of Aristoxenos that perfume filled Alexander's mouth, skin, and clothes—he says this is due to the dry, arid climate which produces spice "since the sun dries up the source of corruption."

If this is meant to be a sublime Platonic myth leaving the hearers gasping and breathless at the new vision opened up to them, it certainly fails in its purpose among Cleombrotos' friends. Demetrios, in a literary allusion to Odysseus among the suitors (*Odyssey*, 21.397), concludes that the man is simply a fraud, who had been around enough to make some good plagiarisms, and that in fact he had stolen the idea from Petron of Himera. Probably only the astronomical mathematical part of the description is meant here, since the Idealist eschatological part is simply a Platonic hodge-podge. At any rate a long digression on the number of worlds is triggered off, which ends in a presentation of the Platonic, Aristotelian, and Stoic one-world theories. During it, Lamprias suggests moderately the possibility of a limited number of worlds. His argumentation is curiously theological: a large number of worlds would be far too much for an already overworked providence. He ends asking that they bear in mind in such difficult questions the old maxim in the Academy of healthy scepticism (431a).

We must now ask what Plutarch himself endorsed. First of all, he hardly endorsed the necessity of human sacrifice for *daimones*. Even here Cleombrotos guardedly puts the idea as a supposition of ancient heroes: "they would not have . . . unless they believed..." Yet according to the logic of the passage he should have affirmed that it was indeed necessary to placate *daimones* this way. Plutarch's own sentiment may be expressed by the "in vain" put in Cleombrotos' mouth at this point (417c-d). Supposedly these *daimones* stir up pestilence, crop failure, and civil war if they do not get the soul they want. What could be farther from Plutarch's conception of disease, drought, and civil war than this superstitious nonsense?[14]

---

[13] Plutarch ridicules the association of Numa with *daimones* in *De fort. Rom.* 321b, and more strongly in *Num.* 4, 8, and 15. In *Rom.* 2 he makes fun of a story about a daimonic phallus rising from the hearth which was supposed to father the Roman race. And in *Num.* 4 even stronger than in *Qu. conv.* 717f-718a he objects to sexual intercourse between humans and more heavenly beings. B. MacKay, "Plutarch and the Miraculous," C. F. D. Moule, ed., *Miracles—Studies in their Philosophy and History* (London: 1965), pp. 93-113, suggests that Plutarch here and in *Lys.* 26 (a fraud involving Apollo's parentage) and in the rejection of Romulus' ascension into heaven (*Rom.* 27) is attacking the virgin birth and resurrection of Christ. This is however difficult to believe in view of Plutarch's complete silence over Christianity, and his point here, to debunk Roman claims to divinity.

[14] In *De Stoic. repugn.* 1051 c-d, Plutarch outright rejects the view that *daimones* might be set over good men—a suggestion made by Chrysippos to save divine providence—on the grounds that this would be like a good

The theory of the "others," the theory which sees the *daimones* as simply one stage in the existence of the human soul, seems hard to reconcile with a theory of *daimones* which conceives them as a link in the chain of being, intermediate between men and gods. For this reason it is questionable that because Plutarch believes in the transformation theory he is obligated to a belief in intermediate beings who flit about attempting to disturb human life. It seems better to treat the "others" doctrine as a parenthetical passage giving an alternate theory, and inserted into Cleombrotos' speech so that the little history of daimonology may be complete. This transformation theory is utilized frequently by Plutarch. An example is his distinction between the begotten and unbegotten gods in *Pelopidas* 16 in order to show that Apollo was not born at a place asserted by some local chauvinists. It is this doctrine which is utilized at the end of the *Life of Romulus* in order to rationalize the apotheosis of Romulus, without at the same time offending Roman eyes. In Plutarch's account Romulus' body did not rise with his soul, but his soul was able to take part in certain purifications and transformations, in this way—like many virtuous men—he could truly have been said to be divine; i.e. Plutarch is applying the ideas of the hero cult in Greece to Roman legend. The same doctrine underlies the fate of the soul after death as it is described in the myths of Plutarch's *De facie in orbe lunae*, *De genio Socratis*, and in allusions to the afterlife elsewhere in his writings.

The whole discussion of the death of the *daimones* in *De defectu* is hopelessly confused, and elsewhere Plutarch has nothing to say about this subject. The topic in *De defectu* generates more heat and smoke than light: Demetrios at 415f thinks that the *ekpyrosis* is implied; Heracleon understands "death like men" (418e); and it is never very clear what relation vice has to shortening their life (420c-e); Ammonios constantly thinks of them as souls—which for a Platonist are immortal—and the whole extinction business seems to go over his head; as referee in the dialogue he asks Cleombrotos to please return to the flight and migration of the *daimones* (420d-e).[15]

---

king's ruling irresponsibly through evil satraps. Babut, *Plutarque et le Stoïcisme*, pp. 291-92, discusses the passage briefly but overlooks the anti-demon emphasis here, as strong as anything in Plutarch.

[15] A lost debate over the effect of passion on immortality may be at stake here. At least M. Pohlenz, *Vom Zorne Gottes* (Göttingen: 1909), pp.

In contrast to his lack of interest in their death, Plutarch seems
to have been very much intrigued by the similarity in the mixed
nature of the moon and that of the *daimones*. In *De facie in orbe
lunae*, the servant of Cronos gives the highest praise to Xenocrates
for having solved the difficult problem of the moon's position
in the universe through a theory of density and mixture which
he reached "by a divine insight into Plato's thought" (θείῳ τινὶ
λογισμῷ τὴν ἀρχὴν λαβὼν παρὰ Πλάτωνος, 943f).[16] This does not mean
that Plutarch believed in *daimones* other than those which are
human souls in some disguise; but in the *Amatorius* he describes
the moon as a place "where mortality is blended with immortality"
(764d), and it is the moon which in both *De genio Socratis* and *De
facie in orbe lunae* receives the souls after death into an atmosphere
particularly conducive to their new state.

What can we make of the *eidola* affair? Democritos' own position
is confusing for scholars, but it is not very likely that Plutarch
thought the *eidola* really resembled *daimones*.[17] Philippos, who

---

137-38 (cf. Soury, pp. 35-36), detected this, holding that Plutarch had given
up the earlier teaching making the two (passion and immortality) compat-
ible (see Chalc. *Diss.* 154), under the pressure of Carneades, Panaitios,
and Poseidonios who rejected it as contradictory. Ammonios, however, at
420d-e disproves satirically the argument—supposedly from the Epicureans—
that vice causes a speedy death. Probably spoofing in *Brut. an.* 989a Plutarch
gives the life span of a crow (used to estimate that of a nymph in *De defectu*),
and in *Amat.* 757e citing Pindar, mentions that the life of a tree nymph
is as long as the tree. The point was probably not that important for Plutarch who elsewhere seems constantly to think of *daimones* as former souls,
i.e. immortal.

[16] Plutarch reveals his high personal estimation of Xenocrates in *Phoc.*
27 where Xenocrates stands undaunted in captivity before the tyrant
Antipater. In *Flam.* 12 he relates a joke made by him to the sons of an
orator who had saved him from prison.

[17] The fragment reads: ἔτι δὲ Δημόκριτος εὐχόμενος εὐλόγχων εἰδώλων
τυγχάνειν ἢ δῆλος ἦν ἕτερα δυστράπελα καὶ μοχθηρὰς γιγνώσκων ἔχοντα προαιρέσεις
τινὰς καὶ ὁρμάς. As repeated in Sext. *Math.* 9.24 and 29 *ta eidola* are said
to be "indeed gigantic and hard to destroy though not indestructible and
they show men the future in advance by their appearance and by uttering
sounds; hence the ancients receiving a presentation of just these *eidola*
supposed that there is a god, though there is no everlasting god apart from
this." Another passage from *Hermippos*, attributed to the 14th Century
Byzantine Catares reads: "Democritos calls the *daimones eidola* and says
that the air is full of them." Cic. *De nat. deor.* 1.12.29 claims Democritos
both held that the *eidola* were gods and that they came from them. Andres
RE Suppl. III, p. 292, and Bailey, *The Greek Atomists*, p. 176, are baffled.
Guthrie, *HGP* II, pp. 478-82, is probably right in rejecting these late sources
for the simpler view that the *eidola* are mere effluences; the manner of
speaking about them in 683b makes them similar to *daimones*, and this

introduces Democritos in the discussion, knows little about philosophy. In the parallel *De Iside* passage giving the list of *daimon*
philosophers (360e) Democritos is omitted. In a discussion on
the evil eye (*Quaestiones convivales* 680c-683b) Plutarch comes
about as near as possible to turning them into *daimones*, but the
whole thing is obviously meant as a joke. When accused of
plagiarizing from Democritos for using effluences (ῥεύματα) to
explain the evil eye, he describes his own effluences as lifeless
while those of Democritos have life (τὸ ἔμψυχον) and volition
(τὸ προαιρετικόν) but adds that in the town of Chaironeia—where
a ghost is seen behind every door anyway—such an hour of the
night is no time to be speaking of thinking and breathing shapes and
visions (φάσματα καὶ εἴδωλα πεπνυσμένα καὶ φρονοῦντα, 682f-683b).

Elsewhere Plutarch is more exact in distinguishing between the
daimones, Democritean *eidola*, and the Epicurean *eidola*. *Quaestiones
convivales* 735a-b contains a discussion in which one speaker,
Favorinus, uses the Democritean *eidola* theory. He describes it
as "polished up like an old mirror," in his attempt to explain
why it is that dreams tend to be nightmarish in autumn. His
solution is not accepted by Plutarch who prefers the *krasis* theory,
for which he is probably indebted to the Aristotelians. In the
course of the discussion, Democritos' eidolology is explained in
greater detail than before, and the very important distinction
between Democritos' theory and the Epicureans' is noted. Here
we learn that Democritos believed that the *eidola* not only emanated
from material bodies but also conveyed the psychological and
intellectual states of the mind, and that the Epicureans refused
to go along with Democritos on this point. This *Quaestio* helps to
explain why Cleombrotos in *De defectu* can heap such scorn on
the soulless (ἄψυχα) *eidola* of the Epicureans, which he sees emanating
from dead bodies to haunt the world for centuries. In contrast
to those of the Epicureans, Democritos' *eidola* seem to have life:
they are "ὥσπερ ἔμψυχα" (735b). There is, however, a narrow
line between ὥσπερ ἔμψυχα and ἔμψυχα, and the popular mind
may have failed to see the distinction. At any rate in a passage
in the *Lives* in which Plutarch explains how he must keep his star

lack of clarity is probably what is responsible for the confusion of the later
sources. But one should not forget the literary heritage, Achilles' words
on seeing the shade of Patroclos (*Il.* 23.104): ψυχὴ καὶ εἴδωλον, ἀτὰρ φρένες
οὐκ ἔνι πάμπαν.

pinned to the virtues of his heroes, he claims that Democritos, by praying that he receive only benevolent *eidola*, actually was introducing superstition into philosophy (πρὸς ἀπεράντους ἐκφέροντας δεισιδαιμονίας εἰς φιλοσοφίαν, *Timoleon* 1). But perhaps Plutarch intends some humor here since even the lifeless Epicurean doctrine receives a bit of flailing from Cleombrotos (φλεδόνας καὶ σκίας ἕλκοντες εἰς φυσιολογίαν, 420b-c).

Perhaps more important is the question whether Plutarch adhered to the daimonological interpretation of the myths as expressions of the work of *daimones*. In answer to this question perhaps the best thing to say is that if Plutarch ever did hold the theory he probably dropped it later in favor of the allegorical interpretation. Heracleon in *De defectu* yields to Cleombrotos on the grounds that he had the authority of Plato behind him for the daimonological interpretation of myth. How did Plato, who tended to treat the myths as nonsense, get associated with the daimonological interpretation of myth? There is a hint in *De Iside* 360e as to how this came about. Here the chthonic deities mentioned in Plato's *Laws* (717a) are described in terms given the *daimones* in later authors. Moreover, when in *De Iside* (360e-f) Plutarch makes use of the daimonological theory, the gods Isis and Serapis are identified with two Greek chthonic deities, Persephone and Pluto. Since Isis and Serapis are described as gods who had once been *daimones* it is easy to see how one would conclude that Persephone and Pluto, Plato's chthonic deities, were also *daimones* at one time.

However, it should be noted that in *De Iside* Plutarch does not endorse this daimonological theory. He only regards it as better than the "notorious" Euhemerist interpretation. The allegorical interpretation is the only rational method with which to understand the myths and avoid superstition. This is what Plutarch tries to get across to Clea, the adressée of the piece: [18] they must

---

[18] For Plato's interpretation of myth see *Rep.* 377a-392a where he even goes so far as to attack the allegorical interpretation. Plato—whose objection is that many of these stories terrify children—even rejects the stories about the heroes. In *Phaedrus* 229c-230a, Socrates claims that he has no time to spend on such nonsense but must rather inquire into whether he has a nature more gentle than that of the Typhons, thus heeding the Delphic maxim "Know thyself." Here we have another example of rationalism and pseudo-science carrying us back into superstition: Plutarch's clever explanations subvert Plato's good sense. On allegorical interpretation of myth in Plutarch, see F. Wehrli, *Zur Geschichte der Allegorischen Deutung Homers* (Leipzig: 1928), pp. 26-40, F. Buffière, *Les Mythes d'Homerè et la Pensée Grecque*

be interpreted in a philosophical and allegorical way, though with pious sensibility (ὁσίως καὶ φιλοσόφως αἰνιττόμενοι, 355c-d). Later Plutarch speaks of the myths as only containing "reflections of truth" about the gods (359a).[19] His own estimate of the Isis myth is proof of his position, and this interpretation is the most important part of the treatise insofar as the interpretation of a myth goes. Here Plutarch gives an explanation, which is purely symbolic or allegorical, and in which he allows some ideas characteristic of *De animae procreatione in Timaeo*—his commentary on Plato's *Timaeus*—to receive prominence. In *De animae procreatione* Plutarch understands creation to be in time; but unlike the creation which Christians are accustomed to, Plutarch's creation is the imposition of *logos* on a soul (*psyche*) which up to this time had existed without it. Previous to this imposition the world had drifted about in disordered movements and gyrations so that it could not truthfully be said to be a *kosmos*. Due to linguistic differences between English and Greek some of this

---

(Paris: 1956), pp. 67-70, J. Pépin, *Mythe et Allégorie* (Paris: 1958), p. 167, and the interpretation of the Circe transformation (not alluded to by Pépin and Wehrli) (*Od.* 10.239-40), fr. 200-201 (Sandbach) Loeb XV, pp. 367-75.

[19] The matter of Plutarch's belief in the diamonological interpretation is much debated but would seem to hinge largely on whether one thinks Plutarch firmly believed in evil *daimones*. Volkmann, *Leben*, pp. 303-10; Eisele, *Zur Dämonologie*, pp. 48-50; and Erbse, "Plutarchs Schrift," p. 311, n.1., hold that the allegorical interpretation is the most important for Plutarch. However Latzarus, *Les Idées Religieuses*, p. 98; Soury, *La Démonologie* p. 229; Moellering, *Plutarch on Superstition*, p. 131; Geigenmuller, "Plutarchs Stellung," p. 251 ff.; and Oakesmith, *The Religion of Plutarch*, p. 132, opted for the daimonological. Jones, *The Platonism*, p. 38, holds a somewhat far-fetched compromise position, seeing Plutarch as another Philo. Flacelière, *Vies* I, pp. 5-11, interestingly notices a euhemerist tendency in Plutarch. Heinze, *Xenokrates*, p. 81; Volkmann, *Leben*, p. 15; Schmertosch, *De Plutarchi Sententiam*, p. 3; and Krische, *Forschungen*, p. 320, thought the daimonological was primarily due to Xenocrates, but there are some problems with how far Xenocrates' influence extends. D. Babut, *Plutarque et le Stoïcisme* (Paris: 1969), pp. 420-422, thinks that Ammonios in *De defectu* is answering the arguments in *Pel.* 21, that if a being is evil morally it cannot be strong physically (420b-c). (Something similar appears in *Brut.* 37). However, the arguments do not seem to run along similar lines: in *Pelopidas* and *Brutus* it is a question of their being disregarded if the world is run by a good God, not of their physical infirmity. Such arguments are discussed by Babut at p. 26 (where he misinterprets the passage from Chrysippos), and p. 291 (where it is correctly stated). Babut believes in a growing acceptance of evil *daimones* by Plutarch. In general, Babut's work contains excellent insights into Plutarch's religious views and how they differ from those of the Stoics.

would be lost on a non-Greek reader; for the Greeks, cosmos implies order. However, Plutarch's position is meant very seriously. In the interpretation of the Isis myth in *De Iside* 373b, Osiris represents *logos* or *nous*, Isis is the nurse or receptacle, and Horos is the world, which results from the union of the two. Plutarch's own ideas enter in when he describes a previous world along the lines of that guided by his "precosmic" soul: Horos is born only after a first imperfect creation, a cripple, had been formed "for at that time there was no world but only an image of a world to be."

The daimonological interpretation receives expression in *Pelopidas* 16, and perhaps more seriously in *De E apud Delphos*. In the first passage, Plutarch states that it is incompatible with his native tradition that Apollo should have ever been a *daimon* who later turned into a god, though Plutarch is not averse to accepting this interpretation for the divinity of Dionysos and Heracles. In the second work, Ammonios gives a long philosophical eulogy of the god Apollo. He takes Apollo to be eternal being, symbolized by the E, which Ammonios understands as Ei, "thou art." Here, Ammonios objects to the conception of Apollo as an inconstant or malicious child building sandcastles along the beach and destroying them as soon as they are built. Rather, according to Ammonios, where such activities seem to be the work of Apollo, they must be attributed to another god or *daimon*, who has been confused with the eternal and irreproachable god (394c). This *daimon*, however, is not a *daimon* which turns into a god; but it is a rather disreputable double, such as those suggested in part of Cleombrotos' speech in *De defectu*. It is surprising to find this sentiment in the mouth of Ammonios. In *De defectu* Ammonios holds that the *daimones* are nothing more than former souls. It is possible, therefore, that the view was held by Plutarch himself at one stage of his life. Ammonios' conclusion is perfect support for the daimonological interpretation: all the confusion has come about by getting the divine mixed up with the daimonic. But the daimonic here is not the intermediate race of spirits, but rather Hades, the hateful god of darkness and sorrow, contrasted with Apollo, the god of light and goodness. And one suspects here that Plutarch is a child of his times, within traditional Greek terminology masking religious ideas of the civilizations around him.

There seems to be nothing of Cleombrotos' *daimones* in the Pythagorean orientated *De genio Socratis*. However, besides the

discussion on the nature of the moon along the lines of Xenocrates' theories, *De facie in orbe lunae* contains some superficial
resemblances to *De defectu oraculorum*. For example, at 944b-c,
Troglodytes are mentioned, such as those who lived near the Red
Sea mystic in *De defectu oraculorum*. Moreover, the hollows on
the face of the moon, within which the *daimon*-souls receive their
purgation, are compared with the cavities in the depths of the
Red Sea, again the region where the mystic lived. But more important, the passage which in *De facie* describes the functions of the
daimones between their incarnations or incarnation and dissolution,
repeats verbatim the description given by Cleombrotos on the
functions and needs of the *daimones*. There is one addition: the
daimones shine forth as saviors on land and sea.[20] And, unlike the
passage in *De defectu*, this one claims that if they act out of envy,
they are punished by reincarnation (944c-d). It seems here that
Plutarch is incorporating all the daimonological material into a
somewhat conflicting whole: the *daimones*—who in Cleombrotos'
description do not seem to be former souls—are now former
souls, but they are endowed with the duties and vices of the great
superior beings of Xenocrates. Having the *daimones* reincarnated
helps to bring the myth in harmony with those of Plato. At any
rate Plutarch could have found the basis for this reincarnation in
Empedocles.

There is also a humorous touch of his own in the description
of the Titans:

> Once in a while the mindless souls of the irascible and intem-
> perate who do not become resolved back into the element of the
> moon quickly—like the temperate souls—in their restlessness and
> emotion are drawn off to the earth, and the moon must charm
> them back; for it is no slight, quiet, or harmonious business when
> with the affective element without reason they seize upon a body
> (ἄνευ νοῦ τῷ παθητικῷ σώματος ἐπιλάβωνται). Such are the
> creatures like Tityos, Typhon, and the Python which seized upon

---

[20] This suggests the influence of the *Lives* since Plutarch piously relates
the appearance of the Dioscouroi when giving accounts of traditional
battles. Cf. *Aem.* 25, *Cor.* 3, *Lys.* 12. These can be found in other authors,
e.g. Dion. Hal. 6.13, Cic. *De nat. deor.* 2.6.3, Val. Max. 1.8.1, Xen. *Hell.*
2.1.28; but in *Them.* 15 he adds to Herodotos 8.64 an account of the mysterious song of Iacchos coming from Eleusis before the battle of Salamis,
and shapes of armed men said to be the Aiacidai (referred to in *Phoc.* 28).

Delphi, void of reason and subject to the affective element gone
astray through delusion (945b-c). (H. Cherniss, Loeb XII, pp. 217-
219).[21]

Here is Plutarch's old precosmic soul in disguise again: the *psyche*
of the world as it wandered in disorder until *nous* or *logos* was given
to it and it became truly the cosmos. Such *daimones* have nothing
to do with Cleombrotos' speech. The same can be said for the
daimones of *De sera numinis vindicta* which are no more than the
infernal torturers of Plato's myths.

In general one cannot conclude from the *Lives* that Plutarch was
overwhelmingly interested in the influence of *daimones* on the
lives of men, or that they had to be feared or placated in some
way. Usually when *daimones* appear, it is in the speech of men who
are suffering under great stress or disturbed under the pressure of
great reversals. For example, we know from *De divinatione* that
Cicero was a rationalist, therefore it is very unlikely that he
believed in the revenge of *daimones*. Yet, in Plutarch's account,
when the hounds are on his trail, Cicero thinks of immolating
himself on the hearth of his enemy Octavius so that an *alastor*
may fall upon him (*Cicero* 47). The sinister Marius, who is contemplating his moves up the political ladder, boasts that he has put
an *alastor* on Metellus through tricking him into putting to death
an innocent friend by casting suspicion on him (*Marius* 8). Perhaps
he expected Metellus to believe the story. However, the mother
of Coriolanus uses the word only symbolically when she says her
son has become an *alastor* to the state (*Coriolanus* 35). Perhaps
we should not take very seriously either the words of the avaricious
senators who claim that a *daimon* of vengeance has been set upon
them when they learn that Otho has taken away their property
(*Otho* 1).

The two *Lives* which could most easily concretize the theories of
Plutarch's daimonological passages in the *Moralia* are the parallel
Dion-Brutus. However, there are serious considerations which
must be taken into account here and which suggest strong reser-

---

[21] Reinhardt, *Poseidonios*, p. 326, correctly noted the contradiction
between these *daimones* and the others, though his interpretation, as Jones
"Posidonius and Solar Eschatology," *Cl. Phil.* 27 (1932), 131, pointed out,
is erroneous in several places. In *Galba* 1 the Roman Empire is compared
to the Macedonian army after Alexander's death—in Demades' phrase,
like a blinded Cyclops—a prey to convulsions and disasters "similar to those
Titanic passions and movements."

vations on the part of Plutarch. The introduction to these two *Lives* states that there is an ancient account (*logos*) that *daimones* attempt to interfere in the lives of virtuous men and frighten them from the path of righteousness, so that these men do not receive a "better portion" than the *daimones* themselves, in the next life. The motive given to these *daimones* is envy, linking it with the *De facie* passage alluded to above. In *De facie* certain *daimones* acted out of envy when they were sent to earth to perform a number of good daimonological functions, including the punishment of evildoers, and had to be reincarnated.[22]

However, when one actually examines the *Lives* of these men, one is puzzled. In the introduction we learn that the greatest similarity in the lives of the two men was the vision of a *daimon*; and this is what triggered off the statement about the ancient account. Yet, it is difficult to see how these visions are the attempts of *daimones* to move the heroes from the path of virtue. In the *Life of Brutus*, the *daimon* seems to be both an evil personal spirit, an *alastor* avenging the murder of Caesar, and possibly even *tyche*, or the *daimon* of Caesar, or even Caesar himself.[23] Moreover, the motive of the *daimon* is not at all clear. Then, Plutarch registers

---

[22] Ziegler, *Plutarchos*, p. 304; Porter, *The Life of Dion* (Dublin: 1952) p. 47; Soury, *La Démonologie*, p. 146 ff.; and Babut, *Le Stoïcisme*, p. 394, think Plutarch accepts the doctrine of daimonic intrusion in human life as presented here. Babut—on the basis that *Pelopidas* is earlier—believes that Plutarch has rejected his anti-superstitious stand in that *Life*, and that this passage confirms his hypothesis that Plutarch moves to constantly greater belief in the *daimones*. Porter—on the basis of a slight verbal parallel with *De Is.* 369b—mistakenly smells out the Zoroastrian great *daimon*. Plutarch gives a similar doctrine of Chrysippos—which he rejects—in *De Stoic. repugn.* 1051c-d. Since both here, and in *Qu. Rom.* 277a when citing Chrysippos he uses the word *daimonia* to describe the *daimones*, but in all three places reverts to his usual terminology when speaking for himself, there is a possibility that the strange *logos* here really comes from Chrysippos and the Stoics. Moreover, in both *Dion-Brutus* and *Caesar* a strong anti-Epicurean, pro-mantic thesis is proposed which suggests a Stoic polemic.

[23] Porter, *The Life of Dion*, p. 97, unjustifiably discounts the vengeance theme, clearly demonstrated by the Erinys sweeping the halls and the proximity in time of Dion's death to his murder of Heracleides, as A. Garzetti's, *Plutarchi Vita Caesaris*, p. xxxix, notes. In Plutarch's account Dion's son—"who always was somewhat queer"—inexplicably jumps from a roof to his death thus extremely disturbing Dion who is now left childless. This conflicts with Plato, *Ep.* 8, 355e, and 357c where the boy is still alive after Dion's death, and Plutarch (?) *Consol ad Apoll.* 119b, where his conduct is a marvel of composure. J. Hani, *Consolation à Apollonios* (Paris: 1972), defends its authenticity.

so much scepticism at parts that one can almost read the *Lives* as anti-daimonological. At the occurrence of the second vision of the *daimon* to Brutus, just before the battle of Philippi, in *Brutus* 48, Plutarch even goes so far as to mention that the most trustworthy witness to the portents connected with Brutus' campaign in Greece never related this vision to Brutus before the battle of Philippi even though he reported the other omens which took place. This is a rather telling argument against the truth of the vision; in the introduction Plutarch tells us that his reason for being inclined to accept the story is that Brutus had been philosophically trained and had related the occurrence to his friends. However, here the witness, Publius Volumnius, is described as a philosopher who had been with Brutus on all his campaigns; presumably he would have been the first to whom Brutus would have recounted the vision. One might object that in the introduction Plutarch is speaking only of the first vision. This may be true, but the second vision is intimately connected to the first. The *daimon* tells Brutus that he will see him at Philippi, and this is the setting of the second vision.

The visions fit the Xenocratic description of the *daimones* in that they are "great and powerful, and of frightening aspect." We may recall that in *De defectu* 416d Xenocrates is said to have described the *daimones* as being midway between men and gods (ὥσπερ ἡ δαιμόνων φύσις ἔχουσα καὶ πάθος θνητοῦ καὶ θεοῦ δύναμιν). In *De Iside* 360e the matter is put more strongly (ἐρρωμενεστέρους μὲν ἀνθρώπων . . . τῇ δυνάμει τὴν φύσιν ὑπερφέροντας ἡμῶν). Plutarch's *daimon* which appears to Brutus (*Brutus* 36) is of a similar nature (δεινὴν καὶ ἀλλόκοτον ὄψιν ἐκφύλου σώματος καὶ φοβεροῦ).[24] Dion's vision is of like size and terrifying aspect (φάσμα μέγα καὶ τερατῶδες . . . γυναῖκα μεγάλην καὶ προσώπῳ Ἐρινύος, *Dion* 55). The vision which appears to Dion is described as being in no way different in aspect and clothing than a tragic Erinys. Since Dion has just murdered Heracleides, and is even portrayed as brooding over this unfortunate event, and the growing plot in the city to avenge the murder, the logical conclusion is that this *daimon* is an avenger of evil. What follows tends to confirm this impression; for the Erinys is pictured as sweeping Dion's halls, and immediately after the vision his only son, in a childlike fit, jumps from a roof to his death.

---

[24] In the parallel passage of *Caes.* 69: ὄψιν εἶδε φοβερὰν ἄνδρος ἐκφύλου τὸ μέγεθος καὶ χαλεποῦ τὸ εἶδος.

The vision scene in *Brutus* 36 has a similar outline, or at least seems to be following similar conventions. Just as Dion had been brooding about the future and past (συνισταμένης δὲ τῆς ἐπιβουλῆς [the murder of Callippos] *Dion* 55), so Brutus is anxious about the coming decision which will decide the fate of the world for centuries (ἐν χερσὶν ἔχων τὰς ὑπὲρ τῶν ὅλων πράξεις καὶ τεταμένος τῇ φροντίδι πρὸς τὸ μέλλον). Since the passage is one of the best of this type in the *Lives* it seems well to give the English translation of it:

> When they were about to cross over from Asia Brutus had a great sign. He was naturally wakeful, and by practice and by selfre-straint had reduced his hours of sleep to few, never lying down by day, and by night only when he could transact no business nor converse with anyone, since all had gone to rest. At this time, however, when the war had begun, and he had in his hands the conduct of a life and death struggle, and was anxiously forecasting the future, he would first doze a little in the evening after eating, and then would spend the rest of the night on urgent business. But whenever he had fully met the demands of such business in shorter time, he would read a book until the third watch, at which hour the centurions and tribunes usually came to him. Once, accordingly, when he was about to take his army across from Asia, it was very late at night, his tent was dimly lighted, and all the camp was wrapped in silence. Then, as he was meditating and reflecting, he thought he heard some one coming into the tent. He turned toward the entrance and beheld a strange and dreadful apparition, a monstrous and fearful shape standing silent-ly by his side. Plucking up courage to question it, 'who art thou,' said he, 'of gods or men, and what is thine errand with me?' Then the phantom answered; 'I am thy evil genius Brutus, and thou shalt see me at Philippi.' And Brutus, undisturbed, said: 'I shall see thee.' (Perrin, Leob, *Lives*, VI, pp. 205-207).

The account given in the *Brutus* gains in a certain richness, but suffers from a lack of clarity in theme, in comparison with the parallel in *Caesar* 69. Here, the *daimon* which protected Caesar through life is said to have tracked down all his enemies until the last one was wiped off the face of the earth. As a proof of this, and of the fact that the murder of Caesar was not pleasing to the gods, Plutarch mentions the vision. Here, Brutus is struck by terror at first, and only after the vision says nothing, does Brutus pluck up enough courage to ask it what it is. Plutarch continues with the report of the second vision, "after which Brutus under-stood his fate and plunged headlong into danger." The common element between the two is the insistence in both of them on

Brutus' anxiety, and on his reduction of sleep to a minimum. The reader's scepticism is further encouraged by the description of the dimly lit tent, the fact that Brutus' servant did not see the vision, Cassius' rationalistic explanation which immediately follows—in which the vision is an hallucination caused by his lack of sleep—and by the absence of the vision in the official report of the portents before Philippi, by the philosopher Publius Volumnius.[25]

Just who the *daimon* is who speaks to Brutus in these visions is also something of a mystery. In *Caesar* 69, Plutarch is careful to distinguish the great *daimon* of Caesar, which is his avenger after death, from the one which appears to Brutus. Among the proofs of this *daimon*'s activity are the following: first, Cassius' suicide with the sword used on Caesar, a great comet which appeared and the weakening of the sun's rays for a whole year, and most of all ("that the murder was not pleasing to the gods") the vision to Brutus. When the phantom speaks, it tells Brutus not that it is the ghost of Caesar, but that it is Brutus' evil *daimon*. It does not even say that it is the avenger of Caesar; and to a large extent, in both *Dion* and *Brutus*, Plutarch has played down the vengeance-murder theme. This evil *daimon* (ὁ σὸς ὦ Βροῦτε δαίμων κακός) of *Brutus* 36, because of the suppression of the vengeance theme, and because of the preoccupation of Plutarch with the *tyche* of Brutus at the time of Philippi, actually seems like Brutus' own *tyche* appearing before him.

There is an interesting passage in *De Stoicorum repugnantiis*,

[25] The vision is related in App. *B.C.* 4.134, but according to E. Gabba, *Appiano e la Storia delle Guerre Civili* (Florence: 1956), p. 135, and index, p. 254, and *Appiani Bellorum Civilium* I (Florence: 1958), pp. xxi-xxxii, following Christ-Schmid, *Grk. Lit.* p. 523, and E. Körnemann, *Klio*, 17 (1921), 33-43, there is little likelihood that one read the other. The *daimon* speaks Greek in Valerius Maximus' version of the story, 1.7.7, in which the vision comes to Cassius of Parma—not the conspirator Cassius, as one might presume from Nilsson—before the battle of Actium. Thus Nilsson, *Geschichte* II, p. 213, thinks the story is from a Greek source. Probably the similarity of names led the story to be transferred to the conspirator Cassius before Philippi, and then to the more prominent Brutus. On this see my "Le songe du Brutus," *Budé Congrès* (1968), pp. 588-96, alluded to in Russell, *Plutarch*, pp. 77-79. Cassius' supposed Epicurean explanation is remarkably unorthodox in terminology, and remarkably like that of Plutarch elsewhere. On Cassius' Epicureanism and that of his friends, see L. Paratore, "La problematica sull' epicureismo a Roma," *ANRW*, I,4 (1973), pp. 116-204, esp. pp. 132-34, and 184-85, where he cites A. Momigliano, "Epicureans in Revolt," *JRS*, 31 (1941), p. 151 ff.

(1051cd) which helps to explain Plutarch's attitude in the *Dion-Brutus*. Here he criticizes Chrysippos who explained such cases as Socrates. Pythagoras, and Zeno—all of whom met an unfortunate end—as due either to oversights in divine providence, such as a few grains of wheat or rye in an otherwise well-run household, or to the presence of evil *daimonia* set over the m.Plutarch found both solutions unacceptable. The language here is interesting. Where apparently quoting Chrysippos he uses, as in *Dion-Brutus* 2 the expression evil *daimonia* (φαῦλα δαιμόνια), but where using his own words, as elsewhere, evil *daimones* (φαῦλοι δαίμονες). The suggestion is that the theory of evil *daimonia* in the introduction to *Dion-Brutus* belongs to Chrysippos ultimately.

In conclusion, *De defectu oraculorum*, the major treatise for that daimonology which has often been propounded as the most Plutarchan, must be used with a very large grain of salt. Only a small part of the dialogue is actually concerned with Cleombrotos' theory; the rest is a long digression on the number of worlds—which is only superficially connected to the rest of the dialogue—and a refutation of the daimonological theory of the operation of oracles. Even if Cleombrotos is not a bungling idiot in the piece, he at least is no intellectual genius, and the rest of the company delight in manifesting his incompetency in handling philosophical and religious problems. His account probably gives a faithful reproduction of the *daimon* theory of Xenocrates, except that it leaves us uncertain as to how much of the superstitious belief in *daimones* was actually part of Xenocrates' teaching. It seems likely that it is much less than some scholars believe. There is also some uncertainty over the question of the *daimones*' preexistence as humans, and over what death for them implies. At any rate Cleombrotos' theories are considered by the company to be rash and unorthodox. We should not be led into making the misleading generalization that they are characteristic either of Plutarch or of the mentality of the Second Century A.D. Both Plutarch elsewhere, and the company here, seem to prefer the concept of the *daimones* as nothing more than former humans; i.e. human souls. There are traces of the daimonological interpretation of myth elsewhere in Plutarch's writings, notably *De E apud Delphos*; but it seems that he abandoned it, if he ever seriously held it, by the time of the composition of *De Iside et Osiride*. Finally, even such passages as those in *Dion* and *Brutus*, which are often used to confirm the argument that Plutarch adhered to the ideas of Cleombrotos, actually indicate a certain confusion or even scepticism as to the nature or existence of these *daimones*. In short, Plutarch did not concern himself much with the intrusion of the daimonic into human life, and his humanitarian nature was offended by certain aspects of daimonological interpretation.[26]

---

[26] The most serious passage in support of the demonological theory is that in the end of Ammonios' speech in *De E* (394a-c). However, the passage is highly poetical, contrasting Apollo-*daimon* and Apollo-*theos* in order to get around the old mythology which might be a hindrance to treating Apollo as the supreme god. Even so, it is difficult to believe that Plutarch held a *daimon* was responsible for the destructive forces of the sun. J. Dillon, *The Middle Platonists*, pp. 191, finds the passage a foreshadowing of the Neoplatonic identification of Hades with the "sublunary demiurge." In this passage Apollo is contrasted with the *daimon* as being *A-pollo* (not many) vs. *Plouton* ("abounding"), but also with other aspects (bright, clear) in other etymological puns. Flacelière, *Dialogues Pythiques*, pp. 7-11 sees some implications here of the worship of Dionysos at Delphi, as opposed to that of Apollo. There is some possibility that Hades here is a place. For the *De animae procreatione in Timaeo*, which has a relationship to Plutarch's Titans etc. on the moon, see the new commentary by H. Cherniss, Loeb, *Mor.* XIII, part 1 (1976), pp. 133-49 (part 2 contains the Stoic questions). Cherniss describes Plutarch's treatment as original rather than over-literal, a skillful manipulation of texts for his own purpose in an arbitrary and contradictory way. See also M. Baltes, *Die Weltentstehung des Platonischen Timaios nach den Antiken Interpreten* (Leiden: 1976).

CHAPTER SEVEN

LAMPRIAS'S REPLY: AUGHT ELSE THAN SOULS THAT MAKE THEIR ROUNDS IN MISTS APPARELLED?

We have seen how Plutarch incorporated the daimonological material which appears in Cleombrotos' speech in *De defectu oraculorum*—and which to some extent can be said to be Xenocratic—into other works of his *Moralia*, and even into the *Lives*. It was suggested, however, that this incorporation was not always doctrinaire, that sometimes Plutarch expresses his hesitancy or indicates the hypothetical nature of the theory, and that at other times he even seems to attack it. In any case the *Lives* and *Moralia* do not reveal a preoccupation with the *daimones* or suggest that these pernicious monsters intrude everywhere into human life, lurking behind every bush, ready to swallow up innocent and guilty alike.

Cleombrotos is, however, only one of the principal speakers in *De defectu*. There is another who figures just as much, Plutarch's brother Lamprias. We must now assess his role in the dialogue, analyze the ideas he represents and attempt to determine how representative his thought is of that to be found elsewhere in Plutarch. The solutions which Lamprias proposes are applications of the principles of *aporroia* (effluence or radiation), *pneuma*, which is sometimes identical with *anathymiasis* (vapor, exhalation, breath), and *krasis* (mixture, constitution, or temperament). Another important concept which is central to the speech of Lamprias is the understanding of a *daimon* not as a great independent being of an order higher than man, but as a creature identifiable with the human soul itself, either in its present state of incorporation in the body, or prior or posterior to that union. The speech of Cleombrotos which preceded that of Lamprias admittedly gave a confused account of the nature of the *daimones*, and it was not clear whether Cleombrotos meant to exclude the idea of *daimones* as human souls. Yet, the speech is primarily concerned with a presentation of the daimonological conceptions of Xenocrates, and it is difficult to understand Xenocrates' *daimones*, which are "greater in nature and more powerful than men," and an intermediate race between men and gods, as identifiable with human souls. Certainly such an identification makes unintelligible Xenocrates' statement about their constitution being different from that of men.

First of all, in order to assess Lamprias' position, one must notice the dramatic superiority of Lamprias.[1] From the end of the mystic's tale to the conclusion, he plays the principal and almost sole role in the dialogue.[2] It is even dedicated by Lamprias to Terentius Priscus, though this style of introduction by Plutarch is not quite as peculiar as it might seem at first sight. Moreover in spite of some mistaken conclusions to the contrary by modern scholars, Lamprias sees himself throughout as a thoroughgoing Platonist—as Plutarch did himself—not as the proponent of some new or foreign doctrine, or as a syncretist willing to abandon Plato at the first opportunity for the lures of Aristotelianism or Stoicism. It is Cleombrotos, not Lamprias, who with his attack on the Platonic explanations of *physis* and *hyle* sets himself at odds with Platonism, and Lamprias who not only comes to the defense of these principles but explains that this is the only way to solve the decline of the oracle (414e, 414d). It is also Lamprias who rebukes the Cynic, Planetiades, for casting aspersions on the benevolence of the divinity and for his overpessimistic view of mankind. Moreover, Lamprias' philosophical competence is revealed in his unearthing of the plagiarism in the apparently heaven-sent account of the nature of the world in the Red Sea mystic's story— which otherwise might have passed unnoticed—and who in the

---

[1] In Qu. conv. 726e he is described as snobbish and good-humored (ὑβριστὴς δὲ ὢν καὶ φιλογέλως φύσει), and in 635b as having a preference for the Peripatetics over the Epicureans (πρὸ τοῦ Κήπου κυδαίνοντι τὸν Περίπατον καὶ τὸ Λύκειον) not—as Ziegler, *Plutarchos*, p. 10, puts it—a Peripatetic himself necessarily and though Ziegler claims he was a priest at Lebadaia—as Cherniss points out (Loeb, *Mor.* XII, p. 4), this is not necessarily true: 431d can be taken to mean simply that Lamprias had a conversation there. Ziegler otherwise treats him as a man of importance, a kind of double of Plutarch. Flacelière, *Dialogues Pythiques*, p. 87, simply repeats the words about Lamprias at 635b on his Aristotelian tendencies, rather than being more specific, and regards his "naturaliste" explanation as inspired primarily by Aristotelian ideas on *pneuma*.

[2] Ziegler, p. 10, points out that Hirzel and Wilamowitz thought the dedication by a person in a dialogue was striking; Wilamowitz called it unique in Greek literature; and Christ and Hirzel had adopted the view that Lamprias was the real or reputed author. However, Ziegler aptly notes that the *Republic* is dedicated by Socrates to Apollodoros.

long discussion on the number of worlds treats with complete confidence the complex cosmological theories of the Platonic, Aristotelian, and Stoic schools, and finally, is able to contribute an original solution of his own and defend it with considerable acumen. Even a superficial glance at the dialogue reveals the superiority of Lamprias. Though modern scholars tend to cast a myopic gaze upon the words of Cleombrotos, his speech in fact takes up only six Stephanus pages of the dialogue, while sixteen, or a ratio of almost three to one, are devoted to Lamprias.[3] Moreover, Cleombrotos' speech is largely an unspeculative *résumé* of Greek daimonology, almost a handbook; it concludes with a preposterous pseudo-myth that leaves at least some of his friends unimpressed. Lamprias covers a vast range of philosophical speculation: the nature of the *daimones*, the multiplicity of worlds, the natural place theory, the extent of divine providence, the cosmological significance of the pempad, the nature of *aporroia* and *krasis*, the inspiration of the oracles, and the distinction between Apollo and the sun, which concludes the dialogue on a note of dignity and religious piety.

On the other hand, Cleombrotos' speech is a bungling thing. It is objected to by the other speakers, ridiculed, called a preposterous hypothesis, anti-scientific, and plagiaristic; during the course of it he is unable to speak at one point, and at another a friend must come to his rescue. Lamprias speaks with dignified authority and receives respect from the group. The master of the Academy, Ammonios,

---

[3] Muhl, *Plut. Stud.*, p. 69, correctly understood Lamprias to be Plutarch's principal speaker in the dialogue, but Hirzel, *Der Dialog* II, p. 192, argued that the two views of Cleombrotos and Lamprias were of equal weight. Soury, *La Démonologie*, p. 109-10, allots only a page and a half to Lamprias' position while giving one hundred to Cleombrotos. Ziegler, p. 10, with some vacillation gives "einen hervorragenden Anteil" to Lamprias. Flacelière, *Sur la Disparition*, p. 10 and 300, shifts back and forth between making Lamprias representative or not, but sees Cleombrotos as a person with notorious intellectual insufficiencies. Goldschmidt, "Les Thèmes du De Defectu Oraculorum," p. 300, criticized Flacelière for contradicting himself, holding that Lamprias was "l'interprète attitré de l'auteur" (p. 19), but that his synthesis was "superficiel et décevant" (p. 47). Goldschmidt holds that Lamprias' doctrine is perfectly coherent, and Platonic. In *Dialogues Pythiques*, pp. 85-87, Flacelière expresses the view that *De defectu* represents the balance of his researches on divination, borrowing from all but the Epicurean school, before he came to a satisfactory conclusion, that of *De E* and *De Pythiae oraculis*. He also feels that through inadvertance, as in the case of Theon in *De Pythiae oraculis* at moments Plutarch substitutes himself for the literary personage, without warning the reader.

9

at one point asks him to continue his exposition, and the others express approbation during it, or ask for further elucidation. At the end of it Philippos pays him the high compliment that it has indeed been very thought-provoking.

But is Lamprias' speech representative of Plutarch or is it merely a hodge-podge of rationalistic Aristotelianism and Stoicism, a temporary, hypothetical solution which Plutarch was toying with, and largely inconsistent with anything that he wrote before or after?[4] First of all, it is correct that Plutarch regarded himself as a champion of Platonism; but it is erroneous to regard the dialogue as a duel between the Academy represented by Cleombrotos, and the Peripatos and Stoa represented by Lamprias. As we have already mentioned, Cleombrotos, not Lamprias, is dissatisfied with Plato and his daimonology. Though claiming support from Plato, Cleombrotos presents a theory of evil *daimones* which is non-existent in Plato; and he substitutes *daimones* for gods in the myths, which Plato treated as absurd falsehoods. Cleombrotos himself regards the origins of the new theories as foreign, and after already slighting Plato's doctrine on matter (414f-415b), is later unimpressed with the logic behind Plato's argument that there might be as many as five worlds (422a).

In contrast to the hostility to Platonism in certain aspects of Cleombrotos' speech, the Platonic substratum of Lamprias' speech is clearly revealed in his discourse on the nature of the cosmos and the imposition of order upon it (423c-424c). The passage reminds one of *De animae procreatione in Timaeo*. Plutarch's innovation here is the existence of a precosmic soul, a *psyche* without *nous*, which wandered about in erratic and disordered fashion under the

---

[4] It is interesting how scholars have interpreted Lamprias' speech here. P. Amandry, *La Mantique Apollinienne à Delphes* (Paris: 1950), p. 217, speaks of "le stoïcien Lamprias," and Flacelière, *Sur la Disparition*, p. 10, writes in a similar vein. Goldschmidt, "Les thèmes," p. 300, —as noted before—recognized the speech to be basically Platonic. Hirzel, *Der Dialog* II, p. 192, had earlier regarded the speech as a "Concordanzversuch," which— on the basis of a similar doctrine in Arist. *De somn.* 456b 9 ff., 463b 19, and 464a 27—he attributed to the Peripatetic Dicaiarchos. However, R. Jones, *The Platonism*, pp. 35-36, corrected Hirzel's misunderstanding of the description by Lamprias of the soul as a *krasis* or *harmonia*. Flacelière, *Sur la Disparition*, p. 16, objects to Von Arnim's attribution of the speech to Poseidonios, and notes the resemblance of parts of Lamprias' theory to Arist. *Meteor.* 1.3. 340b 27, and *De mem.* 432a; he also points a finger at Lamprias' statement at 434b that the Aristotelians believed that all the changes which took place in the earth could be attributed to an *anathymiasis*.

guidance of opinion and imagination until *logos* was imposed upon it; only then the world received its true soul, and could be said to have been created in time. Much of what Plutarch says elsewhere on the creation of the world, and even his myths themselves, are made intelligible if this conception of the creation of the universe is kept in mind. This explains Lamprias' particular words on the subject in *De defectu*. At 424a-425e, Lamprias also rejects the natural place theory so dear to Aristotle, as he does again in *De facie in orbe lunae* (923f-924f), where he is also Plutarch's principal spokesman in a dialogue, and where—far ahead of his time—he argues for the natural attraction of bodies for one another.

His defense of the efficacy of divine providence, in *De defectu oraculorum*, and his rejection of *tyche* as playing a significant role in the destiny of the universe is again in the Platonic tradition. So also is his assault on the Epicurean atomic theory—something which appears frequently in Plutarch's writings and in particular in his anti-Epicurean ones. The attack on the Stoic Chrysippos for making the earth the center of the universe, and, therefore, indestructible (425d), and for concluding that there must be a multiplicity of Zeuses or Zens if there should be a multiplicity of worlds, is so characteristic of Plutarch's attack on the Stoics in *De Stoicorum repugnantiis*, that it could be moved bodily into that work. Moreover, Lamprias' discourse on the five worlds theory (427a-e) is almost a repetition of the speech of the youthful Plutarch in *De E* (389f-390a), as is the commentary (428c-d) on the five superior categories of being in Plato's *Sophist* (256c), a commentary which again is strikingly similar to that in the youthful Plutarch's speech in *De E* (391b).

Finally, at the end of his cosmological speech, Lamprias makes it quite clear that he never felt he was deviating from the path of Plato, nor that he ever believed himself anything else than an Academician:

> But if in any other place we have recalled the Academy to our mind, let us do so here as well and divest ourselves of excessive credulity (τὸ ἄγαν τῆς πίστεως) and, as if we were in a slippery place in our discussion about infinity, let us merely keep a firm footing. (431a, Babbitt, Loeb, *Mor.* V, p. 461).

Even the theory proposed by Lamprias for the inspiration of the oracle—which has seemed so Aristotelian to some scholars, so

Stoic to others—actually is based on Plato, for whom alterations in the physical state of the body are regarded as vitally necessary for prophetic inspiration.

Lamprias' speech also serves to establish the relationship between the three Pythian dialogues.[5] At the end of *De defectu oraculorum* (433d-e), Lamprias—after arguing against the Stoic identification of Apollo and the sun earlier in the dialogue—concludes by saying that certain considerations and objections must be postponed until another time, among them the question which Philippos had raised about Apollo and the sun. This is the main question, or at least the conclusion and high point of *De E apud Delphos*,[6] in which, Ammonios, not Lamprias, is Plutarch's representative. It seems very logical to conclude that *De E* is meant as the continuation of *De defectu*, either because Plutarch had already written it and the final state of *De defectu* is meant to serve as an introduction to *De E*, or because he genuinely meant to write about this question of Apollo and the sun but had not worked out the details yet. The latter seems more logical since it otherwise is strange why Ammonios and not Lamprias should answer the question. The distinction between Apollo and the sun appears in *De Pythiae oraculis* (400d), this time as though the reader were already acquainted with it, though it is put into the mouth of Philinos rather than Lamprias or Ammonios. It is for this reason that the traditional order (*De Pythiae oraculis, De E, De defectu*) seems suspect and that the real order of composition

---

[5] The significance of the discussion about Apollo and the sun as an important link in establishing the chronology of the composition of the Pythian dialogues was recognized by Hirzel, *Der Dialog* II, p. 197, who argued for the order *De def., De E, De Pyth.* Flacelière, "Plutarque et la Pythie," p. 72 ff., may be right in his belief that the Pythian *logoi* mentioned in the dedication of *De Pythiae oraculis* may refer to no more than the *De Pythiae*. The piece may have attracted the attention of the Emperor Hadrian who was interested in promoting solar religion. On this see M. Thornton, "Hadrian and his Reign," *ANRW* II,2 (1975), pp. 432-76, who sees the Pantheon as designed to introduce and magnify the Sun. Trajan had given Plutarch the *ornamenta consularia*, and Hadrian made him procurator of Greece, both honorary titles. See Jones, *Plutarch and Rome*, p. 34, and Flacelière, "Hadrien et Delphes," *CRAI* (1971), 168-185.

[6] On this see note 2 to chapter V. Ziegler, pp. 15-16, and Sandbach, Loeb, *Mor.* IX, p. 219, make no reference to whether Ammonios truly came from Egypt. Dörrie felt that the identification of the Forms with God and contrast between the changeable world and God, rather than the world of Forms was unorthodox. Dillon is impressed with the dualism and suspects Persian influence.

was *De defectu, De E,* and *De Pythiae oraculis.* Lamprias' speech on this point also forms a link with some other essays since the idea of the sun as the image of the good, by which the souls which gaze upon it are freed, figures prominently in the eschatological myths of *De genio Socratis* and *De facie in orbe lunae,* and the matter is alluded to in *Ad principem erudiendum* (780e) and *De latenter vivendo* (1130a). There can be little doubt that the question was important for Plutarch and formed one of the lynchpins of his Delphic theology.

We must now turn to the principal solution of Lamprias to the prophetic problem. This is given in pieces throughout the dialogue and is developed and given in its ultimate form at the end, in which he argues that a prophetic vapor or *pneuma,* rising from the earth affects the Pythian priestess. If she has the proper disposition (*krasis*) to induce the state of prophetic ecstasy, she will be able to achieve contact with the divine world; the *pneuma,* however, is material and will, therefore, eventually dissipate itself, leaving a wasteland where once there was a flourishing center of oracular activity. At the end of his speech, Lamprias is willing to allow *daimones* the minor role of regulating the *krasis* of the *pneuma,* but even if this is not ridiculous—and Lamprias never explains how *daimones* could possibly regulate it—it seems more a polite concession to Cleombrotos than a serious modification or addition which has anything intrinsically to do with Lamprias' prophetic theory (436d-438e).

In *De Pythiae oraculis,* even though the problem of inspiration is somewhat different, the *daimones* are nowhere mentioned; complete silence reigns over their activity. Such a state of in- articulation about their whereabouts would seem to be an indication, not that the prophetic theory of *De defectu* was suddenly cast aside and replaced by a more impressive one, but rather that all along Plutarch had little truck with the *daimon* theory as a literal interpretation of prophetic inspiration. One might justifiably wonder whether for Plato the *daimones* as a "ministering race of prophecy" were in any way less allegorical than that budding Eros, the *élan vital* of love and procreation. One might also justi- fiably wonder whether for Plutarch the *daimones* are meant to receive anything else than allegorical significance in the prophetic context. Certainly Plutarch's Eros is largely allegorical in the *Eroticos,* his essay on love.

That the use of the theories of *krasis*, *pneuma*, and *aporroia* reached alarming proportions in Plutarch's "scientific" explanations is evident from the vast number of subjects to which these theories were applied.[7] The one surprising exception is Plutarch's refusal to treat light as an emanation when he discusses this point in his long astronomical treatise, *De facie in orbe lunae*. These theories of *krasis*, *pneuma*, and *aporroia* are often considered by scholars to be characteristically Aristotelian, though such theories have their origin in Plato's writings or are often as much Platonic as Aristotelian in their application. At one place Lamprias is said to have had a good acquaintance with Aristotelianism, and this may be the reason why he was chosen to be the principal speaker in *De defectu oraculorum*; but in the opinion of at least one modern scholar Plutarch had an outstanding knowledge and appreciation of Aristotle, which has often been neglected by those who comment upon Plutarch's philosophical competence.[8]

---

[7] Two scholars to note the importance of these theories in Plutarch are H. Dörrie and G. Soury. Dörrie in "Emanation," K. Flasch ed., *Parusia* (Frankfurt: 1965), pp. 119-41, records a number of passages in which the *aporroia* theory appears: the evil eye, 681a; magnetism, 1005e; the stingray 978c; the perception of the ink fish, 96f, 916d; the effect of the herb *erygion* on goats, 776c,f; and the tracking ability of dogs, 917e. Soury, "Les questions de table et la philosophie religieuse de Plutarque," *REG*, 62 (1949), 320-27, makes the somewhat exaggerated claim that in Plutarch a link between "homme et cosmos" rests upon the antipathy and sympathy of all things, which is communicated through some sort of *pneuma*. His examples are sometimes trivial, but they do show the extent to which Plutarch went with the theory: air cools water, *Qu. conv.* 6.4; the sweet fruit of the fig tree comes from bitter sap, 5.9; lambs bitten by wolves have tender flesh, 2.9; and a cock suspended from a fig tree tastes best, 6.10. Unfortunately, he follows Reinhardt in making Poseidonios the source for the souls' affinity with the moon, and Von Arnim for making the same philosopher the source of the divination theory in *De defectu*.

[8] R. Jones, *The Platonism*, p. 20, n. 77, notes the Aristotelian influence on Plutarch's conception of *hyle* at *De fac.* 944e, *De Is.* 372a, and *Amat.* 770b; of reproduction at *De Is.* 374b (in which the female has only a passive role); the definition of imagination at *De an. proc.* 1024f; the argument against Plato's Ideas at *Adv. Col.* 1115c; time at *Qu. Plat.* 1007a; and the definition of soul in *Adv. Col.* 1006d. Jones may be mistaken in attributing a commentary on the *Topics* and *Categories* to Plutarch: these listings in the Lamprias catalogue may actually refer to volumes of Aristotle in Plutarch's library. G. Verbeke, "Plutarch and the Development of Aristotle," pp. 236-47, I. Düring and G. E. L. Owen, eds., *Aristotle and Plato in the Mid-Fourth Century* (Göteborg: 1960)—a 1957 symposium which took place at Oxford—notes that 70 pages of Aristotle are preserved in Plutarch, that he was acquainted with the esoteric works (*Phys.*, *Met.*, *Top.*, *De cael.*, *De an.*, *Eth.*, *Pol.*, *Ath. Pol.*, *Prob.* and *Mir. ausc.*), and that his com-

The *aporroia* theory profoundly impressed Plutarch for its ability to explain the rapidity with which that ancient and modern disaster, the plague, could spread through the world with such alarming results. Both in *De sera numinis vindicta* (558e), and in the *Life of Pericles* (34) the theory is used to explain the rapidity of the great plague at Athens:

> And there are other forces with a capacity for contagion and transmission incredible in its rapidity and the great intervals covered that reach one object by passing through another. We, however, are amazed at the intervals in time, not those in space. And yet is it more amazing that a disease which had its origin in Ethiopia should have raged at Athens, killed Pericles, and attacked Thucydides, than that justice after the crimes of the Delphians and Sybarites, should have found her way to their children? (De Lacy—Einarson, Loeb, *Mor.* VII, pp. 243-65).[9]

Among other uses of the *pneuma* theory is Plutarch's explanation of the belief that the soil is drenched by rain after a battle with great carnage has taken place (*Marius* 21). Here, there is a possibility, as in *De defectu*, that the reader is offered a choice between a *daimon* or *anathymiasis* (εἴτε δαιμονίου τινὸς τὴν γῆν καθαροῖς καὶ διϊπετέσιν ἁγνίζοντος ὕδασι καὶ κατακλύζοντος, εἴτε τοῦ φόνου καὶ τῆς σηπεδόνος ἐξανιείσης ὑγρὰν καὶ βαρεῖαν ἀναθυμίασιν, ἢ τὸν ἀέρα συνίστησιν εὔτρεπτον ὄντα καὶ ῥᾴδιον μεταβάλλειν ἀπὸ σμικροτάτης ἐπὶ πλεῖστον ἀρχῆς), but it would be against Plutarch's normal usage to write *daimonion* when he means *daimon*, and the style of the rest of the religious digressions suggests that Plutarch means the scientific explanation to be taken as a substitute for

---

ments on Aristotle's psychology in *De virtute morali*, which point to the development of Aristotle's thought away from Plato, were centuries ahead of his time. Verbeke believes Plutarch may have been less acquainted with the *Metaphysics*, since this is not cited by him when giving Aristotle's criticism of the Platonic Ideas. For more on Plutarch's Aristotelianism see D. Babut, *Plutarque. De la Vertu Éthique* (Paris: 1970), p. 66, who cites the unpublished work of S. Etheridge, *Plutarch's "De virtute morali", A Study in Extra-Peripatetic Aristotelianism* (Harvard: 1961), and M. Pinnoy, *Aristotelisme en Antistoïcisme in Plutarchus "De virtute morali"* (Louvain: 1956), and *De Peripatetische Thema in Plutarchus "De virtute morali"* (Louvain: 1966).

[9] The theory behind the plague is found also in *Qu. conv.* 700d and 776f, and among other writers: Arist. *Hist. An.* 610 b 29, Theophr. fr. 174, Plin. *N.H.* 8.203f., Antig. *Hist. Mir.* 107, and a scholion on Nicand. *Ther.* 645, and Lucretius, 6.1085-1286.

superstitious belief.[10] The principle is extremely important to Plutarch, and is, therefore, enunciated at great length by Lamprias in *De defectu* (435e-437c), and elsewhere in Plutarch's writings. The gist of it is that a purely supernatural explanation should only be offered as a last resort, and that it is the principal purpose of an intelligent thinker to examine what instrumental or natural causes might be involved. In similar style, the color permutations of the octopus are based on *aporroiai*, something close to the idea of *anathymiasis*.[11] Finally the opening of *De Pythiae oraculis*, with its interest in the sharpness of the Delphic air and its peculiar effect on bronze, the end of *De Iside et Osiride* with its attention to the effect of drugs on the mind, and the central part of *De facie in orbe lunae* with its inquiry into the composition of the moon, are unintelligible without an understanding of these theories of *pneuma*, *anathymiasis*, and *aporroiai*.

The *krasis* theory is used to explain the constitution of the world—both in *De defectu oraculorum* (430b-d) and *De animae procreatione in Timaeo* (1012aff.)—the nature of a balanced personality (φύσει δ' εἰς πᾶσαν ἀρετὴν εὖ κεκραμένος τὸ ἦθος, *Num.* 3),

[10] The exposition on religious method is extremely important to Lamprias and consumes considerable space in the dialogue. Failure to appreciate it may be behind so many misunderstandigs of the speech. The theory is similar to that in the digression in *Nic.* 23 on the course of Greek philosophy and its culmination in Plato; and is expounded in shorter form by Florus in *Qu. conv.* 680c-683b and by Ammonios in *Qu. conv.* 720d-722c. The basis of it is that one should not settle for a religious, inexplicable cause, until the scientifically observable causes, which are usually instrumental, have been exhausted. This type of religious explanation appears in the *Lives* frequently: *Cam.* 6 and *Cor.* 38 on speaking statues; *Rom.* 2-4 and 27-28 on the birth and apotheosis of Romulus; *Cam.* 20 on the objects of the vestal virgins; *Pel.* 21 on human sacrifice; *Mar.* 36 on bird portents; *Mar.* 21 on heavy rains after great carnage; *Nic.* 23 on eclipses; *Lys.* 12 on meteors; *Brut.* 36-37 on Brutus vision; and *Num.* 4 and 8 on the relations between men and gods or *daimones*. For a different interpretation of Plutarch's method see H. Erbse "Plutarchs Schrift *Peri Deisidaimonias*," p. 313, n. 2, and J. Schroeter, *Plutarchs Stellung zur Skepsis* (Greifswald: 1911), p. 41. Schroeter's concept of a sceptical Plutarch has been refuted by P. De Lacy, "Plutarch and the Academic Sceptics," *CJ*, 49 (1953), 79-85. Erbse treats the digressions as a balance between rationalism and superstition, with the balance slightly tipped in favor of the latter.

[11] Plutarch (916d) cites Empedocles (πάντων εἰσὶ ἀπορροιαὶ ὅσσ' ἐγένετο, DK B 89) in support of his view that the octopus is constantly sensing the *aporroiai* which are emitted by all material objects. In Plutarch's view, when the octopus receives a particular emission, it closes its pores; this results in a change of *pneuma*, which then is responsible for the change in the octopus' color.

pleasure (*Non posse suaviter vivi secundum Epicurum* 1091e), defoliation (*Quaestiones convivales* 735e), and the nature of light (*De facie in orbe lunae* 930f and 931e).[12] One of the most interesting passages in the *Moralia* is that of the suicide epidemic of the girls of Miletos, which Plutarch surprisingly uses as an illustration of feminine courage (*arete*). The use of the *krasis* theory for insanity appears also in *Amatorius* 758d-e, but this is nothing compared to the story which appears in *Mulierum virtutes*, a story which also formed the introduction to Plutarch's lost *De anima*. It seems fitting to give it in an English translation as it appears in *Mulierum virtutes* (249b-d).

> Once upon a time a dire and strange trouble took possession of the young women in Miletus for some unknown cause. The most popular conjecture was that the air had acquired a distracting and infectious constitution and that this operated in them to produce an alternation and derangement of mind. At any rate a yearning for death and an insane impulse toward hanging suddenly fell upon all of them, and many managed to steal away and hang themselves. Arguments and tears of parents and comforting words of friends availed nothing, but they circumvented every device and cunning effort of their watchers in making away with themselves. The malady seemed to be of divine origin and beyond human help, until on the advice of a man of sense an ordinance was proposed that the women who hanged themselves should be carried naked through the marketplace to their burial. And when this ordinance was passed it not only checked, but stopped completely the young women from killing themselves . . . (Loeb, *Mor.* III, p. 509).

The most popular conjecture about the constitution of the air, that it had acquired a distracting and infectious constitution (κρᾶσιν ἐκστατικὴν καὶ φαρμακώδη, 249c), was undoubtedly philosophical speculation interjected into a familiar Milesian tale by Plutarch, and has little to do with the interesting cure which saved the girls.[13]

---

[12] In *Alex.* 4 the *krasis* of Alexander's body results in a pleasant odor coming from his skin; in 35 the *krasis* of ivy prevents its growing in Persia. In *Arat.* 4 and *Galb.* 1 good character is described in terms of a proper *krasis*. In *Sert.* 8 the pleasantness of the Isles of the Blest is due to the *krasis* caused by the concourse of the winds at this point in the ocean. In *Phoc.* 2 the proper *krasis* of the earth is caused by the elliptical motion of the sun.

[13] The version of the story in Aulus Gellius' Latin translation, 15.10, and the brief form of it in Polyainos, *Strat.* 8.63., omit the cause of the disease. P. Stadter, *Plutarch's Historical Methods* (Cambridge, Mass.: 1965),

The theory is also used to explain the nature of erratic dreams
in autumn. Here Plutarch prefers the *krasis* theory to the *eidola*
theory of Democritos, "touched up and polished like a mirror"
employed by one of the other speakers (*Quaestiones convivales*
734d-736b). In *De facie* 928f and 943e the *krasis* theory is used
to explain how the moon can maintain its position in the universe,
a theory which is proposed in opposition to the natural place
theory. Moreover, in *Brutus* 37 it is used in Cassius' supposedly
Epicurean explanation of Brutus' vision of the *daimon* which
appeared to him at Abydos before crossing to Greece. Cassius
insists—in a vein similar to the explanation of speaking statues
in *Coriolanus* 38—on some internal sensation or hallucination
similar to those experienced in dreams, due to a state brought
upon Brutus by fatigue which had resulted in a bad *krasis* in
his body. At least this would seem to be the meaning of the words
σοὶ δὲ καὶ τὸ σῶμα ταλαιπωρούμενον φύσει τὴν διάνοιαν αἰωρεῖ καὶ
παρατρέπει, which seem to be equivalent to the ἐν τινὶ δυσκρασίᾳ
σώματος of the sceptics quoted in the introduction, who believe
that visions of *daimones* are hallucinations. The speech not only
is not Epicurean, but it is even contradictory to Epicurean doctrine
both in Cassius' insistence that sensation is deceptive and un-
trustworthy, and in his use of the term *eidola* in a highly un-
Epicurean way.[14] The only thing Epicurean about the speech—

p. 77, is puzzled by the inclusion of the medical (sic) explanation, apparently
unaware of Plutarch's frequent use of this theory. An epidemic of madness
among the women of Pylos is recorded in Herod. 9.34. Herodotos claims
that a seer Melampos demanded half the kingdom to cure the women. He
was refused but the Argives gave in when more women "caught the disease."
Melampos had by this time raised his price to include one-third of the kingdom for his brother, and managed to get this also.

[14] At the beginning of the speech Cassius is called an Epicurean, and he
refers to himself as such. According to *Dion* 1, Brutus was a Platonist,
not a Stoic, though some modern scholars have mistakenly referred to
him as a Stoic. There is much in common in the ancient theories of sensation, but it is still possible to show that Cassius' explanation here follows
more along the lines of the Platonic, Aristotelian, and Stoic explanation
of sensation than that of the Epicureans. It has particular affinities with
the Aristotelian doctrine. Aristotle held that sensation was either true or
for the most part true (*De an.* 428a-b); and a similar theory was held by the
Stoics (Aet. *Plac.* 4.9.4, Cic. *Acad.* 2.7.19); both the Aristotelian and Stoic
schools held that *phantasiai* were often false. Plutarch, who was perfectly
versed in the intricacies of Epicurean sensation theory, ridicules the Epicureans in *Adv. Col.* 1123c for holding that sensation and even hallucination
were true; moreover, he indicates that the Epicureans believed the cause
of error to be the interference of *doxa* between the act of perception and

and only half Epicurean at that—is the conclusion in which Cassius says that it is unreasonable to suppose that *daimones* either exist or that they have human form or voice, but that he wishes they did exist so that he and Brutus might have not only the help of arms, horses, and ships but also the aid of the gods in "our most holy and noble enterprise." It is even possible that this last statement is not Epicurean, but Plutarchan, since the denial of human form or voice to the *daimones* seems suspiciously close to Plutarch's refusal on similar grounds to permit statues to speak.[15]

The inspiration theory given by Lamprias to explain the decline of the oracles is basically the same as that found in *De Iside et Osiride*—where this time a drug is necessary to produce the proper *krasis* (383-384c), and in *Amatorius* 758e where the change in *krasis* enables the soul to rise to high flights of spirit in which it achieves contact with the eternal world. Also important is Lamprias' statement that "all souls possess the prophetic power as an inborn gift but that it only discloses its power in dreams and for some at the hour of death" (432c). This idea is repeated in a fragment of *De anima* (178.3.40-45, Sandbach). Here, Patrocleas claims that sleep is a great gift of *tyche*, in fact, the greatest in this life,

---

the act of assent (1122c). However, here the supposed Epicurean, Cassius, speaks of sensation as deceptive, (οὐ πάντα πάσχομεν ἀληθῶς κ.τ.λ.) and hallucination as frequent (ῥᾷστα ποικίλλειν αὐτὴν κ.τ.λ.). Besides this, the term *eidola* is not employed in the technical sense which is customary among the Epicureans; and the *eidola* are not formed from emissions from outside objects (ἀπ'οὐδενὸς ὑπάρχοντος) but by the mind itself (ὀξυτέρα ἡ διάνοια κινεῖν αὐτήν). The theory developed by Cassius—like Plutarch's theory in *Coriolanus* 38—appears to best reflect a combination of Aristotle, *De An.* 428b and *De somn.* 460-61, in which the image of the wax tablet— so frequently used in Greek sensation theories—is extended to include internal sensations produced indirectly in the imagination. See my article in the *Budé Congrès*, "Le songe de Brutus," pp. 588-97. Ziegler, Teubner, *Vitae* II.I, p. 164, prefers the reading κηρῷ μὲν γὰρ ἔξωθεν ἡ τύπησις to that in the Loeb, *Lives*, p. 206, κηρῷ μὲν γὰρ ἔοικεν ἡ τύπησις, which reproduces the mss. but the emendation may be more subtle than was Plutarch's original thought. See also note 23 to ch. VI.

[15] Soury, *La Démonologie*, p. 147—who accepts the explanation as Epicurean—correctly records the note of scepticism but misunderstands the point of the digression, claiming that after initial idealism Plutarch falls back into superstition ("il aime mieux, s'il faut, pencher vers la superstition"). The Epicurean element is obviously that of the first *Kyria doxa* (τὸ μακάριον καὶ ἄφθαρτον οὔτε αὐτὸ πράγματ᾽ ἔχει οὔτε ἄλλῳ παρέχει ὥστε οὔτε ὀργαῖς οὔτε χάρισι συνέχεται) DL 10.139, which only appears at the end of the speech when Cassius says he wishes gods and *daimones* interfered in human affairs since they would be on the conspirators' side.

since in sleep a temporary separation of soul and body is obtained. This fits in with the theme of *De anima*, the nature of death as the escape of the soul from the bond of the body and, therefore, a great blessing. Patrocleas describes the blessing of sleep as a qualified one: in sleep the soul is only able to take off "like a runaway slave" ready to return, but in death the final liberation is achieved. This tendency to restrict normal inspiration to an experience achieved when one is asleep helps to explain why Plutarch—who often is sceptical of prophetic statements in the *Lives*—includes a very large number of prophetic dreams. The words of Patrocleas also aid in our appreciation of the reason why so many of these dreams take place just before the death of the hero. Supposedly at this time not only does a change of *krasis* take place, but the two lines of separation of the soul from the body, that in sleep and that in death, are converging.

The explanation of the extinction of the oracles and particularly of the decline of the oracle at Delphi in Lamprias' speech of *De defectu oraculorum*, relies, then, upon two principal strains of the Platonic inspiration theory: first, the requirement that some sort of *pneuma* affect the mind (*Timaeus* 86e-87a); and second, that outside of states of insanity or dreaming a physical alteration must take place in the body itself (*Timaeus* 71a-72a).[16] Moreover, the position of Lamprias in the dialogue was actually supported by the Delphic legend: as he points out, the shepherd Coretas, who first discovered the prophetic spot, was affected by "nothing other than the place" (435d). It remains for Lamprias to explain why a Pythia is required, since if the place alone is sufficient, anyone ought to be capable of receiving the inspiration. But Lamprias—somewhat illogically it would seem—escapes from the difficulty with the claim that a certain *krasis* is also necessary to receive the *pneuma*, and the Pythia is one suitably endowed with this necessary condition. The prophecy, then, remains both divine and daimonic (ἔστι δὲ θεία μὲν ὄντως καὶ δαιμόνιος οὐ μὴν ἀνέκλειπτος οὐδ' ἄφθαρτος, 438d). But even if one is not willing to equate *daimonios* with *theia* here as part of a hendiadys, then one cannot rule out the possibility that "daimonic" is the symbolic representation of those prophetic

---

[16] The theory appears in *Amatorius* 758d-e, this time in Plutarch's own mouth, where he claims it is a resume of the *Timaeus* (86e-87a). Cf. *Phaedr.* 244a ff. and 265a and *Rep.* 503a. The *Amatorius* passage stresses *krasis* and *pneuma* (δυσκρασίαις τισὶν ἢ συμμίξεσιν πνεύματος βλαβεροῦ).

forces which Plato incorporated allegorically as *daimones*, rather than as a proof that Plutarch believed the *daimones* literally hung around the shrines sifting the *pneuma* through their gossamer fingers. The shrine, then, remains both mortal and immortal: it is eternal in its inspiration, temporal and material in its *pneuma*.[17] It is for this reason that Plutarch can dispense with the *daimones*. They explain nothing for one when one eventually arrives at the core of the problem of disease, evil, or prophecy. They may serve to dress up a tale or a philosophical explanation, but at heart they are only peripheral to the explication of a philosophical difficulty.

If this view is accepted, then the chronological order recommended for the composition of the Pythian dialogues by Hirzel and Flacelière offers a high probability that it is logically correct; and the acceptance of such a chronology makes it easier to understand why the *daimones* should be absent from *De Pythiae oraculis* and should receive only short shrift in *De E apud Delphos*. This new understanding of the Pythian dialogues would also serve, then, as an indication that much greater weight is to be given to Plutarch's position in his commentary on Chrysippos (*De Stoicorum repugnantiis* 1051d), where Plutarch is willingly to admit that necessity (*ananke*) is a reasonable explanation—provided it is not carried to excess—for those slips in divine providence in which good men suffer an evil fate, but that it is utterly repugnant to accept the view that evil *daimones* should be given control over the lives of good men—"as though a good monarch would not

---

[17] Plutarch was not the author of the *pneuma* theory as an explanation of the functioning of the oracle at Delphi, but its origin seems to have taken place not long before his time. H. W. Parke and D. E. Wormell, *The Delphic Oracle* I (Oxford: 1956), pp. 19-24—noting its late development—point out that it first appears in Lucan's *Pharsalia* (5.111, 6.425) where it seems to be inspired by the description of vapors at the Sibyl's cave near Cumae as depicted in Vergil's *Aeneid* (6.9-76). Cicero is acquainted with the *pneuma* theory in general—*terrae vis, terrae anhelitus* (*De div.* 79 and 114)—but he ridicules the idea that the dissipation of the *pneuma* and not a decline in gullibility is responsible for the cessation of the oracles (*De div.* 117-18). Pausanias, 10.5.6, Diodoros, 16.26, and Dio Chrysostom, 72.12 all swallow the theory. E. Will, "Sur la nature du pneuma delphique," *BCH*, 56 (1942), 161-75, and R. Flacelière, "Sur la nature du pneuma delphique," *REG*, 56 (1943), 72-111, believe that the theory is Stoic since Cicero refers to it as such. However, Lamprias regards it as Platonic and Aristotelian, and there seems to be no reason why one should dispute that it at least receives its inspiration from these philosophies.

be held responsible for the excesses committed by his appointed satraps."

For much the same reason, Plutarch has no truck with the Great Daimon, Ahriman, of the Zoroastrians, except insofar as the Zoroastrian religion—in the debased form of it which Plutarch describes—gives a symbolic representation of the balance of good and evil in the universe. As such Zoroastrianism is on a par with the dualism of Heracleitos and Empedocles or the Pythagoreans. Zoroastrianism in Plutarch is not a "dangerous digression" from the path of traditional Greek philosophy, but rather the opposite.[18] Long previous to Plutarch, Zoroastrianism had been adapted into Greek thought as a representation of dualistic metaphysical principles. Thus, Plutarch readily includes Zoroastrian material in *De Iside et Osiride* (369b-370c) with no fear of acting outrageously. Where Zoroastrianism has any real value for Plutarch it is little more than an interesting enunciation of Plato's *Laws* (896d ff.), a work which Plutarch believes Plato wrote in his old age to express in sharper form the dualism of his earlier works (370f). The explication of the Zoroastrian system in *De Iside et Osiride* falls entirely within a dualistic philosophical framework, even if what gives the passage its special interest is the inclusion of the exotic Zoroastrian lore.[19] In the balder and shorter treatment of

---

[18] The "dangerous digression" is Soury, *La Démonologie*, p. 63. He was criticized by M. Pohlenz, *Gnom.*, 21 (1949), 350, for attributing a dualistic system to Xenocrates. Others to overemphasize the Zoroastrian element are W. H. Porter, *The Life of Dion*, pp. 47-48; B. Latzarus, *Les Idées Religieuses de Plutarque*, pp. 66 and 98; J. Beaujeu, "La religion de Plutarque," p. 210. On the other hand, J. Hani, "Plutarque en face du dualisme Iranien," *REG*, 77 (1964), 489-525; and R. Del Re, "Il Pensiero Metafisico di Plutarco: Dio, La Natura, Il Male," *Stud. Ital. di Filol. Class.*, 24 (1950), 33-64, correctly see Plutarch as a traditionalist. Nilsson, *Geschichte*, II, p. 679, notes how the Persian religion in the Hellenistic period was interpreted according to the Greek spirit. More recently, M. E. D. Phillips, "Plutarque, interprète de Zorastre," *Budé Congrès*, pp. 505-11, comparing Plutarch's account with the Zoroastrian texts, finds that, with some minor exceptions, Plutarch has correctly reproduced the Persian texts, but has missed the spirit of the *Frashkart*, the great apocalyptic struggle between the two gods, Ahriman and Ohrmazd. Griffiths, *Plutarch, De Iside et Osiride*, pp. 20-23, and 74, finds Plutarch sympathetic, influenced by the sources, and like everyone else, prejudiced by his own upbringing. For more see J. Hani, *La Religion Égyptienne dans la Pensée de Plutarque* (Lille: 1972).

[19] Plutarch relates or mentions the origin of Oromazes from light, Areimanios from darkness, the perpetual war with its periods of successive domination of three thousand years, the six gods created by Oromazes, the rival gods of Areimanios, the twenty-four gods put in the egg, and the

the system in *De animae procreatione in Timaeo*, the stark interest in the dualism of Zoroastrianism, rather than its more unique religious aspects is even further brought out. Zoroaster first appears as Zaratras—Plutarch apparently did not realize he was the same as Zoroaster—and he is the teacher of Pythagoras (1012e-d). One should remember that Pythagoras invented a remarkable dualistic system, but Plutarch failed to grasp the connection between Pythagoras and Zoroaster on this score. However, in the second instance where Zoroaster appears in the work, his contribution to philosophy is said expressly to consist of his enunciation of a dualistic system of good and evil (1026a). Plutarch's interest in the *daimon* is, therefore, almost wholly philosophical in the sense that the *daimon* is a symbol of the principle of evil in the universe.

This may be the reason why Plutarch scarcely mentions the Zoroastrian sect in his *Lives*.[20] The amount of credence which Plutarch gave to the Zoroastrian beliefs in *De Iside et Osiride* may remain something of a mystery, but one would have to soar rather far astray on the aberrant wings of *Wissenschaft* to claim that the source of the evil in the world was a real, great horrendous *daimon* in struggle throughout the aeons with the beneficent deity.[21] The influence of Zoroastrianism upon Plutarch was very

---

flight of Oromazes beyond the sun, the penetration of the egg by Areimanios' gods, and the eventual destruction of Areimanios to come. The description of the egg, which resembles that of the Orphic cosmogony, is apparently due to Greek cosmogonists rather than to the Persian text.

[20] In *Pomp.* 24 the rites of Mithra are said to have been celebrated by the pirates near Olympos (in Asia Minor) and to be continuing to Plutarch's time. In *Artax.* 3 Plutarch mentions that the Magi taught the young Cyros, and in 4 Cyros swears by Mithra. In *Alex.* 30 Oromazes and Mithra are the gods of Dareios. In *Num.* 4 Zoroaster appears as a political genius on a plane with Lycurgus and Solon (cf. Diod. 1.94.2). F. Cumont, *The Mysteries of Mithra* (New York: 1956), p. 36, and J. Feibleman, *Religious Platonism* (London: 1959), p. 143, misconstrue the *Pompey* passage.

[21] R. C. Zaehner, *The Dawn and Twilight of Zoroastrianism* (London: 1961), pp. 123-24, sees Plutarch's exposition as a "halfway house between catholic Zoroastrianism and the Mithraism we meet with in the Roman Empire;" and he notes that Plutarch is silent about the most important rite, the great bull sacrifice. In the most authoritative work on the subject today, *Cultes, Mythe et Cosmologie dans l'Iran Ancien* (Paris: 1963), pp. 10-15, Marijan Molé—who otherwise seems to contradict Zaehner on every important point—has little to say about Plutarch's text; but agrees with M. Bienveniste, *The Persian Religion according to the Greek Texts* (Paris: 1929), and "Un mythe zervanite chez Plutarque," *JA*, 215 (1929), 287-96, that Plutarch is describing a form of Zervanism. They base their argument

small indeed. Even where we might suspect that he has drawn from this religious belief as in *De sera numinis vindicta*, where the souls of the damned—or more properly of those undergoing purgation—are thrown into pools of molten metal, we must be very cautious.[22] After the long digression on the infinity of worlds in *De defectu oraculorum*, Ammonios—to make a transition back to the subject of the *daimones*—asks if they are "aught else than souls that make their rounds in mist apparelled" ("οἴει γὰρ ἕτερον τοὺς δαίμονας", εἶπεν, "ἢ ψυχὰς ὄντας περιπολεῖν καθ᾽ Ἡσίοδον ἠέρα ἐσσαμένους," 431c). This is the note on which Lamprias ends the dialogue, and which forms the basis for the myths of Plutarch's major religious treatises. Lamprias draws the logical conclusion from the principle that souls are *daimones*: if souls severed from the body are *daimones*, then they must also possess the prophetic faculty while they are in the body, since they are the same souls and *daimones* are supposed to know the future. Lamprias then argues that because of the impurity or cloudiness of the minds of most men they are not able to exercise this faculty, but that in dreams and particularly at the hour of death the prophetic faculty comes to many men (431e-f).

The theory enunciated by Lamprias here—and which undoubtedly represents Plutarch's deepest thoughts on the subject of inspiration—is in the clearest possible terms said to rest upon a conception of the *daimones* as nothing more than human

---

on the sacrifice offered to Ahriman as well as to Orhmazd. J. G. Griffiths in his introduction to *Plutarch, De Iside et Osiride* (Cambridge: 1970), pp. 18-52, notes that Plutarch, who was not much influenced by his own "Sitz im Leben" in describing the Egyptian religion, used sources which described a religion no longer practiced in exactly the same way in his own day. This should be kept in mind in analyzing Plutarch's comments on Mithraism. Griffiths, pp. 47-82—mainly following Bidez-Cumont, *Les Mages Hellenisés* (Paris: 1938) and Zaehner—has little to add, except that he thinks the egg in the Zoroastrian cosmogony may be due to Egyptian influence. On this now see R. Turcan, *Mithras Platonicus, Recherches sur l'Hellénization Philosophique de Mithras* (Leiden: 1975); ch. 2, "Le témoignage de Plutarque," pp. 14-22, stresses the Platonic intrusion of the mediator concept.

[22] In *Datastan i Denik* 31.10, at the final rehabilitation the souls of the damned pass through a river of molten metal to obtain purification and join the saved where they live with them in harmony forevermore. In *De sera* the avaricious souls are punished by being cast first in hot gold, then cold lead, then back in hot gold. This symbolism in *De sera* represents the difference between Greek wit and Persian seriousness.

souls. As such, it is an acceptance of the theory of the "others," which had been mentioned in passing in Cleombrotos' review of Greek daimonology earlier in De defectu oraculorum (415b). As we may recall, this theory claimed that human souls passed through transformation stages and that the two highest stages were that of daimon and god. The interpretation of the daimon as nothing more than the human soul is also perfectly in accordance with Plutarch's explanation of the legend of the apotheosis of Romulus at the end of the Life of Romulus (28).[23] Here he objected to the crass explanation of the legend in which Romulus' body literally ascended to heaven, and proposed rather, that the soul alone rose through progressive purifications. Plutarch does not state what these purifications are or how they take place, but he claims that in them the soul becomes progressively more immaterial (ἄσαρκος), pure, and holy. He also finds this spiritual purification to be the explanation of Heracleitos' enigmatic statement that the dry and best soul flies from the body like lightning from a cloud, whereas the soul, which—"like a heavy and misty vapor (anathymiasis)—is weighted down and surfeited with body, is set loose and rises only with difficulty."

A similar statement of the soul rising up like vapor and the superiority of the dry soul appears in De esu carnium 995e. However, in all these cases we must be on our guard lest we jump to the conclusion that Plutarch in these instances conceives of the psyche as something material. It is not altogether impossible that he thought in terms of a material psyche and an immaterial nous; and this is the first impression one gets from some of his myths. But outside of the myths he seems to be treating the physical ascent of the misty soul as something symbolic of the moral ascent of the spiritual soul. It is curious that Plutarch uses this Stoic,

---

[23] Plutarch often cites Heracleitos in support of his own favorite ideas. See W. C. Helmbold and E. N. O'Neil, Plutarch's Quotations (Baltimore: 1959), p. 34. De an. 178.4 (Sandbach) can be added to their citations; here Heracleitos is said to have believed that ignorance about the end is the bond linking us to the body. The statement about the dry soul appears also in De es. carn. 995e and De def. 432f. In Qu. Plat. 999e, Plutarch combines two favorite sayings from antiquity, Menander's ὁ νοῦς γὰρ ἡμῶν ὁ θεός and Heracleitos' ἦθος ἀνθρώπῳ δαίμων and interprets them to fit his own conception of Socrates' daimon as given in the myth of De genio Socratis (ἢ θεῖόν τι καὶ δαιμόνιον ὡς ἀληθῶς αἴτιον ὑφηγήσατο Σωκράτει τοῦτο ·.ῆς φιλοσοφίας τὸ γένος).

materialistic sounding terminology to express the spirituality of the Platonic conception of the soul. Perhaps he desired to introduce a slightly original and more updated expression of the ascent of the soul such as is found in the Platonic description, or else the matter may have been commonplace enough by this time so that no eyebrows would be raised. At any rate it is erroneous to think that Plutarch has unconsciously fallen into Stoicism on this point, or to imagine that he has cribbed a Stoic.

In approaching Plutarch's eschatological myths the two points most to be kept in mind are the conception of the human composite as an entity consisting of *soma*, *psyche*, and *nous*, and the identification of *daimon* with soul, or with the higher part of the soul, *nous*. It is the distinction between *psyche* and *nous* which permits such elaborations as the affinity of the *psyche* for the moon, and its death there, whereas the *nous* continues intact and seems to have an affinity for the sun. The distinction between *psyche* and *nous* is also extremely important for the conception of the world soul as it appears in *De animae procreatione in Timaeo*, Plutarch's commentary on Plato's *Timaeus*. Here, Plutarch is interested in clearing up the paradox that Plato—in contrast to almost the entire body of Greek philosophy—seems to be advocating the temporal creation of the universe. Plutarch escapes from this difficulty by a new interpretation of what it means to be created in time. In this interpretation creation is the temporal point at which the soul (*psyche*) of the world—which of course always had a "body"—received *nous*, and was thereby directed in orderly movements; only then could it correctly be called a world (*kosmos*, i.e. order). Plutarch's thought here is facilitated by the traditional Greek tendency to think in micro- and macro-cosmic terms, and by his own tendency to elucidate a difficult passage in Plato by interpreting it in the light of another.

The world soul thus acts like Plato's human soul; it is enticed and captivated by the material pleasures of the corporeal world so that it forgets the Ideas, which alone matter, and of which it once had a vision. It is in the light of this that Plutarch interprets a passage of Plato's *Politicus* (273d-e) and uses this in turn to elucidate Plato's conception of the world soul in the *Timaeus*: after a period of time the world begins to turn in a reverse direction to its original motion (*Politicus*), but by lifting up its eyes to the Ideal world which it has forgotten the world can correct its direction and proceed on its original course (1030c).[24] (In the *Politicus* God gives it a shove in the proper direction.) The anthropomorphism of Plutarch's interpretation is so severe that Plato's statement about the reverse turn to the world has to mean that the *nous* of the world soul has lost sight of its original divine inspiration.

The threefold division of man which we see in Plutarch's myths — into *soma*, *psyche*, and *nous* — appears in other essays in his *Moralia* as well. In *Non posse suaviter vivi secundum Epicurum* (1096e) he uses the very unusual expression that *nous* is the sense organ (*aistheterion*) of the soul. In *De virtute morali*, an essay in which he objects to the simplistic monism of the Stoics, he reverses the normal direction of the microcosm analogy: just as the world soul needed to be joined to *nous* before it could truly come into existence, so the human soul must be joined to *nous* (441d-e).[25]

---

[24] Eisele, *Zur Dämonologie*, p. 50, rather vigorously described the nature of the precosmic soul calling it "die reale dämonische Macht," and "der wirkliche Dämon im Gegensatz zu Gott." G. Vlastos, "The Disorderly Motion in the Timaeus," R. E. Allen ed., *Studies in Plato's Metaphysics* (London: 1965), p. 394, also gives something of a false impression, speaking about it as "the evil precosmic soul." However, it is described correctly by P. Thévenaz, *L'Âme du Monde le Devenir et la Matière chez Plutarque* (Paris: 1938); J. Helmer, *Zu Plutarchs De animae procreatione in Timaeo* (Wurzburg: 1937); P. Merlan, "Beiträge zur Geschichte des antiken Platonismus," *Philol.*, 89 (1934), 197-214; R. Jones, *The Platonism*, pp. 68-ff.; and R. Del Re, "Il pensiero metaphysico." According to Del Re, p. 47, it is "non intrinsecamente e necessariamente cattivo;" and Thévenaz observes (p. 119): "n'est malfaisante ni par perversion ni en vertu d'un dessein bien réfléchi: elle n'a rien d'un Satan." The matter is discussed by J. Dillon, *The Middle Platonists*, p. 206, who thinks the appearance of the irrational world soul in both Plutarch and Albinus may suggest it is older than both, though he leaves open the possibility that Albinus read Plutarch. He sees the Indefinite Dyad as the positively evil principle in Plutarch's system, while the irrational soul is the cause of evil." See also H. Cherniss, Loeb, *Mor.* XIII, 1, pp. 133-49.

[25] Plutarch's psychology has been treated by H. Mounard, *La Psychologie de Plutarque*, a thesis condensed in *Ann. de la Univ. de Paris* (Paris: 1960), pp. 341-42. She understands Plutarch's *daimon* as the mind itself and the purpose of morality as letting this part of the soul triumph. She also correctly sees the myths as statements more of Plutarch's psychology than of his daimonology. G. Verbeke, "Plutarch and the Development of Aristotle," pp. 235-38, notes how Plutarch took much of his psychology from Aristotle. In the same volume, O. Gigon, "Prolegomena to an Edition of the *Eudemus*," pp. 19-23, suspects the influence of Aristotle's *Eudemus* on Plutarch's myths. This view is novel but possible. Dillon, *The Middle Platonists*, p. 195, is also impressed by Plutarch's accomodation of Aristotelian ethics into his works. D. Babut, *Plutarque. De la Vertu Éthique*, p. 142, notes how commentators have failed to relate *De gen. Soc.* 588f-589a to *De virtute morali*, a work with strong Aristotelian influence.

Important in these soul analogies is an idea which must be considered characteristically Plutarchan, the use of a cable or rein with which the soul is attached either to *nous* or *logos*. The idea of a rein appears at 446a-c; and in *Animine an corporis affectiones sunt peiores* (501d), *De amore prolis* (493e), and *De tranquillitate animae* (465b), the soul is conceived of as a ship which is kept from being swept over the sea or dashed downstream on the river current only by its cable.

It is possible that there is some development of this idea in Plutarch's ethical and religious treatises. An earlier form of the analogy would seem to be in *De anima* (177.2) where the soul's cable is attached to the body rather than to *nous*, and where it is cut in the process of death. A tangential idea—which appears in a somewhat different sense in *De genio Socratis*—is that in sleep the soul can take off like a runaway slave, but only in death is the cable definitively cut. Timon, the principal speaker, muddles the analogy later on when he says the only bond which keeps us in the body is the fear of death, "like Odysseus clinging to the fig tree out of fear of Charybdis." In the *Moralia* the soul is also compared to a light of various degrees of intensity. For example, in *De latenter vivendo* (1129d-e) on the approach of sleep, reason (*logismos*)—like a fire going out in the hearth—tosses about and flickers in its own fantasies, "just enough to signify that the man himself still lives." [26] This concept also is important to the myths, and sometimes the cable and light analogies are even combined.

Some of the ideas which figure in Plato's myths might be reviewed here. In the *Phaedo* myth well-ordered souls are carried along by a *daimon* guide. At *Phaedrus* 248c "the meadow" is located at some undefined place outside the vault of heaven. In the *Gorgias* the souls retain the bodily welts and scars of their previous vice on earth, and in the *Timaeus* souls are sown on the planets and stars, and *nous* is called our *daimon*. Plutarch's originality consists largely in his preoccupation with the moon as the site of the under-

---

[26] *De ser.* 563f, 564d, *De gen.* 591f. In the last case, the contaminated souls, which resemble stars, have an irregular motion as well. In *Non poss.* 1087f, the pleasures of the flesh are compared to shooting stars; in 1105d, the light of reason which is veiled by mist—and, therefore, indistinct and wavering—takes wing like a bird gazing upward.

world, and the equation of the souls themselves with *daimones*. These eschatological myths from *De sera numinis vindicta, De genio Socratis*, and *De facie in orbe lunae* have offered a fruitful ground of inquiry for many generations of scholars, each of whom has been led by his own personal tastes and by those of the age in which he lived. This seems fair enough, but the debate over the interpretation of Plutarch's most important myths has left a battlefield weighted with a particularly large number of corpses. Here is no place to enter into a discussion of the myths in detail or to examine the complicated issues involved in the study of each dialogue. But it may be illuminating to study how Plutarch's thought apparently moved away from the eschatological conceptions or descriptions of Plato, even if we have no way of knowing whether the actual chronological sequence of the major religious dialogues corresponded exactly to a continuous drift from Plato. The main difficulty is that the details and emphasis of a myth are dependent upon the exigencies of a theme, and each of Plutarch's dialogues develops a different theme. For this reason it is often difficult to determine whether the omission or inclusion of a particular detail is a conscious divergence from a Platonic parallel, or whether it is simply dictated by the nature of the theme. Yet, all the details of a myth are not demanded by a particular theme, and for this reason it seems that often we have a justifiable basis of comparison.

The anti-Epicurean essay, *De latenter vivendo* (1130c-e) does not contain a real myth of the type contained in Plutarch's most important religious dialogues, but it does give a mini-myth with some interesting eschatological geography. Here the eschatological navigator is given a rather vague map to travel with: the good souls drift toward an Elysion described as a great and flowery plain. Yet, Lethe is not a stream crossed by the souls on their way to reincarnation—as in Plato—but leads rather to a bottomless pit which sucks the evil souls into a deep chasm of "obscurity, oblivion, and utter effacement." Though Plutarch means to pun on one of the Greek words of the title (λάθε βιώσας "live obscurely"), one cannot but admire the agility with which he rearranges the solemn *eschata*. Again, *De anima* (?) (201) where he attempts to give a mystical interpretation of the Circe story in the *Odyssey*, the Elysian fields are located in the sky, or more precisely, on the surface of the moon lit by the sun, while the sun—as the guardian of birth and death—receives an important role.[27] Moreover, the souls wander not under the earth or even in some vague meadow but rather in the celestial regions of airy space until their rebirth in a more corporeal form;[28] in the meantime *logos*—another important Plutarchan entity—where it cannot keep the souls altogether from palingenesis, like a good benefactor at least tries to assure their reincarnation in some reasonable form.

Now let us turn to one of the most important parts of this study, an examination of the myths of Plutarch's major religious dialogues. The myth which least drifts from Plato's eschatology is that which is contained in *De sera numinis vindicta*. Here, the eschatology is somewhat restricted by the theme of divine punishment, but this in itself does not completely excuse the almost entire lack of originality in certain details. The myth is related by a personage named Aridaios, whose name itself seems to be taken from one of Plato's dialogues (*Republic* 615e). Like Er in the *Republic*, he is

---

[27] This contains a pun on 'Ηλύσιον Πεδίον, with 'Ηλύσιον as though derived from "Ηλιος. The vision of the souls and the geography of Plutarch's myths are modeled on passages like *Phaedrus* 248a-e where Plato speaks of Hestia at the center, and the plain of truth. He does not speak of a vision of the *logoi*, but the divine intelligence is nurtured on mind and pure knowledge (νῷ τε καὶ ἐπιστήμῃ ἀκηράτῳ) while the souls which fall feed only on opinion (τροφὴ δοξαστική). On this see W. K. C. Guthrie, *A History of Greek Philosophy* IV (Cambridge: 1975), pp. 421-27. For the style of Plutarch in these myths, particularly the emphasis on color, see Russell, *Plutarch*, pp. 71-72, for his language in general, pp. 8-41, an excellent treatment; for technical points of language, see Griffiths, *De Iside*, pp. 10-16, A. Corlu, *Plutarque*, *Le Démon de Socrate*, pp. 92-109, and Hamilton, *Alexander*, pp. lxvi-lxix.

[28] Philip of Opos' (?) *Epinomis* 984d-e—which attempts to link the forms of life with the five elements—describes two classes of *daimones*, one constituted of *aither* and the other of air. Aristotle in *De cael.* 270b 5 ff. and *Met.* 1074 a 38 ff. mysteriously speaks of his *aither* theory as being in accordance with religious belief. In *De gen. an.* 761 b 8.23, he refers enigmatically to a fourth category of superior beings who live on the moon. All this reveals a natural drift toward Plutarch's second death and moon eschatology. In an excellent recent book on *De facie*, H. Görgemanns, *Untersuchungen zu Plutarchs Dialog De facie in orbe lunae* (Heidelberg: 1970), stresses the originality of Plutarch as a scientific thinker, noting that his conception of the moon as earth and the shadows there as due to cavities, was in opposition to the approved speculation of his time. Görgemanns also sees the astronomy of the *diatribe* as only loosely connected to that of the myth (which is outside the scope of Görgemanns' thesis). F. H. Sandbach, *CR* 33 (1973), 32-34, sees the myth as rather closely related. See also H. Martin, "Plutarch's *De facie*, The Recapitulations and the Lost Beginning," *GRBS*, 15 (1974), 73-88.

struck by a blow [29] which leaves him for dead, projects him into the world beyond, and permits him to relate the mysterious and unbelievable wonders of the world beyond the grave in which the most unconceivable blessings are contrasted with the terrifyingly sadistic punishment of the wicked. The experience—during which he had received a new name, Thespesios (the inspired one)—causes him to change his life, which had been one of utmost depravity, to an exemplary one of virtue and edification (563d-568a). In *De genio Socratis* a device similar, but slightly different from the blow on the head is used to project the narrator into the nether world: a man returns from an incubation experience in the cave of Trophonios in Lebadaia (590b).

However, in *De facie in orbe lunae*, Plutarch dispenses altogether with the Platonic machinery necessary to supply the appropriate leap to the never-never world. Here, the key to entering the afterlife is taken from the same material as that which we find in *De defectu oraculorum*. In that dialogue Demetrios (419e-420a) had spoken at some length about an isle off the coast of Britain where Cronos was imprisoned and where *daimones* ministered to his every need. In *De facie*, it is a servant of Cronos from this very island who relates how the souls after death are carried to the moon to undergo purgation and reincarnation, or their eventual release from *nous*, at which time they are assimilated back into the element of the moon (941a).

Not only the technique used in *De sera numinis vindicta* to get the myth narrator, and thereby the reader, into the other world, but also the major constituent elements of the myth reveal a great lack of originality and an exceptionally heavy dependence upon Plato. As in all Plutarch's myths, the souls rise through the heavens.

---

[29] "Ardiaios"—close to Plutarch's "Aridaios"—appears appropriately in *Rep.* 615 e-f, as one of the souls undergoing punishment for his wickedness. In quoting the Republic at this point Justin Martyr, *Coh. ad Gent.* 27.25d, Clement, *Strom.* 5.14.90, and Eusebios, *Praep. Evang.* 13.5, 669d give the form "Aridaios." See De Lacy and Einarson, Loeb, *Mor.* VII, p. 173. The nature of Er the Armenian's apparent death is not mentioned in *Rep.* 614b: he was simply presumed dead after a battle and put upon the pyre 12 days later, at which time he recovered. Plutarch's account, then, introduces something of a subtle innovation. As De Lacy and Einarson point out, (Loeb, *Mor.* VII, p. 271 n.c) Plato—(*Tim.* 69c-e)—had described the neck as the isthmus and boundary between the head, which contained the divine part of the soul, and the body; therefore, the blow on Aridaios' neck, severing the connection for a time, has deeper philosophical implications than might at first appear.

This is similar to Plato's *Phaedrus*, but slight differences can be noted. Plutarch stresses the idea of a celestial ocean, and his souls do not rise to the vault of heaven from which they look out on the Ideas. But the slight differences here do not obscure the basic similarity. Likewise we can find exact parallels in Plato for the Plutarchan figures, Dike, Adrasteia, and Poine who determine the fate of the souls (564e-565a), for the description of the welts and scars on the souls (564d-e) and the description of the course of the souls through the heavens as resembling that of spindles (564a) naturally evokes Plato's conception of the heavenly bodies as revolving in spindle-like orbits. Even the humorous reincarnation of Nero as a frog (567f) reminds one of Plato's similar humorous reincarnations: the soul of Nero is in a sorry plight, pierced by incandescent rivets, and they are about ready to give it the body of one of Nicander's vipers which eats its way through its mother's womb, when suddenly a great light shoots forth and a voice commands them to transform him into a vocal creature, frequenter of marshes and lakes—a bit of kindness shown him from the gods for he had been good to his subjects, especially to that nation "most dear to the gods." The other Plutarchan touch in the myth is an echo of *De latenter vivendo*: the incurable souls are relegated to "the nameless and the unseen" (thus to live out the maxim λάθε βιώσας) as their eternal punishment (564f). What is very interesting for the evolution of religious imagery in classical eschatology is the use of Dionysiac themes. Dionysos is said to have brought Semele up here to immortality, but on the other hand reincarnation takes place in a Bacchic grove called Lethe (566a) where the souls "are dissolved away and liquified by pleasure". This is different from the *Amatorius* passage where reincarnation takes place on the moon (766b), though here Aphrodite, a symbol of pleasure, is associated with rebirth. Eros himself, part of the Platonic tradition, liberates. In *De sera* Plutarchan touches are the similarity of the light of the moon to that of the pure souls (564a), and the cable which is used to snap Thespesios back to his body in order to end the myth (568a)—as well as a touch which indicates Plutarch's Delphic theology is at work—Thespesios' inability to ascend to the lofty place where Apollo's oracle is situated because of the shortness of his cable (566d). The actual scenes of torment are also derived from Plato though the extreme form—most striking are the pools of molten metal into which the souls are cast by *daimon* torturers (567b-d) — makes them strikingly similar to much later representations of the underworld. The myth of *De genio Socratis* in contrast deviates considerably from the Platonic mould. The dialogue itself supposedly takes place on the eve of the revolution of Thebes in December of 379 B.C., which hurled the city to a brief period of greatness. The theme of the myth is dictated by the purpose of the dialogue itself, the identification of Socrates' *daimonion* with his own *nous*, the guiding part of the soul. Since the members of the discussion are of the Pythagorean brotherhood, Plutarch has filled the dialogue with Pythagorean overtones,[30] but the Pythagorean interpretation of the *daimones* would seem to be principally in the speech of Theanor in which the *daimones*, independent spirits freed from the cycle of rebirth run along like former athletes, urging the souls to the finish line, or like swimmers who, having escaped the sea and reached the shore are shouting and stretching forth a hand to those struggling yet to reach it (593d-594b).[31] There

---

[30] M. Detienne, *La Notion de Daïmon dans le Pythagorisme* (Paris: 1963)—developing ideas from G. Meautis, *Recherches sur le Pythagorisme* (Neuchatel: 1922) and P. Boyancé, "Les deux génies personnels dans l'antiquité grecque et latine," *Rev. de Philol.*, 9 (1935), 189-202—has attempted a new reconstruction of Pythagorean daimonology. The work relies heavily on *De genio Socratis* and *Qu. conv.* 8.7 and 8.8—our principal sources for Neopythagoreanism—which may project later Pythagoreanism back into an earlier period. Moreover, Detienne, like Soury, has a tendency to snuff out a *daimon* everywhere. Thus, he writes about *De gen.* 585e: "Theanor avait dans son sommeil rencontré le *daimonion* de son confrère qui lui avait signifié sa mort" (p. 44). On this see Sandbach's article, "Three Notes on Plutarch's Moralia," *CQ*, 6 (1956), 87-88, which correctly interprets the passage to mean that "*to daimonion*"—i.e., the divinity—"had revealed the death of Lysis." The same type of misinterpretation is given Iamb. *V.P.* 247 (Detienne fr. 17, p. 173). His hypothesis of a pre-Platonic Pythagorean lunar daimonology which influenced all subsequent ones also rests on slim evidence (Aet. *Plac.* 2.30.1 and *SVF* 404.10, where the inhabitants of the moon are said to be five times greater than men and leave no excrement). Detienne's work is valuable for its collection of the fragments. For Plutarch's relationship to the Pythagoreanism of his time, see Whittaker, "Ammonius on the Delphic E," *CQ*, 19 (1969), 185-92, who cites H. Thesleff, *An Introduction to the Pythagorean Writings of the Hellenistic Period* (Aabo: 1961).

[31] In his article, "Xénocrate et la démonologie pythagoricienne," *REG*, 60 (1958), 271-79, Detienne correctly casts doubt on Heinze's claim that Xenocrates was the originator of the daimonological interpretation of myth, but one must remain suspicious of Detienne's claim that the identification of the human *nous* as the real *daimon* in the Timarchos myth of Plutarch's *De genio Socratis* represents early Pythagoreanism. It seems

is also talk of a personal protective *daimon* for Epameinondas.
However, the real Plutarchan conception, and that which forms
the basis of the myth, is that of the soul which is carried or directed
from above by its *daimon*, its own *nous*, floating above the soul
like a cork (592a-b). For "those who understand it correctly"
this is not only in ourselves "as the image is in the mirror", but
rather is external and should be called (a?) *daimon*. The eschatological geography is also more fully developed. The souls ascend
through a sealike heaven as in *De sera numinis vindicta*, but
metempsychosis takes place on the moon, and the moon's affinity
with the souls or *daimones* is stressed (591b-c). The road to Hades
becomes the side of the moon opposite the sun, and "the turning
point of birth" is also located on the moon (591b). In a more
startling development of the lunar imagery, the moon passes
over the "Styx" from which the better souls are rescued as they
manage to cling to it, but the unclean slip off in terror and con-
sternation (591c). Four unusual first principles (ἀρχαί) of all
things—"of life, of motion, of generation, of destruction"—are
introduced; and a peculiar chain suggesting the future hypostases
of the Neoplatonists and Gnostics and of great difficulty for
eschatologists is described: the link between the second and third
archai is provided by Nous at the sun with the link between the
third and fourth provided by Physis at the Moon (591b).[32]

very likely that the myth represents Plutarch's ideas, or at least later
Pythagoreanism rather than the earlier form. Guthrie, *HGP* I, pp. 317-19,
and D. A. O'Brien, *Empedocles' Cosmic Cycle* (Cambridge: 1969), pp. 330-
34, wisely leave the matter vague: they underscore the importance of
Empedocles upon subsequent theories about the *daimones* without trying
to reconstruct the daimonology of a particular philosophy from descriptions
of the *daimones* in later writers. At 588d-589f Simmias calls Socrates' *daimonion* "the voiceless speech of the *daimones* which only daimonic men can
understand," and Theanor believes in personal protective spirits (593a-
594a). The theories of the Pythagorean Simmias and Theanor may be
Plutarch's attempt to represent the heart of Pythagorean daimonology
rather than the myth proper which represents very likely his own personal
and philosophical identification of *nous* and *daimon* along the lines of his
ethical treatises. A. Corlu, *Plutarque: Le Démon de Socrate* (Paris: 1970),
p. 59, sees *De genio* as written largely under the influence of Neopythagoreanism and Platonism, rather than heavily influenced by any individual source,
and that for the purpose of harmony, contradictory views of demonology
are downplayed. His book contains an excellent introduction on sources,
problems, and scholarship on this work.

[32] The "hypostases" of this passage are most interesting to students
of the development of Neoplatonism. It is discussed by H. Dörrie, "Die
Stellung Plutarchs im Platonismus seiner Zeit," p. 50, and "Zur Ursprung

Plutarch put such a flourish and so much of himself into these descriptions that it seems a shame not to give a taste of it. One should particularly notice his interest in color and music:

When he lifted his eyes the earth was nowhere to be seen; but he saw islands illuminated by one another with soft fire, taking on now one colour, now another, like a dye, as the light kept varying with their mutations. They appeared countless in number and huge in size, and though not all equal, yet all alike round; and he fancied that their circular movement made a musical whirring in the aether, for the gentleness of the sound resulting from the harmony of all the separate sounds corresponded to the evenness of their motion. In their midst lay spread a sea or lake, through whose blue transparency the colours passed in their migrations; and of the islands a few sailed out in a channel and crossed the current, while many others were carried along with it, the sea itself drifting around, as it were, smoothly and evenly in a circle. In places it was very deep, mainly toward the south, but elsewhere there were faint shoals and shallows; and in many parts it over-flowed and again receded, never extending very far. Some of it was of the pure hue of the high seas, while elsewhere the colour was not unmixed. but turbid and like that of a pool. As they crested the surge 'the islands' came back, without, however, returning to their point of departure or completing a circle; but with each new circuit they advanced slightly beyond the old, describing a single spiral in their revolution. The sea containing these was inclined at an angle of somewhat less than eight parts of the whole toward the midmost and largest portion of the surrounding envelope, as he made out; and it had two openings receiving rivers of fire emptying into it across from one another, so that it was forced far back, boiling, and its blue colour was turned to white. All this he viewed

---

der Neuplatonischen Hypostasenlehre," *Hermes*, 82 (1954), 331-42. Dörrie, perhaps mistakenly speaks of a voyage through planetary spheres here. The passage is also discussed by J. Dillon, *The Middle Platonists*, p. 215, who cites H. J. Krämer, *Ursprung*, p. 98, note 250. He takes *nous* to be the demiurgic mind, monad transcendent self-meditating mind. *Zoe*, a life principle, is placed above the demiurgic mind, unexpected but similar to that found in the Chaldaean oracles and later Neoplatonism.

The myth ends with the story of Hermodoros of Clazomenai, whose wife permitted his enemies to burn his body when he was sleeping and his soul was absent. The mystic voice explains that this was not true, but rather Hermodoros' soul (*psyche*) gave slack to his *daimon* (i.e. *nous*) al-lowing it to roam about the world (592d). The man—who is also called Hermotimos in other writers—is mentioned in Arist. *Met.* 984b 19 for influ-encing Anaxagoras in his doctrine of *nous*. Soury, p. 174, makes an interesting point in noting that Hermotimos was supposed to be one of the reincarnations of Pythagoras. Thus, Plutarch skillfully fits his own ideas on the distinction between *nous* and *psyche* into a Pythagorean background.

with enjoyment of the spectacle. But looking down he saw a great abyss, round, as though a sphere had been cut away; most terrible and deep it was, and filled with a mass of darkness that did not remain at rest, but was agitated and often welled up. From it could be heard innumerable roars and groans of animals, the wailing of innumerable babes, the mingled lamentations of men and women, and noise and uproar of every kind, coming faintly from far down in the depths, all of which startled him not a little.

After an interval someone he did not see addressed him: 'Timarchus, what would you have me explain?'

'Everything,' he answered; 'for what is here that is not marvellous?' (590c-591a, Einarson—De Lacy, Loeb, *Mor*. VII, pp. 463-467).

One must truly admit with Timarchus, that everything is marvellous.

The farthest stage of Plutarch's development is reached in *De facie in orbe lunae*, in which the whole eschatology seems to have been transferred to the moon. Hades is somehow constituted by the earth's shadow; the Elysion plain is that part facing the heavens (942e-f). Here the *psyche* is subject to a second death, a gentle dissolution—unlike the first death, the separation of soul from body—in which the *psyche* is resolved into the substance of the moon. The place of purgatory is located in "the gentlest part of the air" called the "meadows of Hades" while the souls, which resemble rays of light, cling to the moon from which they are at times swept off. They are of the same substance as the moon, suffer in gorges called Hecate's recess, which are similar to those in the Red Sea; and some of the souls without mind manage to slip off and must be charmed back; "of such are the Titans, Typhon, and the Delphic Python:" ἐκείνων ἄρα τῶν ψυχῶν ἦσαν ἐρήμων λόγου καὶ τύφῳ πλανηθέντι τῷ παθητικῷ χρησαμένων, 945b). The sun sows *nous* on the moon to create new souls, and the three Fates—Atropos, Clotho, and Lachesis—are located on the sun, moon, and earth respectively.[33]

---

[33] At the present time modern scholars are loath to seek Eastern influence in these myths. E. R. Dodds, *The Greeks and the Irrational*, p. 228, n. 33, J. Kerschensteiner, *Plato und das Orient* (Munich: 1945) and R. Festugière, *Plato et l'Orient*, Rev. de Philol., 21 (1947), 5ff., see no Persian influence on Plato; M. Nilsson, *Geschichte* II, pp. 269-71, considers the new solar religion of the Hellenistic period as more the product of Hellenized Egyptian priests than of Babylonian or Persian influence. It used to be the fashion to see the oriental-born Poseidonios as the father of the new solar religion, but this viewpoint has long been discredited or at least proved untenable. The final blows against the Poseidonios' reconstruction are those by M.

In *De defectu oraculorum*, then, Lamprias presents a theory of the decline of the oracles fully consistent with the religious method outlined by him in his speech: material causes, *pneuma* and *aporroia*, being material and mortal are eventually subject to decay; yet, the whole operation is within the hands of providence and not the result of pure *tyche* or irrational causes. As such the doctrine— even in its details such as the use of *pneuma*, *aporroiai*, and *krasis*— is not inconsistent with Plutarch's writing elsewhere, but entirely consistent. After dispensing with the *daimones* as great monsters essential for the prophetic shrines, Plutarch can indicate their true nature as human souls. This conception is essential to his great religious myths. The human mind itself—as Plato said—is our *daimon*. Beginning with this principle Plutarch can run out several lines in different directions: the mind as the *daimon* capable of receiving the voice of other *daimones* (prophecy); the mind as

---

Laffranque, *Poseidonios d'Apamée* (Paris: 1964) and H. Görgemanns, "De facie und die Poseidonios-Forschung," *Untersuchugen zu Plutarchs Dialog De facie*, pp. 17-18. Earlier, Soury, *La Démonologie*, p. 210,—still under the influence of Cumont and Reinhardt—suspected that the Timarchos myth of *De genio Socratis* was influenced by Persian literature: in *The Book of Arta Viraf*, Arta takes a narcotic which puts him to sleep and during this time his soul leaves his body, to return after seven days so he can relate his experiences. But Plutarch hardly had to go to Persia for a model of this type. There also is little in common between Plutarch's eschatological conceptions and those of the Hermetic literature. At any rate this literature is Hellenistic in its daimonology and largely inconsistent with Mithraism or Chaldaeism. Moreover, there are ideas totally foreign to Plutarch in the Hermetic writings; in Tract 16 *nous* is not subject to the *daimones*, and in 10 it gets a fiery body when it becomes a *daimon*. P. Boyancé, "Les 'Endymions' de Varron," *REA*, 41 (1939), 319-24, reprinted in *Études sur la Religion Romaine* (Paris: 1972), pp. 283-89, attempted to reconstruct a lost work by Varro, called *Endymiones*. Boyancé looks for Stoic and Pythagorean precedents. As he sees it, Varro wrote a humorous work in his Menippean satires which this title in which beings by this name lived below the moon. Boyancé cites Tert. *De an.* 54.2, and 55.4: "sublimantur animae sapientes. . . apud Stoicos sub lunam; in aethere dormito nostra. . . aut circa lunam cum Endymionibus stoicorum."He incorrectly states that according to Diog. Laert. 7.1 the souls of the wise became *daimones*. The text reads: "and they hold that there are *daimones*. They believe too in heroes, that is, the souls of the righteous who have survived their bodies." Relying on A. Delatte, *Études sur la Litérature Pythagoricienne*, p. 275, he cites Iamb. *Vita Pyth.* 30 for the belief of Pythagoreans that their master was a *daimon* who had fallen from the moon. One can also consult L. Rougier, *La Religion Astrale des Pythagoriciens*, Paris: 1959, and J. Guey, "Martial VIII, 50 (51).7, Plutarque De facie 921c et les 'mers' de la lune," *BSAF* (1966), 114-116. Obviously Plutarch drew from a complex background of lunar eschatology.

the immortal part of the soul, turning into a *daimon* as a stage
toward divinity (apotheosis); the *nous* as a *daimon* with an affinity
for the moon and the sun (eschatology). These ideas combined
with the new astronomy, suggested some interesting myths in
which we can see him moving away from Plato's eschatology to
one in which the final resting place of the *daimones'* mortal part
is the moon; however, they themselves while on earth are naught
"else than souls that make their rounds in mists apparelled."
    It would be impossible now to reconstruct the stages between
Plato and Plutarch which led to the type of conception of the
afterlife which we find in Plutarch. Working within a Platonic
framework, he reflects both the spirit and some of the details
of the speculation of his age. The strange use of Dionysiac imagery,
and more importantly the place of the moon are witnesses to these
characteristics in him.[34] He has very skillfully integrated—in a way
that is very literary, philosophical, scientific, and inspired—the
physical and religious cosmos. Older ideas and conceptions of Plato
are given new life. The sun as the image of the Good receives
more direct religious significance; for the sun is the image of Apollo,
himself the name for Being, which is One and can be described
in terms of the Ideas of Plato. A certain simplification and logical
resolution of Platonic thought has taken place, which undoubtedly
had a strong appeal for the men of his time. Though an eschatological myth is always an eschatological myth, a fanciful literary
creation, it is almost incredible how Plutarch put his most developed myth at the end of his most scientific treatise, and how
skillfully this is integrated with the myth itself. *Daimones* as independent spirits might fit into this scheme, but as a matter of
fact they are difficult to integrate. Far more significant are *daimones* as souls which have not reached their final destiny, human
souls with a link to the moon through their material *psyche*. In
such a scheme there is a sense of direction in his philosophy which
was to strongly characteiize later religious Platonism.

---

[34] The transitional ideas in Plutarch's conception of Lethe have been
noted by M. Nilsson, *The Dionysiac Mysteries in the Hellenistic and Roman
Age* (Lund: 1957), p. 123; R. Turcan, *Les Sarcophages Romains à Représentations Dionysiaques* (Paris: 1966), p. 3; and Y. Vernière, "Le Léthé
de Plutarque," *REA*, 66 (1964), 22-32.

CHAPTER EIGHT

THE FORCE OF THE CAUSE WHIRLED ABOUT IN DISORDER AND UNRESTRICTEDLY: DAIMON AND TYCHE IN PLUTARCH

Beside the use of *daimon* to designate a spirit greater than man, or to designate the human soul itself, another meaning for *daimon* figures prominently in the Greek literature of the 5th Century, and this meaning becomes increasingly more important in the Hellenistic and Roman periods.[1] This is the use of *daimon* as an equivalent for or a personification of fortune (*tyche*). The two words, *daimon* and *tyche*, are in fact so closely linked in the Hellenistic period that in his second volume of the monumental *Geschichte der griechischen Religion*, Martin Nilsson entitled the chapter on fortune, "Tyche und Daimon." [2]

If there is any facet of Plutarch's religious philosophy which has been largely overlooked, it is his attitude toward *tyche*; and it is this attitude which is very important for an understanding of his history of Greece and Rome insofar as that is revealed in his biographies, and for his conception of the rise and fall of the great Greeks and Romans.[3] When the subject of *tyche* has not been

---

[1] For the history of *daimon* as *tyche* in the early period, cf. Nilsson, *Geschichte der Griechischen Religion* II, pp. 200-218, and Wilamowitz, *Der Glaube der Hellenen* I, pp. 362-68, and II, pp. 297-311. Wilamowitz notes, II, p. 303, n. 1, a line from a much earlier period, Euripides' *Iphigenia at Aulis* 1136, in which Agamemnon seems to identify *moira, tyche,* and *daimon*: (ὦ πότνια μοῖρα καὶ τύχη δαίμων τ᾽ ἐμός.) An excellent treatment of the history of *tyche* in Greek religion, philosophy, literature, and art can be found in G. Herzog-Hauser, "Tyche," *RE*, Hlbd. 14 (1948), 1643-89.

[2] Both Wilamowitz, *Der Glaube* II, p. 298, and Nilsson, *Geschichte* II, pp. 200-207, believed that the great and often unexpected political changes among the Diadochoi, Alexander's successors, contributed to an atmosphere in which devotion to *tyche* supplanted devotion previously given to other deities. Even a modern historian is impressed by the fluctuation of fortune among the Hellenistic monarchs. Wilamowitz probably exaggerates the struggle of Stoicism and Epicureanism against the *tyche* cult in describing these philosophies as "Kampf gegen den Tycheglauben" (pp. 298-309).

[3] The only attempted monograph on *tyche* in Plutarch is that by E. Lassel, *De fortunae in Plutarchi operibus notione* (Marburg: 1896), which does little more than cite the passages in which *tyche* appears and attempt

altogether ignored, it has at best only been treated as a very side issue, or as something which has little or no importance outside of discussions on three essays on *tyche—De fortuna, De fortuna Romanorum*, and *De Alexandri magni fortuna*. Even these, however, show a certain complexity and difficulty in Plutarch's thought since the first and last are anti-*tyche*, while the second sees *tyche* as responsible in almost every way for the rise of Rome. An attempt will be made here first to show how Plutarch uses the term *daimon* in place of *tyche* or else entangles the two together in an incredible knot. Afterwards Plutarch's meaning for *tyche* and the use of it in his works will be discussed.

Something of the ease with which Plutarch can turn *daimon* into *tyche* is evident from a passage of *De tranquillitate animi* (474b) in which he comments on a famous fragment of Menander:

ἅπαντι δαίμων ἀνδρὶ συμπαρίσται
εὐθὺς γενομένῳ μυσταγωγὸς τοῦ βίου ἀγαθός (ἀγαθοῦ).

(fr. 789 Körte-Thierfelder).[4]

to group these into rough divisions. Lassel also believed, p. 66—as one might expect from a 19th Century German—that Plutarch relied heavily on his sources and that his use of *tyche* was a direct reflection of them. He concluded that Plutarch is less *tyche*-conscious when following Phylarchos —which Lassel believed was closely utilized for *Pyrrhos, Aratos, Agis* and *Cleomenes*—than when following Douris—which he believed was cribbed for *Demosthenes*. Lassel's study suffers from two major defects: first, the difficulty of determining the exact meaning of *tyche* in a particular passage, the elusive spread of meaning of the word in any case, and the uncritical confidence in 19th Century *Quellenforschung*. Lassel's general conclusions were also confused. At times he correctly indicates that Plutarch was not as enthusiastic about *tyche* as his source was, but also claims, p. 68, that *tyche* was indispensable to Plutarch as a *deus ex machina* to extricate himself from historical and philosophical difficulties; yet, he sees no basis for this paradox other than the use of sources.

[4] Similar to Menander 789 is *Dyskolos* 281 (Sandbach). F. H. Sandbach, *Menander, A Commentary* (Oxford: 1973), p. 180, notes that it is difficult to distinguish *daimon* here (. . . φέρωσι δ' εὐγένως τὸν δαίμον') from *tyche*; the context is, if a change of *tyche* should occur, men should bear their *daimon* bravely. Soury, *La Démonologie*, p. 150, in remarking on this passage admitted that the concept of double *daimones* was not very developed in Plutarch. In *De genio* the Pythagorean speakers talk only of good *daimones* as personal. The *daimon* which appears to Brutus (*Brut.* 36) says he is Brutus' evil *daimon*, but Plutarch seems to discredit the story. D. A. O'Brien, *Empedocles' Cosmic Cycle* (Cambridge: 1969), p. 331, takes *De tranq. an.* 474b, *De Is.* 370d-e, and *De exil.* 607c in an attempt to identify Empedocles' soul-*daimon* with the Strife-Love figures. Plutarch himself, *De an.* fr. 200, (the interpretation of *Od.* 10.239-240) identifies the Empedoclean *daimon*

Plutarch criticizes Menander here for supposedly implying that *tyche* throughout life is constant and claims that he prefers Empedocles (fr. 122) whose combinations of double *daimones* represent to Plutarch the changing or shifting *tyche* of life; this in Greek is usually represented as "good or evil *tyche*." Plutarch is applying that very loose kind of literary criticism for which the Greeks are famous. Menander's actual words at this point are that "at birth a *daimon* stands by each man, the good mystagogue of life; for one should not believe that there is such a thing as an evil *daimon* which harms one's life, or that God is evil—rather He is entirely good; those who have an evil character, create many conflicts in their life, and show their stupidity in all things, [text corrupt here] lay the blame on their *daimon* and speak ill of it, although they themselves are to blame." Plutarch is very arbitrary in his literary interpretations, and this is an example of it. Menander's advice is very sound. The fact that Plutarch does not oppose a real evil *daimon* instead of a *tyche-daimon* to Menander's interpretation may be evidence that he basically is in agreement with Menander here, and not all that preoccupied with evil spirits as some scholars would have us believe. The whole theme of *De tranquillitate* is that fortune is constantly ebbing and flowing, or in more Greek terms, that one constantly encounters good and evil *tyche*; the best advice that the wise man can give is to encourage mortals to keep a cool head whether good or evil *tyche* should at a particular time be one's lot.

There are innumerable examples in Plutarch's work where the two words *daimon* and *tyche* seem to be interchangeable, and often one cannot help suspecting that the use of one word or the other is for stylistic reasons. This is, however, not to deny that *daimon* sounds more mysterious, usually allows the remote possibility that there is a real spirit lurking about, and is used less frequently than *tyche*. For example, in a work entirely concerned with *tyche*, *De fortuna Romanorum* (330d), the *daimon* recalls the soul of Alexander the Great before he has a chance to do the Romans in. Likewise, in the same essay the Greeks had to struggle against an envious *daimon* (as does Priam, *De fortuna* 97d). Something similar would be at stake in *Mulierum virtutes* 258b, where describing

---

which "clothes the souls with flesh" as "the fate and nature of reincarnation." For Plutarch's use of Empedocles see J. P. Herschbell, "Plutarch as a Source for Empedocles Reexamined," *AJP*, 92 (1971), 156-84.

the evil *tyche* of a Theban woman after her city's conquest by
the Macedonians, Plutarch writes that "Camma bowed to (the)
daimon which demanded the surrender of her property."
The interchangeability of the two words is very evident in the
extremely strong *tyche* passage at the end of the *Life of Marius* (46).
Marius is portrayed on his deathbed as a drunken sot, maddened
by his ambition and former glory; he jumps on his bed and waves
his arms around as he violently commands imaginary troops,
anxious to set out on the first impossible mission. In a magnificent
piece of philosophic-literary moralizing on the use of one's *tyche*,
Plutarch comments that "the wretched Marius, though showered
with many opportunities and blessings in his life, lamented his
tyche to the end, but the noble Plato on his deathbed thanked
his *daimon* and his *tyche* that he had been born a Greek and not
a barbarian and that he had lived in the time of Socrates." [5] So,
concludes Plutarch, evil men throw away the present opportunities
while they lament the past or dream about the future. A similar
linking of *daimon* and *tyche* occurs in a passage in the *Life* of the
more noble Brutus (40). Brutus tells Cassius that "when young
and inexperienced in the world, he had blamed Cato for committing suicide, on the grounds that it was impious and unmanly
to yield to the *daimon* and not to accept what happens, but that
in the present *tychai* he was of a different mind and no matter
what might happen, he would go forth with praise for *tyche* because
of the role he played in the assassination of Caesar, "which brought
both him and his country liberty."
     In one case we can compare three parallel passages for the use of
the words *daimon* and *tyche*, and possibly see a story getting better
and more mysterious in the telling. Pompey had won a resounding
victory at Dyrrachion when Caesar with fewer and poorer provisioned troops tried to surround the enemy. However, for reasons
which seemed inexplicable to Plutarch, Pompey did not immediately

---

[5] Also mentioned as thankful for his *tyche* is Antipater of Tarsos, a Stoic
philosopher mentioned by Plutarch in *De tranq. an.* 469d-e. The whole
passage may be influenced by Poseidonios of Apamea, cited here for the
disease and death of Marius. He was at Rome on the occasion of Marius'
death, and his history, continuing that of Polybios, was used by Plutarch.
See Flacelière, *Vies* VI, p. 154. For Poseidonios' influence on Plutarch,
much disputed, see Babut, *Plutarque et le Stoïcisme*, p. 20 and pp. 216-18.
For his influence at Rome, G. Verbeke, "Le stoïcisme, une philosophie
sans frontières," *ANRW*, I, 4 (1975), pp. 3-42. See also T. F. Carney, "The
Changing Picture of Marius in Ancient Literature," *PACA*, 10 (1967), 5-22.

follow up his victory and put an end to Caesar. *Pompey* 66 may
or may not be after *Caesar* but is before *Cato minor*. Here only
strategic reasons are given in the account. In *Caesar* 39, however,
Caesar blames Pompey's failure on his "excessive caution or on
a great work of *tyche*," and claims that if the other side had had a
general, they would have won. Finally, in *Cato minor* 54 the *daimon*
of Caesar is said to have taken away the total victory of Pompey
by relying on Pompey's caution and disbelief at his great success.
Similarly in *Dion* 4 (the) *daimon*, not human calculation, brings
Plato to Sicily; but only shortly before in the same chapter, this
has been attributed to "(a) divine fortune" (θεία τύχη).
An interesting example of this interchangeability, similar to
that in the passage about Dyrrachion, appears in a story about
Antony told in both *De fortuna Romanorum*, an early essay, and
in the *Life of Antony*. In *De fortuna Romanorum* 319f-320a, we
are told that a friend of Antony's, who prided himself on divination, noted that Antony continually lost when he gambled
against Octavius; and, therefore, he told Antony that his *daimon*
feared Octavius and that his *tyche* would go off with Octavius
unless Antony stayed away from his rival. In the version which
appears in the *Life* (33), a number of elements have been changed
to give a greater aura of mystery. Here an Egyptian astrologer
informs Antony that his *tyche* is great and splendid in itself, but
that it cowers before that of Octavius. Plutarch adds that later
events proved the man right since Antony continually lost when
gambling with Octavius.
Some scholars, looking only at the *Antony* passage, have inflated
the whole thing into a daimonological conflict between two protective spirits, and then employed the passage in proof that Plutarch
envisaged the events of the world as involving struggles between
the protective deities of great men.[6] However, one cannot rule
out the possibility that the difference between the account in
De fortuna Romanorum and that in *Antony* represents a difference
in the exigencies of the works themselves. In the first Plutarch
would only be interested in the role of *tyche* in Antony's life. In

---

[6] Soury, *La Démonologie*, p. 141, and Erbse, "Plutarchs Schrift," 312,
base the double *daimon* theory in Plutarch on this text. However, they even
see deep daimonological significance in a relatively innocent expression
like κατὰ δαίμονα in *Aem.* 12 where it is an obvious substitution for κατὰ
τύχην.

the second other elements are at stake: the rivalry between Antony
and Octavius, which ended in the surprising victory of the younger
man; Antony's Egyptian connections, which also were responsible
for his defeat; and the necessity of underlining to a greater extent
than in *De fortuna Romanorum* Antony's ill-fortune in his later
encounters with Octavius. One might also add to this the necessity
of motivation for Antony's departure from Octavius at this point
in the narrative. These ends are achieved by the substitution of
an Egyptian astrologer who acts "on Cleopatra's behalf," for a
friend, and by inverting the narrative so that the Egyptian's
prediction is proved by events, rather than the reverse, as in the
more prosaic version of *De fortuna Romanorum*. Here the friend
deduces Antony's luck from the course of his losses in gambling
with Octavius.

The rivalry between the two *daimones* becomes more prominent in
the *Life* version, by slightly downplaying the reference to Antony's
tyche. Plutarch begins by mentioning that Antony's *tyche* is great,
but from this point concentrates exclusively on the *daimon*. The
daimon, which is identified with his *tyche*, is said to cower before
Octavius, even though it is spirited and lofty (γαυρὸς ὢν καὶ ὑψηλός).
This character description certainly fits Antony himself. One could
imagine well from Plutarch's treatment of Antony how the older
man must have felt humiliated by the younger. Moreover, in the
Life Plutarch constantly propounds the view that Cleopatra
was Antony's downfall, and this theme appears even in the little
vignette given in the incident related here. We learn the advice
was "either as a favor to Cleopatra, or dealing truly with Antony."
And the prediction is made not by an anonymous friend but by
a seer from Egypt, who "cast nativities" (τῶν τὰς γενέσεις ἐπι-
σκοπούντων), a practice associated with Egypt. Later, the Egyptian
context is underlined again: "and indeed events seemed to testify
in favor of the Egyptian." Here we have a characteristic technique
of Plutarch's biographies, the incorporation and adaptation of
apparently trivial matter in order to illuminate the central theme.
In so doing, Plutarch is not above changing and adapting an
original account, provided that this adaptation does not do violence
to the truth.

Sometimes the matter is even more complex. For instance, in
De fortuna Romanorum 324b we have a passage in which Plutarch
is speaking incessantly of the Roman *tyche* so that there can be

no doubt that *daimon* will refer to *tyche*. Here he says that the "great *daimon* of the Romans (ὁ 'Ρωμαίων μέγας δαίμων) blew fair not for a single day, as it did in the case of other nations, but continuously." Caesar is also a person noted for his *tyche*, and this is especially underlined in *De fortuna Romanorum* (391c-d). But in *Caesar* the great *daimon* of Caesar (ὁ μέγας αὐτοῦ δαίμων) is a rather complex entity: it seems to be both his *tyche*, a personal *alastor* tracking down his enemies "on land and sea until every last one was killed," and one might even suspect that it is the ghost of Caesar himself. This *daimon* sends forth another *daimon*, that which appears to Brutus before Philippi and claims it is Brutus' evil *daimon*!

This confused use of *daimon* appears frequently where the action in a *Life* is taking place on Oriental soil. It may be worthwhile to give the instances of this in order to show how they differ somewhat from the ordinary type of reference one finds in the rest of the *Lives*. For example at times the Orientals seem to believe that they have a personal *daimon* watching over them. Dareios on the occasion of the death of his wife, Stateira, laments the evil *daimon* of the Persians (*Alexander* 30), but is told by the eunuch Tireos that he should not blame this *daimon*. In a particularly sinister and bloody context, Sparamizes, the eunuch of Parysatis, the mother of Cyros, acting as an agent-provocateur, manages to trap Mithridates, the murderer of Cyros, into uttering a statement which will cause his death. On so doing he bids the company to toast the *daimon* of the king (*Artaxerxes* 15). There follows the hideous torture of Mithridates. In the *Life of Lucullus* (27), Tigranes, the general of Mithridates, at one crucial point makes the mistake of thinking a feint retreat by the Romans is genuine. His general, Taxiles, reluctantly disillusions him, saying he wished something so unexpected might fall to his *daimon*. Similarly, in a passage from the *Sulla* which seems to have behind it Sulla's *Memoirs*, Mithridates in his meeting with Sulla at the Troad tries to blame the war upon the *daimones* and the Romans, and is promptly rebuked by Sulla (*Sulla* 24). In such cases one suspects that Plutarch has reflected the local color of some genuine Persian sources. In other cases where we are on Persian soil it is difficult to tell. Plutarch suggests that Alexander's murder of Cleitos was due to the evil *daimon* of Cleitos—thus differing from other ancient authors (*Alexander* 50).[7] His phrasing is interesting: it was through his bad fortune (*dystychia*) that his anger and inebriation offered an excuse to the evil *daimon* of Cleitos. Plutarch may here be attempting to remove the theme of the vengeance of Dionysos from the *Life*. In a section of the *Life of Crassus*, heavily influenced by Cassius' own account of the Parthian defeat, Cassius asks the treacherous Parthian guide who is leading the Roman army farther and farther into the desert, what evil *daimon* has brought him to Crassus (*Crassus* 22).[8] Later in his life, in *Brutus* 37, after Brutus has seen the midnight phantom of his evil *daimon* before the crossing into Macedonia from Abydos, Cassius is introduced as an Epicurean, and claims it is ridiculous to believe that such creatures exist. The speech seems to be a creation of Plutarch for the occasion,

---

[7] Plutarch's words in *Alex*. 50 run *tyche* and *daimon* in close proximity: τὴν αἰτίαν καὶ τὸν καιρὸν οὐκ ἀπὸ γνώμης ἀλλὰ δυστυχίᾳ τινὶ ταῦθ᾽ εὑρίσκομεν πεπραγμένα τοῦ βασιλέως ὀργὴν καὶ μέθην πρόφασιν τῷ Κλείτου δαίμονι παρασχόντος. The insertion of *daimon* at this point may be Plutarch's touch; Arrian, at least, (4.8) blames the murder on the wrath of Dionysos who was offended because Alexander had sacrificed to the Dioscouroi. In *Alex*. 13, Alexander himself attributes the death of Cleitos to Dionysos. Flacelière, *Vies* IX, p. 7, believes that in the background is the vengeance of Dionysos for the sack of Thebes, his birthplace, and that Alexander's role as Neos Dionysos was meant to offset this. Plutarch has largely suppressed this theme. One can point to *Sol*. 27 where in the discussion between Solon and Croisos on the blessed life, Plutarch omits the Herodotean line about the gods being envy (τὸν θεῖον πᾶν ἐὸν φθονερόν τε καὶ ταραχῶδες, 1.32); and he changes the wording of Herodotos slightly so that *daimon* rather than *theos* is responsible for eventual prosperity (ᾧ δὲ εἰς τέλος ὁ δαίμων ἔθετο τὴν εὐπραξίαν τοῦτον εὐδαίμονα νομίζομεν.). The change is skillful enough so that the traditionalist would see in it an exact rendering of Herodotos, but so that others would see *tyche* rather than the divinity as responsible for man's misfortune.

[8] A passage similar to that in *Crassus* appears in *Sertorius* 25; the Roman conspirator against Sertorius, Perpenna, asks the other senators what evil *daimon* led them to sit in a wretched Spanish court when they previously could not put up with Sulla's treatment. This part of the *Crassus* seems heavily influenced by an account which must ultimately go back to Cassius, possibly his memoirs. See Flacelière, *Vies* VII, p. 194 and 234.
In *Phocion* 30 Demades arrives at the court of Antipater (ὑπὸ δαίμονός τινος ὡς ἔοικεν) at the most inopportune time, and with his son is cruelly put to death: a letter had been intercepted in which Demades had called Antipater a rotten old thread. Erbse, p. 306, makes this *daimon* equal to that which leads Caesar to his death at the base of Pompey's statue in *Brut*. 14 and *Caes*. 66. This is, however, far too risky a conjecture, since Plutarch is stressing the time coincidence in the *Demosthenes* passage; but in *Brutus* and *Caesar* it is the coincidence that Caesar should collapse before a statue of his arch rival Pompey, whom he had caused to end in a miserable death.

possibly based on the knowledge that Cassius was an Epicurean, but it is interesting that the vision takes place in Asia.

The theme of *daimon* and *tyche* also runs through Plutarch's extremely sympathetic treatment of the last days of Pompey in chapters 74, 75, and 76 of that man's *Life*. Cornelia, the young wife of Pompey, whom he loved intensely, had lost her first husband, Publius, the son of Crassus, in the desert of Parthia. Plutarch's readers may have been expected to have read the touching account of the tragic cavalry charge of Publius in the *Crassus*. After the defeat at Pharsalos, Pompey rushes to Mytilene where he had left her. Cornelia, who had expected his victory, is crushed, and terrified with the observation that no sooner had Pompey associated himself with her than he fell on evil days. She believes her "heavy *daimon*" has affected Pompey asking him "why he came to see her and did not leave her to her heavy *daimon*, her who had filled him with so much *dystychia*" (*Pompey* 74). Pompey kindly comforts her with a little exposition on the mutability of *tyche*: she had met him when his *tyche* was at its height, thinking that it always had been that way. He weakly concludes with the argument that since his *tyche* is so bad it can hardly do anything but improve (75). This is followed by a discussion supposedly with the philosopher Cratippos, which undoubtedly Plutarch did not have in his sources; for he says that at the time he did not want to discourage Pompey, but he might have asked him if he would have used his *arete* any better than Caesar, given his *tyche*.

In the next chapter Plutarch concludes that Pompey's reason for going to Egypt rather than Parthia —which he had contemplated—was to protect his young bride from the Parthians in case something should go awry, "if there was any calculation involved at all, and some *daimon* was not leading him on that fateful trip" (76).

Similarly in one of the strongest passages in praise of *tyche* in the *Lives*, *Timoleon* 16, Timoleon's friends speak about the *daimon* which protected *Timoleon* from an assassin; but this is identified with the *tyche* "which directs all things, using the apparently most disparate elements to achieve its designs and bringing them together in a way incomprehensible to the observer, until all has been accomplished." In the particular occurrence, an assassin about to slay Timoleon, is at the very moment killed by his own personal enemy. A modern historian might look for an agent provocateur or some semblance of double-cross; Plutarch—who registers no trace of suspicion—unquestionably accepts the event as a great work of *tyche*. He notes, as though deeply impressed, that Timoleon in thanksgiving dedicated a shrine to Automatia and his house to the Hieros Daimon (36).[9]

Now that we have seen the easy interchange between the use of the words *daimon* and *tyche*, we can penetrate a bit further into the philosophical presuppositions which they imply. By so doing we may be better able to formulate the influence of the glorification of *tyche* in the Hellenistic and Roman period upon Plutarch's historical conceptions, at least insofar as these appear in a biographical work. As is characteristic of the entirety of his thought, so here certain contradictions and paradoxes, like ugly weeds in an otherwise orderly garden, begin to pop up here and there. However, as a guideline, a general principle can be stated: where he is thinking in philosophical terms, and realizes that he is on strictly philosophical ground, he is liable to have one eye on the bogey of Epicureanism, and the very mention of the word *tyche* leads to a tirade against it; on the other hand where he is on historical grounds and the use of the concept does not seem to represent a philosophical position, he has no qualms about assigning a large role to *tyche*. He may even go so far as to indicate that this miracle of *tyche* is indeed proof of the existence of providence.[10]

---

[9] Nilsson, *Geschichte* II, p. 203, sees Timoleon, in his devotion to *tyche*, as an important forerunner of the Hellenistic monarchs. *De se ips. laud.* 542e mentions Timoleon's devotion, but in this passage "Agathos" rather than "Hieros" is used to describe the Daimon.

[10] *To automaton* does not appear very frequently in Plutarch. Aristotle made a distinction between *tyche*, which operated through rational causes, and *to automaton*, which operated through irrational causes such as in the production of animal prodigies: δῆλον ἄρα ὅτι ἡ τύχη αἰτία κατὰ συμβεβηκὸς ἐν τοῖς κατὰ προαίρεσιν τῶν ἕνεκα τοῦ. διὸ περὶ τὸ αὐτό ἐστι τὸ αὐτόματον καὶ ἡ τύχη αἰτία ὧν ἂν ἢ νοῦς αἴτιος ἢ φύσις. *Phys.* 2.5.197a 5; and ἐπεὶ δ' ἐστὶ τὸ αὐτόματον καὶ ἡ τύχη αἰτία ὧν ἂν ἢ νοῦς γένοιτο αἴτιος ἢ φύσις *Phys.* 2.6. 198a 5. Ross, *Aristotle* (London: 1923), pp. 75-78, pointed out that Aristotle himself was sometimes inconsistent in his use of the distinction. Plutarch roughly adheres to it; e.g. in *Alex.* 35 "naphtha" does not catch fire ἀπ' αὐτομάτου., and in *Sert.* 1 the coincidence that several great generals had only one eye is attributed to *to automaton*. Plutarch is inconsistent, however, in the way he speaks about its relationship to divine providence. In *De Pyth. orac.* 398b-d, the fact that statue portents do not come about through *tyche* or *to automaton* is a proof of divine intervention; in *Timol.* 12 the fact that the portents took place through *to automaton* is a proof of divine intervention, but in 16, where human factors enter to save his life, it is a case of *tyche*, described in terms usually reserved for providence.

Thus, what to our minds often appears totally inconsistent and contradictory can often be explained through the nature of the matter to which Plutarch is directed.

There is an interesting passage in *De audiendis poetis* (23e-24c), which not only gives a rough working definition of *tyche* but also an indication of Plutarch's attempt to reconcile the concept of providence with the fact that good men often appear to suffer more than they deserve. Plutarch argues that one cannot blame the unjust Fate of some virtuous men on God (Zeus), but rather these must be attributed to fate (*heimarmene*). However, Plutarch adds illogically that if men lead a life of self-control they will be rewarded with success and not suffer unjustly. Part of his difficulty is with poverty, which obviously has afflicted a large number of good men in the past. Plutarch argues rather unconvincingly, that poverty does not come from the gods but from *tyche*. It is difficult to see how on any grounds poverty, at least at birth, can be attributed to *tyche* and not to providence, but this does not daunt Plutarch. It is at this point that Plutarch explains that earlier men confused providence and *tyche* "in much the same way that the words divine and daimonic are used to designate men" rather than the gods, but that the concepts really are quite distinct. Plutarch's definition stresses the indefinite and apparently illogical course of this causality: *tyche* is the force of a cause carried about in a disorderly and unrestricted way (τὴν τῆς ἀτάκτως καὶ ἀορίστως περιφερομένης αἰτίας δύναμιν). Even he must have been later dissatisfied with the muddled account of *tyche* and providence given here.

The matter is not much more clarified by the explication of *tyche* by Lamprias in *Quaestiones convivales* 9.5 (739e-740f). Here Plutarch attempts to get at the heart of what was meant in the eschatological myth of Plato's *Republic* by "the casting of lots by the souls" to obtain their reincarnation. Lamprias argues that since Plato speaks about goodness and wickedness obeying no master (617e), it must mean that the choice of our life depends upon our free will. Already this is somewhat baffling to us, and the matter does not get easier. Lamprias' next statement is that the necessity of fate (εἱμαρμένης ἀνάγκη) is responsible for the good life of those who choose correctly, and the evil life of those who choose wrongly. Apparently Lamprias conceives the selection of a life to mean not whether one is born in this or that family, but as the selection of the whole entity of good and evil acts which make up a man's life. Next he adds that the way the lots fall introduces *tyche*, which puts one into this or that society, and therefore, predetermines those things which are dependent upon a person's education and environment. In the actual fall of the lots, Lamprias rules out any higher cause such as *heimarmene* or providence (*pronoia*); this would make the casting of lots, "which signifies *tyche* and *to automaton*," meaningless. It is difficult to say how seriously this passage should be taken, but it does seem to be an attempt to defend certain principles: that virtue and vice are not dependent upon *tyche*, that *tyche* plays a relatively small role in the moral essentials of life, and, perhaps, that providence must be absolved from complete responsibility for evil in the world. *Tyche*, then, is relegated to the relatively small role of placing one in this or that society, which, however, the individual can to a great extent either escape or benefit from.

Plutarch's essay devoted entirely to *tyche*, *De fortuna*, is even more bald and unsatisfactory.[11] Apparently only concerned to rebut the Epicureans, he rules out any important position for *tyche* in the creation of the world, the accomplishment of heroic acts, the development of *arete*, or the creation of artistic masterpieces. A somewhat similar approach, though for different reasons, appears in *De Alexandri magni fortuna*.[12] Due to the execution

---

[11] The source of the essay is uncertain. Ziegler, p. 88, thought that the influence upon the essay was largely Stoic. It is possible that some of the ideas go back to Theophrastos; at 97c Plutarch cites a line from Chairemon, τύχη τὰ θνητῶν πράγματ' οὐκ εὐβουλία which appears also in Cic. *Tusc.* 5.25. Cicero adds: "vexatur idem Theophrastus et libris et scholis omnium philosophorum quod in Callisthene suo laudaris illam sententiam 'vitam regit fortuna, non sapientia'." Ziegler believes the essay was a youthful work published by Plutarch's heirs.

[12] Some think the second part of the essay is not genuine; but Ziegler, p. 87, supports its authenticity. He notes that the topic of Alexander's fortune seems to have been a favorite of the rhetorical school (*Rhet. ad Her.* 4.31; Cic. *De or.* 2.341, *De fin.* 2.116; Liv. 9.17-19; Dio. Chrys. 1-4, 64; Ael. *Var. Hist.* 3.23; Iul. *Conviv.* 320 ff.). Tarn, *Alexander* II (Cambridge: 1948), app. 16, thought that Plutarch's *Life of Alexander* was in opposition to the theme of *De fortuna Alexandri*; but A. E. Wardman, "Plutarch and Alexander," *CQ*, 5 (1955), 96-107, rightly opposes Tarn's position. J. R. Hamilton, *Plutarch. Alexander* (Oxford: 1969), p. xxxi, goes too far in saying that the essays are "epideictic display pieces devoid of any serious purpose;" Plutarch's patriotism toward Greece and its heroes went deep. Jones, *Plutarch and Rome*, pp. 67-71, is impressed by the knowledge of Rome in the young Plutarch. He sees the origin of the ideas in Polybios, but notes a view peculiarly Plutarch's—that Rome "was a stable element

of Callisthenes, a nephew of Arisottle and a former member of
the Aristotelian Lyceum, the Peripatetic school is supposed
to have created a portrait of Alexander which was extremely
hostile: it depicted him as a person of a fiery temperament
given to alcoholism, whose successes were largely due to *tyche*.
The purpose of *De fortuna Alexandri* is to counter this view, and
Plutarch goes beyond it to make Alexander a philosopher in action
whose unification of the peoples of the world and whose promotion
of Greek culture was worth more than the ivory-towered pro-
nouncements of the scholars. The *Life* tones down this idealized
portrait of Alexander which we meet with in the essay, but in
it Plutarch is nonetheless reluctant to let *tyche* play any large role
in Alexander's successes. In this respect the *Life* presents a great
contrast to the history of Curtius Rufus who never stops harping
on Alexander's *fortuna*.[13]
It is quite a shock after these two essays to pick up *De fortuna
Romanorum* and find Plutarch ready to attribute all the Roman
successes to their *tyche*. However, we are probably unable to get
a proper perspective of this work due to our lack of knowledge
about the circumstances which caused its production. It is very
likely that Plutarch did not mean to put the Romans in a derogatory light, or to contrast Greek *arete* with Roman *tyche*.[14] It

in the chaos of history, 'an anchor in storm and change,'" p. 70, a reflection
of Plutarch's world. He also finds the basic thought reflected in his mature
works.
  [13] In *Alex.* 19 Plutarch denies that the sea along the Pamphylian coast
retired miraculously for Alexander as he marched by in contrast to Callisthenes (*FGH* 124, fr. 31); Josephus, *AJ* 2.348; Appian, *BC* 2.622; an anonymous writer (*FGH* 151 fr. 1,2); Arrian, 1.26.2; and Strabo, 14.3.9.66. Curtius
displays an element of mental derangement in describing Alexander's
tyche. Cf. 3.4, 3.8, 3.9, 3.11, 3.12, 4.5, 4.9, 4.25, of his history to see how he
is able to attribute almost anything good or evil to *fortuna*. In Diodoros
17.35 the captured wives of Dareios are victims of *tyche* and when Alexander
contemplates the fall of the Persian, he marvels at ἡ μεταβολὴ τῆς τύχης;
but even such mild admiration for *tyche* is largely avoided by Plutarch.
  [14] F. Kraus, *Die Rhetorischen Schriften Plutarchs und ihre Stellung im
Plutarchischen Schriftenkorpus* (Munich: 1912), p. 15, ff., had argued that
Plutarch meant to contrast the favorable *tyche* of the Romans and Caesar
against the unfavorable *tyche* of Alexander and the Greeks. Ziegler, *Plutarchos*, p. 84, argues against this view; however, it is hard to deny that
this thesis of contrasting *tychai* is at least somewhat implicit. It is true,
though, that in *Alexander-Caesar* Plutarch makes no attempt to contrast
the *tychai* of the two heroes. Ziegler, p. 84, argues that the essay must be
early since Plutarch alludes to an inscription at Chaironeia set up by Sulla
after his victory over Mithridates there: καὶ τὰ παρ' ἡμῖν ἐν Χαιρωνείᾳ τρόπαια

is even possible that *De fortuna Romanorum* represents only half of a debate, the other half of which is lost, or that Plutarch would have been quite willing to defend the Roman *arete* against its detractors who attributed all its greatness to *tyche*. Yet, there is a passage in it which must have haunted him to the end of his life:

> But the great *daimon* of the Romans blew not for one day, nor was it at its height for only a brief time, as was that of the Macedonians, nor was it a land breeze only like that of the Spartans, nor a sea breeze like that of the Athenians, nor late to rise like the Persians, nor quick to cease like the Carthaginians, but rising up from the first beginnings grew up with the city, increased in strength with it, governed with it, and remained constant on land and on sea, in war and in peace, against barbarians, and against Greeks (324b). (Babbitt, Loeb, *Mor.* IV, pp. 365-67).

The rest of the piece is a recital of innumerable occasions on which *tyche* came to the rescue of the Romans, and of testimonies to their great *tyche* on the part of their own leaders.

The essay is considered to be youthful, but at the same time it contains many similarities of thought with certain passages in the *Lives*. It is rhetorical and naive, and this is the general basis for dating a work as early where we have no other indications as to its date of composition. At the same time at 316e-317b it contains the type of reference to Plato's *Timaeus* such as we find in Plutarch's philosophical works. One might also notice the great interest and knowledge of antiquities in Rome.[15] One might

---

κατὰ τῶν Μιθριδατικῶν οὕτως ἐπιγέγραπται. (318)d. In Ziegler's view this is proof that the essay must have been published by his sons or heirs. However, Ziegler's argumentation here is faulty; in *Sul.* 34, the identical line appears, and this is in a work presumably written in Plutarch's mature period.

[15] The date and number of Plutarch's trips to Rome are uncertain. Ziegler, pp. 17-20, thinks Plutarch was in Rome toward the end of the 70's and again in the beginning of the 90's, but that he may have even been there more frequently. Plutarch mentions his visits to Rome in *Qu. conv.* 7.7.1 (727b) and *De soll. an.* 973e. Many of the allusions given by Plutarch in the essay can still be found in extant well-known Roman writers: e.g. 318a, *tyche* takes off her sandals and wings as she approaches the Tiber (Hor. *Carm.* 1.35); 318b, Metellus is taken to his grave by his four sons (Cic. *De fin.* 5.82, *Tusc.* 1.85; Vell. Pat. 1.11.7; Val. Max. 7.1.1; Plin. *NH* 7.13.59, 44.142.1); 318d, Marcellus' temple is described (Liv. 27.25, 29.11; Val. Max. 1.1.8; Cic. *Verr.* 4.121, *De nat. deor.* 2.61); 319b, the temple of Fortis in Caesar's gardens is mentioned (Suet. *Iul.* 83); 319b-c, Caesar's pursuit of Pompey is put on Jan. 4th (Luc. *Phars.* 5.406ff); 320c, Romulus disappears during an eclipse of the sun on the Capratine nones (Var. *Ling. lat.* 6.18). There are also a number of details in common with *Ant.*, *Cam.*,

wonder how he could be so well-informed on them at a very early period of his life. Moreover, there are many common points of interest with the *Lives* which suggest a considerable knowledge of Roman history for a Greek. One should hesitate then to make the essay as early as suggested by some scholars, though the *Lives* tend to tone down the exuberance of the essay and give a more balanced picture.[16] Thus it is possible that it came after works such as *De esu carnium* but before the mature period in which the *Lives* were written.

Some examples of the "watering down" of the *tyche* enthusiasm of the essay are worth mentioning as an example of Plutarch's technique and development. In 319c-d an anecdote is related about Caesar as an indication that Caesar was convinced of his own extraordinary *tyche*. In dire straits during his campaign against Pompey at Dyrrachion, being besieged by Pompey, Caesar decides to set out in a small boat across the Adriatic to get reinforcements.[17] However, a dreadful storm comes up, and the pilot begs Caesar to return. In the essay, Caesar tells the pilot not to worry "since he is carrying Caesar and Caesar's *tyche*." In the *Life of Caesar*, when relating the same incident, Plutarch

---

Cor., Luc., Marc., Num., Pomp., Rom., and *Sul.* It seems difficult to believe that Plutarch would have so much information on Roman antiquities at an extremely early date in his life. On the other hand he strangely does not mention Sulla's temple to Fortuna at Praeneste. We also find his trips to Rome in *Demos.* 2, *Qu. Rom.* 275b-c, *De exil.* 602c, *Praec. ger. reipub.* 805a, and *Adv. Col.* 1126e. He describes being present in the Theatre of Marcellus while a dog act was going on before the Emperor Vespasian, but Jones, *Plutarch and Rome,* p. 21, suspects a white lie since the anecdote is told in Suetonius, *Vespasian* 19 (or did Suetonius get it from Plutarch?). On the date of *De fort. Rom.,* on *De curios.* 522d-e (Rusticus), see Jones, pp. 67, 23.

[16] There are, of course, many similarities also. For example in both *De fort. Rom.* 318e-f, and *Cor.* 37 Plutarch sees the devotion paid by the Romans to the Fortuna Muliebris as significant for the astounding fortune the city experienced from the earliest days of its history. Even in *Rom.* 8, where Plutarch ridicules the stories of the miraculous origin of Rome, he grants that the *tyche* of Rome would seem to prove that it had a divine origin. The best discussion of his attitude toward Rome is that in Jones, pp. 122-30. For a modern attack on anti-Roman clichés see Chester Starr, "The Roman Place in History," *ANRW* I,1 (1972), pp. 3-11.

[17] The story also appears in Appian, *BC* 2.9. Suetonius, *Caes.* 7—who puts the dream during Caesar's quaestorship in Spain—interprets it to mean that he will achieve mastery of his mother, the world, and sees it as a proof of Caesar's good fortune (ipse prosperrime semper ac ne ancipiti quidem umquam fortuna praeterquem bis dimicavit). For more details see ch. X, note 11.

adds that Caesar was forced to turn back, achieved nothing at
Dyrrachion, and almost lost his entire army through his folly (38).
It is true that in the early chapters of the *Life* (32, 43, 53, 57),
Caesar's *tyche* is seen to be extraordinary; however, *tyche* does
not save him from retribution for the death of Pompey. In the
essay (319d) part of the remarkable *tyche* of Caesar is his escape
from retribution of any kind for his rival's death ([τύχης] ἔργον
ἦν ἵνα καὶ Πομπήϊος πέσῃ καὶ Καῖσαρ μὴ μιάνθῃ). Yet, in the *Life*
of both Brutus and Caesar (*Brutus* 14, *Caesar* 66) Plutarch underscores as heavily as possible the fact that Caesar seemed to be
led to the theatre of Pompey as retribution for the death of Pompey.
This comes out as clearly in *Brutus* as in *Caesar*. In *Brutus* 14 there
is something divinely mysterious about the place (ἐδόκει δὲ καὶ
τὸ τοῦ τόπου θεῖον εἶναι πρὸς αὐτῶν); it contained the very image of
Pompey, and thus it seemed that some *daimon* was leading Caesar
to his place of execution (ὥστε καὶ δαίμων τις ἐδόκει τὸν ἄνδρα τῇ
Πομπηΐου δίκῃ προσάξειν). In *Caesar* 66 the number of coincidences
which precede the murder are not ruled out as acts of chance
(ἀλλὰ ταῦτα μὲν ἤδη που φέρει καὶ τὸ αὐτόματον), but the place of
the assassination, in the very theatre of Pompey and before his
statue, is the work of the (a?) *daimon* (παντάπασιν ἀπέφαινε δαίμονός
τινος ὑφηγουμένου καὶ καλοῦντος ἐκεῖ τὴν πρᾶξιν ἔργον γεγονέναι). At
last Caesar collapses at the feet of the statue of his rival, pierced
by three and twenty blows, and wets the pedestal with his own
blood, so that the action appears as an unmistakable proof of
retribution (καὶ πολὺς καθήμαξεν αὐτὴν ὁ φόνος ὡς δόκειν αὐτὸν
ἐφεστάναι τῇ τιμωρίᾳ τοῦ πολεμίου Πομπηΐου).[18]

In the *Life of Antony* also we find how a modification has come
upon *De fortuna Romanorum*. At 319f in the essay, Antony's downfall is attributed to *tyche*, and part of this is said to be his unfortunate association with Cleopatra. But in *Antony* 36 his fall is the
moral degeneration of a great soul through lust and pleasure—the
type depicted by Plato in his *Phaedrus* (254a)—"as though Antony
had come under the influence of drugs or magic." He is singularly
silent about the role of *tyche* in the battle of Actium, though he

---

[18] Plutarch is alone of extant classical authors in seeing divine retribution
in this incident. Cicero, *De div.* 2.23, mentions that Caesar fell at the base
of Pompey's statue, but the only significance he sees in it is that we are
better off not knowing the future. Valerius Maximus, 1.1, Suetonius, *Caes.*
81, and Appian, *BC* 21.149, do not refer to the coincidence.

reports the intriguing incident of Augustus before the event encountering a man named Fortunatus with his ass Victor (or as Plutarch puts it, Eutychos and Nikon) (65). In 66 he describes the soul of the lover as dwelling in the body of the beloved: "he was dragged along by the woman as if he had become incorporate in her." Antony abandons the battle at the sight of the fleeing Cleopatra, giving up once more the role of commander for that of a lover. Plutarch was undoubtedly influenced by Augustan propaganda, but the portrayal is necessary to his theme of Deme-trios and Antony as models of extravagant vices, six of which he names, but the first that they were *erotikoi* (*Demetrios* 1). Yet he does not abandon altogether the lesser theme of the contrast between the *tyche* of Augustus and Antony.

A number of small corrections are also made in the Roman *Lives*, which taken together tend to correct the exaggerated picture of *De fortuna Romanorum*. In making these corrections Plutarch reveals the logical difficulties he was encountering and the ever present danger of being led into a trap which he has himself constructed. The advocacy of a blind *tyche* directing the affairs of history has the great advantage of extricating himself from the position that the Romans were morally, and militarily superior to the Greeks. It also escapes the difficulty that providence allows the innocent to suffer. However, a world run by *tyche* involves a renunciation of the Platonic belief in a beneficent providence, and it is this providence which he advocates so strongly in op-position to *tyche* in his anti-Epicurean works. On the other hand if he insists that the operations of *tyche* are really the hand of providence, then he is faced with the repugnant but immediate conclusion that the Romans had a manifest destiny to conquer and rule over the entire world. It also involves a denial of divine justice. God would be responsible for destroying a race superior in culture, humanity, and political development. He would be substituting in its place one which had achieved its position through the exercise of great cruelty and barbarity in certain stages of its expansion. Moreover, God would support a process which doomed some very noble Greeks to an ignominious death. There is good reason then for Plutarch's attitude to remain ambivalent, and we can find both supernatural support for the Roman Empire and assertions that it was largely due to *tyche*.

However, in one area of his history Plutarch goes to some lengths to remove the supernatural. This is in his treatment of early Roman history. In *De fortuna Romanorum* the divine parentage of the Twins is treated as a great gift of *tyche*, as is Numa's supposed association with Egeria—the nymph who instructed him in governing the Romans, and the outcry of the geese who saved the Romans when the Gauls were climbing to the citadel (320b, 321b-c, 324d). However, in *Romulus* 2-3, Plutarch ridicules the stories that Romulus had a divine parent, and in *Camillus* 27 he explains that since geese are easily frightened, they became alarmed at the approach of the Gauls. In the essay Plutarch had treated the Egeria legend as a *pia fraus*, but he saw her as a symbolic representation of Numa's *tyche*. In *Numa* 4 and 15 the whole relationship between Numa and Egeria is treated as a *pia fraus* and nothing more.

A reassessment of another type occurs in the *Life of Aemilius Paullus*. This *Life* itself is what could be called a *tyche Life*, so Plutarch's reasons for altering his view in the essay cannot entirely be attributed to a change in emphasis. For some inexplicable reason Plutarch claims that Aemilius was a favorite of *tyche* since he led back the army without a wound, celebrating a tearless victory over Perseus, the Macedonian king (νίκην ἄδακρυν θριαμβεύων, *De fortuna Romanorum* 318b). However, in *Aemilius* 21 Plutarch vividly describes the terror which was felt by Aemilius as the Macedonian phalanx began to sweep the Romans before them, and he records the Roman losses in the battle.[19] Aemilius' triumph in Rome is turned into a bittersweet celebration with cries of victory and thanksgiving contaminated by those of sorrow and dismay. Aemilius loses two sons just at the moment of the triumph, and he attributes this to "the gods, an evil nemesis, or *tyche*." Earlier he felt the divine was jealous of his successes and sooner

---

[19] In *Aem.* 18, Plutarch records the frightening appearance of the Macedonian troops, and in 19 he records that the charge of the enemy left an impression on Aemilius which he never forgot. In 21 Plutarch describes the battle as a "great struggle" in which Marcus Cato almost loses his life. However, the losses he records are relatively low, citing Poseidonios (*FGH* 233 F 3) for 100 fatalities for the Romans and Nasica (*HRR* I 48-FGH 233 F 3) for 800. This Poseidonios was not the famous philosopher, but one who lived before him and wrote, as a contemporary of Perseus, a laudatory history of the king. Livy, 44.42, 7-8, gave the losses as 100 (mostly Pelignians!), but admitted there were many wounded. In writing the *Life* Plutarch seems to have come into contact with a letter of Cato to his son, as an eyewitness account. See Flacelière, *Vies* IV, pp. 96 and 245.

or later would demand retribution, and had pontificated on the mutability of *tyche* (*Aemilius* 34 and 35).

The conclusion one must arrive at is that Plutarch is a schizophrenic when it comes to *tyche*. In his great religious treatises he has no truck with it. In *De defectu oraculorum*, for example, Lamprias argues against an infinity of worlds on the basis that they would be more than enough for providence to handle and would therefore be governed by *tyche* (423c). He begins the *De E apud Delphos* with the assertion that the prominence of the letter was not due to *tyche*. Central to the thesis of *De Pythiae oraculis* is a debate over the Epicurean position that portents are the result of *tyche* (397f-399f). The occasion for the essay *De sera numinis vindicta* is the dismay felt by Plutarch's friends after hearing an Epicurean argue the case for *tyche* very convincingly; Plutarch must demonstrate that the delay in divine justice is actually a proof of providence, not the opposite (548c-549b).[20] The introductory speaker in *De genio Socratis* asserts the independence of *arete* from *tyche* (575b-d). The Pythagorean speakers who follow Archedamos argue that the culprits who unlawfully exhumed the remains of Alcmena were punished by *to daimonion*; they are most eager to demonstrate that the fate of these men had nothing to do with *to automaton*.

There is, then, a dichotomy between Plutarch's historical writing and his philosophical works over *tyche*. Probably what happened was that without his knowing it his philosophical speculation simply did not fit the hard realities of history as he came to examine it ever more closely. According to his philosophy, providence somehow or other directed all important human events, and for this reason *tyche* could not run along independent of the divine power. Moreover, his ethical principles demanded an independence of *arete* from *tyche*. Yet, he could not bury his head in the sand. When it was raised, he saw how numerous scoundrels had risen to glory and power on the heels of *tyche*, and how many admirable people and states were shunted aside or done to death in some mysterious association of coincidences. Most important

---

[20] There is a textual difficulty here. Scholars seem divided over whether one should read Ἐπίκουρος or Ἐπικούρειος for the name of the person who presents these views. Since in *De facie* 928e a man named Ἀριστοτέλης puts forward the Peripatetic theories, Cherniss, Loeb. *Mor.* XII, p. 6, prefers to retain the reading which would give us "Epicurus" rather than "an Epicurean."

of all, the Greeks had come to naught again and again, whereas
their barbarian patrons to the west seemed to survive every crisis.
Plutarch often indicates that the Roman greatness consisted in
their unity in the face of peril, whereas the Greeks threw away
their best hopes in the contentiousness of internecine strife, but
he still could not rule out the twists of *tyche* and her treachery
toward the Greeks.

His attitude, therefore, is consistent only in that it is constantly
unresolved. There are numerous assertions to the contrary in the
hope that the reader will see the hand of providence. Yet *tyche*
ultimately seems to decide the fate of both Rome and Greece. An
example of this is the end of the Republic on the battlefield of
Philippi. Throughout the account of this event in *Brutus* (37-51),
tyche seems to be haunting the heels of the conspirators. Just
on the eve of the battle, news comes to their enemies that Brutus'
navy has won a great naval victory that would virtually prevent
all supplies coming to Octavius' camp. Yet, in Plutarch's words:
"*tyche* kept this knowledge from Brutus and Cassius, and if they
had known, they would surely have never resolved upon battle,
for they were well provisioned and in a secure position, whereas the
enemy were encamped in the marshes, and it was now getting
colder and more unbearable for them". Brutus never learns of
his *eutychia* until 20 days after. But this is subordinated to a
higher cause, "as it would seem" since one man rule (*monarchia*)
being necessary, rather than that of the many, God decided to
remove from the scene the only person who stood in the way.
When a deserter informs Brutus of the victory, he refuses to
believe him (47). When the battle does commence, they barely
miss slaying Octavius when his camp is taken; and later Cassius
commits suicide thinking Brutus has also suffered a setback.
Plutarch attempts to subordinate these incidents to providence,
saying that *tyche* kept back the knowledge of Brutus' naval victory,
but in the same breath adding that monarchy was necessary and
Brutus was the last obstacle to its inauguration (47). In the second
chapter of the syncrisis (55) he even goes farther in his assertion
that the end of the Republic was something fostered by the gods:
Caesar is "a good and gentle physician sent by the *daimon*" —
which here, unusually for Plutarch, is used to mean the divinity.
But Plutarch's attempt to convince us that the inception of the
Empire was an act of divine providence is not entirely compelling,

and in doing so he is forced to stress rather than underplay the role of *tyche*. An Epicurean could equally assert that these coincidences prove just the opposite.

The statement in *Brutus* about the inevitability of the Empire and the apparent favor given to its inception by the gods finds an echo in *Pompey*. Chapter 74 and the beginning of 75 include a discussion over Pompey's ailing *tyche*, between Pompey and his unfortunate young wife, Cornelia. Plutarch then relates that the philosopher Cratippos came down to see Pompey who at this time was staying just outside Mytilene. When Pompey began to complain about providence, Cratippos humored him and tried to encourage him rather than engage him in an argument at this inappropriate moment. However, Plutarch adds that Cratippos might have pointed out to Pompey that the political mismanagement of the Republic demonstrated that the state needed *monarchia* but that there was no evidence Pompey would have had more dexterity in his use of *tyche* than Caesar. The passage ends with an enigmatic statement which some editors and translators understand as "such matters should be left to the gods," while others understand it as "such divine matters should be left for discussion elsewhere." It is also uncertain whether the phrase is meant to go within or after the hypothetical speech of Cratippos.[21] At any rate, the *Brutus* and *Pompey* passages would seem to indicate a belief on Plutarch's part in the inevitability of the Empire and the providential inception of it, which were marked by the mysterious operations of *tyche*.

---

[21] The Greek reads: ἀλλὰ ταῦτα μὲν ἐατέον ὥσπερ ἔχει τὰ τῶν θεῶν. Perrin, Loeb, *Lives* V, p. 313, points to the difficulty imposed by the phrase: "Sintenis² follows Amyot in including this last sentence with the words supposed to be spoken by Cratippos: 'But these matters must be left to the will of the gods'." Perrin himself, more convincingly, leaves the line outside the hypothetical speech of Cratippos ("But this matter of the divine ordering of events must be left without further discussion"). Cratippos was a Peripatetic philosopher of Pergamon whose distinction seems to have outpaced his originality since we know nothing of his philosophy. Our only knowledge of him in fact comes from Cicero, who honored him highly, presented him with Roman citizenship, and put his son into his school at Athens—with the advice that he had an exceptional privilege in being able to attend his lectures. The son, however, seems to have become interested in less abstract things (*De off.* 1.1, 3.2; *Brut.* 250). See also C. Schneider *Kulturgeschichte des Hellenismus* I (Munich: 1967), p. 964, who sees Cratippos as an important link between Hellenistic culture and Roman education, and K. Büchner, *Cicero* (Heidelberg: 1964), p. 432. He is mentioned by Plutarch elsewhere in the *Lives* in *Cic.* 24 and *Brut.* 24.

The tension which exists in the *Lives* between Plutarch's philosophical repugnance to the glorification of *tyche* and his historical tendency to allow it a major role is evident in his judgments on Crassus' Parthian debacle. After Crassus' first defeat, which still leaves him with a large part of his army intact, Crassus utters a speech which undoubtedly has been composed for the occasion by Plutarch. He is generally loath to foist speeches upon his heroes, but on this occasion Crassus comforts his troops by telling them that they should not be discouraged at the terrible hour which they are now experiencing because he alone was responsible for it; they are to take comfort in the fact that the great *tyche* and glory of the Romans is still in their possession. But he reminds them that the Romans rose to greatness by the patient acceptance of suffering in the midst of reverses, not only through the aid of a beneficent *tyche* (*Crassus* 26). The speech gives the principal lines of Plutarch's attitude toward the rise of Rome: patient acceptance and unity under adversity, joined to a benevolent *tyche*. In the next chapter Crassus cowers on the ground during the night while covering his face with his cloak so as not to reveal it to his soldiers. Plutarch attacks the mistaken impression that Crassus was a victim of an unjust *tyche*, claiming that in fact Crassus was simply a victim of his own foolish ambition. Plutarch is thus faithful to his general principle that moral degeneracy or virtue constitute the most powerful forces for failure or success. However, if he had left it at that, we might absolve him from the superstitious belief in *tyche* which he shows elsewhere. But in the syncrisis (5) he expresses his profound amazement that even Crassus with all his greed and stupidity could sink the high flying Roman *eutychia*.

The powerless struggle of the Greeks to overcome an unjust *tyche* can be detected in a number of passages, and it seems worth our efforts to look into these. However, it would be misleading not to indicate that the blame for human failing is primarily the lack of *arete*. Therefore, it seems best to commence with a passage of this type. In *Flamininus* 11, after Philip has been defeated by Flamininus at Cynoscephalai, there is a joyous description of the declaration of liberty for the Greeks at the Isthmian games. On this night, as Flamininus is surrounded by well-wishers toasting his success or thanking him for his prodigality, he expounds what undoubtedly is Plutarch's well-considered conclusion about the causes for the decline of Greece and the meteoric ascendancy of Rome. *Flamininus* lays the blame not on the injustices of a callous *tyche* but on the eternal contentiousness of the Greeks, which led to the indiscriminate slaughter of their best generals on the fields of Hellas and constantly betrayed their best interests:

> And here, their pleasure naturally increasing, they were moved to reason and discourse about Greece, saying that although she had waged many wars for the sake of her freedom, she had not yet obtained a more secure or more delightful exercise of it than now when others had striven in her behalf, and she herself, almost without a drop of blood or a pang of grief, had borne away the fairest and most enviable of prizes. Verily, they would say, valour and wisdom are rare things among men, but the rarest of the blessings is the just man. For men like Agesilaus, or Lysander, or Nicias or Alcibiades could indeed conduct wars well, and knew how to be victorious and commanders in battles by land and sea, but they would not use their successes so as to win legitimate favour and promote the right. Indeed, if one excepts the action at Marathon, the sea-fight off Salamis, Plataea, Thermopylae, and the achievements of Cimon at the Eurymedon and about Cyprus, Greece has fought all her battles to bring servitude upon herself, and every one of her trophies stands as a memorial of her own calamity and disgrace, since she owed her overthrow chiefly to the baseness and contentiousness of her leaders. Whereas men of another race, who were thought to have only slight sparks and insignificant traces of a common remote ancestry, and from whom it was astonishing that any helpful word or purpose should be vouchsafed to Greece—these men underwent the greatest perils and hardships in order to rescue Greece and set her free from cruel despots and tyrants. (Perrin, Loeb, *Lives* X, pp. 353-55).

A similar sentiment appears in *Agesilaus* 15 where Plutarch castigates the internecine strife of the Greeks which recalled Agesilaus from Persia just as "*tyche* was flying high," only to squander the lives of more great generals on the battlefields of Greece.

However, even the *Agesilaus* passage does not omit *tyche* altogether, and the importance of *tyche* is apparently the deciding factor in a number of other passages in the *Lives*. In chapters 11, 17, and 26 of *Nicias*, the failure of the Athenian expedition to Sicily is attributed in no small part to *tyche*. In chapter 17, alluding to the numerous victories of the Athenians against the Syracusans until their ultimate defeat, Plutarch cites a verse of Euripides that the Athenians were successful eight times until the gods turned against them:

οἵδε Συρακυσίους ὀκτὼ νίκας ἐκράτησαν.
ἄνδρες ὅτ᾽ ἦν τὰ θεῶν ἐξ ἴσου ἀμφοτέροις

Plutarch claims that it was not only eight times but many more, and then adds to Euripides' statement about the gods' turning against the Athenians, "or *tyche*" (πρὶν ἐκ θεῶν ὄντως ἢ τύχης ἀντίστασίν τινα γενέσθαι). And in the syncrisis (5), where he is setting Nicias off against Crassus, he complains that Crassus had all the benefit of the great Roman *tyche* but squandered it, whereas Nicias had to do his best with the meager Greek *tyche* at his disposal.

An even more fatalistic view of the Greek *tyche* is apparent in *Philopoimen, Phocion, Cicero*, and *Demosthenes*. In *Philopoimen* 17, while commenting on the collapse of the Achaean league, Plutarch notes that the Roman *tyche*—which here in the style of *De fortuna Romanorum* he designates as *daimon*—seemed to be ever increasing its momentum (ἡ δ᾽ ἰσχὺς ἐπὶ πάντα πολλὴ μετὰ τοῦ δαίμονος ἐχώρει) while the *tyche* of the Greeks was gradually eliminating that country from any serious role in history (τὸ τέλος ἐγγὺς ἦν εἰς ὃ τὴν τύχην ἔδει περιφερομένην ἐξικέσθαι).[22] The best that Philopoimen could do was to struggle bravely, like a good steersman, against an adverse tide. A few lines later when a friend asks him to defect to the Romans, Philopoimen asks him bitterly why he is so eager to see "the fated end of Greece." At the beginning of the *Life of Phocion*, Plutarch apologizes for Phocion on the basis that the *tychai* of Greece rendered his *arete* obscure. At the end of the *Life* (38) he compares the death of Phocion to that of Socrates "since the fault, and *dystychia* of the city were the same in both cases." In *Cicero* 4, Cicero's teacher Apollonios laments the *tyche* of Greece which had permitted her eloquence to pass to Rome.

---

[22] Plutarch sometimes writes as though he believes in the cyclic theory of history, but he probably is not to be taken too literally. In *Brut.* 31, describing the fate of the Xanthians under the siege by Brutus, he writes εἱμαρμένην περίοδον διαφθορᾶς ἀποδιδόντες τὴν τῶν προγόνων ἀνενεώσαντο τῇ τόλμῃ τύχην. This refers to their similar self-destruction on the approach of the Persians in Herod. 1.176. In the introduction to *Sertorius* Plutarch attempts to explain how it is that several great generals in history were one-eyed. Since the examples of coincidences which he gives are rather puerile, we must give Plutarch the benefit of the doubt, and presume that he is more interested in literary dressing than pure philosophical speculation; he claims that matter and time are infinite and *tyche*, which is constantly flowing now one way now another, can work upon such matter to produce similar results.

Such a statement is undoubtedly trivial, but there are others, to which we must attach greater significance. Among these would be Plutarch's comment on the *tyche* of the Greeks before the battle of Thermodon in *Demosthenes* 19. Here he reflects that some "daimonic *tyche*" was about to extinguish the flame of Greek liberty. Depending upon which reading of the manuscripts one takes, this *tyche* is either an alternative to, or interwoven with the cyclic theory of history: τύχη δέ τις ὡς ἔοικε δαιμόνιος ἢ περιφορά (Ziegler) πραγμάτων εἰς ἐκεῖνο καιροῦ συμπεραίνουσα τὴν ἐλευθερίαν τῆς Ἑλλάδος (Some mss. give ἐν περιφορᾷ).[23] Virtue would have little to do with the fall of the Greeks at this point in their history. One cannot help associating such sentiments with that which concludes *De fortuna Romanorum* (326a-c): Alexander the Great did not conquer the entire world because *tyche* removed him from this life while he was still young and had not completed all his designs; it would have been inevitable that Rome would have fallen under Greek sway; Alexander would surely have turned westward against Rome, and at that date the city would have been in no position to put up successful resistance against him.[24]

---

[23] Soury, *La Démonologie*, p. 150, has no trouble snuffing a *daimon* out of this passage and constructing a whole philosophy of history from it ("La démonologie appliquée aux Vies nous conduit donc, nous le voyons surtout ici à une philosophie de l'histoire en raccourci"). With the exception of the very special *De E* 394c, it is difficult to prove that Plutarch is using *daimonios* to mean "of the *daimones*" rather than "divine" or "mysterious." The use of *daimonios* to describe *tyche* can be seen already in Aristotle: εἰσὶ δέ τινες οἷς δόκει εἶναι μὲν αἰτία ἡ τύχη ἄδηλος δὲ ἀνθρωπίνη διανοίᾳ ὡς θεῖόν τι οὖσα καὶ δαιμονιώτερον (*Phys.* 2. 198b). P. Merlan, "Greek Philosophy from Plato to Plotinus," *Cambridge History of Later Greek and Early Medieval Philosophy*, p. 34, n. 1, insists that the word *daimonios* means "full of demons" in *De div. per somn.* 463b 12-15; but in a passage on divination one must always be ready to sense allegory, even if one is willing to take *daimonios* as "full of demons" and not "divine," since from the time of Plato's *Symposium daimones* are associated with divination. Whether one is to take these literally or symbolically is another question. One of the sceptics is Dodds, *The Greeks and the Irrational*, p. 134, n. 4: "I cannot agree with Boyancé (*Culte des Muses*, 192) that when Aristotle calls dreams *daimonia* he is thinking of the Pythagorean (? post-Aristotelian) doctrine that they are caused by *daimones* in the air (see n. 53). And Boyancé is certainly wrong in claiming Aristotle as an unqualified believer in mantic dreams."

[24] E. H. Carr, *What is History* (London: 1961), p. 99, n. 2, mentions Plutarch's essay as an example of "might-have-been" history. Since one of the major reasons for writing the *Lives* was to prove to the Romans that the Greeks had generals and statesmen equal to theirs, it is difficult to accept Hamilton's view (*Alexander*, p. 31) that Plutarch did not seriously think that Alexander with better *tyche* might have changed the course of history.

Having discussed some of the philosophy behind the use of *tyche* in the *Lives*, we can now turn to the actual application of it in particular *Lives*. There are several which are especially affected by the *tyche* theme, and one might justifiably ask why this is so. Since relative chronology does not exercise much of a role, Plutarch is either more influenced by his sources than he ought to have been, or he was genuinely intrigued by the role that *tyche* played and felt no harm could be done by dramatizing it. Among such *Lives* are *Sulla*, *Aemilius-Timoleon*, and *Demetrios*.

Sulla is portrayed as a darling of *tyche* in *De fortuna Romanorum* (318c-d), and this view is not contradicted in the *Life* of the general. Plutarch records the monument Sulla had erected at his hometown, Chaironeia, in which his *tyche* was loudly proclaimed — something which may have left a youthful impression on him. He may have been influenced through friendship for Sextius Sulla of Carthage who may have had a real or imagined relationship to Sulla, may have been overwhelmed by the testinomy of Sulla's own *Memoirs*, or may simply not have thought out the *Life* very well. At any rate, where we would expect the theme of power corrupting followed by lurid descriptions of the miserable end of the hero, we find *tyche* triumphant to the end. Plutarch does give us a vivid, baroque description of his death in which Sulla surrounded by the partners of his dissolution becomes the victim of a horrible disease: night and day his companions cannot remove the worms which issue from his body. But retribution is not underscored, and he is fortunate to the end, for the wind comes at the proper time to permit the hero to pass away in a blaze of glory. Plutarch was not lacking in precedent if he wanted a retribution life. "Crimen deorum erat Sulla felix," writes Seneca (*Consolatio ad Marciam* 12.6) and others asked how one who died such a horrible death could be counted *felix* (Pliny, *Natural History* 7. 138).

In chapter six we have a long discourse on *tyche* in which Sulla contrasts himself with Timotheos, the son of Conon of Athens, who was punished by *to daimonion* for failing to attribute his triumphs to *tyche*.[25] The story of Timotheos might be an addition of

---

[25] In the passage Sulla, who continually praises his *tyche*, is contrasted with Timotheos, the son of Conon of Athens. According to the story, Timotheos reacted in anger to his enemies who asserted that all his victories were due to *tyche* and who even went so far as to have a painting commissioned in which he was portrayed as sleeping while *tyche* swept cities into a net for him; after his next victory he proclaimed that surely *tyche* had no part

Plutarch who includes it in *Regum et imperatorum apophthegmata*
187c, but as an example of a clever retort to one's enemies. However, Nepos had written a life of him.[26] In the *De fortuna Romanorum*

in that. Plutarch adds that "it was said that, after this, *to daimonion* punished Timotheos by depriving him of all further success, and that he was
eventually driven from the city." Sulla's *Memoirs* are also mentioned in
An. sen. resp. 786 d-e, where they are responsible for the information that
Sulla was so excited on entering Rome that he could not sleep. The story
of Timotheos seems to be Plutarch's addition. It is mentioned in *Reg. et
imper.* 187c but with a slightly different emphasis; Timotheos says that
if he captures such cities when asleep, what will he do when awake. In
De Herod. malign. 856b, Plutarch censures historians for slander, "such
as those who slandered Timotheos by attributing all his victories to *tyche.*"
This would seem to represent a different tradition, but Plutarch does frequently alter the meaning of an example to suit his context.

Unfortunately Flacelière has little to say about Sulla's use of *Epaphroditos*
for *Felix*, when dealing with Greeks. The matter puzzled the ancients
(cf. Appian, *B.C.* 1. 452). K. Latte, *Römische Religionsgeschichte* (Munich:
1960/1967), pp. 187-188 and 279-280, sees Sulla's *tyche* as an internal
force emanating from within him and expressing the guidance of the divine
powers—which Latte takes to be a new development of the personal and
individual in Roman religion: Venus, the symbol of grace or favor of the
gods is closely related to *fortuna* in war, the proof of that favor. He believes
there are missing links but that the Hellenistic concept of Tyche was important. Venus, the patroness of Pompeii—Sulla's foundation—was represented there with the turret crown and steering oar made famous by the
Tyche of Antioch (so her picture from the Via Abbondanza: M. H. Swindler,
AJA, 27 (1923), 302. This Venus Felix differed from the Aphrodite of
Aphrodisias, a statue of the Artemis type, which he also erected. But one
should note that Tyche was also identified with this type of Artemis (cf.
G. Herzog-Hauser, "Tyche," *RE*, Hlbd. 14, p. 1686. The representation of
Venus in the elephant chariot at Pompeii dates from the last years of Nero.
There is another interesting connection which has not been explored. With
one exception Tyche does not appear on Attic vases, but here, an Attic
lekythos, she is one of the companions of Aphrodite, and thus appropriately
Epaphrodite (See G. Körte, *Arch. Ztg.*, 37 (1879), 95), and Apelles had
painted a picture in this style with Tyche accompanying Aphrodite (Herzog-
Hauser, p. 1688). One might also ask whether Sulla's "Bellona, Ma, Selene"
statue, brought back from the Orient, might not also be identified with
Tyche through the Artemis connection.

[26] Since the story of Timotheos is treated differently in *De Herod. malign.*
856b, one might ask why. In the 19th Century many scholars regarded
the work as spurious, but it is accepted by modern scholars as genuine.
Yet, there are some more puzzling divergences. At 855d Plutarch criticizes
Ephoros for reporting that Pausanias tried to involve Themistocles in
treachery; but in *Them.* 22 Plutarch follows this version of Ephoros. At
856b he criticizes those who attributed insincere motives to Thebe in the
assassination of her husband Alexander; but in *Pel.* 35 her motives are
not pure, and the murder is performed with a touch of sadism. At 871c he
criticizes Herodotos for accusing Themistocles of taking bribes at Salamis;
but in *Them.* 21 Plutarch not only accepts the charge as true, but expands

Plutarch attributes to Sulla rather ironic lines from the *Oidipous Tyrannos* (ἐγὼ δ᾽ ἐμαυτὸν παῖδα τῆς τύχης νέμω. 1080). But in both the essay and the life he strangely omits any mention to the great shrine of Fortuna Primigenia built on the ruins of Praeneste. This is odd in view of the fact that Plutarch gave some attention to this siege in the *Life* and presumably had spent quite a bit of time in Rome. It is no coincidence that the passage contains some of Plutarch's most extravagant praise of *tyche*.

The parallel *Lives, Aemilius-Timoleon* are also marked for the emphasis which is put upon *tyche*. *Tyche* is mentioned prominently in *Aemilius* 2, 10, 12, and 24, and particularly in 26 and 27 where Aemilius expresses the very superstitious fear that his victories will stir up the resentment of *tyche*. When his two sons die at the moment of his triumph, he does in fact attribute it to the retribution of this force and offers thanks that nothing more serious has happened. It is possible that Plutarch was inclined to accept the story because it fits in with his own desire to combat the archaic view that success stirs up the jealousy of the divinity. *Tyche* takes the onus off God. However, the mutability of *tyche* undoubtedly crept into the *Life* through the influence of Polybios, who at 29.21 in his history introduces the fall of the Macedonian king Perseus, over whom Aemilius triumphs, as an astounding work of *tyche*. He refers the reader to a book of Demetrios of Phaleron on *tyche* which was supposed to have predicted the fall of the Macedonian empire. Apparently Polybios expected his readers to be just as unimpressed as we are, so he adds that Demetrios predicted the fall just at the moment when the Macedonians had conquered the world, and no one would ever have dreamed that their empire would collapse. For Polybios it was a divine utterance

upon it. At 871c-d Herodotos is accused of slander for giving the first prize at Salamis to the Aiginetans rather than to the Athenians; but in *Them.* 17 Plutarch does the same. At 855c he praises Thucydides for overlooking Cleon's faults; but in *Nic.* 7-9 Plutarch goes to all lengths in ridiculing and degrading Cleon. Less telling is his description of the Egyptian myths as worthless stories at 857d, though in *De Iside et Osiride* and elsewhere he takes them seriously as containing certain rays of truth. Ziegler, pp. 234-35, not only supports the authenticity of the work, but treats it as a mature work. It seems very difficult indeed to explain the inconsistencies if it were written at the same time as the *Lives*. H. Homeyer, "Zu Plutarchs De malignitate Herodoti," *Klio*, 49 (1967) 181-187 sees the essay as part of traditional literary controversy. Recently A. Podlecki, *Themistocles* (Toronto: 1975), p. 69, n. 7 has raised the question of authenticity.

(ὥσανει θείῳ τινὶ στόματι περὶ τοῦ μέλλοντος ἀποπεφοίβακεν), and worthy of the most serious attention.[27] The parallel, *Timoleon*, is also filled with *tyche*, particularly in chapter 14 on the mutability of *tyche* and in chapter 16, where Timoleon is saved from an assassin when the latter is recognized by a personal enemy and killed on the spot. Here *tyche* in the eyes of those who marvel at it seems to be superior even to providence as it takes elements totally disparate and weaves them together in mysterious ways to achieve the desired and unexpected result. *Tyche* also saves the Corinthians from the Carthaginians as Timoleon attempts to cross into Sicily (20); it crowns Timoleon's efforts with success (21); he dedicates an altar to Automatia and his house to the Hieros Daimon (37);[28] and the *Life* closes in old age with the assertion that Timoleon's blindness was an hereditary ailment, not something attributable to *tyche*.[29] Some

[27] The extant parallel sources seem split over attributing retribution to *to daimonion* or *tyche*. Appian, *Mac.* 19, and Zonaras, 9.24, speak of the nemesis of *to daimonion*. However, Valerius Maximus, 5.10, speaks of *fortuna*; Diodoros, 30.23, mentions *tyche*; and such is the account of Livy, 45.4, in which Perseus is an example of the *casus humanus* or *sors humana* which is subject to *fortuna*. The account of Perseus in *Reg. et imper.* 198b is somewhat different since Perseus cuts a nobler figure: he spurns the idea of walking in the triumph, and does not cringe and complain about his *tyche* as in *Aemilius*. There is a hint of a nobler Perseus in *Aem.* 34 where his friends seem to have the highest regard for him as he walks in Aemilius' triumph, and in *Aem.* 37 where Plutarch gives alternate versions of his death, in one of which he starves himself. The friendlier version may be due to Poseidonios who is cited in chapter 18 as one of the sources of the *Life*, and who in 19 is said to have written a history of Perseus in several books. Here Plutarch, after giving the version of Polybios in which Perseus is a distasteful coward who flees the battleground, adds that of Poseidonios in which Perseus had received such a bad wound just before that his friends tried to keep him from entering the battle, but even so rode forth without armor, and having received a serious glancing blow which ripped off his clothes, was forced to retire. In general Plutarch follows the hostile source, probably Polybios, in which Perseus is portrayed as an avaricious scoundrel. Plutarch's text is remarkably close to that of Livy. See Flacelière, *Vies* IV, pp. 59-65, who sees Plutarch using Polybios while keeping an eye on Poseidonios.

[28] Diodoros, 31.10, also cites Demetrios at this point. H. D. Westlake, "The Sources of Plutarch's Timoleon," *CQ*, 32 (1938), 67 ff, on a guess attributes the digression to the influence of Clearchos. Plutarch was well acquainted with the life and work of Demetrios of Phaleron. Cf. *Demos.* 9 and 11, *Cam.* 1 and 27, *Lyc.* 23, *Sol.* 23, *Arist.* 1 (where he treats of Demetrios at some length), 5, and 27; and details of Demetrios' life are given in *Demet.* 8, 10, and *Phoc.* 35.

[29] Wilamowitz, *Der Glaube* II, p. 304, n. 2, refused to accept this reading, which appears in the parallel passage in *De laud. ips.* 542e as "Agathos

have thought that Plutarch was greatly influenced by the Sicilian
historian, Timaios of Tauromenion.[30] But it seems doubtful that
Timaios was inclined to attribute everything to *tyche*. In *Dion* 36
Plutarch even castigates Timaios for reviling Philistos, Dionysios'
general, when Timaios should have seen that *tyche* was to blame
for his misfortune.[31]

Daimon." However, Ziegler, in the Teubner text of the *Life*, treats "Hieros
Daimon" as correct. In *Praec. ger. reipub.* 816e, the shrine to Automatia
is mentioned but not the dedication to the Hieros Daimon. In this essay
Timoleon's dedication is treated not as a sincere expression of religious
belief, but as a political expedient to escape the envy of his rivals.

[30] Both the use of Timaios as a source for the *Life*, and the religious
beliefs of Timaios himself are hotly disputed by modern scholars. M. J.
Fontana, "Fortuna di Timoleonte, Rassegna delle fonti litterarie," *Kokalos*,
4 (1958), 323, concluded that Timaios was chiefly responsible for Plutarch's
portrait of Timoleon. Others are more sceptical. Cf. T. S. Brown, *Timaeus
of Tauromenium* (Berkely: 1958) and "Timaeus and Diodorus' 11th Book,"
AJP, 73 (1952), 337 ff.; N. G. Hammond, "The Sources of Diodorus Siculus,"
CQ, 32 (1938), 148 ff.; and H. D. Westlake, "The Sources of Plutarch's
Timoleon," *CQ*, 32 (1938), 67 ff. Hammond is particularly critical of Laqueur's
article for Pauly "Timaios," *RE* 6a (1936), pp. 1076-1203; and Brown
argues that we cannot be sure that we have even one direct quotation
from Timaios. As far as Timaios' religious views go, scholars are also split.
Gomme, *Commentary on Thucydides* I, p. 82, and Bury, *Ancient Greek
Historians*, p. 169, argued that Timaios was principally interested in divine
retribution, and this seems to be the viewpoint of Laqueur, p. 1191, who
attacks the view of Reuss, *Die Bedeutung der Tyche* (Constance: 1880),
p. 8, that Timaios exalted *tyche*. Polybios, 12.24, castigates Timaios for
being full of "womanish superstition," but the fragments we possess do not
indicate that he was any more superstitious than other historians of the
time. Nor do the fragments indicate that he was preoccupied with *tyche*.
Moreover, where Diodoros and Plutarch are both supposed to be following
Timaios, Diodoros has little to say about *tyche*. Polybios' testimony about
Timaios' belief in omens and dreams at 12.12 and 12.24 seems contradictory:
in the first passage Timaios is blamed for criticizing Callisthenes, who had
incorporated the portentous activity of ravens and many dreams into his
history; but in the second Polybios accuses Timaios of writing in this way.
Flacelière, *Vies* IV, pp. 3-15, believes that Timaios' laudatory account is
responsible for the strangely hagiographic nature of this life with its great
stress on omens, portents, and *tyche*,—treated as synonomous with providence. However, Timoleon's erection of a shrine to *Tyche* and *To Automaton*
suggests that at least he thought of it as different from providence. K.
Meister, "Die sizilische Expedition der Athener bei Timaios," *Gymnasium*,
77 (1970), 508-17, feels that Plutarch's criticism of Timaios is justified.

[31] It does not seem possible to use *Dion* as proof that Timaios—who
was presumably the major source for parts of this *Life*—exalted *tyche*.
In 26 *tyche* is responsible for a wolf stealing an important message for
Dionysios which had been left unguarded in the messenger's lunch sack;
in 29 Dion stands on a sundial to harrange a crowd, "thus indicating a speedy
change of *tyche* to come;" and in 50 Plutarch says that success in war

We can hardly help agreeing with Plutarch that the life of Demetrios was one in which *tyche* often exhilarated or disenchanted this great monarchial nuisance. Demetrios had already associated with *tyche* in *De Alexandri magni fortuna* 338a (Δημήτριος δὲ ᾧ τῆς 'Αλεξάνδρου δυνάμεως ἡ τύχη σμικρὸν ἀποσπάσασα προσέθηκε . . .).[32]

However, Demetrios is one with his parallel degenerate, Antony, and is to be portrayed—as Plutarch states in the introduction to the two *Lives*—as a powerful nature which is subject to powerful vice if it should fall. In the final chapter of the *Life of Demetrios*, Plutarch indicates that in fact *tyche* does not really do such persons much good anyway since they only use it to feed the fires of their lust and avarice.

Another theme which is prominent in the *Lives* is the struggle between *arete* and *tyche*. In general, Plutarch seems to favor some combination of the two as necessary elements in the acquisition of greatness, but his expressions vary. In *Lucullus* 33, the hero's *tyche* is a more important factor in the victory over Mithridates than the military superiority of the Roman army. However, in *Pelopidas* 25, Pelopidas' victory is due to *arete* and *tyche*, and in *Timoleon* 36 Plutarch puts this view in a neat phrase (ἀρετὴ εὐτυχοῦσα). In *Pompey* 50, after noting Pompey's reception of the grain commission and his famous saying "navigare necesse est, vivere non est," Pompey's success is attributed to his courage attended by *eutychia*.

Some sort of a struggle seems to have been going on in Plutarch's mind over this idea. It seems that in the end he decided that the virtue of the philosophers is inaccessible to the mortals who grace the pages of his *bioi*. In *An vitiositas ad infelicitatem sufficiat*— which seems to be an early essay—we get the stolid intellectual

must always be shared with *tyche*. However, this is not convincing proof that Timaios—if he is the source for these passages—was a *tyche* historian. Even wider from the mark was Busolt (*Hermes*, 34 (1899), 280-297, who claimed that the use of *to daimonion* was "echt timaisch," p. 296, and attempted to use this word as a touchstone for Timaean passages. *To daimonion*, however, is one of Plutarch's favorite words for retribution or revelation passages; see ch. XII, note 13 for texts.

[32] This influence of the historical sources is evident from Diodoros' whole approach to the Diadochoi, one in which he never ceases marvelling at the *tyche* of these monarchs: ἀγαθὴ γὰρ ἡ τύχη τοὺς μέγα φρονοῦντας παραδόξως σφῆλαι καὶ διδάξαι μηδὲν ἄγαν κατελπίζειν (15.33). Polybios lets *tyche* play a prominent role, especially in the early history of Rome and introduces Scipio Africanus as "a great instrument of *tyche*" (2.2.).

doctrine: the philosophic soul is untouched by *tyche*; if a soul is
affected by *tyche* it must have within itself "some festering wound
of its own" (499f).[33] In *De tranquillitate animi* (475d-476a) *tyche*
is conceived of as touching only the top of what we would call
an iceberg. Plutarch uses a different terminology: "*physis* contains
something out of the reach of *tyche*, and the corruptible and per-
ishable part is very small; *tyche* can bring sickness, poverty, or
disgrace, but it cannot make the good valiant, or the high-souled
man base or cowardly, mean, ignoble, or envious, nor can it deprive
one of tranquility." This is followed by the somewhat mysterious
statement that the harbor is always near at hand and we can
swim from our body as from a leaky boat.[34] The passage thus makes
concessions to the experience of real men; their virtue is not impreg-
nable to *tyche* in every respect.

   Modern biographers like to indicate the development of character
and to discover the internal stresses responsible for the change or
disintegration of that character. In contrast, there was a tendency in
ancient biography to regard character as stable. Plutarch does not
escape altogether from this tendency though modern commentators probably overemphasize the static element in his character
study. The tendency to regard personality as stable and changes
as only apparent is revealed in the *Life of Aratos*—an early *Life*
if we are to trust the cross-references.[35] Here, the change in Philip's

---

   [33] Both the Stoic and Epicurean schools claimed that even on the rack
the wise man is free (DL 10.118). In *Cat. Min.* 67, Plutarch relates that
on the night of Cato's death when a Peripatetic objected to the Stoic paradox
that only the good man is free and all evil men are slaves, Cato became so
angry that the company, which realized he was planning to take his life,
became extremely depressed. Though Plutarch relates Cato's death with
great tenderness and sympathy, he does not exactly register his approval,
and he predicts that Caesar would have pardoned him.
   [34] Helmbold, Loeb, *Mor.* VI, p. 231, n.c, interprets the passage to mean
that Plutarch approves of suicide in certain cases, and alludes to "the
admiration Plutarch expresses for Demosthenes' suicide" in *Cicero and
Demosthenes* comp. 5. However, it is difficult to make all out of the *Cicero
and Demosthenes* passage that Helmbold sees in it. Perhaps a different interpretation can be given to the *De tranquillitate* passage. In *Non posse* 1103e,
Plutarch is arguing against the Epicurean idea of extinction at death, and
uses the same analogy of swimming from a leaky boat; however, here he
takes "the harbour near at hand" to be "a blessed afterlife," and there is
no suggestion of suicide. The "leaky boat" would easily suggest the frailty
of old age.
   [35] The relative chronology of the *Lives* depends to a large extent on one's
attitude toward accepting the cross-references contained within them.
J. Mewaldt, *Gnomon*, 6 (1934), 431ff., argued that they were genuine and

character appears to be nothing more than the revelation of true character which up to this time had been concealed. Lifted up by *tyche* he revealed many inordinate desires. According to Plutarch (*Aratos* 49), good fortune had laid bare the virtuous mask he had constructed; when *tyche* turned his way, all the inner hideousness of his soul revealed itself.

Yet, there are indications that Plutarch did not entirely accept the thesis that character was basically unchangeable. The *Life of Pericles*, according to Plutarch's word in the introduction, is part of the 10th set of parallel *Lives*. Here Plutarch struggles with the problem of an apparent change in Pericles' character from a rationalistic, unsuperstitious thinker to a believer in magic (*Pericles* 38). According to the story here, Pericles was suffering bitterly from the plague which eventually caused his death, and therefore, permitted the women to put an amulet around his neck. Apparently Plutarch's source was Theophrastos; for he mentions in connection with this incident that Theophrastos had raised the question in his *Ethics* whether it was possible that character is affected by fortune and by the afflictions of the body, and criticizes Pericles' conduct here. It is hard to see how the answer could be anything but yes, especially since Pericles was in Plutarch's eyes the enlightened rationalist and the walking image of Zeus (*Pericles* 6, 39). Unfortunately, he has failed to reveal more of an intimation of his own opinion here. In *Eumenes*, a work which was written after *Pericles*, we again find the revelation theory. Adversity revealed that Eumenes' character was true and not sham (*Eumenes* 9). The ending of *Tiberius and Gaius Gracchus* is more ambiguous. Noting how the mother of these men never shed a tear when she

---

that the cross-references referred to *Lives* which were published in groups at a particular time. His view was opposed by C. Stoltz, *Zur Relativen Chronologie der Parallelbiographien Plutarchs*, and he is supported by Ziegler, *Plutarchos*, pp. 262-66. More recently C. P. Jones, "Toward a Chronology of Plutarch's Works," *JRS*, 61 (1966), 61-74, has returned to Mewaldt's theory, with some modifications. In spite of the excellent work done by Jones, there are some difficulties with accepting all his conclusions. For instance there are some striking discrepancies between the interpretation given the Vestal fire in *Num*. 9 and 11, vs. that in *Cam*. 20; yet, in Jones' theory, these *Lives* were published at the same time. Moreover, Jones is forced to accept the word γέγραπται in *Num*. 9 as referring to a *Life* about to be written. Stoltz had made *Theseus-Romulus* very late, and Jones early. There are no cross-references involved here, but only a puzzling statement by Plutarch in the introduction that after traversing delineated historical material he was now embarking on the legendary.

came to relate their fate, Plutarch claims that though *tyche* can "prevail" over *arete*, it cannot take away from *arete* the patient and untroubled acceptance of evil, and he expresses his belief that the aristocratic heritage of "a noble nature, honorable birth, and good rearing" are the greatest aids to the development of this composure (*Tiberius and Gaius Gracchus* 19).

The most mysterious and difficult passage on this whole subject appears in *Sertorius* 10 where Plutarch tries to reconcile the savage manifestations of Sertorius' character at the end of his life with the reputation he had attained for mildness. There is a parallel to the *Sertorius* passage in the *Life of Sulla*. After Sulla's entry into Rome he decided to take vengeance on his enemies. In Plutarch's description of the event, Sulla orders 6000 survivors of the siege of Antemnae, who had surrendered because of Sulla's pledge of good treatment, to be executed in the Circus; as the screams of the dying reach the ears of the senators and they panic, Sulla tells them not to be disturbed since on his orders "a few wicked men were being admonished." Plutarch finds Sulla's conduct here out of accordance with his previous gentleness, which stood out in sharp contrast with the harshness of Marius throughout his life, and he is afraid it might confirm the belief that power corrupts (*Sulla* 30).

Plutarch varies his terminology when speaking about the elements of *arete*, but some help to understanding his terminology can be found in *Mulierum virtutes* 243b-d. Here he explains that *physis* is responsible for the differences in *arete* between members of the same or the opposite sex: *arete* must be shaped to fit the *ethos* and *krasis* of the body. *Physis* is thus a kind of substratum, over which *krasis* and *ethos* are overlaid. In *De virtute morali*, *ethos* is also something more superficial than *physis*: it is the result of *logos* putting limitation and order on *pathos*. In *Sertorius* 10 Plutarch reaffirms the revelation theory, but he would seem to exclude Sertorius from the realm of those lofty possessors of true virtue: Sertorius was always cruel but hid his real nature with a cloak of virtue because of the exigencies of political life; true *arete*, that which is pure and unblemished (καθαρῇ καὶ εἰλικρινής) and firmly based on *logos*, can never be turned by *tyche* into the opposite.

Such is the type of thinking we are accustomed to in Plutarch's writing, and what commentators are referring to when they speak about the staticism of his character treatment. However, as

Plutarch continues in the *Sertorius* passage he seems to develop a new understanding of human conduct which offers an alternative to the simplistic and unworkable hypothesis that one can possess undaunted philosophical virtue or be guilty of crass deception. This does not seem to be entirely consistent with the passages we have treated so far, and it seems to be a radical departure from the revelation theory, which many scholars see as his only explanation of character. Plutarch adds in the *Sertorius* passage that an escape can be made through the horns of the dilemma. Between crass vice and the pure philosophical virtue there exists a middle ground of noble but not pure virtue, and to prosperity and adversity one can add great unexpected blows of *tyche*. In such a situation one can conceive of a noble or worthy person (φύσεις καὶ προαιρέσεις χρησταί), but one who is not possessed of philosophical virtue, yielding to the enormous injustice arrayed against him and turning for the worse when great misfortunes unworthy of the man come about; in such cases it is not impossible for a nature to fit its *ethos* to the *daimon*—to give the peculiar language Plutarch uses here (τῷ δαίμονι συμμεταβαλεῖν τὸ ἦθος). This may have been what Theophrastos was driving at in his puzzled analysis of the effect of the plague on Pericles' character.

The abandonment of the philosophical idea of unshakable virtue has startling consequences for any subsequent analysis of character in the *Lives*. The advocacy of a noble, but not perfect, virtue is not a negation of the theory of *De virtute morali*; it still maintains that philosophic virtue is untouched by any *tyche* when that virtue is pure and unblemished. But it is in effect saying that the old philosophical definitions about *arete* and *tyche* are of no practical value in political biography. Plutarch has no doubt that Sertorius was a good man but suffering a change in character under the enormous blows of an unfair *tyche*, became vicious to those who had injured him.[36] We possibly have here the case of reflection

---

[36] The *Sertorius* passage is treated by D. A. Russell, "On Reading Plutarch's Lives," *Greece and Rome*, 13 (1966), 139-54, who does not seem to be entirely consistent. Following V. Cilento, *Transposizioni dell' Antico* (Milan: 1961), p. 108, and the opinion of such authorities as F. Leo, *Die Griechisch-römische Biographie*, p. 188, A. Dihle, *Studien zur Griechischen Biographie*, p. 160, D. R. Stuart, *Epochs of Greek and Roman Biography*, p. 121ff., and H. Erbse, "Plutarchs Schrift *Peri Deisidaimonia*," 400, n. 1. Russell states that Plutarch is insensible to real changes of character, but can only envisage a revelation of what previously lay hidden: thus—in Russell's view—having made up his mind about the true character of his

upon the realistic situations of those characters Plutarch tried to idealize in the *Lives* modifying the ivory towered speculation of the philosophers reflected in the *Moralia*.

A passage in the *Life of Cimon* tends to confirm this belief that Plutarch had developed a new theory. Some domestic troubles at Chaironeia undoubtedly left a deep impression on all its inhabitants. Now the passage needs a bit of background. The Roman governor had been murdered by a young man named Damon who had resisted his advances. Though the townspeople had trapped Damon in the baths, where he was murdered, they still feared reprisals from the Romans but were saved by the intercession of Lucullus. Out of gratitude they erected a realistic statue of the Roman general, which, Plutarch claims, served him as a model for his own biographical treatment. A handsome portrait, but one which does not omit those blemishes which give strength and identity to a work, is the ideal. He adds a statement that may have far-reaching consequences: we should be indulgent rather than over-critical in the assessment of great men "since human nature produces no *ethos* which is unqualifiedly good and pure" (εἰ καλὸν οὐδὲν εἰλικρινὲς οὐδ᾽ ἀναμφισβήτητον εἰς ἀρετήν, *Cimon* 2).[37] The

---

hero and indicated it in the opening chapter of a *Bios*, Plutarch proceeds to show how the traits worked themselves out in the rest of his life. Russell, p. 146, interprets the *Sertorius* passage to mean that though true and pure philosophical virtue cannot be subverted, that many good and noble natures suffer a change. But his interpretation of the *Sertorius* passage actually runs counter to the thesis sometimes seen, the static portrayal of character in Plutarch's *Lives*. Russell's interpretation of Plutarch's ethical works— that *ethos* may change but not *physis*—receives a new twist in the *Sertorius* passage. He does not mention the *Cimon* passage. One textual difficulty should be noted. Ziegler, Teubner, *Vitae* II-I, p. 265 returns to the reading of the mss., γινομένων πονηρῶν (*Sert.* 10.24) but Coraes' correction γιγνόμενον πονηρόν may be right. A. Wardman, *Plutarch's Lives*, pp. 132-37, sees Plutarch as wavering in the *Sertorius* passage, and interestingly notes Plutarch's inconsistency: when change is for the good it is change, when for the bad, revelation of true nature. Flacelière, *Vies*, VI, pp. 17-18, is also impressed by the pattern of degeneration of character through access to power (power corrupts), considering it a foundation of Plutarch's political philosophy, a heritage from Aischylos, Herodotos, and Plato. One can also see the discussion on *physis* and *ethos* in B. Bucher-Isler, *Norm und Individualität in den Biographen Plutarchs* (Bern: 1972), pp. 79-80. The passage may be influenced by a contrast in *physis/tyche* behind Philemon, fr. 95: all men are alike by *physis* but *tyche* makes them different. See Herzog-Hauser, p. 1658.

[37] The event took place, as Flacelière notes, in 88-87 B.C. while Q. Baetius Sura was setting up resistance to the first Pontic invasion. Cf. Flacelière, *Vies* VII, pp. 3 and 261-262; M. Holleaux, *Ét. d'épigr. et d' hist. gr.* I, p.

vagueness of the statement might even lead one to suspect that Plutarch gave up altogether the philosophical axiom of the wise man on the rack. However, in the context and in the light of the *Sertorius* passage, it probably referred to politicians and generals rather than to philosophic moral giants.

Not only for Plutarch alone, but also for his characters *tyche* is a tremendously important consideration. His heroes keep tab on their *tyche* much as a modern politician scrutinizes the opinion polls. When they believe it has turned against them, they hope for its return; when they think it has abandoned them ultimately, they give up the last hope and take their lives or plunge to an ignominious death. Such concern for *tyche* is particularly apparent in *Marius, Pompey,* and *Antony.* Therefore, it seems worthwhile to note how the swing of *tyche* proceeds. In all these *Lives,* with a few retrogressions, it moves steadily upward until in the end it abandons the hero. However, there are some differences. As Plutarch notes in the introductory chapter of *Marius,* Marius experienced some rather extraordinary fortunes in the course of the Civil Wars. As a matter of fact he was in and out of power far more than one might expect, at one point completely abandoned and destitute, at another back for another consulship. In 7 *tyche* introduces him into history at an opportune time; in 14 he is elected consul for the fourth time because the Romans have great confidence in his *tyche;* in 19 the order to attack is never given but through *tyche* the men make contact with the Ambrones and destroy them; in 24, 26, and 27 Marius' *tyche* saves the Romans from the fury of the Teutones. From here on his *tyche* turns against him, and Plutarch criticizes Marius for having an unbounded faith in it. In 40 it helps him escape to Africa; but the final part of the *Life* sees him deserted by it; and in the last chapters Plutarch paints him as a miserable figure gone mad in his insatiable lust for power while lamenting the *tyche* which had given him more consulships than any other Roman; and he is contrasted with Antipater of Tarsos and Plato, who praised their *daimon* and *tyche* to the end.

The upswing of Pompey's *tyche* is similar; but, unlike that of Marius, once his *tyche* has left him, it never returns. In fact in chapter 46 Plutarch is impressed with the great contrast between

---

153. Flacelière rejects the opinion of J. van Ooteghem, *L. Licinius Lucullus,* p. 37, n. 3, denying its authenticity. Bucher-Isler, *Norm und Individualität,* pp. 9-10, uses the passage as a basis for her treatment of Plutarch.

Pompey's *tyche* in the early part of his life and that in the end; he claims that if Pompey had had the good fortune to die at the middle of his life, he would have been remembered as another Alexander, but that "after this, his *dystychiai* brought irremedial harm and his *eutychiai* only helped others." At Dyrrachion, when Pompey has Caesar on the run, Caesar's *tyche* prevents Pompey from finishing off his rival (66). The *Life* winds down in 73, 74, and 75 with Pompey's discussion with his wife, and with Cratippos; Pompey hopes to the last that his *tyche* will change, but realizes that the odds are against him. It is also possible that the *daimon* which leads him on the fatal trip to Egypt is his own ill *tyche* (76).

The *tyche* of Antony is similar to that of Pompey; but, unlike Pompey, Antony seems to gain no moral good from it; it only makes him unbearable (*Antony* 17, 20, 30, 31). The change of his *tyche* is dramatized in 33 when he is told by a seer to stay away from Octavius since Antony's *daimon* and *tyche* cowers before that of his rival. In 44 a series of disasters makes him believe that he is experiencing retribution for his former glorious *tyche*, and in 65 and 67 Octavius' *tyche* is a terrible threat to the very life of Antony. In 70 Antony tries to imitate the life of Timon, the "heavy-daimoned" (βαρυδαίμων) misanthrope of Athens. Finally, as he dies, his ultimate concern for his *tyche* finds its last expression: he begs Cleopatra not to lament the last reversals of his *tyche* but to remember that he had once been the most illustrious of all men, "not ignobly conquered, a Roman by a Roman" (77).

Other heroes also lament their *tyche* as they see it hurtling them to disaster or death. As Brutus is about to commit suicide he lays the blame on *tyche*, for his country's sake, not for himself, and he prides himself in not letting his *arete* be overcome by it (*Brutus* 52). Cato also feels he has a just complaint against *tyche*. He alleges that the divinity is inconstant since when Pompey was for once on the right side and was trying to preserve his country's liberty rather than destroy it, *eutychia* deserted him (*Cato minor* 53). As Cato is about to die, he indicates that he is aware that his followers are already closely observing the course of *tyche*, but he will give them the benefit of the doubt and attribute their conduct to *ananke*; yet, if they wish him to, he will be their leader until they have tested the last *tyche* of their country (60). They in turn consider it better to die than betray Cato's *arete* which they think no *tyche* will ever be able to overcome. Cato sees that their intention is to defect, and so after quietly reading the

Phaedo he takes his life. In their darkest hours Coriolanus (*Coriolanus* 23), Alcibiades (*Alcibiades* 33), and Demetrios (*Demetrios* 45), Pyrrhos (*Pyrrhos* 22), and Crassus (*Crassus* 52) lament the *tyche* which brought them into irreparable disaster. Finally, though victorious, Eumenes complains of the bitterness of *tyche* and *ananke* which brought him into conflict with a friend in such a way that one or the other must be slain, "thus forcing him either to do or suffer the greatest of ills" (*Eumenes* 7), while Nicias' followers lament the *tyche* which gave to their leader the fate of the basest man (*Nicias* 26).

It should now be clear that Plutarch is entirely representative of much of the literature of his time in both equating *daimon* with *tyche* and in his remarkable interest in the course of *tyche*. Those scholars who have concentrated only on the word *daimon* emerging from the *Lives* have often failed to realize that what they see is only a puff of smoke screening the less dreadful *tyche*, not a Xenocratic *daimon*. It should also be clear that there is a certain ambivalence and tension in Plutarch's attitude toward *tyche* especially in the *Lives*. In his philosophical works, with the exception of the rhetorical *De fortuna Romanorum*, he consistently deprecates *tyche*, which he tends to link with the Epicurean denial of providence. However, in the *Lives* he seems to swing back and forth between admitting that *tyche* decided the course of history, and in asserting that it is no substitute for *arete*. Here, he was to some extent influenced by his sources; but all assertions to the contrary about the subordination of *tyche* to providence or the superiority of *arete* and its invulnerability to *tyche*, it is evident that for Plutarch's philosophy of history *tyche* was a very important element indeed. His complaint over that *tyche* which lifted the Romans to greatness but destroyed the Greeks is only thinly veiled. Even such great scholars as Ziegler and Flacelière have little noted how much the *Lives* depend upon the descriptions of the flow of *tyche* and of the demoralization of Plutarch's heroes when it goes awry. There even is a possibility that Plutarch's historical work—contrary to the opinion of most scholars—brought him face to face with the fact that tragedy changes character. He did not, at least toward the latter part of his biographical opus, clearly look upon character as static. Yet, whatever one holds about the effect of *tyche* on character, the dread seriousness with which both he and his heroes contemplate the ebb and flow of their fortune shows that they are all children of their time.

CHAPTER NINE

AND TO ALL THE SIGN SEEMED EVIL:
OMENS AND PORTENTS

Plutarch prided himself on his rationalism and would have been shocked if someone regarded him as superstitious. Yet, when one reads his *Lives* and even many of his *Moralia* one cannot help but feel that he reflects to an astounding degree a certain complex of popular beliefs in his day. One could cite his faith in portents, the mantic power of dreams, the veracity of oracles, and the immediate infliction of divine retribution. Plutarch's attitude toward these superstitions will be discussed in this and the next chapters. However, as we have seen in treating other religious problems in Plutarch's work, his thought is not as simple as it seems at first. As usual, he has certain criteria, different than ours, by which he judges whether a particular action or belief is superstitious or not. We will also see that the demand to dramatize his biographical sketches may be responsible for the inclusion of some material which he would have omitted if he were acting purely as an historian.

The *Lives* reveal many of those characteristics for which ancient historians have often been justly blamed, namely, the belief in omens, dreams, and oracles. An astute reader may be surprised at the stress placed on retribution for evil. What should be kept in mind, however, is that Plutarch is as much a moralist as an historian even where he is relating rather commonplace historical matter. His major interest is in illuminating the virtues or vices of a hero through the type of "insignificant" detail which he felt was often overlooked by the major historians.[1] Moreover,

---

[1] For Plutarch's purpose in writing the *Lives* see especially *Alex.* 1, *Cim.* 2, and *Per.* 2. It is one of the best covered aspects of Plutarch's work, see: F. Leo, *Die Griechisch-römische Biographie* (Leipzig: 1901), pp. 178-192; D. R. Stuart, *Epochs of Greek and Roman Biography* (Berkeley: 1928), esp. p. 121; A. Weiszäcker, *Untersuchungen über Plutarchs Biographische Technik* (Berlin: 1931); A. W. Gomme, *A Historical Commentary on Thucydides* I (Oxford: 1945),pp. 54-58; C. Theander, "Plutarch und die Geschichte," *Bull. Lund.* (1950-51), 1-86; A. Dihle, *Studien zur Griechischen Biographie* (Göttingen: 1956), pp. 57-76; H. Erbse, "Die Bedeutung der Synkrisis in den Parallelbiographien Plutarchs," *Hermes*, 84 (1956), 398-424; R. Flacelière,

Plutarch's interest as an historian is overshadowed by his philosophical and theological training. One must always remember that he was extremely conservative in his religious thought. During the later part of his life he functioned as a priest at Delphi, and at the end of it was an epimelete there.

Because of these interests, which stem from his conservative religious outlook, the *Lives* in a certain sense are case studies in some of the theories we encounter in the *Moralia*. Without even considering the whole *Moralia* output, one can think of the emphatic belief in the mantic power of dreams put into the mouth of Lamprias toward the end of *De defectu oraculorum* (432c). One can recall Plutarch's belief in portents throughout *De Pythiae oraculis*, or his sincere defense of divine retribution in this life in *De sera numinis vindicta*. We have three essays, the Pythian dialogues, which are meant as a defense and explanation of the Delphic oracle. These dialogues are especially important since it is most likely that all the *Lives* were written when Plutarch was a priest at Delphi.[2]

Plutarque, Vies I, (Paris: 1957), pp. ix-xxxi; H. Martin, Jr., "The Concept of *Praótes* in Plutarch's *Lives*," *Greek, Roman and Byzantine Studies*, 3 (1960), 65-73, and "The Character of Plutarch's Themistocles," *TAPA*, 92 (1961), 326-39; K. Ziegler, *Plutarchos* (Stuttgart: 1964), pp. 266-67; D. A. Russell, "On Reading Plutarch's Lives," *Greece and Rome*, 13 (1966), 139-54; A. J. Gossage, "Plutarch," in T. A. Dorey ed. *Latin Biography* (London: 1967), pp. 45-77; R. Flacelière, *Budé Congrès* (1968), pp. 491-98; Jones, *Plutarch and Rome*, pp. 102-109; Russell, *Plutarch*, pp. 100-116; B. Bucher-Isler, *Norm und Individualität in den Biographien Plutarchs* (Bern: 1972), pp. 9-10, 89-92. All put stress on the ethical aspect of the *Lives*. Needed is a good treatment on how they differ from modern biography. Jones is the best in relating the *Lives* to Plutarch's world and appreciating the importance of the parallel method. This aspect can be seen in A. Momigliano, *The Development of Greek Biography* (Cambridge, Mass: 1971), esp. pp. 96-99.

[2] See C. P. Jones, "Towards a Chronology of Plutarch's Works," 68-70 and 73 for the dating of the *Lives*. Jones regards most of Plutarch's literary work, including the *Lives*, as after 96 A.D. *Theseus-Romulus* and *Themistocles-Camillus* refer to *Quaestiones Romanae* which were written after Domitian's death (see 276e). *Poplicola* of *Solon-Poplicola* refers to Domitian with an hostility which indicates he must be dead. *Aemilius* 25 of *Aemilius-Timoleon* also seems to refer to Domitian as if he were dead. *Brutus* 25 of *Dion-Brutus* refers to *Qu. conv.* 693f, a passage which must have been written after 99 A.D. Jones' dating, p. 69, for *Lysander-Sulla* after 104 A.D., on the basis that it refers to the battle of Orchomenos as having taken place "almost 200 years" before, seems questionable. *Demosthenes-Cicero, Theseus-Romulus, Dion-Brutus, Aemilius-Timoleon, Agis Cleomenes-Gracchi* appear to have been written before 116 since they do not refer to Sossius Senecio, the *adressé* of the *Lives*, as proconsul, an honor which he would have received by this time. The exact date of Plutarch's priesthood at Delphi is uncertain.

Yet, this superstitious exuberance is balanced by some other considerations. Among these are his frequent notices to the reader that other accounts omitted the superstitious material he has just related, or alternate versions of the same dream or portent, and the adaptation of religious matter for the biography in question. At the same time he reveals a strong tendency to eliminate any superstitious matter which is not a direct illumination of the state of mind of his hero or others involved. Particularly when an inner struggle is at stake do we find the relation of dreams and portents.

Another aspect of Plutarch's use of supernatural material is his liberty in reshaping or adapting it. Some introductory comments can be made here about matter which will be treated in greater detail later. No matter what Plutarch believed about the apparitions of *daimones* to mortals, his literary soul could hardly have passed over in silence the supposed apparition to Brutus before his crossing over to Greece from Abydos (*Brutus* 36, *Caesar* 69), and the second apparition before the battle of Philippi (*Brutus* 48, *Caesar* 69). There is some possibility that he used the story even though it was known that it had been applied to a different person, Cassius of Parma, before the battle of Actium. It is not even inconceivable that Plutarch himself is responsible for transferring the apparition to Brutus. Similarly the responsibility for putting Caesar's dream of incest with his mother (*Caesar* 32) at the Rubicon rather than in Spain, and endowing it with different connotations seems to be Plutarch's innovation. Unfortunately we cannot usually compare Plutarch against his sources. Generally the miraculous is an addition to Polybios or Thucydides, and though Nepos wrote lives of Dion, Timoleon, Agesilaus, and other heroes in common with those of Plutarch his biographies are not only exceedingly short, but also tend to be minus those interesting vignettes which are found in Plutarch. Moreover, they almost exclude the supernatural. We have Suetonius' lives of Galba and Otho in common with the lives of the same men by Plutarch; but Suetonius' are shorter, and in any case Plutarch's lives of these men are anything but the best representatives of his biographical work. More helpful as a basis of comparison is Arrian's history of Alexander's conquest of the Persian Empire.

In *An sen. resp.* 792f he refers to himself as a priest at Delphi for "many Pythiads." An inscription erected at Delphi in 117 refers to him as priest and epimelete of the Amphictyons.

Throughout his works Plutarch indicates his belief that some divine agency is responsible for giving signs to men. Usually he assigns some indiscriminate name to it, like *to daimonion*, or *to theion*, but he also uses the words *theos* or *theoi*. The most extreme form of this belief in divination appears in *De sollertia animalium* (975a, 976c). Here, speakers who represent his views argue that not only birds, which are so often evident in divination, but even such lowly marine animals as eels, fish, and crocodiles must be gifted with intelligence since they at all times have played a role in divination. In Plutarch's view such actors could hardly act out their part unless they understood it.

A rather unusual passage, which has not been commented upon by Ziegler but attracted Flacelière, appears in *Sulla 7*. Here, after relating the portents which took place before the Civil Wars, Plutarch gives a supposed Etruscan account of soothsaying. An Etruscan of learning claims that the length of world history is eight Great Years and that in the intervals between the Great Years clear signs are given by *to daimonion*;[3] the rest of the time divination falls into disfavor because of the weakness of the signs. Since the Civil Wars initiated the beginning of a new Great Year, that is, the period of the Empire, it was possible to interpret the signs correctly. The idea appears nowhere else in the Plutarchan corpus, but behind it is certainly Plutarch's belief that the divinity does not demean itself by issuing portents for insignificant events. This principle may excuse the introduction of a rather spectacular

---

[3] The importance of the Great Year in the Etruscan account may disguise some Delphic theology. The Great Year has some connections with the Septerion festival at Delphi elsewhere in Plutarch's work. In *Qu. Graec.* 293c it is explained that the Septerion festival every eight years ritually enacted Apollo's fight with the Python, his flight to Tempe and banishment. In *De def.* 421c Cleombrotos integrates the Great Year into the Delphic legend: the mystic tells him that after slaying the Python Apollo was exiled "not for eight years but for eight cycles of the Great Year." Since Apollo is *the* God of prophecy, Plutarch may have a Delphic ace up his sleeve. Certainly the Great Year originally had nothing to do with the Roman calendar. It was supposed to be the time required for the sun, moon, and planets to reach their original position. It is believed to have a Pythagorean origin and is defined in Plato's very Pythagorean *Timaeus* (39d) where he estimates its length as around 10,000 years. It also was later identified with the time of the Stoic *ekpyrosis*. See Guthrie, *HGP* I, pp. 282, 353, 388, 458. A possibility is that it was introduced into Etruscan divination by Neopythagoreans. Flacelière, *Vies* VI, p. 226, sees strong Neopythagorean influence. Crows and rats were considered prophetic (Aelian, *V.H.* 1.11, Pliny, *N.H.* 8.82.1). Plutarch often uses crows but avoids omens with rats.

number of portents at the end of *Caesar* after the murder of the Imperator. The portents are, then, a sort of fanfare announcing the inception of great events. The most dramatic portents are in fact associated with the rise of Athens, the fall of Persia and ascendancy of Alexander, the end of Greece as a political power, the rise and murder of Caesar, the end of the conspirators, and the fall of Antony and inception of the Imperial period.

We can now take a closer look at Plutarch's technique. First of all, he is very cautious about what he will relate. The vulgar, base, or trivial is eliminated if possible. The portent is accommodated to the hero's career in such a way that it motivates his action rather than detracts from the principal flow of the narrative. As an illustration of this technique we can examine *Sulla* 7. Here Plutarch, in contrast to his usual practice, has followed the plan of Roman historians in grouping together the portents for the event, before the relation of the event itself. But unlike some of the Roman historians, he does not group them together as "portents for the year." The unusual grouping of the portents should stir the reader's curiosity, but Plutarch is not content to stop here. He subtly begins to integrate them into his narrative in such a way that they help to clarify rather than confuse the flow of events for the reader. While the senate is debating, a sparrow flies into the senate house with a grasshopper in its mouth. The symbolic meaning of this incident is immediately clarified by him: the sparrow represents the agricultural patricians; the grasshopper is a type of the urban proletariat. The struggle between Marius and Sulla can now be seen as a clash of economic and political interests. A supernatural disturbance to break up an otherwise peaceful scene is a characteristic of Plutarch's portent technique, but here the symbolic representation of the two classes through the image of the sparrow and the grasshopper is particularly apt—especially for one acquainted with Aesop's fables. We have only to compare this description with that of Appian for the same event (*BC* 1.83) to be convinced of the marked superiority of Plutarch. Appian's portents are mentioned *en bloc* without any attempt at innovation or originality, and they are far more indiscriminate and petty than those of Plutarch.

Another example of Plutarch's skillful adaptation of portents can be seen in *Marcellus* 28. Plutarch is attempting to convey the impetuosity of Marcellus, which is the tragic flaw in his character and will eventually lead to his slaughter. Burning with eagerness to meet Hannibal, Marcellus is hamstrung by the priests at Rome, who keep producing one bad omen after the other to thwart his designs; the air is ever filled with more clouds of ill-boding. The intimation of the interior struggle of Marcellus against the beneficent counsels of the divine will is conveyed by the increasing intensity of the divine intervention in the natural order of the world. Each portent seems to flow into another: lightning strikes a temple; a temple is entered by an animal; an animal utters human speech; a human is born like an animal. As though this were not enough, Plutarch exclaims that Marcellus' one dream was to see himself and the Carthaginian locked together in mortal conflict.[4] As is frequent, he goes out of his way to inform the reader that the hero was "greatly disturbed" by the portents, where other writers leave it up to the intelligence of the reader to grasp this subtlety.

A comparison with Livy reveals that Plutarch used the Livian material but exaggerated it in order to throw Marcellus' impetuosity into greater relief. The ambition of Marcellus appears in Livy 27 and 28; the portents are related in Livy 27.11. The digression on Marcellus' restlessness in Plutarch adequately reflects Livy's estimation of Marcellus' character, but Plutarch takes the liberty to write that Marcellus nightly dreamed that he was meeting Hannibal in mortal combat.

We can also see how Plutarch carefully selected from the portents which Livy relates on the approach of Hannibal in Italy (*Fabius*

---

[4] τοῦτο καὶ νύκτωρ ὄνειρον ἦν αὐτῷ καὶ μετὰ φίλους καὶ συναρχόντων ἐν βούλευμα καὶ μία πρὸς θεοὺς φωνὴ παραταττόμενον Ἀννίβαν λαβεῖν. (28.15). One can gather how Plutarch has exaggerated by comparing him with Livy: Mors Marcelli cum alioqui miserabilis fuit tum quod nec pro aetate—iam enim maior sexaginta annis erat—neque pro veteris prudentia ducis tam improvide se conlegamque et prope totam rem publicam in praeceps dederat (27.37). and: Ceterum consulem Marcellum tanta cupiditas tenebat dimicandi cum Hannibale ut numquam satis castra castris conlatu diceret (28.11). Plutarch inaccurately reproduces Livy's account of Marcellus' delay, in which the priests are afraid to dedicate the temple, not knowing what expiation should be offered *if* lightning should strike. But Marcellus manages to dedicate it anyway and hurries away (27.25).

For a general treatment of Plutarch's sources in both the Roman and Greek *Lives* consult the very balanced account by Theander, "Plutarch und die Geschichte." The problem is extremely difficult, but Theander undoubtedly has a good point in his stress on Plutarch's trips to Rome, and his desire to investigate oral tradition.

Maximus 2, Livy 22). Some of the portents are dismissed by Plutarch as "the usual fulgural portents of the Romans." The others are related because of their supposed rarity. He then gives a list which seems to mimic Livy, but in a censored version. They even are related in Livy's order with the one exception that the rain of stones follows the bloodstained wheat. Yet, there are some omissions which at first may seem curious. In the following passage, the italicized parts of Livy 22.1 are those portents which are used by Plutarch; those which are not italicized are the ones omitted:

> 8   Auge-
> bant metum prodigia ex pluribus simul locis nuntiata; in
> Sicilia militibus aliquot spicula, in Sardinia autem in muro
> circumeunti uigilias equiti scipionem quem manu tenuerit
> arsisse et litora crebris ignibus fulsisse et *scuta duo sanguine*
> 9 *sudasse*, et milites quosdam ictos fulminibus et solis orbem
> minui uisum, et *Praeneste ardentes lapides caelo cecidisse*, et
> Arpis parmas in caelo uisas pugnantemque cum luna solem,
> 10 et Capenae duas interdiu lunas ortas, et aquas Caeretes sanguine
> mixtas fluxisse fontemque ipsum Herculis cruentis manasse
> respersum maculis, et *in Antiati metentibus cruentas in corbem*
> 11 *spicas cecidisse, et Faleriis caelum findi uelut magno hiatu uisum*
> *quaque patuerit ingens lumen effulsisse*; *sortes sua sponte at-*
> *tenuatas unamque excidisse ita scriptam*: '*Mauors telum suum*
> 12 *concutit'*, et per idem tempus Romae signum Martis Appia uia
> ac simulacra luporum sudasse, et Capuae speciem caeli ardentis
> 13 fuisse lunaeque inter imbrem cadentis. Inde minoribus etiam
> dictu prodigiis fides habita: capras lanatas quibusdam factas,
> et gallinam in marem, gallum in feminam sese uertisse.

Plutarch left out the other portents because of some definite ideas about them. The fact that wheat or a crab in Sicily or the shore seemed to light up is hardly a significant factor in itself announcing a great war with Hannibal. Then the locality is in the very superstitious Sicily to begin with. One can also be little impressed with the diminution of the sun's rays here or lightning striking soldiers. He might have left in the story of shields in the sky, but the sun and moon fighting begins to get absurd. At the same time it involves all sorts of scientific problems which should have been recorded elsewhere. He probably could have left in the fountain of Hercules showing drops of blood. The statue portents at Rome are also not insignificant in themselves, since being of Mars and the wolves with the twins they would be associated with Roman destiny. The last portents mentioned are animal and celestial omens which also strain one's credulity. One might argue that certain portents are omitted for economy's sake, but this cannot be the whole reason. Plutarch's reluctance to treat celestial phenomena as portentous has been illustrated in the treatment of eclipses in his writings. We also saw that he had difficulty with statue portents (*Coriolanus* 38, *De Pythiae oraculis* 397e). The point of the debate between Lampon and Anaxagoras in *Pericles* 6 is that animal prodigies are explicable through natural science. It is true that in *Pericles* 6 Plutarch is willing to grant the seer Lampon his day, as well as to praise Anaxagoras who offered a scientific explanation, but the passage still reveals a reluctance to treat such prodigies as important.

The subordination of the portents to the dramatic needs of the *Lives* is another important consideration in any discussion of Plutarch's technique. First of all it should be noted that he seems to prefer a dream to a portent where it is a case of a choice. Caesar's crossing of the Rubicon (*Caesar* 32) is heralded by a dream, not a portent.[5] Dreams occur before the battle of Leuctra (*Pelopidas* 20-21)—where Diodoros (15.53), Pausanias (9.13) and Xenophon (*Hellenica* 6.4) give portents—and they are the most significant supernatural warnings before Pharsalos (*Pompey* 68), and Caesar's murder (*Brutus* 14, *Caesar* 63). The dreams seem to contain portents within them. Antony, before his disagreement and flight from Octavius, dreams that his hand is struck by lightning (*Antony* 16). At this point Cassius Dio (45.7) offers a comet predicting Octavius' future immortality. In *Brutus* 14 and *Caesar* 63 one version of Calpurnia's dream has the gable ornaments fall from the house. Plutarch adds to the dream a flame darting from Pompey's to Caesar's camp before the battle at Pharsalos, but he omits the commonplace portents related by Appian (*BC* 2.68) at this time.

On two significant occasions in the *Life of Antony*, Antony is significantly motiviated and the reader receives an unforgettable depiction of the mood of the participants through the use of portents. It has already been mentioned how Antony's dream of

---

[5] The stress which Plutarch puts upon the dream as illicit (ἔκθεσμον . . . τῇ ἑαυτοῦ μητρὶ μίγνυσθαι τὴν ἄρρητον μίξιν) would seem to suggest that the crossing of the Rubicon was also an act violating decency. The dream is interpreted in Suet. *Caes.* 7.2, Dio, 4.24.2, Artemidor. *Onirocr.* 1.79, Herod. 6.107, Zon. 10.7, and Phot. *Bibl.* 396 as indicating rule over one's country. However, Artemidoros gives a large number of meanings and in Herodotos the dream turns out to be illusory.

his hand struck by lightning (*Antony* 16) was used to motivate Antony's separation from Octavius at that time. Shortly after the dream he hears reports that Octavius is plotting against him. All Octavius' protestations are in vain, their mutual hatred goes into full bloom, and they run about Italy raising armies to battle one another. One must almost assume that the dream is the cause of all the trouble. Another reconciliation takes place in chapter 33. But this time their reconciliation is broken up when a seer tells Antony that his *daimon* and *tyche* fears Octavius' and he should keep it as far away from Octavius' as possible. Antony's fears that the seer may be right are confirmed by his continual losses in gambling to Octavius. Antony takes off without further ado.

Marius is continually motivated by portents which first lift him to undreamed of successes, then to delusions of grandeur, and finally hurl him into the abyss of despair. In *Marius* 3 Scipio taps Marius on the shoulder when he is asked who is to succeed him. Marius takes the incident as a "divine oracle." In 8 the propitiousness of the sacrifices and the words of a seer that "*to daimonion* was revealing incredible success for him" greatly encourage him. While in flight from Sulla's cavalry (36) his recollection of a portent so inspires him that his friends are amazed at his good spirits. He is dying of hunger and despair and only escapes certain death by hiding in a thicket. He then rushes to the seashore where he remembers an incident which had occurred to him while he was young. He had found an eagle's nest with seven young inside, and the seer had predicted that he would hold the highest command and power (τὴν μεγίστην ἀρχὴν καὶ ἡγεμονίαν), i.e. the consulship seven times.

One of the surprising things about Plutarch's relation of this portent is that he did not believe one whit of it himself. He gives Musaios as his authority for the impossibility of an eagle laying more than three eggs, hatching two, or maintaining one. But Plutarch did not rule out the possibility that the portent sustained Marius' hopes, and in any case it helped to express the unexpected morale of Marius at this time. One suspects that Plutarch transferred this portent from the account of Marius' boyhood, in the hope of giving some supernatural motivation to Marius in his darkest hour.

Not long after the recalled portent, Marius falls into a state of uncertainty as to whether he should escape by land or sea (39), but the divine powers come to his assistance once again. He notices that an ass is attracted to water rather than to its fodder, and concludes that *"to daimonion* is indicating a way of escape by sea rather than by land." But evil does not triumph forever, and after a series of monstrosities, Marius falls sick before the approaching footsteps of Sulla. The beginning of the end for him is signified by the execution of Sextus Lucinus, "a great sign of coming ills" (45). When he tries to sleep, he is only tormented by a nightmare in which he keeps hearing a voice, "Dreadful is the lion's den, even when the lion's away." Not even the most ghastly drunken debaucheries can cure his insomnia, and he dies of pleurisy brought on by his alcoholic excesses. At least that was the opinion of Plutarch's authority here, Poseidonios. The *Life of Marius* is punctuated, underlined, and dittoed with the supernatural much in the way that the careers of Homer's heroes are symbolic of another celestial battle-ground. In an age which had done away with polytheism in certain intellectual circles, the new supernatural machinery has a special importance.

It has been mentioned that Plutarch likes to break up an other-wise peaceful scene with the disturbing intrusion of an ill-boding portent. An example of this appears in the *Life of Sulla* where the relation of the portent at first seems so pointless that it appears Plutarch included it out of perverse delight in his own technique. Here (*Sulla* 27) he is in the midst of an idyllic description of the area around the Nympheion at Apollonia, a scene of pastoral charm in the midst of deep grass and abundant water but with an ominous touch, for fonts of fire shoot up.[6] Suddenly the picture is interrupted by the appearance of a bleating satyr which is led into Sulla's presence and leaves him with a sickening feeling of revulsion. Normally such a psychological shock demonstrates that the gods have tolerated the hero's success long enough and a contrary course is in the wind: the ring of good fortune has been broken, and the reader must be painfully informed of it. No conceivable literary or thematic reason seems to justify the inclusion

---

[6] On this see Flacelière, *Vies* VI, p. 340. The phenomenon is described in Dio 41.55, Aelian, *V.H.* 13.16, and Pliny, *N.H.* 2.106. There was no reason to take it as particularly portentous. Later (27.8), Sulla sees a vision of two goats (mss.) or two armies (Ziegler, Flacelière) fighting like men. The correction is based on Julius Obsequens 57 and Aug. *De civ. dei* 2.25 (*acies*), (in Greek τράγοι vs. στρατοί). The Penguin and Loeb editions have "goats."

of the satyr portent. It is inconceivable that Plutarch himself believed in satyrs, especially at Apollonia. One can only conclude that he was carried away by the grotesque, Hellenistic fondness to portray these creatures. The description stands out from his pages like a small piece of ancient baroque, a bit of literary, almost statuary persiflage.

But at the same time it introduces a temporary psychological setback for the hero, and such reversals are not uncommon in the pages of the *Lives*. We next learn that Sulla is apprehensive that when his troops reach Italy they will quickly disperse. However, at Tarentum he is buoyed up when the sacrificial victim's liver contains the impression of a laurel wreath, and when he sees either two armies or two goats fighting just like men—depending upon our fancies in textual criticism—rising in the Campanian sky and floating gradually away.

Another characteristic of Plutarch's portent technique is the skillful piling up of ever intensifying portents until the hero is left in a state of complete psychological collapse, unable even to take the most elementary logical steps to protect his own interests. One feels that the gods are using portents to manipulate men almost as though they were puppets on a string. This is most surprising in view of the fact that Plutarch's philosophy embraced the freedom of the will and responsibility for one's moral actions. Disturbing portents which continue at some length until the hero has been totally demoralized appear especially in the *Lives* of *Alexander*, *Antony*, *Brutus*, *Caesar*, *Cicero*, *Crassus*, *Demosthenes*, *Dion*, and *Nicias*. They are, therefore, worthwhile studying from the standpoint of Plutarch's technique.

In general Plutarch does not pay too much attention to portents in the early part of the *Life of Cicero* though he is our only source for a portent seen by Cicero's nurse when the lad is young, a *phasma* which predicts his future greatness (*Cicero* 2). He is also our only source for a Stoic-sounding response from the Delphic oracle which assures Cicero of his future success: he is to make nature, not the opinion of the multitude, his guide in life (5). One might also be mystified by the sign which Plutarch found to resolve the orator's dilemma over the Catilinarian conspirators. A flame leaping up while the women are sacrificing is responsible for Cicero's ordering their execution (20).[7] Finally in his dark hour

---

[7] Cicero's wife Terentia is a Roman Lady Macbeth who drives Cicero on to the questionable execution of the Catilinarian conspirators, a woman

as he sets out in exile he is encouraged by another portent. As he is sailing into Dyrrachion and about to disembark for the trip to Greece, an earthquake and tidal wave—movements in the earth—announce to the seers that his exile will not be stable (32).

But the masterpiece of Plutarch's portent description is the death scene of Cicero, which takes place at the end of the *Life*. The death of the hero is foreshadowed by the appearance of a flock of crows or ravens (*korakes*).[8] These also become symbols of the whole of nature in sympathy with the afflicted. In their puzzling and contradictory movements they express not only the hero's irresolution and coming death, but they also reveal the distress of the cosmos as manifested in the animal world, and the contrast between man's inhumanity to man and the gentleness of the beasts. Plutarch jokingly opposes the bestiality of men to the humanity of animals in the *Gryllos* (989a), where crows are especially praised for their fidelity. One suspects that the *Cicero* passage might be a conflation of two different types of treatment of the crows, one which saw them as mere portents and another which treated them as part of the cosmic sympathy. One might even suspect that the rhetorical school was behind the sympathetic treatment

---

of "great ambition," who together with Publius Nigidius incites Cicero against the conspirators; it is she who reports the flame to Cicero. Dio, 37.35, says *to daimonion* sent the portent, but Plutarch actually leaves its supernatural quality rather ambiguous (ἐκ τῆς τέφρας καὶ τῶν κατακεκαυμένων φλοιῶν φλόγα πολλὴν ἀνῆκε καὶ λαμπράν). Earlier writers like Sallust, Appian and Cicero himself, do not mention the incident. A clue to its origin is in Servius, *Buc.* 8.105, where Servius claims he found it in a poem of Cicero: "the altar trembled and a flame sprang up as Terentia poured the libation." A poetical conceit may have turned into a portent. Plutarch omits the statue portents associated with Cicero in Dio. 45.17 and 46.33, as well as the large number of portents for the proscriptions recorded by Appian, *BC* 4.4 (one of these portents was the end of an Etruscan soothsayer who was so depressed at what he saw in the future that he held his breath until he died!). Plutarch (*Cicero* 14) blandly notes that *to daimonion* seemed to be foretelling the future by earthquakes, lightning, and visions. His words are probably modeled on Cicero's *In Cat.* 3.8.18 ("visas nocturno fasces ardoremque caeli ut fulminum iactus ut terraemotus relinquam"). Dio, 37.9.1, abounds in portents for the conspiracy, including animal and statue portents, but Sallust, *Cat.* 50-53, omits them.

[8] Translators seem undecided on whether to translate *korakes* as crows or ravens. They arc used as a portent by Plutarch in *Cic* 4, *Alex.* 27 and 73, *T. Gracch.* 17, and *Nic.* 13. In *De soll. an.* birds are praised for their ability in divination. In *Pomp.* 25 and *Flam.* 10 *korakes* flying over the heads of a crowd are brought down but Plutarch regards this not as an omen but as due to the shock of the sound waves.

of the crows and that all Plutarch had to do was borrow it from a ready-made source. This at least was the conclusion of one recent work. However, this is certainly to deny a great amount of originality to him, and the whole passage harmonizes so perfectly with his *Moralia* and with his fondness for crows as portentous conveyors of the divine messages that one is on slippery ground in having recourse again to the thief named *Quellenkritik*.[9] At any rate a simpler version in which the crows are indications of evil seems to be behind the pecking of the crows on the ship's cable as an evil portent (καὶ πᾶσιν ἐδόκει τὸ σημεῖον εἶναι πονηρόν, 47). The rest of the passage portrays them as helpful and sympathetic to Cicero. Here is the portent scene in a recent translation of the *Life* (48).

(Cicero has tearfully parted from his brother Quintus; there follows a description of Quintus' betrayal by his slave. Cicero goes to Astura and sails down as far as Circaeum with a favorable wind. Suddenly he changes his mind against the advice of his pilots who want to sail on, "either because he feared the sea, or had not entirely lost faith in Caesar." He proceeds twelve miles in the direction of Rome. Again he loses his resolution, goes back to Astura, passes a night "with his mind full of terrible thoughts and desperate plans"—including the idea of killing himself on the hearth of Octavius in order to bring a curse on him. At last he goes to Caieta where he has a summer villa, "a most agreeable place to go to in the summer, when the Etesian winds are so pleasant." It is here that chapter 48 begins).

---

[9] Dio, 47.8, omits portents for Cicero's death. Appian's account is simpler and more straightforward: the *korakes* try to warn the slaves that their conduct is not pleasing to the gods. H. Homeyer, *Die Antiken Berichte über den Tod Ciceros und ihre Quellen* (Baden-Baden, 1964) has given an elaborate account of the sources used. She believes that it owes much to the rhetorical school, and that Tiro must be responsible for the death scene since no one else would have known the places mentioned so intimately. However, E. Badian at the Regional Meeting of Ancient Historians at the University of Michigan, May 7-8, 1971, sharply criticized Homeyer's study as an outdated piece of dubious *Quellenkritik*. A similar sharp criticism of her attempt to find a ready-made secondary source for Plutarch's *Alexander* is to be found in Hamilton, *Plutarch, Alexander*, pp. xlix-l. See also Homeyer's, "Ciceros Tod im Urteil der Nachwelt," *Altertum*, 17 (1971), 165-174. Plutarch stresses the evil of Antony's nature: when the head and hands are posted on the rostra, the Romans see in them the soul of Antony. His own essays on animals, including the stress put upon their role in divination, and the conceit that they are more humane than humans, certainly influenced his passage on the death of Cicero. Particularly the crow gets high praise in these essays.

In this place also there is a temple of Apollo, a little above the sea, and from the temple a flight of crows rose up into the air with a great noise and came flying at Cicero's ship as it was being rowed to land. They perched on either side of the yard, some croaking and some pecking at the ends of the ropes, and everyone regarded this as a bad omen. Cicero, however, disembarked, went to his villa, and lay down to rest. Then, while most of the crows perched round the window, making a tremendous noise with their cawing, one of them flew down on the bed where Cicero was lying with his head all covered up, and little by little began to drag away with its bill the garment from his face. When the servants saw this they reproached themselves for standing by as spectators waiting for their master to be murdered, and doing nothing to defend him, while these wild brute creatures were helping him and caring for him in his undeserved ill-fortune. So partly by entreaty and partly by force, they took him up and carried him in his litter towards the sea. (Rex Warner, *Plutarch, Fall of the Roman Republic*, p. 318).

(In the next paragraph human savagery and treachery is depicted at its worst: Quintus' freedman, Philologos, who had been educated by the hero betrays Cicero and points out his escape route to the soldiers; Herennius, the assassin, and Popillius, who had once been defended on a charge of parricide by Cicero, as he looks steadfastly at them—"in the pose he was most famous for, with his chin resting on his left hand, but his hair long and covered with dust and his face filled with anxiety;" those present turn their heads as the mortal blow is dealt and his head and hands are cut off).

The career of Alexander is accompanied by a portentous under-current of supernatural prodigies. The culmination of them at the end of the *Life* drives the hero into superstitious despair. In chapters 2, 3, 14, 17, 26, 27, favorable portents accompany his birth, initial successes, and the overthrow of the Persian Empire. But finally a number of extremely disturbing and annoying portents undermine his moral fiber. In 57 the sight of a lamb with a tiara and testicles growing out of its head puts a shudder through his spine; he imagines that *to daimonion* is about to leave his powers to an impotent heir. He is frightened enough to have himself purified by Babylonian priests. His apprehensions, however, are for a time greatly alleviated by the discovery of petroleum (i.e. *naphtha*—which they slightly underappreciate) by a Macedonian soldier who was digging a trench for his tent near the Oxos river; the seers declared that oil was given by God as an aid to toil. Later a series of portents begins to cloud the horizon again. *Korakes*

begin to act ominously and fall dead at his feet. There is no lobe
in the liver of the sacrificial victim. Alexander's favorite lion is
kicked to death by an otherwise despicable creature, an ass. A
mysterious person is found impiously sitting upon his throne,
and when questioned the person claims that the God Serapis
had commanded him to do as he did (73).[10] By chapter 75 Alexander
is now the perfect image of that cowering creature, the superstitious man of De superstitione (πρὸς τὰ θεῖα ταραχώδης γενόμενος
καὶ περίφοβος τὴν διάνοιαν). Frightened by the slightest cause
which might be construed as portentous, he fills his house with
incensors, sacrificers, and diviners. In a vein characteristic of the
anti-superstition essay, Plutarch concludes that just as disbelief
in the divine is to be condemned so also is deisidaimonia which
"like water always running to a lower level . . ." The text breaks
off here but we can easily conclude what Plutarch had in mind.

One would like to know what the source was for Alexander the
deisidaimon. The somewhat elaborate story of the man on the throne
may perhaps have no more ample a source than a version like that
we find in Arrian (7.24). It is also not inconceivable that the
picture of diviners filling the house is merely an elaboration of
something similar to Arrian's (7.30) "oracles as well as dreams and
visions of different persons were supposed to have foretold Alexander's death." [11] It would be rash to deny that Alexander became

---

[10] This is the only reference to Sarapis (or Serapis) in the Lives, and has
raised much discussion. Arrian, 7.26, mentions an all-night vigil and con-
sulation of the shrine of Serapis before Alexander's death. Wilcken, Philologus, 53 (1894), 119, believed the thing an anachronism due to Ptolemaic
propaganda, but L. Pearson, "The Diary and Letters of Alexander the Great,"
G. T. Griffith, ed. Alexander the Great, the Main Problems (Cambridge:
1966), p. 10, disagreed, believing the incident not to have much propaganda
value and to be an easily detected fraud. On this problem, the historical
value of Alex. 76 and Arrian 8.26.2 here, more recently J. Stambaugh,
Sarapis under the Early Ptolemies (Leiden: 1972), pp. 9-11, inclines to the
view that the shrine was that of a native god later identified with Sarapis,
but against C. B. Welles, "The Discovery of Sarapis and the Foundation
of Alexandria," Historia, 11 (1962), 271-98, (that Alexander introduced this
worship into Persia). Stambaugh believes that Alexander found Osiris
worshipped at the site of Alexandria, and built a shrine for him there as
Osiris-Apis, later Hellenized as Sarapis in his lifetime. W. Hornbostel,
Sarapis (Leiden: 1973), pp. 44-45, comes to a similar conclusion: Sarapis
was the interpretatio graeca for Osiris from very early times. Nock, Essays,
p. 140, places it in the 3rd Cent.
[11] Many of the final portents are mentioned as well in Arrian, 7.18ff.,
and Diodoros, 17.116. Plutarch omits portents over the capture of Thebes
though Diodoros, 17.10, gives the rather startling one of blood covering

superstitious at the end of his life, but Plutarch is not squeamish when it comes to exaggeration.

We can leave the difficult problem of sources, for Plutarch has died with his secret. Some insight into the nature of Plutarch's use of portents as a tool to biography can be seen by comparing his *Life of Alexander* with Arrian's history of Alexander's conquest. In general it can be said that the thematic viewpoint is the same in the two authors. Some exceptions occur. In describing the death of Cleitos (4.8), Arrian suggests the hand of the god Dionysos, but Plutarch (*Alex.* 50) desires to remove the impression that the anger of Dionysos was responsible for Alexander's slaying of the old general, and lays the blame on Cleitos' evil *daimon*. Another difference is a somewhat more marked anti-Chaldaean attitude in Plutarch, particularly in recounting the last days of Alexander.[12]

the Phocian temple at Delphi. Plutarch alone relates the lamb-with-testicles prodigy and the dream before Alexandria. Arrian 3.3, used the more superstitious account of Aristoboulos that serpents led the way through the desert to the shrine of Ammon, over that of Ptolemy. Plutarch—who seemed to like *korakes* in divination—lets them lead the way. Arrian complains here about the diversity of accounts over the Ammon trip. Plutarch did not accept the account of Alexander's divinity, and attempts to downplay it on every occasion. He does not state what Alexander's aim was in going out into the desert (*Alexander* 26-26), but when Alexander meets the priests his question is whether his father's murderers are still alive. The prophet there keeps twisting his innocent questions into claims of divinity. Even when pushed Alexander exclaims that God is the common father of all men, though he treats the best men (οἱ ἄριστοι) as his special sons. Arrian gives Aristoboulos as his source for the ribbon portent (7.23), similar but somewhat different in Diodoros 17.116. Aristoboulos is also the source for the man on the throne. Only Plutarch mentions the name of the man (Dionysios). H. Berve, *Das Alexanderreich auf Prosopographischer Grundlage* (Munich: 1926), believed it was connected with the Saccae festival described by Dio, 4.66 (cf. *RE*, 1A, p. 1769ff.) where a condemned criminal was permitted to act as king before his execution. Perhaps Plutarch's account contains a hint in the name Dionysios. Some source may have linked the event to the wrath of Dionysos, itself an element entering through the *interpretatio graeca* in which Sarapis was identified with Dionysos. There must also be some relationship to Alexander as Neos Dionysos. On the importance of this see A. D. Nock, "Notes on Ruler Cult, I-IV," *JHS*, 48 (1928), 21-43, reprinted in *Essays on Religion and the Ancient World*, pp. 134-57 (pp. 144-52 on Neos Dionysos). Nock, pp. 140-44, sees no contemporary evidence for Alexander equating himself with Neos Dionysos, even finds counter evidence, and suggests the idea goes back to Cleitarchos. This is damaging to Flacelière's suggestion, *Vies* IX, pp. 7-8, that Alexander portrayed himself as Neos Dionysos to avoid retribution for Thebes. Plutarch only hints at this theme.

[12] Diodoros, like Plutarch, is suspicious of the Chaldaeans. In 17.112 he writes that through the use of astrology they had predicted Alexander's

Plutarch's Alexander is one of pious belief steadily turning toward superstition brought on by increasing portents. He, therefore, reports a large number of portents in the *Life* but at the same time, on occasions, shows more restraint than Arrian. Like Arrian he relates the story of the sweating statue of Orpheus—probably one not to his taste—but locates it not at Pieria as in Arrian (1.11.2) but in Leibethra and explains in some detail how the statue symbolized the coming conquest by Alexander. He reports the story of the Gordian Knot rather sceptically (18) and omits three portents associated with this event in Arrian (1.27.5-29). Arrian is puzzled by the contradictory accounts about Alexander's trip to visit the shrine of Zeus Ammon, but superstitiously accepted Ptolemy's account about two snakes leading the way (3.3ff.). Plutarch discreetly lets the army be directed by a pair of *korakes* (*Alexander* 26-27). Another trivial incident, a swallow perching on Alexander's hat, is taken seriously by Arrian (1.25) as portentous of coming treason. Plutarch—if he were aware of the story—ignores this insignificant event. Arrian (4.4) also on two occasions portrays a rationalistic Alexander whom we do not find in Plutarch: while Alexander is about to attack the Scythians the seers claim that the sacrifices are unfavorable, but Alexander gives the command to attack rather than be a laughingstock like Dareios. Another note of scepticism appears in Arrian's treatment of Alexander and the Babylonian priests (7.16): Alexander believes that the Chaldaeans are trying to obstruct his entry into Babylon because they wish the construction of the temple of Baal to be delayed as long as possible so as to offer more opportunity for peculation;[13] when they say that

---

death but said he was promised a slight lease on life if he helped reconstruct the temple of Baal; on no account was Alexander himself to enter Babylon. In Ps. Callisthenes, 3.31.4, Serapis appears in a dream to warn Alexander, and there are more elaborate portents than in Plutarch. See Hamilton, *Alexander*, pp. 202-04. The anti-Chaldaean attitude comes from Aristoboulos, who himself may have used Cleitarchos and Ptolemy (Hamilton, pp. liv-lv).

[13] The *Lives* reveal little interest in foreign religions. For example, *Antony* and *Pompey* tell us next to nothing about the Jews, even though their failure to fight on the sabbath—criticized in *De superstitione*—may have been largely responsible for Pompey's capture of Jerusalem. Possibly it was only late in life and after writing *Alexander* that Plutarch developed this interest. Certainly *De Iside et Osiride* is one of his latest works, and it is here that we find almost all of his knowledge of foreign cults and customs. His explanations of Jewish religion and history in the *Symposiacs* (4.5,

they have an oracle of Baal commanding Alexander not to enter the city, he responds sardonically with a rationalistic verse of Euripides (μάντις ἄριστος ὅστις εἰκάζει καλῶς, fr. 973). Perhaps these stories could not be harmonized with Plutarch's portrait of Alexander *deisidaimon*. The second passage is perhaps important since outside of a reference to the line of Euripides in Cicero's *De divinatione*, the only occurrences of the fragment are in works of Plutarch (*De Pythiae oraculis* 399a, *De defectu oraculorum* 432c). In both cases the line is taken to be an introduction to a kind of anti-divination manifesto.[14]

It is a characteristic of the *Lives* to preserve many portents which we do not have in the extant histories. Undoubtedly Plutarch justified them on the grounds that they illuminated the mind of the hero, but also he desired to prove the fact of divination. In any case he would have been less obligated, since he was writing biography not history, to follow the canon of Thucydides and Polybios on the omission of portents. Moreover, Arrian's history starts with the campaign in Persia itself whereas Plutarch begins with Alexander's birth and childhood. At any rate Plutarch includes a large number of portents not recorded in Arrian. Included are those at Alexander's birth (1), his setting out for Asia (14), and before the battle of the Granicos, where Alexander changes the name of the month to avoid an unlucky day. He records a

---

and 4.6-669e-672c) are a disappointment: in the first, he somewhat correctly adduces that the Jews abstain from pork for hygenic reasons, but shows that he has never read their own writings; in the second the speakers identify Jahweh with Dionysos. However, to be just to Plutarch here, one should note that the *Symposiac* breaks off at this point and he might have concluded with a discussion on the God of the Jews being invisible and unrepresented in *eikones*—something which he would have approved of heartily. Arrian, 3.4 ff., Curtius, 4.7, and Diodoros, 17.50, offer a rather weird description of what was in the temple of Ammon. Arrian mentions the use of salt; Curtius speaks of an immense grave there, and the worship of the god as a figure resembling a huge navel fastened in a mass of emeralds and carried in a golden boat; Diodoros mentions an image in a boat carried by 80 priests. Perhaps the silence of Cleombrotos in *De defectu oraculorum* when asked about the contents of the shrine is indicative of Plutarch's own lack of knowledge.

[14] Cicero writes: vide igitur ne nulla sit divinatio. Est quidam Graecus vulgaris in hanc sententiam versus—bene qui coniciet, vatem hunc perhibeo optumum. (*De div.* 2.5). In *De Pyth.* 399a the Epicurean Boethos uses the verse to support his viewpoint that prophecy is only the result of *tyche*. In *De def.* 432c Lamprias argues that irrationality is involved in prophecy but that not just guessing is involved but following *nous*, the higher part of the soul.

bronze tablet found at Xanthos predicting the end of the Persian
Empire (17). Then we have a portentous dream of Dareios before
the battle of the Granicos (18), and another before the founding
of Alexandria (26). Certainly the eclipse before the battle of
Gaugamela serves as a portent (31). Before the murder of Cleitos
the unpropitious actions of some sacrificial animals signal his
doom (50). A lamb with something resembling a tiara and testicles
on its head is treated as a frightening prospect of Alexander's
inability to put a son on his throne (57). A number of ugly portents
at Babylon and the growing superstition and suspicion of Alexander
fill out the last chapters of the *Life* (73-75).[15] Some of these portents
and portentous dreams are not in Arrian. But there is one puzzling
omission. In Arrian while Alexander is sailing on a pleasure cruise
up the Euphrates, a ribbon from his diadem floats from his head
and lands on a reed near the tomb of a dead king. The incident
is supposed to predict approaching evil (7.22.2). Perhaps it simply
was not in his sources, though one thinks it would be in Nearchos
whom he used as much as in Ptolemy whom he did not.

One of Plutarch's greatest contributions to Greek narrative
literature is his genius in using portents in such a way that they
illuminate the milieu of the civilization he is describing. He enables
the reader to sympathize with those involved, to appreciate the
culture depicted, and to see events through the eyes of the participants. An especially moving example of this type of description
is that in *Phocion* 28, the entry of the Macedonian garrison into
Athens at the very time when the Eleusinian mysteries are being
celebrated. The thematic idea of the passage is first boldly stated:
"the entry of the Macedonians was not dictated by either political
or military expedience, but was rather a brute display of arrogant
power." We are then told that this was the month Boedromion
and that the Eleusinian mysteries had been interrupted by this
dread event. The glory of the celebration in the past is then contrasted with the present misery of the city. At this point, Plutarch
mentions how the dye on the sacred fillets came out sallow instead of bright red, and how a mystic had been mutilated by a

---

[15] With Arrian Plutarch relates: the sweating statue of Orpheus (14),
the Gordian knot (18), the dream at Tyre (24), the clod dropped by a bird
to fulfill the prophecy of Alexander's wound at Tyre (24), portents on the
visit to Ammon (26), the eclipse before Gaugamela (31), the spring of oil
at Sogdiana (57), and portents before Babylon (73 ff.).

fish which destroyed the lower part of his body while he was attempting to wash his sacrificial pig in the water. The symbolism is then quickly indicated: (the) God revealed that the Athenians would be deprived of the lower part of the city. This was the meaning of the oracle of Dodona which warned them about guarding the extremities of their city.[16] It is necessary to read the passage in the original to gain its full effect. Still, the significance and uniqueness of the portents related are what gives the passage its strength. All of them are intimately connected with Athens, and undoubtedly could be deeply appreciated by one who had actually been initiated in the Eleusinian mysteries. Even so, a modern reader, many hundreds of years removed, can gain an appreciation of what the event meant to the original participants who stood by and watched the Macedonians haughtily ride into the great but fallen city at this time.

A similar technique is used to illuminate the career of Antony; this time the portents reflect the soul of a person rather than a city. In the introduction to *Demetrios-Antony*, Antony is described as possessing a great nature which—due to faulty education and the lack of self-control—succumbed to titanic vices. He is the walking image of the undesirable features of the god Bacchos in his vices, and of some of the desirable ones in his virtues. An unforgettable impression is left upon the reader by the Plutarchan description of Antony's entry into Ephesos in *Antony* 24. Antony rides in drawn by lions and surrounded by Bacchantes, flute players, dancers, men and boys dressed like Satyrs and Pans; the whole city is decorated in jubilation for a bacchic orgy. This is in a way the high point of Antony's career though Plutarch adds that at the time some saw Antony not as Dionysos the Giver of Joy and Beneficent (χαριδότης καὶ μειλίχιος) but also as Dionysos the Carnivorous and Savage (ὠμηστὴς καὶ ἀγριώνιος), and he quotes from Sophocles (*Oed. Tyr.* 4) to the effect that Antony's extravagance filled the city not only with paeans but also with groans (for those who had to pay for it). The turning point of his career, at

---

[16] Perrin, Loeb, *Lives* VIII, p. 209 takes the pig not the mystic to have been mutilated. The Greek reads otherwise, but Perrin may be right. A few changes in endings could rectify the problem, if it is there: μύστην λούοντα χοιρίδιον ἐν Κανθάρῳ λίμενι κῆτος συνέλαβε καὶ τὰ κάτω μέρη τοῦ σώματος ἄχρι τῆς κοιλίας κατέπιεν. I. Scott-Kilvert, *The Age of Alexander* (Hammondsworth: 1973), p. 242, translates as it stands.

the battle of Actium, is well prepared for by the Dionysos portent at this time. Plutarch relates that on the Acropolis was a scene with a statue of Dionysos in it called the Battle of the Giants, and that just before the battle the wind tore this away and dashed it to the ground. Plutarch quickly reminds the reader that Antony had always associated himself with Dionysos.

In chapter 75 of this very long *Life* we arrive at the final portentous scene in Alexandria. The type of supernatural incursion is characteristic of the *Lives*. This is a night scene in which the hero is trying desperately to compose himself for the great strategic decisions to be made on the morrow. He only asks for the comfort of a few hours sleep, but he is tormented by supernatural intrusions which destroy the last bit of his composure, and thereby the last hope of success. Here Antony, who had been refused in his slightly unrealistic challenge of a personal duel with Octavius, decides on battle, but the tears of his friends persuade him to postpone the engagement. It is at this point that Plutarch makes use of all the Dionysos material again to symbolize the complete abandonment of Antony by the powers that be:

> It is said that at dinner he told his slaves to fill his cup and serve him more generously than usual, for no man could say whether on the next day they would be waiting on him or serving other masters, while he himself would be lying dead, a mummy and nothing. But when he saw that his friends were weeping at these words, he told them that he would not lead them into action, since he did not expect that he would come out of the battle victorious or safe, but rather looked to it to assure him of an honourable death. That evening, so the story goes, about the hour of midnight, when all was hushed and a mood of dejection and fear of its impending fate brooded over the whole city, suddenly a marvellous sound of music was heard, which seemed to come from a consort of instruments of every kind, and voices chanting in harmony, and at the same time, the shouting of a crowd in which the cry of Bacchanals and the ecstatic leaping of satyrs were mingled as they went. The procession seemed to follow a course through the middle of the city towards the outer gate which led to the enemy's camp and at this point the sounds reached their climax and then died away. Those who tried to discover a meaning for this prodigy concluded that the god Dionysus, with whom Antony claimed kinship and whom he had sought above all to imitate, was now abandoning him. (Ian Scott-Kilvert, *Plutarch, Makers of Rome*, p. 340).

One can have no doubt that the "those who tried to discover a meaning" is Plutarch himself, who as usual wants to leave the reader perfectly clear about the purpose for relating the portent.[17]

The next chapter (76) illuminates the portent scene in its own way: Antony's fleet no sooner meets that of Octavius than it raises its oars in salute, goes over to Octavius, and the two fleets head for the city against Antony. No sooner has Antony witnessed this betrayal than his cavalry also goes over. In a fit of spiritual and intellectual blindness he rushes in on Cleopatra, claiming that she has betrayed him to the very men he was fighting for her sake. Antony's conduct here is in significant contrast to the earlier scene of betrayal at the battle of Actium. At that time Domitius Ahenobarbus had defected to Octavius just before the battle, sailing over in a boat before Antony's very eyes; but Antony nobly ordered his servants and the rest of his luggage to be sent after him (63). The last shreds of Antony's good nature disappear as he rushes in on Cleopatra, ready to blame her for his own stupidity. The supernatural Bacchanalia which departed at night through the gates of Alexandria has been as demoralizing for his character as the flame which darted from Pompey's camp to Caesar's before the battle of Pharsalos was for Pompey (*Caesar* 43, *Pompey* 68).

There can be no doubt that Plutarch believed the future was revealed through portents. They fill the pages of his *Lives* and have left an unforgettable impression on all the readers of them. On the other hand there is a certain highly independent rearrangement and adaptation which strikes a modern reader as somewhat inconsistent with a really serious belief in the phenomenon. For example most Christians would be rather horrified if someone rewrote the Gospel miracles, adapting them to suit his fancy, even though this is to some extent what the original writers of the Gospels did themselves. Plutarch both varies the effect and the nature of these portents. There is, for example, a rather marked difference in effect between the *Life of Brutus* and *Life of Caesar* over the vision which appears to Brutus at Abydos and Philippi. In the first there is no hint of retribution involved. Brutus remains

---

[17] Compare the subtlety of Plutarch's portents with the stupidity of Dio's (50.8): an ape and an owl in various Roman temples, strange doings with the chariot of Jupiter and the statue of Victory, an 85 foot long snake killed in—naturally—Etruria, and finally a statue of Antony gushing blood after the battle. Plutarch also mentions the destruction of a Heracleion at Patrai, and attempts to link this with Antony's association with Hercules, an association which Plutarch is really not much interested in elsewhere in the *Life*.

undaunted, and doubt is cast on the reality of the vision (*Brutus* 36, 37). After the initial shock Brutus calmly asks the phantom who he is.[18] In *Caesar* 69 the vision is associated with divine retribution: having seen it a second time Brutus "understood his fate and threw himself into danger" (συνεὶς ὁ Βροῦτος τὸ πεπρωμένον, ἔρριψε φέρων ἑαυτὸν εἰς τὸν κίνδυνον). Moreover, in Valerius Maximus (1.7.7) the vision appears not to Brutus before the battle of Philippi, but to Cassius of Parma before the battle of Actium. Since Valerius was one of Plutarch's sources for the Roman *Lives*, there is no reason why Plutarch should not have known Valerius' version.

Given Plutarch's belief in divination, it should be no surprise that the portents always indicate what will happen, and no one ignores them with impunity. There would hardly be any point in relating them if it were otherwise. In this sense Plutarch shows the contrast between sophisticated, rationalistically grounded superstition and the more primitive type of the Roman annalists. They simply reported the portents for the year. After one notices that portents seem to occur every year, and that they usually are so vague and indiscriminate—such as animal or fulgural portents—that they could apply to almost anything, one can hardly remain anything but sceptical. However, Plutarch's attempt to make them relevant, significant, and really predictive of the future adds a new credible dimension to them. For example, if Dionysos was really associated with Antony, the portents associated with the statue or processions of Dionysos have real meaning for Antony, and a symbolic literary value whatever one believes about portents in themselves.

---

[18] Actually, Plutarch wants to have his cake and eat it too. Since Brutus is a hero, and a philosopher as well, he must be depicted as unperturbed by the vision, but at the same time a blow must be struck against Epicureanism. Therefore, bees fill the camp of that Epicurean, Cassius, shattering his confidence in his beliefs and filling his army with *deisidaimonia* when all the efforts to dislodge them fail (*Brut.* 39). The bees ominously appear again before the second phase of the battle (48). Having had an opportunity to visit the site of Philippi one summer—one of the few sites which is virtually untouched in its setting, and gives one a good idea of the misty marsh described by Plutarch—I was struck to see bees protruding from the eyes of a statue which was lying on the ground; Cassius' troubles with the bees came immediately to mind. In *Dion* 14 an explanation of the portent is given: bees on the stern of a ship indicate that an undertaking will prosper for a short time then fail. This is what happens in both *Lives*. No attempt in the *Lives* is made to have parallel portents; and as a matter of fact, in the introduction to *Dion-Brutus*, Plutarch thinks it an extraordinary mark of *tyche* that both men were visited by a vision of a *daimon*.

As a matter of fact there are some notable *causes célèbres* of heroes who obstinately refuse to heed the portents. Flaminius (*Fabius* 2, 3),[19] the Athenians before Syracuse (*Nicias* 13, *Alcibiades* 17, 18), Demosthenes before Chaironeia (*Demosthenes* 19), and Crassus on the Parthian adventure (*Crassus* 16, 17, 23) are constantly warned but obstinately rush to their doom. Very memorable passages in the *Lives* are the scenes of irresolution between superstition and scepticism before the deaths of Tiberius Gracchus and Julius Caesar. In *Nicias* 23-24, Plutarch had followed and even elaborated on the indecisiveness of Nicias before Syracuse because of superstition, which he found in Thucydides (7.50). But in *Gracchus* and *Caesar* he takes an opposite course. As Tiberius begins to go into the forum where he is shortly to be murdered he is disturbed because the birds which are used for the auspices refuse to leave their cage. He then remembers an omen which had happened earlier; serpents had crawled into his helmet and laid and hatched eggs there. He is now "more disturbed." As he leaves his house he stumbles on the threshold. *Korakes* fighting on the rooftop cause a stone to roll at his feet. Tiberius wants to turn back but a friend taunts him with the ridicule he would get if he told the assembly that he could not come because he was afraid of a crow, while at the same time they would think he was putting on tyrannical airs (*T. Gracchus* 17). The omen of the serpents' eggs in the helmet is rather puzzling here. Probably in Plutarch's source the omen was about Tiberius' death and came in an earlier chapter, but Plutarch who preferred to relate it at the hour of death, has Tiberius "recall" it in much the way that Marius (*Marius* 36) recalls in flight the omen about the seven consulships which happened to him as a youth. The commonplace stumbling omen is given more graphic and horrifying overtones by the description of the nail of the big toe being broken and blood spurting through Tiberius' shoe.

The description of Caesar's irresolution and final ill-fated decision to enter the senate meeting is close to the description in *Tiberius*. Plutarch relates that fulgural portents and oddities in

---

[19] Flaminius, like Pelopidas and Marcellus, is undone not by failing to heed the portents so much as by his own rashness. Flaminius is a person overcome with false confidence arising from his early success. Fabius on the contrary, maintains his equilibrium but is just as sceptical of the portents because of their ἀλογία (*Fab.* 2).

the flight of birds were reported but that he did not think they were
worth mentioning "for such a great event." He then mentions men
appearing to be on fire, the lack of a heart in the augural victim,
Calpurnia's dream, and the inability of the seers to obtain good
sacrifices. At last he orders Antony to dismiss the senate (*Caesar*
63). But Brutus and the other conspirators act upon Caesar in much
the way that Blosius of Cumae worked upon Tiberius. They imply
that his superstitious fears are a disguise for tyranny, or if true the
product of a crazed mind. The conspirators mock the seers and ask
Caesar sarcastically if they should return when Calpurnia has better
dreams. Caesar has been caught on their hook. He does not even
bother to look at the warning handed him by Artemidoros the
sophist, and sarcastically points out to the seer that the Ides have
come and nothing has happened (64, 65). One might wonder why
Plutarch was willing to mention the men on fire here, but not in
Fabius when giving the portents for Hannibal coming into Italy.
He gives his source here as Strabo, and Strabo may be responsible
for the other portents as well. Perhaps Plutarch felt the greatness
of the event justified the inclusion of the fire portent. It is also
somewhat odd that he felt compelled to explain to the reader
why the missing heart was a bad omen. Apparently he could
not have expected his Greek readers to understand this without a
commentary. But the ultimate effect of both these passages is the
horror of attempting to evade divination.[20]

Some other unlucky sceptics could be mentioned. Pyrrhos
makes the rash—and always unfortunate boast in antiquity—
"One omen is best, to fight for Pyrrhos," a remodeling of Hector's
unfortunate blasphemy in the *Iliad* (12.243). This comes before
his ill-fated attack on Sparta where he returns lucky to have
escaped with his life (*Pyrrhos* 29). The final chapters are punctuated

---

[20] There are some apparent exceptions to going in the face of portents
but they do not cause much difficulty. Timoleon manages to convince
his troops—who pass by mules laden with parsley—that parsley is not only
used to decorate graves but for victory (*Timol.* 26). Alcibiades returns to
Athens on the Plynteria, the unluckiest day for the Athenians, but no ill
comes (*Alc.* 34). Agesilaus ignores an eclipse and the death of his general
Peisander, pretending to have been victorious (*Ages.* 17). In the first case
Timoleon may be legitimately using a portent. For the Plynteria, we have
Plutarch's ridicule of unlucky days as superstition in *Qu. Rom.* 269e and
Cam. 19, where he shows that both propitious as well as unpropitious
events happened on so-called unlucky days. Finally, Plutarch did not
believe eclipses were portents and in any event believed in the *pia fraus*.

with graphic portents shattering the hopes of the hero: a vision of the city filled with corpses and gore, the slaughter of an eagle, sacrificial animals licking their own gore (31) and the sight of a bull and wolf fighting, an omen which he had earlier learned would be the sign of his death (32). Demosthenes not only disclaims the portents but even the warnings of the Delphic oracle. The carnage of Chaironeia is proof of the value of divination (*Demosthenes* 19). At times Plutarch even lets his belief in divination contradict his theme. For example, in *Agesilaus* 6 he discredits the human sacrifice dream of Agesilaus at Aulis and regards Agesilaus as noble in not fulfilling the immoral request. Yet, the Boiotians interrupt his substituted sacrifice as he sets out for Asia, and he leaves "full of ill-boding, anticipating that his expedition would come to naught." [21]

Plutarch's attitude toward portents should now be reasonably clear. Once again we see that superstitious belief is reinforced by the sophistication of thought in the Hellenistic and Roman periods. Between Plato's ingenuity and Plutarch's eclecticism stands the full ponderous weight of Stoicism in unbending affirmation of the belief in divination. The refined monotheism and the exalted nature of the divinity in Platonism constructs a basis for the miraculous: God's ways are not our ways; there is no comparison between the human and the divine; those who challenge his power detract from His divinity. At the same time the sympathy of the whole cosmos, the doctrine taught by the Stoics and accepted by Plutarch to a large degree, offers another basis for divination. Like a bow the cosmos can sense vibrations in any part, and the goodness of the divine leads to a natural inclination to reveal the future to its friends. The Epicureans' attempt to combat this belief in a certain sense only fostered it since from their time it was impious and atheistic not to believe in portents. Plutarch's reserve in relating the miraculous by limiting portents to great events in

---

[21] Plutarch seems to be overinfluenced by Xenophon, *Hell.* 3.4.3, where Agesilaus is disturbed by the sacrifice. Since Xenophon had not related the dream, his account does not suffer from inconsistency. Pausanias—who like Xenophon does not record the dream (3.9.1)—shows Agesilaus as similarly depressed by the sacrifice. The eclipse before the battle of Gaugamela has the effect of a portent, but Plutarch could hardly have been expected to surmount his sources here. Cf. Arrian, 3.7.6, Curtius, 4.10.2, Pliny, *NH* 2.180, and Cicero, *De div.* 1.121. For more technical information on the eclipse see Hamilton, *Alexander*, p. 81.

the life of an individual or country only gives the belief a greater aura of respectability.

Thus two principles of Plutarch's use of portents are very evident. The first is the absolute belief in divination through portents. The second is the adaptation of portents so that they serve a distinct literary purpose. For this reason portents appear prominently throughout the *Lives*, very often where no other extant source reports them. They invariably turn out to be true indications of the future, and no one runs in the face of them with impunity. At the same time Plutarch reveals his dislike for commonplace or vulgar portents. Where the portent is an obvious challenge to one's reason he is inclined to omit it. Thus, he is willing to allow crows, or ravens, to lead Alexander to Siwah, but not snakes. Generally the portents are not exceptions to the law of nature but simply ordinary occurrences which have special meaning for a particular person or city at a particular time. Thus he does not mention a huge snake found in Etruria of such enormous dimensions that one would be forced to laugh, but concentrates rather on such things as stumbling, the activities of crows, the drinking habit of an ass, the symbolic activities of statues where not too much is required for belief, portents within dreams—or dreams themselves—the darting of a flame, an earth tremor, the finding of oil, disturbances at sacrifices. The portents are used to motivate the hero in that the hero is elated or depressed by them. Undoubtedly this was very necessary for Plutarch in view of the lack of material available to portray the psychology of a hero at a given time. Some classical historians resorted to long imaginary speeches partly to supply this need. Plutarch's technique here is interesting and rather well-developed. The fact that he seemed to rely so much on Sulla's *Memoirs* in writing that hero's *Life* is evidence that he desperately wanted to find material expressing what the hero thought at a certain time, not just what he did. In many *Lives* the hero is elated or carried up and down by portents and dreams, only to be crushed at the last moment by a series of ill-boding ones. One must also be impressed by his use of portents to describe the mood of a city and his close interrelationship between the portents and the symbolism he has created for the hero. Though there is seldom an attempt to render exact parallelism in the portents—as in *Dion-Brutus*, where the appearance of the *daimon* to both men is not an entirely successful experiment—

there is an attempt to maintain a consistent tone and style through-out the *Parallel Lives,* and to impress his personality upon them.

Great latitude is allowed in the selection and narration of these portents. Where they detract from a literary account they can be modified or omitted. Where they dress it up, one can take a few liberties in the name of drama or personal color. It is questionable whether scholars have been aware of the great care and selection used for the *Lives* in regard to portents. Those like statue, animal, and celestial portents, which did not fit Plutarch's taste, are generally omitted. Where they do not motivate or illustrate the mind of the hero or reveal the psychology of the situation, he has little use for them. At the same time he seems to delight in narrating these supernatural flourishes, almost for their own sake. What would the deaths of Alexander, Caesar, Marius, Cicero, and Antony be if portents were omitted from the *Lives* of these men? Or would we be better off if he had felt the portents for the battles of Pharsalos, Philippi, Gaugamela, or Antony's last stand at Alexandria were beneath him?[22] We pass them off as humorous and interesting aberrations of a more gullible and primitive age, but these men of Plutarch's day took them seriously because they had created philosophical systems of great complexity to explain them. These described the exalted state of the divine, and the mantic power of an immortal human soul, which was capable in certain purified persons of receiving predictions of the future from the divine. And such a possibility was rational because the cosmos existed through a harmony of its divine, human, and irrational elements.

Plutarch's use of portents may also give a hint concerning his approach to the artistic structure of the *Lives.* They have too often been treated from almost purely moralistic and historical viewpoints as far as the parallelism goes, and on this basis have often received a negative judgment. The use of portents reveals

---

[22] To some extent there is a pattern for the distribution of supernatural occurrences in the *Lives.* Since Plutarch tends to reproduce portents even when well known, such as in *Alexander, Theseus,* and *Caesar,* one can presume that he would have used more if he could have found them in his sources. He seems to have liked dreams, particularly before death. There is also a rather equal distribution between Greek and Roman *Lives,* perhaps indicating an attempt at parallelism. In the *Dion-Brutus* a conscious attempt was made at this. The numbers refer to portents, but sometimes several are used rather than one in a particular chapter. The absence of portents in *Philopoimen* might reflect Polybios. It is surprising how often he makes use of eclipses.

GREEK LIVES

	Birth	Battle or Start of Career	Death
Ages.	3	6, 17 (eclipse)	30 (oracle)
Ag. Cleo.			
Alc.		17, 18	39 (dream)
Alex.	2-3	14, 17, 18, 24, 25, 31 (ecl.), 57	73-75
Arist.		11, (includes dream), 18	
Cim.			18
Demet.		19 (dr.), 29 (includes dr.)	
Demos.		19 (or.)	29
Dion		24, 27 (soothsayer)	55
Eum.		6 (includes dr.)	
Lyc.		5 (start of career)	
Lys.		12, 20 (alleged dr.), 29 (or.)	death follows 29
Nic.		13, 23 (eclipse)	death follows 23
Pel.		21, 22 (incl. dr.), 31 (ecl.)	death follows 31
Per.	3 (dr.)	6 (start of career)	
*Philop.**			
Phoc.		8 (or.)	28
Pyr.		11 (dr.), 25 (sacrifice)	29 (dr.)
Sol.			
Them.		10 (engineerd by T.), 12, 15	
Thes.	3 (oracle)		
Timol.		8, 12, 26	

ROMAN LIVES

	Birth	Battle or Start of Career	Death
Aem.		17 (ecl.)	
Ant.		60, 65, 75	75 followed by death
Brut.		36, 39	48
Cam.		5 (sacrifice)	
Cat. maj.			
Cat. min.		42, 52 (prophecy)	
Caes.		32 (dr.), 42, 43, 47, 52 (subverts or.)	63, 69 (after death)
Cic.	2 (dr.)	20	
Cor.		3	
Cras.		16, 17, 23	23 followed by death
Fab.		2	
*Flam.**			
T. Grach.			17
G. Grach.	1 (dr.)	11 (at founding of Carthage)	
Luc.		10, 12 (unlucky day), 23 (incl. dr.), 24, 27 (dr.)	
Marc.		3 (or.), 4, 6 (gets around omen), 12, 28	29
Mar.		3, 4 (start of career), 18	45 (dr.)
Num.		8 (for constitution *pia fraus*)	
Pomp.		68	
Popl.			
Rom.	2 (incl. dr.)		27 (eclipse)
Sert.			
Sul.		5 (career), prophecy), 7, 9 (dr.), 27, 28 (dr.)	37 (dr.)
Arat.		43	
Artax.			
Galb.			24 (sacr.)
Otho.		4	

*Both are taken from Polybios, a "scientific historian" not that keen on relating the supernatural. The choice of Philopoimen and Flamininus, vanquished and victor, from the same source, is most interesting, and gives a different type of artistic harmony than we find elsewhere.

a continuity of artistic tone between paralleled *Lives*. One interesting point is the lack of portents altogether in two *Lives*, *Philopoimen-Flamininus*. This set is particularly striking since both come from Polybios, they are the only case of contemporaries vanquished and victor in the parallel series. Toward the end, Plutarch is extremely laudatory of the Greek, critical of the Roman. The apparitions to Dion and Brutus were an obvious attempt at parallelism (though these things may have been taken no more seriously within the confines of Greco-Roman literature than the almost humorous transitions of Ovid in his *Metamorphoses*). Portents at the end of *Alexander-Caesar*, *Nicias-Crassus*, and *Demosthenes-Cicero*, give a consistent, almost symphonic tone, something obviously popular in Hellenistic literature, a great success with Ovid, and reflected in the art of such things as the Pegamon altar and Trajan's column. The artistic nature of Plutarch's parallelism, in fact the picking up of certain themes through many *Lives* certainly deserves more attention. This aspect of his writing has been seriously undermined by too narrow concentration on historical and moralistic aspects, and even printing Roman or Greek lives in chronological series and separate. Taken together, in a certain sense, his work is a biographical *carmen perpetuum*.

CHAPTER TEN

STILL FEELING THE EFFECTS OF HIS DREAM:
THE DREAMS OF THE LIVES

Now that Plutarch's attitude toward portents has been discussed, it is necessary to backtrack somewhat. The question of dreams arose earlier in connection with *De superstitione*, where trust in the mantic power of dreams seemed to be attacked. There also was seen to be a close connection between the use of portents and dreams. However, the study of *De superstitione* and related passages made it clear that Plutarch did not attack the reliability of all dreams but only those of the superstitious and that in fact he put incredible trust in the mantic power of dreams, especially when they came near the hour of death. We have also seen Plutarch's preference for dreams over portents, and his tendency to put a portent in a dream, such as in *Antony* 16 where lightning strikes a man's hand. It seems, then, worthwhile to direct more attention to this problem of dreams. Since one of the richest sources—if not the richest—of dreams in classical literature is the *Lives*, it would be folly not to attempt to make some sense out of these dreams. One word of caution is probably in order, namely, that it is difficult to say what is typical. The dreams reported by Aelius Aristides or Galen are quite different, almost exclusively concerned with healing. Yet, one should think that Plutarch's dreams —which cover a large temporal, geographical, and cultural span— must be more representative of classical civilization as a whole than those of Aristides.[1]

---

[1] Very helpful is the chapter, "Dream Pattern and Culture Pattern" in E. R. Dodds, *The Greeks and the Irrational* (Berkeley: 1951), pp. 102-134. One can also consult pp. 40-46 of his *Pagan and Christian in an Age of Anxiety* (Cambridge: 1964) for useful insights into dreams. Several studies are primarily concerned with the healing dream. Among them, A. Taffin, "Comment on rêvait dans les temples d'Ésculape," *Bull. Budé*, 4 (1960), 325-367; C. A. Meier, "The Dream in Ancient Greece and its Use in Temple Cures;" G. von Grünebaum, ed., *The Dream in Ancient Society* (Los Angeles: 1966), pp. 303-319; A. Behr, *Aelius Aristides and the Sacred Tales* (Amsterdam: 1968); and G. Michenaud and J. Dierkens, *Les Rêves dans les "Discours Sacrés" d'Aelius Aristide* (Brussels: 1972). Other studies: B. Büchsenschütz, *Traum und Traumdeutung im Altertum* (Berlin: 1868); O. Hey,

Artemidoros, Macrobius, and other late writers divided dreams into three classes, and these three categories may be useful in illuminating Plutarch's dreams.[2] However, the reliance which both ancient and modern authors have put upon these categories may be dangerous. According to the ancient authors, dreams can be divided into the following: the symbolic dream, which is enigmatic, metaphorical, and unintelligible without interpretation; the vision (*horama*), a straightforward enactment of coming events; and the oracular dream (*chrematismos*), in which a relative or other respected person reveals without symbolism the course of a coming event or the actions to be performed or avoided by the dreamer. The difficulty with using these divisions is that, in Plutarch's case at least, they invariably seem to overlap. One wonders whether the divisions, then, correspond as much to reality as they do to Artemidoros' pseudo-scientific bent. However, as Dodds points out, dreams represent culture patterns, and it is the culture patterns which should most concern us. Moreover, the dream which most distinguishes the ancient from the modern dreamer is the oracular dream. This is the most characteristic dream of the classical

Der Traumglaube im Altertum (Munich: 1908); J. B. Stearns, *Studies of the Dream as a Technical Device in Latin Epic and Drama* (Diss. Princeton: 1927); J. Hundt, *Der Traum bei Homer* (Greifswald: 1935); J. Volten, *Demotische Traumdeutung* (Copenhagen: 1942); H. Steiner, *Der Traum in der Aeneis* (*Noctes Romanae*, 5) (Bern: 1952); A. L. Oppenheim, "The Interpretation of Dreams in the Ancient Near East," *TAPhA* 46 (1956), 179-255; A. M. Esnoul, ed., *Les Songes et leur Interprétation* (*Sources Orientales*) (Paris: 1959); M. Weidhorn, "Dreams and Guilt," *Harv. Theol. Rev.*, 68 (1965), 69-90, A. Brelich, "Le rôle des rêves dans la conception religieuse du monde en Grèce," R. Caillois and G. E. von Grünebaum eds., *Le Rêve et les Societés Humaines* (Paris: 1967); pp. 282-289; P. Frisch, *Die Träume bei Herodot* (Meisenheim: 1868); R. Lenning, *Traum und Sinnestäuschung bei Aischylos, Sophokles, Euripides* (Diss. Tübingen: 1969); R. van Lieshout, "A Dream on a *kairos* of History. An Analysis of Herodotos, Hist. VII, 12-19; 47," *Mn.*, 23 (1970), 225-249; R. J. White, *The Interpretation of Dreams, The Oneirocritica of Artemidorus* (Park Ridge: 1975); N. Lewis, *The Interpretation of Dreams and Portents* (Toronto: 1975). Much of the matter in this chapter has been treated in my article "The Dreams of Plutarch's *Lives*," *Latomus*, 34 (1975), 336-349.
[2] Artemidor. 1.2, p. 5 Hercher; Macrobius, *In somn. Scip.* 1.3.2; Ps. Aug. *De spiritu et anima* 25 (*PL* 40.798); Ioann. Saresb. *Polycrat.* 2.15 (*PL* 199. 249a); Nicephoros Gregoras, *In Synesium de insomn.* (*PG* 149. 608a). The passages are collected and discussed by Deubner, *De Incubatione* 1 ff. The definitions quoted in the text are from Macrobius. For more on this matter see Dodds, "Dream Patterns and Culture Patterns" in *The Greeks and the Irrational*, pp. 102-34, and the introduction by R. J. White, *The Interpretation of Dreams*.

world, outside of the healing dream, and here Dodds' observations are entirely supported by the study of the dreams which appear in the *Lives*.

Around fifty dreams—depending on how one counts them— occur in the *Lives* even without the inclusion of *Marcellus* 28 where Plutarch turns Livy's comment that Marcellus was impetuous into a nightly dream in which Marcellus imagines he is locked in deadly conflict with Hannibal, *Dion* 9 where Dionysios is said to have executed his courtier Marsyas for dreaming that he had assassinated Dionysios, and *Antony* 27 where it is related that Octavius was saved in the first engagement at Philippi by the dream of a friend which warned him to withdraw before the battle.[3] The most numerous type of dream is the symbolic though often this type falls into another category as well. For example, in *Cimon* 18 a bitch warns Cimon of his approaching death. The appearance of a speaking personage suggests the oracular dream, but in the case of Cimon's dream the matter is put so enigmatically that the dream must also be thought of as symbolic. In *Timoleon* 8 two goddesses, Persephone and Demeter instead of speaking to the dreamer act out a part in which they indicate that they are favorable to Timoleon's enterprise to liberate Sicily. Likewise in *Eumenes* 6 two Alexander the Greats, each with a different pass-word, appear in a dream to Eumenes and engage in battle. Eumenes is able to observe which password went with the victorious Alexan-der in the dream battle, and by using the proper one for his own battle, is assured of victory. The personages belong to the oracular dream but they do not speak. In *Brutus* 20 (*Caesar* 68) Caesar attempts to lead the unwilling Cinna to dinner, and Cinna is unable to prevent himself being led into a dark void. In *Cicero* 44 Jupiter without speaking acts out a role in which it is indicated that the young Octavius will rise to greatness. In *Pompey* 73 where the hero is fleeing from Pharsalos, he appears in a dream to a Roman pilot in Egypt, indicating by his posture and clothing that he has suffered an ill fate; the next day the man recognizes

---

[3] In the Greek *Lives*: *Ages.* 6, *Alc.* 39 (where an alternate is given); *Alex.* 2 (2 dreams), 3, 18, 24, 26, 50; *Arist.* 11, 19; *Cim.* 18, *Cleom.* 7 ; *Demet.* 4, 19, 29; *Demos.* 29; *Eum.* 6; *Lys.* 20; *Pel.* 21; *Per.* 3, 13; *Pyr.* 11, 29; *Them.* 27, 30; *Timol.* 8; In the Roman *Lives*: *Ant.* 16, 22; *Brut.* 20, (*Caes.* 68), *Caes.* 32, 42 (*Pomp.* 68), 63 (with an alternate); *Cic.* 2, (possibly not a dream), 44, *Cor.* 24, *G. Gracch.* 1; *Luc.* 10, 12, 23; *Mar.* 45, *Pomp.* 32, 68, (*Caes.* 42), 73; *Rom.* 2; *Sul.* 9, 28, 37.

Pompey immediately, because of the dream, and takes him on board. It is an interesting and not untypical case of the use of dreams for motivation, as well as for conveying psychological states without the type of documentation which a modern biographer might have. In *Sulla* 9, the goddess called Selene—among other names for an eastern goddess Sulla picked up in the east— hands Sulla a firebolt and tells him to strike his enemies with it. Heracles, in a dream to Alexander before Tyre, simply stretches out his hand toward the city (*Alexander* 24).

Another characteristic of Plutarch's dreams, which does not exactly correspond to Artemidoros' description, is that the symbolic type rarely needs interpretation. Since Plutarch is using them for dramatic illustration of his narrative, they would probably be self-defeating if they were too complicated for his readers to grasp at once. Still, it is possible that Artemidoros is exaggerating slightly when he says that the symbolic dream needs interpretation. At any rate, the symbolism of Plutarch's dreams is almost patently evident. As noted above in connection with his portents, the great value of the supernatural machinery seems largely to consist in the symbolism with which the imagery can illuminate great events either in the life of a hero or the destiny of a nation, and it would be self-defeating to make this symbolism too complicated to be understood.

Toward the end of *De defectu oraculorum* (431e-433e), Lamprias indicates a firm belief in the mystic relationship of death to prophecy, and especially to that prophecy which is the result of dreaming:

> Souls therefore, all possessed of this power, which is innate but dim and hardly manifest, nevertheless oftentimes disclose its flower and radiance in dreams, and some in the hour of death, when the body becomes cleansed of all impurities and attains a temperament adapted to this end, a temperament through which the reasoning and thinking faculty of the souls is relaxed and released from their present state as they range amid the irrational and imaginative realms of the future. It is not true, as Euripides says, that
>
> The best of seers is he that guesses well;
>
> no, the best of seers* is the intelligent man, following the guidance of that in his soul which possesses sense and which, with the help of reasonable probability, leads him on his way. But that which foretells the future, like a tablet without writing, is both irrational and indeterminate in itself, but receptive of impressions and pre-

sentiments through what may be done to it, and inconsequently grasps at the future when it is farthest withdrawn from the present. Its withdrawal is brought about by a temperament and disposition of the body as it is subject to a change which we call inspiration. Often the body of itself alone attains this disposition. (F. C. Babbitt, Loeb, *Mor.* V, pp. 467-69: * should be "best of guessers").

Plutarch's belief here seems to be fully borne out by the dreams which he narrates in the *Lives*; for it is especially at the death of a hero that we find a dream, and frequently these are predictions of the death itself. Sometimes they are sufficiently detailed so that they reflect the manner of death. For example, Plutarch gives two versions of the dream which Alcibiades was supposed to have had before his murder. In one of the versions of his death the house where Alcibiades is staying is set on fire, and he rushes forth only to run upon his enemies' lances (*Alcibiades* 39).[4] Thus, there is some resemblance to one of the dreams in which he imagines an enemy cutting off his head while his body is on fire.

A similar type of vague vision of the future is evident in *Alexander*. Before the murder of Cleitos, Alexander has a dream in which he sees the victim sitting in black robes surrounded by his sons, "and all are dead" (*Alexander* 50). Not long after, while entertaining his generals at a banquet, Alexander in a heat of passion slays Cleitos. Perhaps the posture of Cleitos in the dream is meant to suggest the banquet. There is less similarity as far as the sons are concerned; at least there is no evidence that they were later executed by Alexander. After the death of Cleitos, the seers attempt to excuse Alexander by alleging that the deed was fated, as proved by the dream and portents; and Callisthenes tries to tell Alexander that he should not become depressed with the

---

[4] See note 12 to chapter II. 431e-433e is influenced by Plato, *Apol.* 39b. Plutarch gives two versions of Alcibiades' death and two dreams to go with them. In the first, his death is politically motivated: Lysander prevails upon the Persians to kill him; they set the house on fire and cut him down as he comes out. In the second version brothers of a girl he has corrupted kill him for personal reasons in the same circumstances of the burning house. In the first dream Timandra, Alcibiades' mistress, applies cosmetics to his head which she holds in her hands; in the second he sees Pharnabazos' men cutting off his head and his body on fire. Diodoros, 14.11, and Nepos, 10.2, omit the dreams. Justinus, 5.8.13 claims Alcibiades was burned to death in the house. The ultimate sources are supposed to be Apollodoros and Timagenes of Alexandria. It is interesting how often in the *Lives* the circumstances of a hero's death were swept up in conflicting versions.

incident since he is above the law (52).[5] At any rate there is a very convincing surrealistic quality to the dreams. Alcibiades, like many other heroes, dreams of his own death. Fortunately for posterity these dying heroes all managed to convey the dream to someone before their death (even if it were not always in one version). Let me quote from my article on the subject:

The nature of these dreams can be clarified by studying their use for two events which are similar in nature, the assassination of Caesar in *Caesar*, 63 and Alcibiades in *Alcibiades*, 39. In *Caesar* the dream comes not to the victim, but to his wife, Calpurnia, who sees herself holding her murdered husband in her arms. We have no evidence that Calpurnia ever did hold the murdered Caesar in her arms. In any case, it is not reported by Plutarch. Interest in a direct vision of the future, to establish a direct revelation of the details of the assassination through the dream was not his intention. His symbolic intention is further demonstrated by the alternate dream related in which the controversial pediment on Caesar's new house collapses.

The *Alcibiades* dream is similar but more interesting in its technique on several counts. Plutarch's principal intention in the *Caesar* passage was to construct an atmosphere of apprehension, suspense, and distress before the assassination, while underscoring the ironic hesitation which almost saved Caesar's life. At the same time the dreams illustrate the validity of oneiromancy, with the lurking suggestion that had Caesar been less sceptical and rationalistic he might have averted his doom. Though the *Alcibiades* is not one of Plutarch's most exciting or vivid lives and the death scene in particular is rather vague and imprecise, the dream experiences have a striking surrealistic and convincing quality. As in *Caesar* two dreams, perhaps from different sources, are related. There was no doubt about how Caesar died, but there were two versions of Alcibiades' assassination; both dreams, however, seem to go with the first version. Whether intended or not, the two dreams offer a complementary picture of the future. In the first dream the hero sees himself dressed in the clothes of his mistress Timandra—daughter of the famous Lais of Corinth—who holds his head in her arms

---

[5] The Cleitos incident figures large in *Alexander*. Truesdale Brown in "Callisthenes and Alexander," *Alexander the Great, the Main Problems*, pp. 19-51, suggested that the whole affair is unsatisfactory from an historical standpoint. He thinks it reflects the characteristics of the symposium genre (the murder takes place at a banquet), which have distorted the reality. However, Hamilton, *Alexander*, p. lxvi, disagrees, and believes he has the consensus of scholars on his side. Probably the basis of the affair is factual, but Plutarch—who himself resented the idea of Alexander's divinity—has probably blown up this element of the debate over Alexander's divinity and dramatized the banquet scene.

"whitening and painting his face as though it were a woman's."
In the other he sees the Persians cutting off his head and his body
burning. What are we to make of all this? Much is clarified by the
murder itself. The Persians sent to execute Alcibiades set fire to
the house and Alcibiades ran out naked with sword in hand only
to fall under a shower of spears, while Timandra later covered the
corpse with her own clothes (χιτωνίσκοις) and gave it a splendid
funeral. The part of the woman's clothes, cosmetics, and burning
of the body is suggestive of the funeral preparation, but the connection is rather loose; especially since decapitation is not mentioned,
there seems to be no attempt to describe a direct vision of the future
murder. The dream seems at least equally to symbolize the frustration, helplessness, and ignominy of Alcibiades. The horrible
reversal of sexual roles is a brilliant stroke depicting the inglorious
end of the swashbuckling but somewhat effeminate general. Thus
the dream is an intriguing mixture of symbolism and literalism.
Perhaps the omission or distortion of source material has contributed to this effect, but the result is fascinating and one might
suspect that the author approved of the result. (*Latomus* 39, 1975,
pp. 339-340).

Dodds implies that the anxiety dream was not frequent in Greek
literature, but such a view hardly seems to be justified by Plutarch's
selection of dreams before death. Several at least of the dreams of
death have strong undertones of anxiety. In *Demosthenes* 29 before
his death at the hands of Archias, Demosthenes dreams that the
two are engaged in a dramatic contest; Demosthenes plays his
role brilliantly but is denied the prize because the stage settings
of Archias are superior. At the end of *Sulla* (37), Sulla's son quite
openly tells him to put aside his anxious fears (παύσασθαι τῶν
φροντίδων) and to come join him and his mother, who had just
died.[6]

---

[6] Plutarch relied heavily on Sulla's *Memoirs* for this *Life* and the sentiment of many parts of it must reflect the *Memoirs*. In this chapter Plutarch
informs us that Sulla was down to the 22nd book of the *Memoirs* and still
working on it only two days before his death. Among the last words seem
to have been a Chaldaean prediction that he would die at the height of his
good fortune. The dream of Sulla in which his son appeared is taken from
this 22nd book. Apparently Sulla believed in a pleasant afterlife since the
son beckons him to a place of peace, and Sulla is not disturbed by the
dream even though the son appears in shabby clothes. Dreams apparently
were a striking part of the *Memoirs*. The introduction to the *Memoirs*
especially stressed the power of dreams; in *Sul.* 6 we learn that the dedication
had been to Lucullus and in it Sulla had said that one should rely on nothing
so much as that *to daimonion* revealed in dreams. In *Luc.* 23, after Lucullus'
dream of Autolycos at Sinope, Plutarch has Lucullus exclaim that Sulla

One could think also of the terrifying dream of Cinna which is related in *Brutus* 20 and *Caesar* 68. Plutarch thought it valuable enough to relate it as the last event in the *Life of Caesar* before the closing retribution chapter:

> There was a certain Cinna, however, one of the friends of Caesar, who chanced, as they say, to have seen during the previous night a strange vision. He dreamed, that is, that he was invited to supper by Caesar, and that when he excused himself, Caesar led him along by the hand, although he did not wish to go, but resisted. Now when he heard that they were going to burn the body of Caesar he rose up and went thither out of respect, although he had misgivings arising from his vision, and was at the same time in a state of fever. At sight of him one of the multitude told his name to another who asked him what it was, and he to another, and at once word ran through the whole throng that this man was one of the murderers of Caesar. For there was among the conspirators a man who bore this same name of Cinna, and assuming that this man were he, the crowd rushed upon him and tore him to pieces among them. This more than anything else made Brutus and Cassius afraid, and not many days afterwards they withdrew from the city. (Perrin, Loeb, *Lives* VII, pp. 603-605).[7]

was certainly right in regarding nothing as more certain or worthy of belief than that revealed in dreams. One suspects that Plutarch wrote this off his head, deducing that Lucullus should have said this, but it is certainly possible that Lucullus made some such remark. Sulla died in 79 B.C. Lucullus gave up his command in 66. Judging by Plutarch's fondness to use *to daimonion* in revelation contexts (10 times out of 15 occurrences in the Greek *Lives*, 9 times out of 20 occurrences in the Roman *Lives*) the *Lucullus* version, which omits *to daimonion*, may be closer to the wording of the *Memoirs*. Erbse, "Plutarchs Schrift *Peri Deisidaimonias*," 305, distorts the meaning of this passage. Claiming that it proves Plutarch believed in the constant incursion of *daimones* in human life, Erbse writes: "so berichtet Sulla in seinen Erinnerungen er habe sich auf nichts so fest verlassen wie auf die nächtlichen Befehle seines Daimon." Only once in the *Lives* (*Caes.* 69) does Plutarch use *to daimonion* to mean a *daimon*: this is in reference to Brutus' vision ("*to daimonion* departed"), and it is quite possible that it means "the mysterious thing;" elsewhere *to daimonion* almost certainly refers to the divinity. On the *Memoirs* see Flacelière, *Vies* VI, p. 216. He defends Plutarch against Carcopino, *Sylla ou la Monarchie Manquée*, pp. 9-10, who felt Plutarch was completely taken in by them. Plutarch interestingly omits the gruesome torture and murder of M. Marius Gratidianus, supposedly in retribution of Marius' forcing suicide on L. Catulus (Val. Max. 9.2.1). See Flacelière, p. 345. For the importance of the dream in *Sul.* 6 to Sulla, see M. L. Vollenweider, "Der Traum des Sulla Felix," *SNR*, 39 (1958-9), 22-34.

[7] The expression undoubtedly refers to the afterlife and reflects a phrase of Parmenides. In the introduction to his philosophy (B1.18), the philosopher is led on his mystic voyage to the world beyond, through doors which swing open to a χάσμ' ἀχανές. The description became a model for

The dream as related in shorter form in *Brutus* contains a more loaded eschatological phrase: Caesar leads Cinna into a limitless dark place where he follows unwillingly and in terror (εἰς ἀχανῆ τόπον καὶ σκοτεινὸν αὐτὸν δ' ἄκοντα καὶ τεθαμβημένον ἔπεσθαι, *Brut.* 20).

The anxiety dream also appears in less unfortunate circumstances. In *Demetrios* 19 we have the only dream of running in the *Lives*. Antigonos—at the age of eighty years—is elated by Demetrios' successful attack on Cypros and decides to launch a full-scale attack on Ptolemy. But the dream of a friend—prefaced with Plutarch's words that this was to predict the outcome of the struggle—reflects the doubts of his army. In the dream Antigonos with his army is competing in a race in which they must run back and forth. Antigonos starts out well, but as he runs on his strength gradually begins to fail him; he becomes weak as he rounds the turn and collapses over the finish line. Plutarch adds the expected commentary: "events verified the vision since Antigonos and Demetrios ran into trouble at sea, lost many of their ships, and returned without accomplishing much." The dream illustrates the curious characteristics of anxiety, prediction, and vision of the future which we find in so many dreams of the *Lives*. Though Demetrios' dream is symbolic, it is sufficiently vague to escape immediate understanding of the future. The reader would hardly guess that Antigonos would have to turn back. We should think that in some land struggle he would have won a Pyrrhic victory. In this sense interpretation is an important factor.

A brilliant, more personal, and very convincing type of this anxiety dream appears in *Pompey* 32 in which Mithridates' coming political and military debacle is depicted through a shipwreck scene on the Pontos. One should notice the setting of the dream for local color and the sudden shift in mood appropriate to the surrealism of a dream:

---

subsequent portrayals of the other world. See J. S. Morrison, "Parmenides and Er," *JHS*, 75 (1955), 59-68. Parmenides meant the place to be something like the world of Forms we encounter in Plato, but in the description of it in Plutarch, it has become identified with the underworld. The dream is not mentioned by other authors but possibly came from L. Crassicius of Tarentum, surnamed Pasicles, a freedman, who was active in the theatre, ran a school, and published a commentary on Cinna's *Zmyrna*. Plutarch does not seem to be aware of Cinna's place in Roman literature. On this see J. Granarolo, "L'époque néotérique ou la poésie romaine d'avant garde," *ANRW* I, 3 (1973), pp. 299-302.

Next, however, Pompey caught up with him (Mithridates) near the River Euphrates and camped close by him. Fearing that he might give him the slip again by crossing the river first, he drew up his army and led it out about midnight. At this time Mithridates is said to have had a dream showing him what was going to happen. He dreamed that he was sailing on the Pontic Sea with a fair wind behind him, and that he was already in sight of the Bosporus and was talking gaily with his fellow passengers, as one might be expected to do in one's pleasure in finding oneself really and certainly safe; and then suddenly he seemed to see himself, with all his companions gone, being tossed about on the sea, clinging to a small piece of wreckage. While he was still dreaming and feeling the effects of his dream, his friends came to his bed and woke him with the news that Pompey was attacking. There was nothing to be done except to fight in defence of the camp, and so his generals led out their forces and put them in order of battle. (Rex Warner, *Plutarch, Fall of the Roman Republic*, p. 169).

One cannot help but feel that Plutarch's source said nothing about Mithridates rising immediately to battle Pompey. The very Plutarchan touch helps to explain why he lost. One can recall Brutus and Cassius leaving the city after Cinna's dream and death (*Brutus* 20, *Caesar* 68), and Antony leaving Octavius after his hand is struck by lightning in a dream (*Antony* 16). It is simply amazing how many defeats in Plutarch's description of great battles of the past are psychologically grounded in these dreams of coming disaster.

Not all these symbolic dreams are unpropitious. We have the favorable vision of the priests at Corinth who see the goddesses Persephone and Demeter accompanying Timoleon to Sicily (*Timoleon* 8), and Themistocles' dream before his escape to Persia (*Themistocles* 27).[8] In the latter dream a snake turns into an eagle and deposits the hero near a herald's wand; Themistocles is thus sufficiently encouraged to try his luck at the Persian court. Other dreams of this sort are Cicero's dream of Jupiter picking the young Octavius out of a crowd of Roman boys (*Cicero* 44) (Plutarch claims that Cicero was later able to identify the boy on sight).[9] Sulla, on the march from Nola to attack Marius at Rome, dreams

[8] Thucydides, 1.137, only mentions an encouraging letter. Plutarch's dream here is a typical example of his fondness for them and his use of them to motivate a departure to another place.
[9] The dream was well known but with some variations: in Suetonius, *Aug.* 94.9, and Dio, 45.2, Jupiter casts an image of Rome into the boy's lap.

that Selene put a firebolt (κεραυνός) in his hands and told him to strike his enemies (*Sulla* 9). As she names them one by one, they are smitten, fall, and vanish away. "Encouraged by this vision" Sulla relates the dream to his friends and marches in good spirits on Rome. It is possible that this dream came from Sulla's *Memoirs*, and that Plutarch has in fact missed part of the point of it. As he relates in the same chapter, Sulla's troops ran into stiff resistance as they entered the city: the mob took to the rooftops and pelted them with stones, and they were ordered by Sulla to fire their "firebolts" (πυροβόλοι) which turned part of the city into an inferno. Plutarch, who tries his best to excuse Sulla, attributes the incident to Sulla's anger, but he cannot help but lodge a protest against this act of cruelty which destroyed "friends and enemies, innocent and guilty alike." But he seems to miss a possible allusion to the firebolts. Perhaps the allusion was used in the *Memoirs* to justify the action.

The symbolic dream, therefore, needs little interpretation and is usually prefaced anyway with Plutarch's comments as to its meaning. At least the dream is clear as far as the general outcome is concerned, even if the prediction is unclear about the details. Plutarch's interest, however, seems to be rather exclusively concerned with the general outcome or rather gross implications of a dream. On a few occasions where the dream is still obscure he provides the reader with a seer to unravel its dark meaning, even if the dream was undoubtedly well-known, such as Philip's dream that he had put a seal on Olympias' womb (*Alexander* 2). There are more dreams which require interpretation. In *Pyrrhos* 29 we have a dream of lightning striking a city. The dream is similar to that which one of the Theban conspirators in *De genio Socratis* has on the night before the liberation of Thebes from the Spartan garrison. At that time the dream turned out to be propitious, but Pyrrhos, who dreams of lightning striking Sparta, ignores the ominous interpretation of a friend and runs into disaster, being lucky to save his life. It is clear to the reader before the result, that Pyrrhos lacks caution, and his bold statement, "One omen is best, to fight for Pyrrhos," is clearly a sign of his spiritual blindness. Another uncertain dream appears in *Demetrios*. Antigonos dreams that Mithridates has stolen a golden crop which he has sown. Plutarch is quick to point out that Mithridates was to reap the fruits of Antigonos' efforts (*Demetrios* 4). Plutarch's interest in the dream centers around the figure of the early Mithridates as the founder of the dynasty of Pontic kings, but he relates that Antigonos took the dream so seriously that the unsuspecting Mithridates was only saved by the friendly Demetrios who wrote "fly" on the ground with his spear. One technique to depict the uncertainty is to have the hero come to the true interpretation of a dream after a preliminary false start. Thus, Pompey before the battle of Pharsalos dreams that he entered his theatre to decorate a statue of Venus. Pompey is at first elated, but then he remembers that Venus was a patron of Caesar, and his confidence is shattered (*Pompey* 68, *Caesar* 42).[10]

Plutarch rarely indicates any uncertainty himself about the meaning of a dream. However, in one case he seems to have thrown his hands in the air. In *Cimon* 18, Cimon sees an angry bitch which barks at him and tells him that he will soon be a friend to her and her whelps. Plutarch explains that Astyphilos of Poseidonia—who undoubtedly was his source for the dream—interpreted it to indicate the approaching death of Cimon. Plutarch's uncertainty suggests that we have an actual dream of Cimon which puzzled him at the time and not mere literary dressing.

One of the places where Plutarch seems to have taken great liberties and to have not only used his greatest powers of embellishment, but also to have injected his own idea of the hero into a dramatic passage is at the crossing of the Rubicon in the *Life of Caesar* (32). The historical narrative differs considerably from that in other ancient authors, and Plutarch injects, alone of extant authors, a most interesting dream. Let me quote once more:

> The most blatant manipulation of a dream for biographical purposes—so far as we can judge—is Caesar's dream of intercourse

---

[10] When Appian relates the dream (*BC.* 2.68) he does not give the place in which Pompey decorates the statue. Perhaps Plutarch filled it out from his own conjecture as to where the statue should have been. In *Brutus* and *Caesar* he lays special stress on Pompey's theatre and statue as the place of Caesar's murder. The text in *Caesar* does not give more than the introduction to the dream, and its place in the theatre. Most editors fill it in from the *Pomp.* 68 passage, but Ziegler lets it stand (Teubner, *Vit.* II-2). However, since the dream is barely intelligible as the text stands, Ziegler's version seems overly conservative. Plutarch should have seen the place himself, and if Caesar was not killed under the statue, may have been taken in by his guides. K. Schefold, "Cäsars Epoche als Goldene Zeit Römischer Kunst," *ANRW*, I, 4 (1973), pp. 944-69, gives on p. 964 an interesting description of the statue of Venus.

with his own mother (*Caesar*, 32.9), treated in a strikingly original and effective manner. Plutarch transfers the dream from Caesar's quaestorship in Spain—where the authorities had put it (Suetonius, *Caesar*, 7.2, Cassius Dio, xli, 24)—to the night before the crossing of the Rubicon. He dispenses with the sole, propitious interpretation given it by Suetonius and Dio—mastery over one's country, leaving this interpretation possible, but suggesting the ill-boding meaning it had for Hippias before Marathon in Herodotus, vi, 107 where Hippias took the dream to prophesy his success and death in his motherland at a rich old age, but died shortly after. The reader might think of Caesar's horrible murder to come before he had settled down to rule in his own country (69. 1), though five years and several chapters separate the event. Plutarch's description of the dream as "unlawful" is significant, and the immediate tone is one of anxiety, lawlessness, and ruthlessness—a man who would not hesitate to rape his own mother if that meant supreme power, and there is the hint, as in the *Pompey* dream of Mithridates, that the gods were working through the dream to push forward the course of destiny, as the dream seems to motivate his fateful decision. (p. 346).

It is interesting that Plutarch does not explain what meaning he got out of Caesar's incestuous dream of intercourse with his mother the night before crossing the Rubicon (*Caesar* 32). Perhaps Plutarch thought the dream was self-evident, or else—the opposite—that it was too confusing.[11] At any rate he says nothing,

---

[11] Artemidoros, *Oniroc.* 1.79, has a field day with the dream. He criticizes previous interpreters for sloppy groundwork in failing to take into account the sexual positions in the dream and the circumstances of the dreamer. His own basic pseudo-scientific outline can be given here: a jealousy is indicated if the mother loves the father; if the father is sick the dream is an indication that the father will die; if the dreamer is poor and the mother rich he will either inherit wealth or become rich himself; if the mother is dead, death is indicated for the dreamer; if she resists, bad news is in store for the dreamer; if the mother is motionless—a difficult dream for Artemidoros—she represents "birth, *tyche*, or some *daimon*;" if the mother is on top of the dreamer he will probably die since she represents the earth; if the dreamer is sick at the time, he is going to die. Prominent in Artemidoros' account is the dream's political significance in which power over one's country is indicated. This is the significance given the dream by Dio, 41.24 and Suetonius, *Caes.* 7. See White, *The Interpretation of Dreams*, pp. 61 and 64. Other significant references to it: Soph. *O.T.* 981-982, Paus. 4.26.3, and see Dodds, *Greeks*, pp. 47 and 61-62. The whole passage at the Rubicon has been heavily reworked by Plutarch or his source, probably Pollio to some extent, and differs greatly from that of other classical authors, especially in the tone given the ἀνερρίφθω κύβος. On this see J. Taillardat, "Comica," *REG*, 64 (1951), 4-9; E. Hohl, "Cäsar am Rubico," *Hermes*, 80 (1952), 246-49, M. Gelzer, *Caesar* (tr. Oxford: 1968), p. 193, note 3,

though Suetonius (*Caesar* 7) feels obligated to explain the dream to the reader. It may also be that Plutarch felt he had to suppress Suetonius' interpretation, which gave it a propitious meaning; Plutarch was more interested in the approaching tragedy to the Republic, and in Caesar's ambition, which knowing no bounds eventually brought about his murder. The Greek reader might recall the death and disappointment of Hippias, who had the sinister dream before the battle of Marathon (*Herodotos*, 6.107).[12] In Plutarch's ambiguous relation of the dream, the soul of Caesar is laid bare: his ruthless ambition would not stop at raping his mother if this stood in his way to power.

Only one riddle dream appears. Before the capture of Tyre in *Alexander* 24, Alexander is baffled by a dream in which he manages to coax a satyr into his hands. The seers correctly interpret the dream to mean that Tyre will soon fall (σὰ γενήσεται Τύρος).[13]

In spite of the impression that one gets from Artemidoros that the *horama*, or straightforward vision-dream is common in Greek literature, it is difficult to find a clear-cut case of it in Plutarch. There are three cases where it is approximated. In *Aristides* 19 Plutarch repeats a dream found in Herodotos: a Lydian sent to the temple of Amphiaraus by the Persian general Mardonios has an

---

and F. H. Sandbach, *Menander, A Commentary* (Oxford: 1973), pp. 690-691, with different interpretations of the meaning of the phrase. The saying seems to come from Menander *Arrephoros* fr. 59 (Sandbach), where it is difficult to tell whether it emphasizes the decision or the future risk. Plutarch seems here to have it parallel the dream; i.e. Caesar is a gambler who will stop at nothing. This seems to be the meaning of something similar, ἀναρρῖψαι used with μάχην in *Caes.* 40, with κύβος in *Brut.* 40, and with κίνδυνος in *Nic.* 11, *Demos.* 20, *Brut.* 54, *Arat.* 4, and *Pomp.* 74, where an act of desperation is implied, and the act refers to the future. All except the *Nicias* passage refer to famous battles (Pharsalos, Phillipi, Chaironeia), with which readers of the *Parallel Lives* would be familiar. All but the *Nicias* passage use the aorist infinitive ἀναρρῖψαι. The likelihood is that the perfect is meant to emphasize the action (see L. A. Post, "Dramatic Uses of the Greek Imperative," *AJP*, 59 (1938), 30-59. The dream emphasizes—like the saying—Caesar's rashness rather than decisiveness. I am grateful to Prof. E. N. O'Neil for helping locate the passages.

[12] In Herodotos 6.107 Hippias, the Athenian aristocrat who is trying to have himself installed at Athens as a Persian puppet, has the dream before the battle of Marathon. Hippias at first believes he will return to power and die peacefully, but later he loses a tooth and after searching in vain for it he concludes that that little bit of soil is all he or the Persian will ever have of Greece.

[13] The text has been reconstructed here by Ziegler from Zonaras who has σὰ Τύρος ἔσται See Teubner, *Vit.* II-2, p. 184.

incubation dream in which the servant of the god stands by him and commands him to depart; when he refuses, the man crushes his head with a rock. We learn that this was the manner of Mardonios' death later.[14] In *Caesar* 63 Calpurnia holds Caesar's murdered body in her arms. However, in both cases certain incidents in the dream do not match those in reality; Calpurnia never held her husband in her arms, and Mardonios could hardly have concluded from the Lydian's dream that he was to be slain by a stone from a Greek soldier. The third case, the dream in which Alcibiades' mistress holds his head in her hands and applies cosmetics to it, is less obvious (*Alcibiades* 39). Did it signify emasculation, or the dressing of the body for the funeral?[15]

The oracular dream is indeed common, appearing twenty-three times in the *Lives* if we can include some dreams which have already been classified as symbolic. One of the first types to strike one's attention is that in which the oracle is delivered by a mysterious voice. Such a voice commands Agesilaus to sacrifice his daughter at Aulis (*Agesilaus* 6). Another mysterious voice tells Marius in an enigmatic verse that he is to watch out for the return of Sulla (*Marius* 45). An anonymous voice in a dream also assists Cleomenes to power. He has contemplated usurping power at Sparta and is fearful that his plot has been detected when a man reports that a voice in a dream has indicated that the best arrangement for Sparta would be that depicted in the dream—one chair standing in place of the usual four chairs of the ephors (*Cleomenes* 7). But later, when Cleomenes finds the man is in good faith, he goes along with his original plan, removes the chairs and conducts

---

[14] It is possible that Plutarch for some reason or other is attempting to pick a bone with Herodotos, whose account differs. In Herod. 8.135, Mys, the Carian, visits the shrine of Ptoan Apollo overlooking Lake Copais to have the dream. Plutarch gives an account similar to that of the *Life* in *De def.* 412 a-b, but Babbitt has everything confused in his note on it (Loeb, *Mor.* V, p. 363, n. a.). Flacelière, *Sur la Disparition*, p. 224, is undoubtedly right in refusing to correct Plutarch's text on the basis of Herodotos. If there is any place where Plutarch exercises independent judgment it is in his treatment of Herodotean material.

[15] Dreams appear frequently before the death of a hero, a characteristic which illustrates Plutarch's belief in the mantic power of the soul at this time. Cf. *Alc.* 39, *Alex.* 50, *Arist.* 19, *Cim.* 18, *Demos.* 29, *Caes.* 63, 68, *Brut.* 20, *Mar.* 45, *Sul.* 37. Dreams before great battles rate highest in frequency, cf. *Ages.* 6, *Alex.* 18, 24, *Arist.* 11, *Demet.* 19, 29, *Eum.* 6, *Pel.* 21, *Pyr.* 11, 29, *Timol.* 8, *Ant.* 22, *Caes.* 32, 42, *Luc.* 10, 12, 23, *Pomp.* 32, 68, *Sul.* 9.

business there with confidence that his usurpation is seconded by the gods (10).

The oracular dream is in no way restricted to the Greek *Lives*. From the earliest to the latest Roman period described by Plutarch in his biographies we find the dream. Among dreams in the early period is one in *Romulus*. In chapter 2 of that *Life* Hestia appears in a dream to Tarchetius, an early king of Italy, in one of the many conflicting stories of Roman origins. Plutarch regards the whole thing as myth (μυθῶδη παντάπασιν) but undoubtedly related it as important for conveying the Roman mentality about their origins, the barbarism of the early state, and the conflicting sources about it. In the story a daimonic *phallos* had risen from the hearth and remained there for many days. The Etruscan sooth-sayer who was consulted ordered Tarchetius to command his daughter to have intercourse with it. But the girl refused and Tarchetius threatened her with death. The whole dreadful dilemma was resolved by a dream in which Hestia commanded Tarchetius to release the girl from the threat, and the maid—whom the girl sent in to do the job—gave birth to the twins. No wonder Plutarch regarded it as rather fantastic. Luckily he gives us his source for the story, "a certain Promathion who wrote a history of Italy." Plutarch writes the story with tongue in cheek but the sentimental ending, with the god appearing in a dream to save someone, is not uncharacteristic of his own writing.[16]

The *Romulus* dream is very straightforward in that Hestia speaks directly. Most of the other dreams involve some sort of enigmatic conversation or symbolic gesture. It would seem that Plutarch's source for the dreams in the *Life of Lucullus* was particularly captivated by the oracular dream. At any rate, while Lucullus is engaged at the siege of Cyzicos in his campaign against Mithridates, the goddess Persephone appears in a dream to the town clerk, a man named Aristagoras, and tells him she is bringing

---

[16] Some scholars think the dream represents a genuine very ancient layer of Roman thought with Ethruscan origins. E. Gabba, *Entretiens Fondation Hardt*, 13 (1966), p. 148 ff., speculated that Plutarch was affected by the Etruscomania of the late Republic. T. J. Cornell, "Aeneas and the Twins: The Development of the Roman Foundation Legend," *Proc. Camb. Philol. Soc.*, 21 (1975), 1-33, in an interesting and well researched article on Roman origins accepts a late date (1st B.C.) for Promathion. For Vesta see H. Himmel, "Vesta und die Frührömische Religion," *ANRW* I,2 (1972), pp. 397-420.

"the Libyan fifer against the Pontic trumpeteer." Only after a wind from Africa destroys the Pontic king's siege engines can everyone breathe easier. The goddess Athena later, looking quite battered, appears to the citizens of Ilion and exclaims that she has just come from helping the Cyzicenes (*Lucullus* 10). Then, after the capture of Cyzicos while Lucullus is camped at the Troad he pitches his tent in the sacred precinct of Aphrodite. In the night the goddess stands over him in his sleep and says "Why are you sleeping, great lion, when the fawns are there for the taking?" Lucullus wakes quickly and acting on the divine assistance destroys Mithridates' fleet which is attempting to escape (12). Later in the *Life*, when he is engaged before Sinope, an anonymous figure in a dream stands beside him and asks him why he is sleeping when Autolycos (the founder of Sinope) has come to see him. Lucullus is puzzled as to what this is about, but after taking the city he later finds a statue of Autolycos lying on the sand of the beach. Plutarch at this point fills in the reader on who the legendary Autolycos was, and then adds the surprising note that Lucullus on seeing the statue recalled that Sulla in his *Memoirs* had related that nothing was more trustworthy than that which was signified in dreams (*Lucullus* 23). It is possible that Plutarch is writing this off the top of his head, but one should remember that Sulla's *Memoirs* were dedicated to Lucullus and that in the dedication Sulla had told him to rely on nothing so much as that which *to daimonion* signified in dreams (*Sulla* 6). The most logical deduction is that Plutarch is filling in on the *Life of Lucullus* from the information he got in Sulla's *Memoirs*—unless of course, Lucullus wrote his own *Memoirs*. It is also possible that the statue of Autolycos was in the possession of Lucullus' family and the story of the dream had been attached permanently to it. At least this would help to explain Plutarch's ability to identify the artist.

As a matter of fact, the oracular dreams seem to speak more in riddles than the oracles themselves. In rewriting the battle of Plataia, however, we find the reverse. The oracle must be clarified by a dream. Plutarch records a very complicated oracle given by Delphi before the battle. Fortunately, Zeus Soter appears in a dream in the nick of time to the seer Arimnestos and explains the puzzling contradictions (*Aristides* 11). In *Themistocles* 30, Cybele puzzles the hero by telling him in a dream that he is to avoid "the lion's head;" he escapes disaster when he remembers the dream on getting to a town of that name where his enemies are lying in ambush for him.

Yet, thank heaven, the gods do not always speak in riddles. The *phasma*—which possibly appears in a dream—seen by Cicero's nurse simply tells her the child will achieve greatness (*Cicero* 2). Alexander, in a dream to Pyrrhos, candidly tells Pyrrhos that he will help him (*Pyrrhos* 11). In the only healing dream of the *Lives*, Athena appears in a dream to Pericles to instruct him on the cure of a workman who had fallen from the Parthenon during its construction (*Pericles* 13). Zeus Ammon tells Lysander to raise a siege (*Lysander* 20). And before Sulla's death his son appears to him in a dream and tells him to come and join himself and Metella, Sulla's wife, who had previously died (*Sulla* 37).

Though the oracular dream appears in both Greek and Roman *Lives*, it is interesting that the appearance of gods in the dreams is more or less restricted to Greeks or to Romans when they are on Greek or Oriental soil. There are two exceptions. One is the appearance of Jupiter to an early Roman where Jupiter expresses his displeasure over a procession preceded by a slave who was being beaten (*Coriolanus* 24). Jupiter also, without speaking, picks out the young Octavius from a crowd of youngsters, in a dream to Cicero (*Cicero* 44). Otherwise we must move over to Greek territory to find a god speaking. There is an incident in the *Life of Sulla*, where the goddess described by Plutarch as Selene, Athena, or Enyo, appears to Sulla in a dream while he is on the march from Nola to Rome (*Sulla* 9). But this is a goddess whom Sulla has undoubtedly picked up on his travels in the East. It is difficult to say what conclusions should be drawn from the rarity of Roman oracular dreams in which gods appear, but it seems to suggest that the phenomenon was not very indigenous to Roman thought.

Alexander apparently was a frequent personage in the oracular dreams, if we can judge by his appearance to the generals Demetrios (*Demetrios* 19), Pyrrhos (*Pyrrhos* 11), and Eumenes (*Eumenes* 6). In each case his appearance has to do with a revelation of the outcome of a battle. One must suspect that many a Hellenistic general told his troops that Alexander had appeared to him in a dream the night before and assured him of success in a coming battle, or perhaps spread the rumor that Alexander in a dream to his rival had warned of defeat. Two dreams take place in sacred precincts, that of the Lydian who is sent to the temple of Amphiaraus—a dream taken from Herodotos (*Aristides* 19)—and that of Lucullus in the sacred precinct of Aphrodite at the Troad (*Lucullus* 12). In the first, the servant of the god speaks; in the second, Aphrodite reveals herself openly, standing over Lucullus to speak her enigmatic verse.

There are many indications that Plutarch felt much safer when relating dreams than he did relating portents. Even so, as he does when introducing portents, he usually prefixes the dreams with the hedging "it was said." Only on three occasions does he definitely attack the reliability of a dream. In *Lysander* 20 he refuses to accept the report that Lysander's real reason for abandoning the siege at Amphytai and sailing to Libya was a dream in which Zeus Ammon appeared to Lysander and told him to go there. Plutarch indicates this is his personal opinion, but he mentions that Ephoros thought differently and that he will give Ephoros' version later. In 25 he does so, accepting Ephoros' interpretation of Lysander's relationship with the shrine of Ammon as an attempt to bribe his way to the throne. Plutarch himself believed Lysander's primary reason was his fear of returning to the subjection of the ephors. In *Agesilaus* 6 and *Pelopidas* 21 Plutarch obviously had to reject the idea that the gods could be asking in a dream for human sacrifice, but he does not reject the idea that the gods in the dream were asking for some sacrifice. Perhaps the use of a mysterious voice in the first instance, and the inconsequential Scedasos and his daughters in the second, is meant to detract from the possible divine authority of the dreams.

In two cases he asserts that the dream was true because of the unsuperstitious character of the recipients (*Coriolanus* 24, *Caesar* 63). In the first, the man who reports the dream is one "not given to superstition" and in the second he reports that Calpurnia was never given to "feminine superstition" (γυναικισμὸν ἐν δεισιδαιμονίᾳ,). This is undoubtedly meant to lend credibility to the dreams. The phrases are especially interesting since Livy's account of the *Coriolanus* dream does not use the qualifying phrase.[17] We have no other sources on Calpurnia which mention her lack of superstition. The addition then, seems to be Plutarch's fancy. Naturally

---

[17] The lack of superstition is apparently Plutarch's touch, judging not only by Liv. 2.36, but also by Val. Max. 1.7.4, and Dion. Hal. 7.68-69, which omit mention of the recipient's mentality. The dream fits Plutarch's own genuine humanitarian feelings.

it would have made little sense for Plutarch to include a large number of dreams which he felt were spurious, and he undoubtedly expected his readers to use a grain of salt. Moreover, the interpretation of a dream is just as important as the dream itself. He ridicules Mithridates, whose body was found with books of dream interpretations not only of his own dreams but of those of his wives (*Pompey* 37). Since the dreams involved with Alexander's divinity were repugnant to Plutarch's own views on the subject, he makes short shrift of them (*Alexander* 1).

Plutarch's personal, philosophical belief in dreams expresses itself in the *Lives* to an extraordinary degree. Once again we find that the rejuvenation of an ancient superstition is aided by the philosophical advances of several centuries of sophisticated thought. The belief must be pared down, trimmed up, based on rational principles. For Plutarch these are the spirituality of the soul, the nature of sleep which effects a temporary separation of soul and body, and the desire of the divine in its goodness to communicate with men. It is no coincidence that in one of his most developed myths, that of *De genio Socratis*, Timarchos is able to experience the vision of the other world while he is sleeping, and the myth ends with the story of a man whose soul—"or rather *nous*"—was able to roam while he slept, returning to report news from all the world. In general Plutarch's dreams in the *Lives* bear out the conclusions and suggestions of scholars like Dodds. However, there would seem to be more stress on anxiety in these dreams than Dodds implies, and symbolic dreams tend to be more obvious than he suggests. Moreover, it is questionable whether the *horama* dream, or straightforward vision of the future, in the literal sense is really very common. At least Plutarch seems to avoid it altogether.

As we have found in the case of portents, Plutarch uses considerable liberty in the selection and adaptation of dream material in order to suit the exigencies of the *Lives*. In general, though he seems to have favored divination through dreams over all other types, he exercises caution. Dreams are usually reserved for predictions of the future greatness of the hero, for important decisions in his life or before great battles which decide the destiny of nations, and for the coming death of the hero. The *Lives* particularly exemplify the *Moralia* tenet that dreaming is most accurate as one approaches death since it is at that time that the soul comes closest to purification. The oracular and the healing dream are the most characteristic types in Greek literature. Plutarch's silence over the healing dream—not only in the *Lives*, but also in the *Moralia*—may be an indication of his disbelief in it. On the other hand healing dreams would normally serve little purpose in his type of writing. As always, he is interested in material which will illuminate the character of the hero, and for this reason the dreams are often expressive of the dreamer's personality. Moreover, they are often used as motivation necessary for a particular action. In this connection one can cite Caesar's dream at the Rubicon, Antony's dream before his departure from Octavius, Brutus' and Cassius' decision to abandon Rome, Pompey's half-hearted stand at Pharsalos.

His attitude is difficult for us to grasp, with its implicit faith in the veracity of dreams along with stress on their prophetic quality as the most important element in them, and then the almost bizarre and baroque use of them to communicate the inner feelings of men in an area where his biographical sources were weak, combined with the greatest liberty in manipulating and embellishing them for literary purposes. He probably is in sympathy with Sulla when Sulla writes in his *Memoirs* that nothing could be so much relied upon as that which *to daimonion* revealed in dreams (*Lucullus* 23, *Sulla* 6). In fact, this element in Sulla's character may have been responsible for Plutarch's incredible whitewashing of some of his deeds. Thus the *Lives* here closely reflect the spirit of the *Moralia* where he selects dreaming as the most worthy form of divination. The inclusion of so many dreams in the *Lives*, often where we can find them in no other source, is not just a coincidence. In contrast, Plutarch seems reluctant to include many portents occurring in other sources. He expected the reader to believe them, yet leaves belief in an individual occurrence dependent upon a covering "it was said."

Perhaps Plutarch's major contribution, and a magnificient one at that, was the use of the dream in a period of individualism, to lay bare the recesses of a hero's soul when the lack of intimate details in his sources, often centuries old, must have been a perplexing frustration. That he found so many interesting dreams is a tribute to his ingenuity. Unconsciously or consciously he seems to have used the canons of older history and biography to write about men almost his contemporaries, thus giving an artistic balance to the *Greek and Roman Lives*. With centuries separating him from Homer we see him using, though in a more sophisticated fashion, many of the elements constitutive of dreams in the *Iliad* and *Odyssey*, such as the appearance of the recently departed to the dreamer (itself as old as the Gilgamesh epic) and above all, what appears to be the manipulation of history and of fate by the gods working upon the minds of men by sending dreams. Here also, Plutarch reveals that fascination with the interaction of the human and the hidden divine, that dual motivation and dual causality affecting human affairs and divine destiny—at least as it is seen by modern eyes investigating an alien culture. In this way we can appreciate both the change and continuity of classical civilization, a theme of classical history and biography expressing itself in different ages through Homer, Herodotos, and Plutarch. Partly this was so because he believed that his own age represented something significant, the end result of the gods working through human blunders and what seems to men, capricious circumstances—a peaceful civilized society in which the unity of man had somehow been achieved.[18]

---

[18] G. Devereux, *Dreams in Greek Tragedy, an Ethno-Psycho-Analytic Study* (Berkeley: 1976), came to my attention after writing this. Most interesting is his discussion of the oracular and oedipal dreams in the light of his clinical practice. (They are virtually non-existent). D. Del Corno, *Graecorum de re onirocritica scriptorum reliquiae* (Milan: 1969), besides interesting texts, supplies a full bibliography.

CHAPTER ELEVEN

NOT A PRETENCE FOR COWARDICE: THE DELPHIC ORACLE IN THE LIVES

The divine does not reveal itself through dreams alone but also through oracles, and for Plutarch the oracle of oracles was that at Delphi. It even seems likely that most of the *Lives* were written while he was a priest there. At any rate he is a superb propagandist for the shrine. Delphi shines through the *Lives* like a beacon of inspiration in the darkness of human misery and misunderstanding. The *Lives* are, then, an excellent fund of information on the shrine though we know little of Plutarch's sources, what existed in the archives there, or the exact nature of the antiquities at the time he wrote. Invariably where his account differs from that of another writer, it is biased in favor of the shrine. To a large extent it can be said that the *Bioi* attempt to glorify Delphi where it has already been illustrious, remove the dark spots where it seems to have a tarnished reputation, and demonstrate that not only the origins of the Greek and Roman states, but even the most critical moments in their history are intimately associated with the most famous of all Greek oracles.[1]

Naturally there are fewer references to Delphi in the Roman *Lives* than there are in the Greek, but one should not underestimate their importance. Delphi is mentioned on eight occasions in the Roman *Lives*, and generally something is contributed to our knowledge. An interesting example of the inclusion of Delphi material in a *Life* appears in *Aemilius Paullus* 28. Aemilius arrives

---

[1] The most recent full work on the subject is H. W. Parke and D. E. W. Wormell, *The Delphic Oracle* (Oxford: 1956). The first volume gives the history of the shrine, the second, the oracles themselves. A full bibliography is given at the back of volume one. A more recent study is Parke's *Greek Oracles* (London: 1967), a short and popular work. R. Flacelière, *Greek Oracles* (London: 1965), another popular work, is also more recent than Parke-Wormell. For the history of the shrine one can also consult G. Daux, *Delphes au IIe et au Ier Siècle* (Paris: 1937), and R. Flacelière, *Les Aitoliens à Delphes* (Paris: 1937). On the oracle itself useful works are still P. Amandry, *La Mantique Apollinienne à Delphes* (Paris: 1950), H. Bervé, "Das Delphische Orakel," *Gestaltende Kräfte der Antike* (Munich: 1949), and J. Pollard, *Seers, Shrines, and Sirens* (London: 1965).

at Delphi and orders his statue to be erected on a column which had originally been designated for his defeated rival, Perseus. The column was rediscovered in the early 20th Century and thus modern archaeology is able to vindicate Plutarch's account.[2] Aemilius says his own statue should be erected in place of Perseus', "since the conquered should make way for the conqueror." The *Aemilius* account is an aid in reconstructing Polybios' corrupt text at this point (30.10). Plutarch is, however, more accurate than Polybios; he gives one column rather than several, the location, and Aemilius' saying at the time. Besides this he describes the column correctly as a great rectangle constructed of square blocks of white marble. Later, on the completion of his successful campaign against Perseus, Aemilius returns to Delphi to offer a thanksgiving sacrifice (*Aemilius* 36). This incident is not in Polybios, though Livy (45.41), Diodoros (31.1), and Appian (*Macedonica* 19) record it.

Plutarch is also our only source for other information about the interrelationship between Rome and Delphi, even if at times one must be somewhat suspicious about the validity of what he says. He is our only source for Cicero's ambitious interrogation of the Delphic oracle on how he might achieve greatness, and the Stoic response of the oracle, "Let your own nature, not the opinion of the multitude be your guide" (*Cicero* 5). Chapter 12 of the *Life of Flamininus* mentions Flamininus' dedications at the shrine, but is largely taken up with the inscriptions upon them. We learn (16) that at Chalcis a *Delphinion* was dedicated to Titus and Apollo, and that at the time a hymn had been sung to Zeus, Rome, Titus, and "the good Faith of the Romans" ('Ρωμαίων τε πίστιν). Though the passage savours of political temporizing, Plutarch relates it with decorum. This is somewhat surprising in view of his horror at the "divine honors" paid Demetrios at Delphi in *Demetrios* 10-12. In fact he seems to praise Titus who is designated

---

[2] The inscriptions on the Aemilius monument were described in great detail in the article which announced its discovery, H. Pomtow, "Delphische Neufunde V," *Klio*, 17 (1921), 153-203. Consult also the more recent article in *RE* Suppl. V, p. 104. Justinus, 20.3.1, records a delegation of the Crotonians to Delphi before the battle of Pydna, but this is not recorded in Plutarch or other classical authors. The inscription is still intact: L-Aimilius-L-f-inperator-de-rege-Perse / Macedonibusque-cepet. See Flacelière, *Vies* IV, p. 104, and L. Budde, "Das römische Historienrelief I," *ANRW* I,4 (1975), pp. 805-25, (first part on the Aemilius monument).

a "savior" (ὦ Τίτε σῶτερ) though the appellation savior god is one of his strongest charges against Demetrios, as we shall see. Another Roman relationship with Delphi is recorded in *Marcellus* 8, the sending of a golden bowl to Delphi in thanksgiving for Marcellus' victory over the Gauls. Again Plutarch is our only extant source.

One can detect the reshaping of history in the account of the Romans' relationship with the shrine during the Hannibalic War. Plutarch's intention would seem to consist of underscoring the normalcy of relations between Rome and Delphi at that time, in contrast to the Livian account where Delphi is only consulted as a last resort. In Livy the embassy to Delphi is the result of a superstitious panic (22.55). It follows immediately after the description of religious atrocities: some vestal virgins who had been accused of infidelity to their office were buried alive while others committed suicide and the debaucher, a secretary of the pontiffs, was beaten to death by the pontifex maximus himself; and worse, on the consultation of the Sibylline books, two Greeks and two Gauls were buried alive. Livy excuses the incidents as exceptions to the normal Roman spirit, and on the basis that the actions were done out of superstition at a time of great peril. Only at the end of this chain of events is the consultation at Delphi mentioned.

The account of the delegation in *Fabius* 18 attempts to cut the incident free from the air of panic and immediacy which one finds in Livy. As in Livy (23.11) Fabius Pictor—Livy's source—is sent to consult Delphi as Hannibal sweeps down on Italy. In contrast to Livy Plutarch is curiously silent about Fabius' question and the answer given. He perhaps had good reason to delete it since the oracle did not seem to be informed on which gods the Romans worshipped, and therefore rather stupidly told Fabius that the Romans should propitiate "the usual gods." The rest of the response was a request for a large share of the booty if the Romans should win—not a very inspiring oracle.[3] Plutarch mentions the deflowering

---

[3] The oracle was more blunt in Livy (22. 55-57):

Si ita faxitis Romani, vestrae res meliores facilioresque erunt magisque ex sententia res publica vestra vobis procedet victoriaque duelli populi Romani erit. Pythio Apollini re publica vestra bene gesta servataque lucris meritis donum mittitote, deque praeda manubiis spoliisque honorem habetote lasciviam a vobis prohibetote.

An excellent account of the work and position of Fabius Pictor can be

of the vestal virgins and the subsequent execution of one and suicide of the other, but not the burying alive of the Greeks and Gauls. Rather like Pliny (*NH* 28.12), he puts this incident in the career of Marcellus (*Marcellus* 3) during the panic when the Celtic Insubres were invading. Plutarch's source for the burial was the rite performed in the Forum Boarium during the month of November in his own day when two Gauls and two Greeks were still being ritually buried in a ceremony not open to the public. Perhaps Plutarch was impressed by the ceremony while in Rome. The same story of the burial is told in *Quaestiones Romanae* 283f-284c, but here the atrocities are committed because of the panic felt by the corruption of the vestal virgins. One of them, Helvia, is struck by lightning while riding on horseback, and when found, her tunic is pulled up around her head, "as though on purpose to reveal her nakedness" and her tongue is protruding from her mouth. The names of the other virgins and that of the corrupter are given. The Romans are greatly disturbed after the execution of these virgins and the corrupter; the seers who consult the Sibylline books tell them to bury the unfortunate foreigners. Livy, and Plutarch in the *Lives*, leave the burial causally independent of the vestal virgin incident. It is difficult to decide what it ever went with, but the rhetorical and dramatic possibility of associating the burial with a panic in wartime may have led Livy to associate it with Hannibal's invasion and Plutarch with that of the Insubres. The obstacle to Plutarch's leaving it with the Hannibalic invasion may have been the immediate relation of the mission of Pictor to Delphi. In Plutarch, therefore, one feels that the embassy to Delphi was part of the attempt by Fabius to reinstall those religious practices which had fallen into disuse, and that it was done in order to reinspire confidence in the shaken populace.

---

found in E. Badian, "The Early Historians," T. A. Dorey, ed., *Latin Historians* (London: 1966), pp. 1-38. Badian points out that Pictor's history— which at first did not receive the attention it deserved—left a profound effect not only upon Roman historiography but also upon Roman politics. Pictor attempted to portray the brilliance of the aristocratic patience against the disastrous shakiness of the lower classes, the need for firmness and *fides*, and tried to portray for the Greeks the Roman idea of *clientela*. His use of autobiographical touches and the integration of morality and politics undoubtedly would have appealed strongly to Plutarch, as well as his descriptions of ceremonies and ritual, besides having the advantage of being written in Greek. See now also D. Timpe, "Fabius Pictor und die Anfänge der römischen Historiographie," *ANRW* I,2 (1972), pp. 928-69.

Livy and Plutarch are also not completely in agreement when relating the link between Camillus and the Delphic oracle. In *Camillus* 4—as well as in Cicero, *De divinatione* 1.100, Livy, 5.15, Dionysios, 12.10, and Zonaras, 7.20—the sending of a Roman embassy to Delphi before the capture of the Etruscan city of Veii is mentioned. Plutarch alone names the ambassadors at this time but curiously omits the names of those later sent in thanksgiving with a golden bowl (Livy, 5.28). Moreover, Livy (5.21) records that Camillus prayed before the battle to the Pythian Apollo—apparently on the basis that part of the booty was designated for this god—and to Juno (with prophetic insight, "that you may leave this town")—but Plutarch's Camillus prays to "Zeus and the other gods"—thus obscuring the theme of *evocatio*. Perhaps Plutarch was not convinced that Camillus' devotion to this god could have been that strong, and preferred the more traditional invocation to the Roman Jupiter (Zeus). The deletion of the invocation to the Pythian Apollo may also reflect a desire on Plutarch's part not to destroy the local color which he carefully constructs in his lives of early Romans. Perhaps the original attribution of the prayer to the Pythian Apollo was due to Fabius Pictor, himself a Delphic propagandist, who was part of the delegation sent to Delphi during the Hannibalic War and who on his return made the report to the Senate. He may have projected Delphic relations farther back into Roman history than Plutarch with his more professional interest in the shrine, could fathom.[4]

Plutarch obviously was not happy with Sulla's depredations at the shrine during the Mithridatic War. He has some harsh words to say. Yet he does not introduce the divine retribution machinery one might expect nor even utter a note of surprise, like Diodoros (38.7), that Sulla had escaped nemesis. Some of the sting of the action was removed by Sulla's insistence that this was only a temporary measure and that the shrine would be repaid. Plutarch apparently believed that after the war Delphi was fully compensated by the revenues of the Theban lands which were transferred to Delphi. The actual scene of despoliation is painted in touching

---

[4] The relationship between Rome and Delphi at the time of the capture of Veii seems to have an historical foundation, but the stories about predictions by Delphi on how to capture the city seem to be fictitious, and were apparently modeled on the supposed Etruscan prophecy about the lake drying up. The sources for the golden bowl dedicated at this time all seem to be Roman. See Parke-Wormell, p. 269.

terms. The Phocian Judas sent to do Sulla's dirty work is portrayed as suffering from the stings of his own conscience and attempting to dissuade Sulla by every means possible, including superstition. However, his recourse to the miraculous falls on its face: he informs Sulla that the god was heard to be playing his lyre; Sulla replies sardonically that in such a case the god must be happy and the Phocian should get on with the job (Sulla 12). His tears are recorded with sympathy, before the Amphictyons who contemplate the "royal" treasures being sliced up to be transported on the backs of the pack animals.

The incident of depredation is used to introduce some moralizing on the decline of Roman political morality. Sulla is blamed severely for starting a precedent for other Roman commanders to prey on the shrine, thus introducing a practice which eventually left the oracle destitute.[5] Plutarch claims that the earlier commanders, Flamininus, Acilius, and Aemilius, were men of self-restraint with disciplined troops and that they not only refrained from plundering the shrine but actually added to its treasures. In contrast he regards the later commanders as avaricious demagogues who sold out themselves first and then their country. In his view this degeneracy was both the cause of the Civil Wars and the reason for the great fluctuations in them. He regards the restorations made to Delphi after the war through the appropriation of the Theban lands and the transference of their revenue to Delphi as only a cloak of Sulla's vindictiveness toward Thebes (Sulla 19). Sulla in fact is portrayed as contemptuously insulting the Thebans by staging a dramatic festival in his honor at "the fountain of Oedipus." Plutarch sarcastically notes that the judges had to be imported from outside.

At a later stage in Sulla's career Delphi appears again. As

---

[5] Plutarch mistakenly believed that the urn was one of the dedications of Croisos which had escaped the Phocian plundering. See Parke-Wormell, p. 282, n. 27. They doubt (p. 279) that Sulla ever repaid the debt as Plutarch says he did, but their argumentation here is somewhat loose, and if he had not, one should think that Plutarch would have known this fact and mentioned it. On the statue of Apollo which Sulla carried with him, see J. Gagé, Apollon Romain (Brussels: 1963). This is mentioned by Valerius Maximus, 1.2.3, whom Plutarch seems to be following. Whatever his devotion to Apollo, on returning to Rome he sacrificed to Victoria, Mars and Venus. Flacelière, Vies VI, p. 225, does not bring out very well the connection between Sulla's Venus and fortuna. On this see chapter VII, note 25.

Sulla has settled down for the siege of Marius at Praeneste, Telesinus the Samnite makes a diversionary movement toward Rome in the hope of taking the pressure off Praeneste. In the engagement Sulla comes close to losing his life, and in despair of his situation utters a prayer to the Pythian Apollo. It is directed toward a little golden statue of Apollo which Sulla is said to have taken from the spoils of Delphi and which he always carried with him. Plutarch puts a prayer into Sulla's mouth at this point in which Sulla begs the Pythian god not to abandon him after having raised him up to glory and greatness after so many struggles. Since Valerius Maximus (1.2.3) and Frontinus (*Strat.* 1.11.1) mention the image but not the prayer, one suspects that Plutarch invented it, unless, of course, it came from Sulla's *Memoirs*. The prayer, however, is hardly very efficacious; Sulla's army is battered and the fugitives almost cause the siege of Praeneste to be ended (*Sulla* 29).

The attack on Sulla is unusual. Even here Plutarch is careful to point out that Sulla was an exception to the rule that the Romans treated the shrine well. Plutarch's real desire is to demonstrate that liberality toward the shrine is a part of Roman tradition even if he does have to stretch history a bit. At other times it may simply be that the very nature of parallel lives leads one into a pattern of comparison as much as it does of contrast. One begins instinctively to interpret things in one culture in terms of the other. This seems to be the case in the *Romulus*, where Plutarch seems instinctively to have thought of Rome in terms of Greek *synoikismos*, even going so far as to make something close to a Freudian slip. Let us compare Livy (1.8) and Plutarch on the building of the asylum at Rome:

> Meanwhile Rome was growing. More and more ground was coming within the circuit of its walls. Indeed the rapid expansion of the enclosed area was out of proportion to the actual population and evidently indicated an eye to the future. In antiquity the founder of a new settlement, in order to increase its population, would as a matter of course shark up a lot of homeless and destitute folk and pretend that they were "born of the earth" to be his progeny; Romulus now followed a similar course: to help fill his big new town, he threw open, in the ground—now enclosed—between the two copses, as you go up the Capitoline hill, a place of asylum for fugitives. Hither fled for refuge all the rag-tag-and-bobtail from the neighboring peoples: some free, some slaves, and all of them wanting nothing but a fresh start. That mob was the first real addition to the City's strength, the first step to her future

greatness. (A. De Selincourt, *Livy, The Early History of Rome*, pp. 26-27).

Now let us look at *Romulus* 9:

And in the second place [that after the capture of the Sabine women], when their city was first founded, they made a sanctuary of refuge for all fugitives, which they called the sanctuary of the God of Asylum. There they received all who came, delivering none up, neither slave to masters, nor debtors to creditors, nor murderer to magistrates, but declaring it to be in obedience to an oracle from Delphi (μαντεύματι πυθοχρήστῳ) that they made the asylum secure for all men. Therefore, the city was soon full of people, for they say that the first houses numbered no more than a thousand. This, however, was much later.[6] (B. Perrin, Loeb, *Lives* I, pp. 113-15).

Plutarch has understood Livy's theme, the increase of population at Rome, which was a vital element in the political expansion of the city, but he seems to confuse it with the early struggles of the Greek city-states. He speaks of slaves and masters, creditors and debtors, much in the language about Solon's reforms at Athens. Plutarch seems to be trying to convey how the Romans managed to settle their problems peacefully in contrast to the more violent settlements in some of the Greek states. Thus he connects the asylum business with the rape of the Sabine women, understanding both as institutionalizations of accomodations though in Livy the rape of the Sabine women is an event which followed the founding of the asylum. Probably it is his Greek understanding of early Roman social conditions which also leads him to make a curious addition to Livy's account: the asylum is built in response to a command "worthy of Pytho," and this word, πυθόχρηστος has led translators into implying that the Delphic oracle was at work here. However, the word may perhaps mean no more than "infallible," the reflection of a line from Aischylos' *Choephoroi*, where retaining its link with Delphi it is used in the sense Plutarch wants.[6] Whether Plutarch is primarily to blame for the tenor and

---

[6] Parke and Wormell, p. 265, seem unaware of this passage which attributes a role to Delphi in the origins of Rome. The earliest instance they record is a fictitious deputation sent by Tarquinius Superbus. They feel that the first real embassy was sent at the time of the capture of Veii. The word πυθόχρηστος is used by Pylades to Orestes in *Choephoroi* 900-901:

τὰ πυθόχρηστα πιστά τ' εὐορκώματα
ποῦ δαὶ τὸ λοιπὸν Λοξίου μαντεύματα

vocabulary of the passage is difficult to say, for he may be following one or both of the Greek authors he cites in the passage, the obscure Herodoros Ponticos and Diocles of Peparethos. Livy's account centers precisely on the expansion of population at Rome. Plutarch is sidetracked by religious curiosities like ornithomancy. This may be why the founding of the asylum receives religious connotations and the implausible sanction from Delphi. Later in the *Life of Romulus* (28) there is another reference to Delphi, but it is only the oblique noting of a response of the Delphic oracle as to the disappearance of Cleomedes of Astypalaia, which Plutarch regards as a fable similar to that of the mysterious vanishing of Romulus at the end of his life.

Only five Greek *Lives* fail to note the oracle: *Cimon, Dion, Eumenes, Alcibiades,* and *Pyrrhos.* Much of the matter which he relates about Delphi was the stock and trade of Greek historiography. As such one could count such items as Agesilaus' celebration of the Pythian games at Delphi after his victory over Thebes (*Agesilaus* 19), the mission of the ephors to determine whether the Spartan kings had transgressed in their dealings (*Agis-Cleomenes* 11), Alexander's failure to obtain an audience from the Pythian priestess but her admission that he would be victorious (*Alexander* 14), the mission of the Sicyonians inquiring if they could bury Aratos in their city (*Aratos* 53), the unfavorable prophecies of the oracle before the Athenian catastrophe at Chaironeia (*Demosthenes* 19), Lycourgos' help from the oracle in framing his constitution (*Lycourgos* 5) and the ratification of these plans by Delphi (*Lycourgos* 29), Phocion's claim that he was the

---

where it involves Delphi and "reliable". At 940 Pylades applies the word to Orestes, ὁ πυθόχρηστος φυγάς. By Plutarch's time it might have meant little more than "reliable". He may also have been unconsciously thinking in terms of the parallel events in the *Theseus*, one of the disadvantages, historically, of parallel lives. Flacelière, *Vies* I, p. 69, translates: "confirmé par un oracle de la Pythie". He feels that Plutarch, who alone mentions Delphi, was influenced by a Hellenistic decree which declared the place an asylum (*Sylloge*[3] 550). Both Flacelière and Ziegler at 9.3 give ὁ Θεοῦ 'Ασυλαίου προσηγόρευον, creating a problem, since Plutarch alone speaks of such a god. Perhaps, since Livy 1.8 puts it on the Capitoline Hill, Plutarch wrote, "the asylum of the god" (i.e. Jupiter), possibly giving a transliteration or similar sounding Greek word for the Latin, then at 9.3 later giving a more normal Greek word for it ... τὴν ἀσυλίαν φάσκοντας. He actually leaves the name of the oracle vague: ἄσυλον καὶ φυκτιμὸν ἀπὸ πάντων κατὰ τὴν τοῦ θεοῦ μαντείαν. Perhaps a solution to 9.3 would be: ὁ Θεοῦ (i.e. Jupiter Capitolinus) ἀσύλαιον προσηγόρευον.

one described by the Delphic oracle as alone to oppose Athens' conduct (*Phocion* 8), Solon's relationship with Delphi and the meeting of the seven wise men (*Solon* 4), the oracle to propitiate the heroes Periphemos and Cychreus before Solon's attack on Salamis (*Solon* 9), and the oracle about the wooden wall and Themistocles' interpretation of it at the time of the Persian attack (*Themistocles* 10).

Delphi is so often mentioned in *Theseus* that one might suspect it was supposed to end the entire series of *Lives*. However, the case of Theseus, like that of Agesilaus, posed a problem. In both cases the Delphic oracle had hardly sanctioned their careers: Theseus was not even supposed to be born, and Agesilaus, the lame, was not to be king. Yet, their *arete* forces Plutarch to give them the benefit of the doubt: he finds it difficult to believe that their lives were in complete opposition to the will of the gods. Silly as the supposed divine prohibition seems to us, it was taken seriously by Plutarch. The two unfavorable oracles are duly recorded: Aigeus was not to open the wineskin (*Theseus* 3); Agesilaus was not to be put on the throne, for the oracle had forbidden a lame king (*Agesilaus* 3). Yet, Plutarch's bewilderment is reflected throughout *Agesilaus*, in the syncrisis to *Agesilaus-Pompey*, and in *Lysander* 22. It may be significant that in both *Agesilaus* and *Lysander* he is curiously silent about the origin of the oracle. Did he want to conceal the fact that it came from Delphi? His puzzlement over Theseus is largely confined to the syncrisis to *Theseus-Romulus*.

Plutarch in general regards Lysander as a rather unscrupulous knave, so he naturally would not show too much reluctance to accept the account that Lysander had been fiddling with the Delphic oracle in an attempt to put himself on the throne of Sparta. At any rate Lysander conjures up a rather fantastic plot: he corrupts the priests at Delphi and Dodona, who are to interpret an ancient oracle in his favor; finds a woman of Pontos who is to claim that Apollo has sired her son, a necessary ingredient for the oracle; and hopes that all will converge to leave him on top (*Lysander* 25-26). In the nick of time the plot is foiled. Earlier in the *Life* (18), Plutarch—probably mistakenly—records that Lysander was the first Greek to whom the cities erected altars, made sacrifices as to a god, and the first to whom songs of triumph were sung, and he relates an arrogant insult made by him to a Delphic victor.

We should not be surprised then that Plutarch took the most inimical version of the plot. At any rate Diodoros (14.13), though he alludes to the plot, gives us no details, and the version of Nepos (*Lysander* 3) could possibly be interpreted in Lysander's favor. Here letters are detected which implicate Lysander in an attempt to gain the throne through "some divine favor he had supposedly received." The statement in Nepos does not rule out the possibility of a counterplot, but Plutarch seems to be following closely the hostile version of Douris of Samos, revealed in 18 as the source of the derogatory material on Lysander, in his view a momentous example of cunning and pomposity disguising a sham. Here the parallel technique would be recalled. Read independently of one another, the *Sulla* and *Lysander* do not invite the same interest in comparative treatment of Delphi as they do when read together. One is forearmed for the contemptuous treatment of Delphi by Sulla after reading Lysander's dealings with the shrine. One also wonders whether Sulla's treatment of the shrine did not influence the tone of the *Lysander* passage, and even possibly, the choice of sources.

In the same chapter Plutarch favors Lysander's general reputation for poverty over Anaxandrides the Delphian's statement that Lysander was wealthy because he had deposited a large amount of money at Delphi. Naturally it is difficult for a modern historian to decide who is right, but Plutarch probably had in the back of his mind the possibility that Lysander's friends may have contributed to the sum. At least that is his reasoning in the case of Aristides (*Aristides* 1), where he criticizes Demetrios of Phaleron for regarding Aristides as wealthy. Finally Plutarch mentions the bronze statue of Lysander and the golden stars of the Dioscouroi—which, he says, disappeared before the battle of Leuctra.

The whole account of Lysander's attempt to put Agesilaus on the throne reveals interesting variations in Plutarch's assessment of the situation. The Spartans had received an oracle that they should not elect a lame king, but Lysander directed the oracle against Leotychides, the son of the old king, who was reported to be an illegitimate child. One can spot two traditions about Leotychides, that in Xenophon (*Hellenica* 3.3), which treats him as illegitimate, and that of Pausanias (3.8.4) which holds the contrary. In general Plutarch follows the Xenophonic tradition and emphasizes the popular support for Agesilaus, for example in *Agesilaus* 3. This accords with Plutarch's *De tranquillitate animi* 467f, where Agis is one of those men who accepted sterility with tranquillity; Leotychides is stated to be the illegitimate son of Alcibiades, conceived while the latter was enjoying Agis' hospitality at Sparta. The same is stated in *Alcibiades* 23. But after the battle of Leuctra, the Spartans who sit around waiting for the Thebans to swoop upon Sparta, entertain the superstitious fear that the defeat was due to their flaunting of the clear words of the Delphic oracle about putting a lame king on the throne (*Agesilaus* 30). This superstitious sentiment is reflected again in the syncrisis of *Agesilaus-Pompey*, where Plutarch claims that at all costs the Spartans should have avoided putting Leotychides or Agesilaus on the throne. Thus, there is a certain ambivalence in Plutarch's treatment of the oracle, though this is brought out more strongly in the syncrises.

Another interesting subject in which Plutarch's bias can be noted is his rewriting of the Herodotean history of the activity of the shrine during the Persian War. Herodotos' account is unfriendly in several places, revealing the shrine as ready to court Persian favor and to skirt treachery. In the early *Themistocles* we do not observe many changes from the account of Herodotos, but even here Delphi is seen to be the savior of Greece. After all "logical efforts" have failed, Themistocles uses the oracle of the wooden wall— almost as a *pia fraus*—to persuade the Athenians to abandon their homeland and flee to Salamis (*Themistocles* 10). Yet, the omission of much derogatory material such as we find in Herodotos leads one to see the oracle as the straw which decided the issue in favor of Athens. Herodotos gives a much more hostile version in which the oracle is hell-bent on demoralizing the Athenians: "not even the terrifying warnings of the oracle at Delphi could persuade the Athenians to abandon Greece" (7.140). The duplicity of the attendants of the oracle, hinted at in Herodotos' account of the double consultation, and the advice that the Athenians should "pray to the winds," (7.18) are omitted by Plutarch. Moreover, he is silent on the Persian expedition which was "miraculously" prevented from plundering the shrine (8.35), though other late writers like Diodoros (11.14.2) and Pausanias (10.8.7) are not reluctant to mention the incident.

A more significant reshaping of Delphic history can be observed in Plutarch's account of the battle of Plataia. Herodotos does not give the slightest shred of credit to Delphi for this victory. On the contrary, full responsibility for aligning the spiritual forces on the side of the Greeks goes to an Eleian diviner named Tisamenos (9.34). In Plutarch's version Tisamenos is barely mentioned. Rather, the Delphic oracle tells the Greeks where the battle is to be fought in order to assure victory and what gods and heroes were to be propitiated. Granted that the oracle is extremely enigmatic—in fact a sceptical observer would say contradictory— Zeus Soter manages in a dream to clear up the difficulty so the Greeks can fight in time (*Aristides* 11).[7] Herodotos had said that the Persians according to the oracle would be successful as long as Delphi was not attacked (9.44). Whatever happened to this in Plutarch's account? Finally, Herodotos give us a rather venal "slander" of the oracle: one tenth of all the spoils is to go to Delphi. After the victory a gold tripod is in fact made out of the spoils (9.81). Plutarch relates a more edifying version which omits mention of the tithe and states piously that after the victory all the fires polluted by the Persians were extinguished and relighted from the Delphic flame before the Greeks could sacrifice on the altars erected to Zeus Eleutherios. He adds to this the interesting detail—even if a bit suspicious—that the Plataian, Euchidas, sent to get the fire, expired on the way back and was buried in the shrine of Artemis Eucleia. His epitaph, with its mention of Delphi, is duly recorded (20).

Plutarch also seems to readjust some legends concerning the early history of Greece. Parke-Wormell (p. 85) note two traditions concerning the early Spartan constitution. The first was a romantic projection into the past of the existence in Crete of a primitive ideal Doric civilization, which was used as a model by Lycourgos for the Spartan constitution. The second tradition—which according to

---

[7] The response given by the oracle, according to Plutarch, urged the Athenians to make vows to Zeus, Cithaironian Hera, Pan, and the Sphragitic nymphs; they were to offer sacrifice to the Plataian heroes Androcrates, Leucon, Peisandros, Damocrates, Hyposion, Actaion, and Polyïdos; and they were to fight on their own territory on the plain of Eleusinian Demeter and Core. The difficulties were removed by the "fortunate" discovery of the temples of Eleusinian Demeter and Core in the area, and by the Plataians making a fictitious sale of part of their territory to the Athenians. None of this appears in Herodotos and undoubtedly represents Plataian legend, especially since the Hera, heroes, and nymphs mentioned were honored in Plataian territory. Apparently to underscore the truth, Plutarch gives the oracle in the original Dorian dialect.

Parke-Wormell was accepted by the rest of Greece and was supposedly popularized by the Spartan king, Pausanias—claimed that Lycourgos had received his original inspiration from Delphi. Plutarch in his *Life of Lycourgos* conflates the two traditions but in such a way that there is no doubt that the main inspiration is the Delphic shrine. Lycourgos travels to Crete and is impressed by many of their laws, some of which he later adopts, but he also discovers many contemptible aspects of their civilization. He even gets much information from the philosopher Thales—who, Plutarch tells us, was a lawgiver in secret (*Lycourgos* 4). The Cretan trip forms part of a larger fact-finding commission which involves Lycourgos in voyages not only to Crete, but also to Ionia, Egypt, Spain—and according to some sources Plutarch has seen—even to India where he has conversations with the Gymnosophists.

It is difficult to decide what one should make out of Plutarch's omission of the oracle to the Athenians at the commencement of the Peloponnesian War that they should avoid congesting the city (*Thucydides*, 2.17.1). Plutarch also ignores an oracle recorded by Pausanias. Pausanias had found a trophy at Delphi which was still extant in his own day, commemorating the event, so there was no reason for Plutarch's being ignorant of it. Perhaps he disliked turning Pericles' death under the plague into divine retribution for refusing to heed the oracle. After all, Pericles was for Plutarch the walking image of Zeus. However, all this speculation may be too subtle.

Those who attack or mistreat the oracle naturally do not fare well in Plutarch's accounts. We have already seen the harsh attack on Lysander and Sulla. It was mentioned then that we should be suspicious of the charge, repeated from Douris, that Lysander was the first Greek to whom divine honors were given (*Lysander* 18)[8]. Diodoros (14.13) and Nepos (*Lysander* 3) express no awareness of this sublime arrogance. But Sulla and Lysander are graced with honor compared to the bitter treatment which

---

[8] Nilsson, *Geschichte* II, p. 139, rightly questions the reliability of Douris for these statements about Lysander. He notes that Douris, who lived 100 years after Lysander, is notoriously unreliable. As a tyrant himself, of Samos, he misinterpreted the dedications of Lysander on the basis of later practice. Nilsson suggests that a statue of Lysander as benefactor was put up next to an altar upon which certain sacrifices were to be made and that games were dedicated in his honor. No intention of usurping the role of a god was involved.

the rogue Demetrios receives. Here Plutarch is heavily influenced by the satiric verses of a contemporary of Demetrios, a playwright named Philippides. He was a rival to Demetrios' chief flatterer, Stratocles, and attempted to sling as much mud as possible at the two. All of this, as well as the high praise of Philippides himself, comes out of *Demetrios* 10-12. Plutarch should have been more cautious, but his depressingly low opinion of Demetrios undoubtedly was responsible for taking Philippides' verses at face value.

Demetrios receives no mercy. The Athenians "render Demetrios and Antigonos odious" by bestowing the title of kings upon them, a title not used by the monarchs up to that time. There follows a whole list of "abominable honors" which the two receive: they receive the title savior-gods (σώτηρες θεοί); their names are substituted for those of the eponymous archons; their figures are incorporated into the sacred peplos of Athena; an altar to Demetrios the Alighter (Δημήτριος καταιβάτης) is consecrated on the spot where Demetrios "alighted;" two new tribes are named after Antigonos and Demetrios; and "the most monstrous of desires," the appellation of sacred deputies (θεωροί) the title used for those sent on great official occasions to Delphi, is used for the envoys sent to the two monarchs (*Demetrios* 11). Plutarch continues in 13 with more "horrors:" the month Mounychion was changed to Demetrion, the last day of the month was renamed Demetrias, the Dionysia was called Demetria, and—"the most outrageous horror"—when the question of certain shields at Delphi was raised, it was requested that an oracle be obtained from Demetrios. This must have seemed to Plutarch like the world turned on its head. Many of these changes were actually put into effect, though some with modifications not indicated by Plutarch. Yet, he—and some modern scholars—treat Demetrios' assumption of divine honors somewhat more seriously than the satiric verses of Philippides would seem to warrant. However, Philippides' satire certainly accorded with Plutarch's own low opinion of Demetrios. Perhaps some of the charges were in fact no more than the "elegant and clever bits of obsequiousness" of Stratocles, Demetrios' chief flatterer, and the proposals never got off the ground.[9]

---

[9] Apparently with approval, Plutarch records two *esprits* of Stratocles. In one, when his mistress brought home some brains and neckbones from the market he told her that this was the sort of thing "we politicians" have

Plutarch's credibility comes more into question in the following chapters, when he relies on Philippides "in his abuse of Stratocles" and accepts the story that Demetrios turned the Parthenon into a brothel for his mistress Lamia and her friends (26) and ground special taxes out of the Athenians to keep these girls well supplied with soap (27), adding insult to injury.[10]

Demosthenes' relationship with the oracle before the battle of Chaironeia also strikes a tender spot with Plutarch. According to *Demosthenes* 19, the orator not only rejected the warnings of the Delphic oracle, but accused the Pythia of being in the pay of Philip and attempted to denigrate the shrine by asserting that the great statesmen of the past regarded the oracle as a pretext for cowardice. Demosthenes in the chapter alludes to Epameinondas and Pericles. It is uncertain what he means. Pericles' words probably had something to do with the Persian War, since there is no oracle in the *Life of Pericles* which was rejected by Pericles and later proved to be false. The *Life of Epameinondas* is lost, so we cannot judge by that *Life* if there was some reference to an oracle proved to be false. However, there are in fact recorded two oracles which pertained to Epameinondas and Pericles and which may have been rejected by them. There is an oracle about Epameinondas recorded in Pausanias 8.11.10 which warned him not to go aboard a ship. This probably was a *vaticinium post eventum* for the general's death at Pelagos in the battle of Mantinea. Perhaps in one version Epameinondas had refused to accept the warning.

The reference to Pericles is also very puzzling. In 449 B.C.

to put up with. On another occasion he learned that the Athenians had been defeated, but ordered celebrations. When they learned the truth later and were furious at him, he asked how they could be angry at him for giving them two more days of happiness. The lightness of the touches on Stratocles suggests Plutarch is not one hundred percent serious about his charges against Demetrios.

[10] On this see Nilsson, *Geschichte* II, pp. 150-52, who takes the matter quite seriously, and gives abundant bibliography. Parke-Wormell, pp. 245-46, accept the account of Plutarch at face value. One problem is that the source is the unreliable Douris. Dionysia was not eliminated from the list of festivals, but Demetreia added to it (W. B. Dinsmoor, *Archons of Athens in the Hellenistic Age*, p. 8 and 15). Inscriptions found reveal an agon, sacrifice, and procession, and that an equestrian statue of Demetrios was to be erected in the agora next to *Demokratia* and sacrifice to be offered to Demetrios Soter. Nock, *Essays*, pp. 248-251 ("*Synnaos Theos,*" *HSCP*, 41 (1930) 1-62), taking up the cases of both Lysander and Demetrios, was very sceptical, seeing comic elaboration on something like a statue carried in the procession, and added festivities.

Pericles was involved in a dispute with the Spartans over Delphi. After the Spartans championed the side of the Delphians against Phocis, they accepted the grant of *promanteia* chiseled on the brow of the bronze wolf in the precinct. Pericles avoided a direct clash with the Spartans, but quickly undid their work, put the shrine back under Phocian control, and had the right of *promanteia* awarded to the Athenians as well (Thucydides 1.112.5, *Pericles* 21). Thucydides also records (2.17.1) an oracle given out in 431 B.C. that the Pelargicon was to remain unused. The Pelargicon was the site of a fort in the time of Peisistratos but for ritual reasons was to remain free of habitation. Since the spot was occupied during the plague, the oracle was taken as a warning not to congest the city. Perhaps Pericles had attempted to calm the people down on this occasion. However, it seems odd that Demosthenes would allude to occasions when the oracle was correct. At the same time it does not affect Plutarch's purpose adversely, but rather reinforces it if on the occasions Demosthenes alludes to, the oracle was later vindicated. At any rate Demosthenes' attack on the shrine bears bitter fruit, for the warning against engaging at Chaironea is fully vindicated by the outcome of the battle.

One of the most bitter indictments falls upon Timoleon's mercenaries who had sacked the shrine (in 356 B.C.) but were later enrolled by Timoleon for the conquest of Sicily (*Timoleon* 30). Plutarch justifies Timoleon's use of these men "hated by all mankind" on the grounds of expediency: there were no others to be found. But he feels that they filled a divine purpose in the liberation of Sicily and were no argument against providence since they were quickly disposed of when no longer useful. He concludes that their ultimate slaughter at the hands of the Bruttians was retribution for the earlier sack of Delphi (they received a fitting *dike* from *to daimonion*). Here his bias is revealed again, since Diodoros (16.18) believed that retribution had visited the mercenaries for sacking a sacred town of the Bruttians.

Though it is difficult to tell from the *Lives* what Plutarch actually saw in existence at Delphi in his own time and what had disappeared, we find numerous vivid descriptions of the antiquities there and the history of them.[11] For example, he illustrates the

---

[11] Among the items mentioned in the *Lives*, Pausanias, 10.10 ff., refers only to the gold tripod from the spoils of the Persian War as extant. This had a base which still exists, having been taken by Constantine to Con-

effect of Alexander's anger upon his subordinates by relating how
many years after Alexander's death Cassander happened to see
a statue of Alexander at Delphi and came near fainting. (*Alexander*
74).[12] He attempts to correct the impression that Philopoimen was

---

stantinople. Flacelière, *Vies*, II, p. 100, notes that Plutarch may have
made his correction of Thucydides on the cities taking part at Plataia on
the basis of this inscription. He notes that in *Sol.* 9.2 the Delphic archives
are given as a source. He had a lively interest in statues and paintings
both here and elsewhere as a clue to character. See A. E. Wardman, "Description of Personal Appearance in Plutarch and Suetonius," *CQ*, 17 (1967),
414-20. B. Bucher-Isler, *Norm und Individualität in den Biographien Plutarchs* uses this interest as a basis for her study. He notes that Antony's
statues were meant to give him a resemblance to Heracles (*Ant.* 4), Cato the
elder had reddish hair and green eyes (*Cat. Mai.* 1), the statue of Lucullus
at Chaironeia, with a mixture of realism and idealism is the model for his
Lives (*Cim.* 2), the bronze statue of Flamininus by the side of Apollo from
Carthage opposite the Circus Flaminius showed him with a bit of temper
(*Flam.* 1), Pericles was "squill-headed," therefore shown with a helmet
(*Per.* 3), Phocion had frowning brows (*Phoc.* 5), Pyrrhos did not have many
teeth and the upper jaw was a continuous bone with the teeth separated
by depressions (*Pyr.* 3: a herm at Naples and bust at Copenhagen are
extant to verify this, see P. Leveque, *Pyrrhus* (Paris: 1957), pp. 640, 683,
689, and plate IV, Flacelière, *Vies* VI, p. 29), the statue of Marcellus can
be found in the temple of Athena at Lindos (*Marc.* 30), that Sulla's appearance was revealed by his statues, a gleam of grey eyes, terribly sharp
and powerful, a face covered with coarse blotches of red interspersed with
white, a mulberry sprinkled with meal (*Sul.* 2), that Alexander's favorite
artists were Lysippos and Apelles (*Alex.* 4), that Agesilaus because of his
deformities refused to have his statue made (*Ages.* 2). Other portrait details
are given in *Them.* 22, *Arat.* 3, *Philop.* 2, *Alc.* 1, *Cat. Min.* 1, *Otho.* 18). In
Arat. 13 he tells an interesting anecdote about an attempt to save the
portraits of the kings at Sicyon. A flourish is added to *Cat. Min.* 71 by the
description of the indomitable hero's statue at Utica (Cato erect with sword
in hand), and he ends *Dion-Brut.* (*Brut.* 58, comp. 5) with an anecdote about
Augustus and the statue of the hero at Mediolanum. One should not forget
the death of Caesar before the statue of Pompey (*Caes.* 66, *Brut.* 14). (In
spite of his protestations about natural causes, Plutarch includes a large
number of statue portents.). Recent studies in this area are J. Breckenridge,
"Origins of Roman Republican Portraiture—Relations with the Hellenistic
World," *ANRW* I,4 (1975), pp. 826-53, M. Bieber," The Development of
Portraiture on Roman Republican Coins," pp. 870-898, and R. Winkes,
'Physiognomonia,' Probleme der Charakter-interpretationen römischer
Porträte," pp. 899-926. For the statue of Alexander by Lysippos, which
influenced Plutarch's conception of the hero, see Flacelière, *Vies* IX, p. 33,
and M. Bieber, *Alexander the Great in Greek and Roman Art* (Chicago:
1964). On the Marcellus inscription, see Ziegler, "Plutarchstudien XXII.
Drei Gedichte bei Plutarch," *Rh. M.*, 110 (1967), 53-64.

[12] Plutarch relates Delphi to Alexander's career on three occasions.
In chapter 3 the oracle implies to Philip—who has consulted the shrine
about the meaning of the snake he saw sleeping with Olympias—that
Ammon was the boy's father. In 14 Alexander can get no response from

ugly by referring the reader to the handsome statue of the man at
Delphi (*Philopoimen* 2). An account of Alexander's hunting expedition in Persia is interrupted by a description of the statuary
group at Delphi depicting Alexander's hunt. Plutarch includes the
names of the benefactors and the artists (*Alexander* 40).[13] The
column and statue of Aemilius was mentioned by Polybios (30.10)
and Philopoimen's by Pausanias (8.49), but Plutarch is our only
extant source for this statue of Alexander at Delphi. Plutarch is also
the sole source for our knowledge of the deposit made by Lysander
at Delphi—something he found in the account of a Delphian named
Anaxandrides (*Lysander* 18) and for the tomb of the general beside
the road from Delphi to Chaironeia (Lysander 29). Finally, Plutarch
is responsible for telling us how the Athenians came to put the right
of *promanteia* for themselves on the bronze wolf (*Pericles* 21).[14]

---

the Pythia because he has come on an unlucky day, but on his using violence
on her she exclaims that he is invincible; he takes the utterance as a good
omen. In 37 he is told by the Delphic oracle that he will be led by a wolf,
or possibly a Lycian (λύκος Λύκιος) through Persia. The last incident appears
also in Curtius 5.4.11, Polyainos 4.3.27, and Diodoros 17.68. Justinus,
12.2.3, refers to a poison plot against Alexander which was predicted by
Delphi. Halliday, *The Greek Questions of Plutarch* (Oxford: 1928), pp. 61ff.,
tried to show that the oracle was open most of the year for consultation,
but Hamilton, *Alexander*, p. 35, on the basis of *De E* 398a and *Qu. Graec.*
292e thinks it unlikely. In his view the oracle was only open for consultation one day out of the year, until much later—when it was open each
month. Parke-Wormell, pp. 30-31 leave the impression that throughout
Greek history the Pythia had monthly consultations. But Plutarch's words
make clear that it was only "lately" that the monthly answers were given
and previously it had only been on an annual basis (292a). In *CQ* 37 (1943),
19ff., Parke had maintained that the change took place in 590 B.C.—the
time of the first Sacred War—but Hamilton argues convincingly that the
annual consultation was still in effect in 336; and that the ὀψέ and πρότερον
of 292a are Plutarch's own words.

[13] The dedication on this work was discovered at the end of the last
century. Plutarch tells us that the hunting scene—which was cast in bronze
and included dogs, lions, and Alexander slaying a lion—was dedicated by
Crateros and designed by Lysippos and Leochares. Hamilton, p. 107,
notes that Crateros died in 321 before the work was completed, so its execution was completed by his son of the same name and dedicated at a
Cratereia in Crateros' honor. Since the inscription states that the hunting
depicted took place in the confines of Syria, Plutarch may have erred in
locating it at Sogdiana; but it is also possible that he has conflated two
hunts. The one depicted on the monument probably took place at the royal
hunting reserve at Sidon. The dedication is still extant. See Flacelière,
Vies IX, p. 83, 122, and 239 (*Fouilles de Delphes*, III, 4, no. 137, pl. XXIII).

[14] Plutarch used monumental evidence on several occasions, e.g. for the
location of Cimon's remains (*Cim.* 19). See Guthrie, *The Greeks and Their
Gods*, p. 236. Gomme, *Commentary on Thucydides* I, p. 76, used this passage

It is quite evident, then, that Plutarch felt the need to justify the ways of the oracle to men, and that he did his best to do so. There were certain vexing inconsistencies in the oracle's conduct which irritated other Greek historians. Plutarch invariably eliminates, plays down, or corrects these irregularities. He seemed to be particularly concerned to portray the extent of Delphic influence in Greek history and culture, and to show that from the earliest times the Romans had maintained a favorable relationship with the shrine. Even when treating the outrage perpetrated upon the oracle by Sulla, he is quick to point out that Sulla's conduct was an exception to the normal Roman beneficence toward Delphi, and that even Sulla made retribution for his depredations. One must be cautious then in accepting certain accounts he offers. Certainly the description of Demetrios' relationship with Delphi and his usurpation of divine honors must be somewhat exaggerated. Though modern evidence in general supports Plutarch here, he has probably telescoped events to a great extent and relied upon an extremely hostile source. Unlike many ancient historians Plutarch was intrigued by the possibility of using monumental evidence. He should not be too harshly criticized for his failings in this respect, for he had plenty of companionship.

---

along with *Arist.* 5 and 22 to attack Plutarch's methods. He is defended by Hamilton, *Alexander*, pp. xliii-xlix. In *Arist.* 1 he uses this evidence to determine Aristides' wealth, that of Nicias in *Nic.* 3. In *Arist.* 19, the inscription at Plataia is used to determine the number of cities involved, a painting of the battle of Pallene is used to illuminate that event (*Arat.* 32), a statue for the death of Machanidas (*Philop.* 10); in *Cim.* 7 the *hermai* dedicated to him are indications of his greatness.

CHAPTER TWELVE

CLINGING LIKE BEES OR BATS:
DIVINE RETRIBUTION IN THE LIVES

There is hardly a more characteristic feature of Plutarch's religious outlook as manifested in the *Lives* than his insistence that crime does not pay. Yet, no scholar seems to have given it the attention it deserves. Perhaps too many other questions have obscured the undeniable fact that Plutarch's *Lives* are case histories in crime and punishment. However, his thought is somewhat complex and oscillates considerably between the two poles of vice bringing its own punishment, and vice punished through supernatural intercession.

But before one examines the *Lives*, it will be necessary to take a look at his views on crime and punishment in the *Moralia*. An example of the weight of retribution in Plutarch's writing can be seen in a very Stoic-sounding passage from *De exilio* (610a-b), a work which in itself has little to do with retribution:

> This is the boundary of our native land, and here no one is either exile or foreigner or alien; here are the same fire, water, and air, the same magistrates and procurators and councillors—Sun, Moon, and Morning Star; the same laws for all, decreed by one commandment and one sovereignty—the summer solstice, the winter solstice, the equinox, the Pleiades, Arcturus, the seasons of sowing, the seasons of planting; here one king and ruler, "God holding the the beginning, middle, and end of the universe, proceeds directly as is his nature, in his circuit; upon him follows Justice (Dike) who visits with punishment those who fall short of the divine law;" the justice which all of us by nature observe toward all men as our fellow-citizens (De Lacy-Einarson, Loeb, *Mor.* VII, pp. 529-531).

Certainly there is nothing spectacular in this combination of Plato and later Stoicism. Yet, divine retribution seems to worm its way into everything Plutarch writes.[1] In *Mulierum virtutes* a

---

[1] The tendency is not confined to Plutarch. In Ps. Plutarch *De liberis educandis* (10c-12d), a kind of ancient Piaget, it is recommended that the reward of the just and the punishment of the evil be constantly put before the minds of children. As examples are the suicide of a boy who got the nickname "kicker" after kicking Socrates (undoubtedly a popular story

Thracian officer who had raped a noble Macedonian lady named Timocleia, is lured into a well where she rains stones upon him as he searches in vain for hidden treasure (260b-c). Plutarch approves her conduct with gusto. Children are not spared the sins of their parents.

In *De sera numinis vindicta*, Plutarch's principal essay on crime and punishment, heredity involves one as much in guilt and punishment as it does in property and honors (558d-560a). One of the most vivid scenes in the myth of *De sera* portrays the children of a wicked ancestor rushing upon him in fury for all the punishment they have had to expiate for him on earth:

> Most piteous of all, he said, was the suffering of the souls who thought that they were already released from their sentence, and then were apprehended again; these were the souls whose punishment had passed over to their descendants or children. For whenever the soul of such a child or descendant arrived and found them, it flew at them in such a fury and raised a clamour against them and showed the marks of its sufferings, berating and pursuing the soul of the other, which desired to escape and hide, but could not. . .To some, he said, great clusters of the souls of descendants were attached, clinging to them like veritable swarms of bees or bats, and gibbering shrilly in memory of what they had suffered through their fault. (De Lacy-Einarson, Loeb, *Mor.* VII, p. 297).

Even Plutarch's *Erotikos* (the Greek title of *Amatorius*), which is otherwise devoted to the gentle and sometimes satirical, but in no way somber praise of love, ends with two hair-raising retribution stories. In the first of these Camma of Galatia lures her husband's murderer into the temple of Artemis where she induces him to join her in a cup of poison, then exults over his unexpected death agony (768b-d). The dialogue closes with the death of Empona, the Gallic wife of Sabinus, one of Vespasian's victims. After undergoing a painful pregnancy and bearing him a child in his underground hiding place she was finally discovered along with her husband and put to death. Plutarch claims that divine retribution visited Vespasian by wiping out his family—"in a short time his whole line being destroyed" (770d-771d).

---

with schoolmasters) and the rotting to death in prison of one wit who twitted Ptolemy Philadelphos for marrying his sister Arsinoe, and another who joked about Antigonos the One-Eyed and his cook. The elements of *arete* are said to be the hope of reward and the fear of punishment.

The view does violence to historical fact since Vespasian died peacefully, and Plutarch had to telescope the twenty years it took Domitian to die.

Even a rather innocuous statement by Plato is turned into a manifesto on retribution. Florus, the principal speaker in a *Symposiac*, "what Plato meant when he said God was always doing geometry," upholds the view that it means God uses "geometric" rather than "linear" proportions in the punishment of evildoers (719b-c).

As usual there are variations in Plutarch's thought on the subject. It seems that he never really made up his mind on whether vice in itself was sufficient punishment or at least brought its own punishment with it, or whether some direct act of divine intervention was needed. The *Lives* are always talking about *to daimonion* punishing the culprit. Yet, at the same time one of the general purposes of the *Lives* is to demonstrate that virtue is rewarded and vice punished, and at times Plutarch explicitly points out how the vice of a character brought about his downfall. In three places— *De sera* (554a-555c), *An vitiositas ad infelicitatem sufficiat* 498d, 500a, and *Non posse suaviter vivi secundum Epicurum* 1102e—it is argued that vice suffices and implied that divine intervention is to be taken only symbolically.[2]

The principal theme of *De sera numinis vindicta* is the inevitability with which *to daimonion* tracks down the guilty: "the mills of the gods grind slow but sure," as is alluded to by one speaker (549d).[3] Plutarch throws in a scene of eschatological torment

---

[2] *Non posse* is probably datable to c. 99 A.D.—judging by its dedication to L. Herennius Saturninus, who was proconsul in Achaia in 98-99 A.D. (1107d, PIR² H 126). See Ziegler, *Plutarchos*, p. 126, and Jones, "Towards a Chronology," p. 72. Jones, however, is not convinced that the essay need have been written in Saturninus' consulship. In any case the essay represents one side of Plutarch's thought, and we very probably should not look for the development of ideas here.

[3] Plutarch's speaker quotes the maxim rather obliquely: it actually goes "the mills of the gods grind late but fine" (ὀψὲ θεῶν ἀλέουσι μύλοι, ἀλέουσι δὲ λεπτά). A great deal has been written about *De sera numinis vindicta*. Proclos transcribed and adapted large portions of it in antiquity. See V. Cousin ed., *Procli Philosophi Platonici Opera Inedita . . .* (Paris: 1864), 2nd ed. coll. 76-145. In the 19th Century we find J. De Maistre, *Sur les Délais de la Justice Divine* (Paris: 1858), A. P. Peabody, *Plutarch on the Delay of the Divine Justice* (Boston: 1885), H. B. Hackett and W. S. Tyler, *Plutarch on the Delay of the Deity in Punishing the Wicked*, rev. ed. (New York: 1868), C. W. Super, *Between Heathenism and Christianity* (New York: 1899), and the more recent work by G. Méautis, *Des Délais*

at the end of the essay but throughout he attempts to prove every act of a criminal nature is punished somehow or other in this life. The title suggests the direct intervention of the divine, but in fact vice is usually seen to bring its own punishment; and if retribution comes at all, it is not by a supernatural action on God's part but through the use of human instruments. Those who altogether seem to escape punishment are said to be punished by their own consciences (554e-f). From the modern viewpoint the most distressing part of the essay is the defense of the hereditary guilt theory, which is applied not only to individuals and families but to cities as well.

In the anti-Epicurean essay, *Non posse suaviter vivi secundum Epicurum*, Theon, the principal speaker, adopts the view that God cannot be personally responsible for retribution since such a viewpoint implies that the divinity is subject to passion (1102e). After this apparently Epicurean opening, Theon goes on to argue against *Kyria doxa* 1. Basing himself on Plato (*Timaios* 29e, *Republic* 335d), he argues that the divine (*to theion*) is not subject to anger, but on the contrary its whole nature is to bestow favor: it is not true that the divine is not prey to feelings of anger and favor; rather it is the very nature of the divine to bestow favor and lend its aid, and not its nature to be angry and do harm; the real punishment of the evil is their separation from the delight and pleasure of this relationship to the divine (1102e-1103a). Theon himself is not in favor of illuminating the masses on this point since he believes that the idea of an angry God prevents them from doing more evil, but he regards the divine as incapable of anything other than *philanthropia* (1101d). This was probably Plutarch's official stand on the matter, but it did not prevent him from taking a surprising amount of relish in the punishment of evil-doers, and it is difficult to believe that his reading public consisted so much of *hoi polloi*.

There are several points of contact between *De sera* and the *Lives*, which enable us to see a more pronounced and precise stand on retribution coming out in the essay. For example in *Solon* 12

---

de la Justice Divine par Plutarque (Lausanne: 1935). The recent translation with notes in the Loeb (VII, pp. 170-299) by Einarson and De Lacy has very helpful modern notes and a short introduction to the literature. The essay is referred to in almost every work on Plutarch's religion but usually so exclusively that a balanced view of the subject is not possible.

Plutarch sees no element of retribution in Solon's extradition of the bodies of those who slew Cylon in the sanctuary. But in *De sera* 549a this is supposed to exemplify the futility of retribution upon children, by a speaker who opposes the thesis that God visits his vengeance upon the children of evildoers, a view supported later in the essay. Similarly the treatment of the death of Timoleon's mercenaries who had sacked Delphi is treated in the *Lives* within a retribution context, it is true, but one which is primarily concerned with the *tyche* of Timoleon. There are great variations in how the corrupt text here (*Timoleon* 30.10) should be reconstructed, but all the reconstructions see Timoleon's *eutychia* as figuring prominently. The passage itself begins with a laudatory description of Timoleon's *eutychia*; "from these events Timoleon's good fortune became famous". In *De sera* Plutarch throughout opposes divine retribution to *tyche*, and in the particular passage the mercenaries are explicitly stated to be the instruments of *to daimonion* in removing the Carthaginians from Sicily—in much the way that Dionysios was used for this purpose by the divine—but "they were disposed of when they had outlived their usefulness" (552f). It is possible that Plutarch is overinfluenced by his sources in the *Lives*, but it also seems logical that *De sera* was written with greater reflection, and probably after *Timoleon*.

Another example of the unclear division between *tyche* and *to daimonion* can be seen in the punishment of Callippos, the murderer of Dion (*Dion* 58). Here retribution for the deed is attributed to *tyche* and the gods (οὐ μὴν πολὺν χρόνον ὁ Κάλλιππος ἔγκλημα τῆς τύχης καὶ τῶν θεῶν περίην).[4] The word *tyche* is carefully

---

[4] Both *Dion* 58 and *De ser.* 553d refer to Calippos, the assassin of Dion, as murdered by the sword with which he killed Dion; and *Caes.* 69 mentions that Cassius was killed with the sword with which he killed Caesar, though this is not mentioned in *Brutus*. Remarkable as the coincidences may be for proving divine retribution in this life, one would think the stories fictitious. In Plutarch's *Life of Dion*, Callippos, "after being hated by all men" is killed at Rhegium by Leptines and Polyperchon after an unsuccessful assault on Catana. In both *Dion* and *Caesar* the assassin is killed with the sword used upon his victim, though in *Brut.* 43, Cassius is simply found decapitated, with some suggestion of foul play. In Jones' scheme, p. 67, *Dion-Brutus* was published in the same group with *Alexander-Caesar*, and perhaps some effect at parallelism in the sword incidents may have unconsciously crept in. The syncrisis to *Dion-Brutus* (5) contains a peculiar statement that no one avenged Dion, something which seems to be in conflict with the retribution ending of that life and the statement that Callippos quickly paid *dike* to *tyche* and the gods: καὶ Δίωνος μὲν τιμωρὸς

expunged from the *De sera* version (553d). In *Pericles* and *Pompey* we hear nothing about the hereditary guilt of these heroes, but in *De sera* 533b-c, much is made out of it.

Another example occurs in the *Life of Cimon*. In 6 the death of Pausanias is related. Pausanias had forced the parents of a girl to send her to him at night. When she came in the dark he mistakenly thought someone had come to assassinate him and killed her. For a long time he is troubled by dreams in which she tells him to prepare for his doom. Finally he goes to the *nekyomanteion* at Heracleia to consult her soul. The girl then tells him that he will soon receive his release, implying his death.[5] The relation of the incident in *De sera* 555c is entirely subordinated to the retribution theme. His action, one of *hybris*—which De Lacy-Einarson (Loeb VII, p. 223) getting into the spirit of the piece, translate as "insolent lust"—deserves retribution. His vision is the result of a guilty conscience, and one might draw the conclusion that all such visions are hallucinations brought on by guilt. But in the *Life* the incident is used primarily to indicate why the allies suddenly turned upon Pausanias, and the girl appears to be kindly in her appearance at Heracleia to announce Pausanias' death.

But the most remarkable characteristic of the *Lives* in this regard is the frequency of retribution endings. We have already noted the punishment of Timoleon's mercenaries, which ends the *Life* of that hero. One can cite a great many more. Among them is the death of Alcibiades in one of two very different versions which Plutarch gives. In the preferred version the hero is executed

οὐδεὶς ἔφανη πεσόντος ἀλλὰ Βροῦτον ᾽Αντώνιος μὲν ἔθαψεν ἐνδόξως. The reference seems to be to Antony honoring Brutus by laying a robe over him, whereas Callippos was showered with praise by the Syracusans and Athenians, Dion's pregnant wife thrown into prison where she brought forth a son. Perhaps in the Greek (58.3) τιμωρός is used in a loose sense, meaning honored, or should be amended to τιμῶν. There also is trouble with the line immediately preceding, regarding Plutarch's recollection of Plato's Seventh Letter. (Ziegler, II-I, p. 182). Plutarch followed a source hostile to Heracleides. See G. A. Lehmann, "Dion and Herakleides, *Historia*, 19 (1970), 401-06.

[5] Thuc. 1.94.95 and Diodor. 11.14 do not record the vision. Plutarch, however—who records that it took place at Byzantion and the consultation of the girl's soul at Heracleia—apparently felt the end of Pausanias was too well known to need relating. We have a very good example of his desire to add information rather than repeat well-known history. According to Pomponius Mela (1.19.51), Heracleia was on the Black Sea near the coast of Bithynia and had its nekyomanteion near a river called Acheron. See Flacelière, *Vies* II, p. 22.

at the instigation of either the Persian Pharnabazes or the Spartans working upon Pharnabazes. In the second, which ends the *Life*, and would seem to come from the version published by his enemies, he had raped "a girl of good family" and was run down by her outraged brothers (*Alcibiades* 39).[6] When one takes a second look it is easy to see how this could be tied in with the more likely one in which he dies in the arms of his mistress Timandra. Plutarch preferred to end with a retribution story. Demades meets a horrible end in Macedonia for betraying Demosthenes (*Demosthenes* 31). He learns that "traitors sell themselves first, a truth of which Demosthenes had often assured him, but which he would not believe", and it is this note which ends the life.[7] For the end of the Silver Shields, who delivered Eumenes to Antigonos, Plutarch takes what would seem to be the most hostile version. Antigonos sends them to one of his commanders with instructions to destroy them in every way possible (*Eumenes* 19). This is also the version of Diodoros (19.48), but in the version we find in Polyainos (4.6.15), they were permitted to return to Macedon, except for two of the leaders who were executed. One can only say that wherever we have a retribution death in Plutarch the historian must be very cautious.

Other *Lives* reveal a similar propensity toward this criminal fiction. Those who fail to marry Lysander's daughters after his death are punished, even if it is as trivial as a fine (*Lysander* 30). At the end of *Pelopidas* Plutarch apologizes for the death of Alexander, Pelopidas' murderer, on the grounds that the death came so swiftly; but he thinks the retribution was sufficient "because Alexander was the first tyrant to be murdered by his wife, and his body was outraged after death" (35)[8]. Here Plutarch agrees

---

[6] Ancient authorities disputed the motive behind Alcibiades' murder. Diodoros, 14.11, attributes it to a Spartan conspiracy with the Persians, but he offers Ephoros as his source for another version. In this Alcibiades had uncovered the Spartan plot to help Cyros to the throne against Artaxerxes, but was killed by Pharnabazos who wanted to be first to tell the king. Nepos, *Alc.* 10, seems to follow Plutarch's version but without the dream and the role of Timandra, Alcibiades' mistress.

[7] The connection between the death of Demades and Demosthenes' revenge is pure theological fancy on Plutarch's part. Even Diodoros who is fond of retribution himself, did not see it here (18.48. 1-4).

[8] Plutarch's account is more melodramatic than that in Xenophon, *Hell.* 6.4.35, but basically the same. Plutarch is uncertain of Thebe's motives in assassinating Alexander, but guesses at two rather unidealistic causes. One is her anger at Alexander for executing one of his favorites whom she

with Xenophon (*Hellenica* 6.4.35) but not with Diodoros (16.14). At the end of *Timoleon* (37), Plutarch timidly notes that the general's blindness in old age was "not due to retribution, but to an hereditary illness."

Naturally the punishment fits the crime. We have already seen how this was the case in *Timoleon, Eumenes*, and to some extent in *Demosthenes*. The *Life of Crassus* closes with a series of exterminating murders: Sourena, who betrayed Crassus, is betrayed himself and slain by Hyrodes, Hyrodes himself by his son Phraates —which Plutarch characterizes as *dike* for the treachery of Sourena, and the cruelty of Hyrodes (33). Even Caesar is not spared: his murder in the portico of Pompey's theatre is seen as retribution for his assassination (implied) of Pompey, and he is ridiculed for the ambition in achieving power at such great risk, "from which he reaped no fruit, but only the name, and which aroused envy on the part of his fellow-citizens." But his assassins fare worse. Many portents signify that the murder was not pleasing to the gods: the sun shines weakly for an entire year, a great comet appears, but most of all, the great *daimon* of Caesar seems to avenge him, tracking down all his murderers "on land and sea" until the last is dead—Cassius killing himself with the very sword used on Caesar, and Brutus after seeing the vision of his evil *daimon* at Abydos, and then before Phillipi, understanding his fate and plunging to his death (*Caesar* 69).

Plutarch ends the *Life of Cicero* with probably the most grim version of events after the hero's death: the young freedman Philologos, who in Plutarch's version betrayed Cicero, is forced by Quintus' wife Pomponia to cut off his own flesh and eat it. Handing over the young man to Pomponia was supposedly the one decent thing Antony did. The life ends with a tribute to Cicero's patriotism and greatness as an orator to the grandson of Augustus by the Emperor, mention of the election of Cicero's son to the con-

---

liked. The other is her fear that her sterility will cause her husband to divorce her and marry Jason's widow. The passage is rather surprising in view of the sharp criticism in Plutarch's *De Herod. malign.* 856b where he attacks historians who give base motives to Thebe (those who attribute it not to a noble spirit and hatred of evil, but to jealousy and womanly passion). Here she acts out of dread of faithlessness and her hatred of his cruelty. Things are further complicated by *Amat.* 768b where the main motive for the death seems to be his sexual abuse of the boy Pytholaus (Thebe's brother in *Pel.* 35), who for this reason kills Alexander.

sulate, the prohibition of the family of Antony from using the name Marcus, and the removal of all his statues, "thus *to daimonion* devolved upon the family of Cicero the final steps in the punishment of Antony" (*Cicero* 49). Plutarch must have been aware that he was running at times in the face of more reliable sources, but his desire for retribution overrides his better judgment.

Other Romans are not left unrequited in death. Plutarch had a little trouble finding retribution for Nasica, the prime mover in the death of Tiberius Gracchus, but he has him wander about in exile "hated by all men until he ended his life ignominiously at Pergamon" (*T. Gracchus* 21). One should not have thought Pergamon such an awful place to end one's life, and more observant people believe that he may have been sent to Pergamon to straighten out the affairs of that kingdom, in the light of their dealings with the hero, and their "special relationship" to him. Plutarch has Marius drink himself to death to avoid the torments of his own conscience and fear of the approaching Sulla (*Marius* 45), though to do so he had to telescope events. The final chapter of the life is a disquisition on the insatiable appetite for power and lack of appreciation of the good things *tyche* had given him, contrasting him with the philosophers Plato and Antipater of Tarsos (the Stoic successor of Diogenes of Babylon in the school at Athens, and the teacher of Panaitios). This is followed by something of an afterthought, the end of Marius junior—who had inherited his father's evil traits—at Praeneste, the final words of that *Life* being the grim "he himself killed himself" (αὐτὸς αὐτὸν ἀπέκτεινεν).[9]

Caesar's first task on landing in Egypt is to execute all of Pompey's murderers. One does in fact escape, Theodotos the

---

[9] Plutarch may have an axe to grind here. In *De nat. deor.* 3.81, the case of Marius is offered as proof that providence does not exist: his evil life rewarded by seven consulships and a happy death is not convincing proof of a just providence. The neurotic death of Marius in Plutarch's *Life* is followed by the miserable annihilation of the son—who, Plutarch claims, inherited his father's vices. However, it seems very doubtful that Plutarch had read Cicero's philosophical works. At least his life of the Roman orator is remarkably silent over Cicero's literary and philosophical accomplishments.

According to Livy, *Per.* 88, the younger Marius died in a suicide pact with the youngest son of Pontius Telesinus, the Samnite general. The matter has been studied by J. Bayet in "Le suicide mutuel dans la mentalité des romains," *L'Année Sociologique*, 38 (1951), 35-89, reprinted in *Croyance et Rites dans la Rome Antique*, (Paris: 1971), pp. 130-176, esp. p. 131.

sophist, but he is later overtaken by Brutus and executed "with every possible torture" (*Pompey* 80). Pompey's remains are given to Cornelia to be transported to his Alban Villa—a delicate and sympathetic touch which characterizes much of Plutarch's work. All of Sertorius' assassins are hunted down and slain except for Aufidius, whom Plutarch describes in the manner of Nasica as ending his life in a barbarian village "poor and hated by all men" (*Sertorius* 27). However, Sulla's last illness, in which the worms multiply so fast his friends are unable to remove them, is not meant as a sign of retribution for his former cruelty (*Sulla* 36).[10]

---

[10] Plutarch describes the horrible death of Sulla (*Sull.* 36) in some detail:

By this mode of life he aggravated a disease which was insignificant in its beginnings, and for a long time he knew not that his bowels were ulcerated. This disease corrupted his whole flesh also and converted it into worms, so that many were employed day and night in removing them; what they took away was nothing compared with the increase upon him, but all his clothing, baths, hand-basins, and food were infected with that flux of corruption, so violent was its discharge. Therefore, he immersed himself in water many times a day to cleanse and scour his person. But it was of no use for the change gained upon him rapidly, and the swarm of vermin defied all purification. (Perrin, Loeb, *Lives* IV, pp. 439-41).

Plutarch seems then, more interested in the medical than the moral aspects of the case. Perhaps he had a medical source before him since he follows with the information that Pelias, Alcman, Pherecydes, Callisthenes of Olynthos, Mucius the jurist, and Eunos—the head of the slave revolt in Sicily in 134 B.C.—died of this disease. Plutarch believed in spontaneous generation from corpses so he undoubtedly imagined that Sulla's body literally generated worms. But the last words of the *Life* are all about his good fortune not retribution. This type of medical digression is almost unique in the *Lives*. The disease is found in Arist. *Hist. Anim.* 5.31, Plin. *N.H.* 11.39, and Paus. 1.20.7. Valerius Maximus, 9.3.8, suggests death from hemoptysia rather than phthirasis. Plutarch added to Aristotle's victims, Alcman and Pherecydes. Pliny mentioned Alcman and Sulla; Pausanias mentioned Sulla and Pherecydes. Diog. Laert. 4.4 claims Plutarch also mentioned Speusippos. See Flacelière, *Vies* VI, pp. 227 and 348, who believes Plutarch may have studied medicine in Alexandria. Appian, *BC* 1.192—like Plutarch—describes the splendor of Sulla's funeral. Pliny, however, represents a different tradition. He asks (*NH* 7.138) how the Romans could be so fatuous as to swallow the story that Sulla was always fortunate, a man who had dipped his hands in the blood of so many, had died such a horrible death, and had been cut off by it from finishing his temple on the Capitoline. After this bitter criticism Pliny concludes that Sulla's victims—who died a less dreadful death—were more fortunate: Sulla's death was his own punishment (*erodente se ipso corpore et supplicia sibi gignente*). Plutarch suppresses all this in his rather poorly thought-out *Sulla*. Cicero, *De leg.* 2.56, notes that cremation was rare in Rome at this time, and that Sulla was the first of the Cornelii to have it done. Cicero

There can be no doubt that Plutarch was serious about these endings. One must certainly regret the dark side of his nature which rejoiced in these trivial sadistic tales, often where they were a serious distortion of truth or where unfortunate pawns were caught up in the vengeance or politics of the mighty. One might question Plutarch's intelligence when he swallows the Roman line on men like Philip of Macedon, the slayer of Aratos, who must pay "ample *dike* to Zeus Xenios." In Plutarch's version he is hated by his subjects, kills his only decent son by mistake, and in the end is forced to give his kingdom to an illegitimate son, the child of a seamstress, while the eventual heir Perseus is forced to walk in the triumph of Aemilius Paullus. Plutarch comments that in this way the great line of the Antigonids ended while the descendants of Aratos were still living at Sicyon and Pellene in his own day (*Aratos* 54). One might think that Plutarch would have better attempted to understand the role of Philip or Aratos. At least his Greek sympathies should have questioned the humanity of Paullus in forcing Perseus—who apparently had surrendered on conditions which were later refused by the Romans—to walk in his triumph and to die of starvation in the *carcer*.

A similar lack of perception is evident in Plutarch's description of the end of Aristion, the Greek commander who finally surrendered the Acropolis to Sulla. To be fair to Plutarch, as in the case of Perseus, he allows both a hostile and friendly source to shine through his work, with that splendor of impartiality which he himself confessed to be the bias of his materials. The two sources for the siege are in chapter 14, the whitewash of Sulla's *Memoirs*, and "the memory of the oldest Athenians," 150 years old by Plutarch's time but still graphic in its description of the blood-

---

thought it was to prevent the possibility of desecration of the body since Sulla had previously had Marius' remains scattered. But one would think that Cicero, who should have been prejudiced against Sulla anyway, is mistaken and that if the disease was that horrible, the family had the body cremated for hygienic reasons. The kindly treatment of Sulla in the *Life* could be due to Plutarch's friendship with Romans. Sextius Sulla from Carthage spent considerable time with Plutarch in Rome (*Rom.* 15, *Symp.* 7.7.1, 8.8.1); he appears in *Symp.* 2.3 and 3.3; and he is the principal speaker and narrator of the myth in *De facie in orbe lunae*. Perhaps he had some real or imaginary link with the dictator. More likely, Plutarch was over-influenced by pro-Sullan sources and by the mystical side to Sulla's character in his *Memoirs*, if not by his own aristocratic leanings. The *Lives* are in general anti-Marian. On the period, see E. Gabba, "Mario e Silla," *ANRW* I,1 (1972), pp. 764-805.

bath and the destruction of the artistic treasures of the city. Ambivalent as often, Plutarch is puzzled, attributing it first to some mad delusion of Sulla, fighting "against the shadow of the city's former glory," or to his resentment at the taunts of Aristion against his wife. Aristion himself is described in the vilest terms, undoubtedly from the *Memoirs*, as a compound of licentiousness and cruelty, a sink of the worst of diseases and passions of Mithridates, a fatal malady on the city, etc. Sulla rejects the mission of peace sent by Aristion, claiming he had come "to punish rebels, not to learn history," and here Plutarch's sympathies must have been with his countrymen.

Even though Sulla's atrocities are portrayed in some detail, Plutarch seems to be unable to put them into perspective. He accepts Sulla's excuse that the Academy and Lyceum had to be devastated and the most glorious shrines of Greece—Delphi, Olympia, and Epidauros—had to be sacked because Sulla was in a hurry to prevent the outbreak of revolution at Rome during his absence. Plutarch still believed in Sulla's "mild temperament" (30). Yet, it is no wonder that the memory of the oldest Athenians had not forgotten the siege. Sulla's entry was a furious bloodbath: the bloodshed in the agora covered the entire Kerameikos inside the Dipylon gate, and "according to some" even flowed into the *proasteion* (14). But Plutarch accepts uncritically the thesis, again undoubtedly from the *Memoirs*, that Aristion's fall was pleasing to the gods; for he had to surrender through lack of water, and immediately after *to daimonion* caused abundant rain to fall upon the Acropolis. In many respects this is a most non-reflective *Life*, with sources pulling Plutarch in opposite directions. In spite of all his faults he seemed to see something in Sulla which covered a multitude of sins.

Like a melodramatic playwright Plutarch ends his piece with a clutter of dead bodies on the stage. Galba's murderers are tracked down by the petitions they send to Otho (*Galba* 27). In chapter 27 of that *Life*, Galba himself tumbles out of his litter near the Lacus Curtius and is hacked to pieces, his death followed by several others. In 28 we find the bizarre touch: "the dead bodies all headless in their consular robes were still strewn over the forum."

Throughout the *Lives* individual perfidy and vice finds its own reward. The hapless, and perhaps innocent Greek engineer who sets Amisos on fire to facilitate his escape, is punished by

Lucullus (*Lucullus* 32). Marius' bloody bodyguards are appropriately shot down by Sertorius (*Sertorius* 5). Philip dies of grief
after unjustly putting his son Demetrios to death (*Aemilius* 8).
Perseus is captured since he is too avaricious to pay the costs of
his own salvation (*Aemilius* 12). Alcibiades, who has been rejected
by the Athenians, reveals to their enemies the way to defeat them
(*Alcibiades* 23). Antony's murky career is somewhat redeemed by
his putting to death a man who had stolen a robe he had graciously
laid over the dead Brutus (*Brutus* 53). Hannibal attempts to honor
the impetuous, but courageous Marcellus (*Marcellus* 30); he removes
the ring in order to send it back to Marcellus' relatives, and puts
the ashes into an expensive urn to be returned to Marcellus' son.
However, some Numidians attempting to plunder the trappings
cause the bones to be lost. When Hannibal learns of it, he punishes
the Numidians but feels the gods are responsible for the strange
fate of his good intentions. Plutarch ends the *Life* with a description
of Marcellus' statues, including the flowery inscription at Catana
upon one of them, and praise for the glory of his line.[11] This is
undoubtedly an attempt to offset the impression of retribution
against Marcellus, but it stems from the same mentality which
demands the punishment of the Numidians.

In the *Moralia* Plutarch includes some stories of boys who killed
their lovers, and there is an addition to these accounts in the *Lives*.
At *Amatorius* 768f he mentions Crateas, who slew Archelaus (Plato,
Alcibiades II, 141d, and Aristotle, *Politics* 1311b 8ff), Pytholaus,
who killed Alexander of Pherai (also related in *Pelopidas* 35),
and a boy who killed Periander, the tyrant of Ambracia, after
Periander had taunted him with not being pregnant. Plutarch

---

[11] Is this getting the record straight again? In *De nat. deor.* 3.80, Marcellus'
death is another argument proposed by Cotta against providence. Plutarch's references to his sources here seem very confused. He claims that
Nepos and Valerius Maximus (οἱ περὶ Κορνήλιον Νέπωτα καὶ Οὐαλέριον
Μάξιμον), were his sources for the death of Marcellus, and he gives Livy
and Augustus Caesar as sources for a contradictory version in which Marcellus' son actually received the urn and it was ceremoniously buried.
However, such a version appears in neither Valerius (5.1 ext. 6) nor in
Livy (27.28). Livy himself notes the great divergence of the sources over
Marcellus' death. The funeral eulogy was probably suggested
by Valerius, and Appian, *Hann.* 50, has something similar. Perhaps Poseidonios was responsible for the confusion and Plutarch was following him;
here Poseidonios (*FGH* 87, F 44) is given as the source of the inscription
on Marcellus' statue which had attributed seven consulships to him. (Plutarch explains that in reality two were proconsulships.)

begins *Cimon* 2 with the story of Damon, an incident which took place in his own town of Chaironeia and which he had learned from the old men of the town. The Roman governor had made advances to Damon, and Damon reacted by killing the governor and raising a rebel band to protect himself. The townspeople, in fear of reprisal, lured Damon into the bath where he was murdered. Damon apparently had his revenge on the townspeople since the baths became haunted and they were forced to close it up. At least that is the version Plutarch gives, but one might suspect that it was their only way of giving a monument to Damon. There is a story also in *Demetrios* 24 of a young man, Democles, nicknamed the handsome (ὁ καλός), who escaped from the clutches of Demetrios by jumping into a caldron of boiling water. Since the story has as its source the satirical verses of Philippides, let us hope that in reality Democles only jumped into the bath to avoid an obese Demetrios. Otherwise, he is something of an exception in not getting his revenge.

One might wonder how the generally humane Plutarch could have condoned the stoning of the captive Messenians at the funeral of Philopoimen (*Philopoimen* 21). The funeral is one of the most touching in the *Lives* and reveals the hand of an eye-witness. The bier is covered with ribbons and wreaths so that the burial urn can barely be seen, and the total effect is not merely that of a funeral cortege but also that of a triumph.

It is obvious that Plutarch is faithfully reproducing the pages of Polybios' *Philopoimen*, which is now lost. Apparently Polybios described himself as a young boy marching with pride at the side of the great hero's ashes as they were conveyed to the cemetery (αὐτὴν δὲ τὴν ὕδριαν . . . ἐκόμιζεν ὁ τοῦ στρατηγοῦ τῶν Ἀχαιῶν παῖς Πολύβιος καὶ περὶ αὐτὸν οἱ πρῶτοι τῶν Ἀχαίων). But what about those Messenians who were stoned to death at the time? Plutarch's desire for retribution allows him to approve the archaic barbarism of an Achilles. Or is this another proof that in writing the *Lives* he was often little inclined to challenge his source? More predictable is the vengeance meted out to Philopoimen's murderers. Deinocrates anticipates by suicide—apparently a sign of the divine hand—the fate he deserves, while the others are promptly slain; and those who voted for his torture are themselves tortured. This gruesome scene is, as so often in Plutarch, followed by a contrasting one in which the hero is lauded; in this case there

follows the defense of Philopoimen by Polybios before the Roman
general Mummius.

One might also wish that Plutarch had expressed more pity
for the fallen. He treats Jugurtha as receiving his just deserts
when he is starved to death in the carcer at Rome, a grotesque
scene in which the pitiful maltreatment of the victim—who is not
all that unsympathetically portrayed—contrasts with the rigor
of the author's judgment (ἀξία δίκη τῶν ἀσεβημάτων, *Marius* 12).
Here as often we surely have a reflection of his sources. In *Lucullus*
13 he attributes the wreck of Mithridates' fleet to divine retribution for the sacking of the temple "of Artemis of Priapos", something which apparently was taken from the letter of the highly
theological Lucullus to the senate. He almost gloats over the irony
of Mithridates committing suicide when he learns of the defection
of his son, and seems in accordance with Pompey that he needed
to propitiate the gods to prevent retribution on himself (*Pompey*
42). On Perseus Plutarch, as so often, did not take a clear stand.
He seems to accept the position of Aemilius that Perseus was a
coward who destroyed a kingdom through his own avariciousness,
but an opposite view shines forth, probably from the history of
the king by Poseidonios, in which as Perseus walks in the triumph
his friends and relatives weep not for themselves but for him. He
does not question that Aemilius tried to help Perseus by removing
him from the carcer to another place—where he starved himself
to death, but he also relates another version in which the king is
put to death after much cruel treatment from the Roman soldiery
(*Aemilius* 37). If there is such a thing as symphonic movement
in Plutarch's *Lives*, one might think of the thematic movement
in the end of Jugurtha, picked up here by the end of Perseus.

His attempt to prove that the good are rewarded, by relating
elaborate funerals for the unjustly afflicted, also seems contrived.
Usually, elaborate testimonials to the man's greatness are used to
conceal the fact that crime sometimes does pay. We have already
seen how Philopoimen's death was glossed over through the description of his glorious funeral and the stoning of the Messenians.
Aratos receives a similar funeral in Plutarch's account and is
permitted by Delphi to be buried within the city (*Aratos* 53).
The body of Brutus is treated with chivalrous respect by Antony
(*Brutus* 53). Cato is portrayed as the savior of his country, his
burial is splendid, and a statue of him by the sea "which still

stands there" is described (*Cato Minor* 71). At the end of *Cicero*, Plutarch touchingly describes how a grandson of Octavius was caught reading a book of the dead orator. Expecting a punishment the boy was terrified, but Octavius praised the man and his writings to the skies (*Cicero* 49). Plutarch adds that the punishment of Antony's family was left up to that of Cicero, which promptly set about taking down all of Antony's statues. The *Life* ends with a curious description of vice making its way down through several generations and ending with Nero, who in Plutarch's view came close to turning the whole Empire on its ear (*Antony* 87). Pelopidas is honored in death as the father and savior of his country (*Pelopidas* 34-35). The evil *tyche* which led to Phocion's death is lamented, and his fate is attributed to the same causes which destroyed Socrates; both are said to have been a sin and a misfortune to the city and to have had a lasting effect upon the Athenians (*Phocion* 38).

One peculiar touch which ends a *Life* occurs in *Demosthenes*. Demosthenes committed suicide, so it was really quite difficult to show that virtue in his case was rewarded. But even so Plutarch relates a quaint story about a soldier who hid his savings in the fingers of Demosthenes' statue, and returned after a long absence, "thus offering the local epigramists an opportunity to vie with one another in verse in praise of the incorruptibility of Demosthenes" (*Demosthenes* 31). There is something almost pathological here in Plutarch's attempt to avoid a tragic ending. Good men must not finish last.

In many ways one of the most spectacular passages to gloss over the death of a hero is in *Caesar*. Plutarch never seems to have made up his mind about Caesar's true character, but in the final passage he is absolutely clear that the imperator's death was not pleasing to the gods. In order to put the affair in perspective, he makes two divisions, the divine and the human (τὰ θεῖα, τὰ ἀνθρώπινα). The great *daimon* which supposedly guided Caesar in life acts as his avenger. Of the "human" events, the most marvellous is the death of Cassius with his own sword, which was used to kill Caesar (rather unlikely in itself). Of the "divine" incidents the most remarkable is a comet which shone for seven days after the death of the hero and then suddenly disappeared. Here Plutarch accepted the accounts of prominent Roman writers which are still extant.[12]

---

[12] The story of the comet was really too well known to pass up; see Verg. *Ecl.* 9.47, Serv. *Comm. in Aen.* 8.681 and *Comm. in Ov. Met.* 15. 749ff. and 840ff. Senec. *Qu. nat.* 7.17.2, Plin. *NH* 2.93.94, Suet. *Caes.* 88,

Along with this he mentions the dimming of the sun's rays for a year, during which time it appeared sallow and fruit and crops only half ripened. Since this is the only place in the *Lives* where the death of an historical figure is accompanied by portents, it represents a great concession on Plutarch's part to the Roman mentality.

The "most clear" indication that the murder of Caesar was not pleasing to the gods is the vision of the *daimon* to Brutus before the crossing from Abydos and before the battle of Philippi. It is quite surprising that so much attention and detail is given to the vision in *Caesar*. Moreover, in contrast to the account in *Brutus* where Brutus calmly responds to the vision and shows no effects from it in contemplating his strategy, in *Caesar* Brutus is said to have immediately understood his fate and plunged forward into danger. The two engagements are compressed into one so that "not having been slain in the engagement" he retreats to a lofty crag and commits suicide. The whole business of his initial success related in *Brutus*, is forgotten. The *Life of Caesar* ends with that dire ἀπέθανεν of which the chief conspirator is the subject.

To some extent, then, the *Lives* represent a great historical and theological thesis in their insistence on divine retribution in this life. The guilty, and sometimes their children, are inevitably shown to be punished, even if this involves the distortion of facts, time sequences, and the relationships between persons and events. The *Lives* continually represent vice bringing its own punishment or the divinity finally so exasperated as to intervene itself.[13] The

Obseq. 68, and Cass. Dio. 45.7.1. Still, it is interesting that Plutarch so often uses astronomical phenomena in this way.

[13] *To daimonion* in Plutarch's *Lives* is rather busy. The cognates have a slightly different, though sometimes related meaning or context. *Daimonios* or *daimoniôs* in *Alex.* 52, *Artax.* 13, *Marc.* 17, *Num.* 5 and 20, *Rom.* 28, and *Sert.* 20 seems to mean little more than marvellous, but in *Demos.* 19—with *tyche* (a similar use in *Popl.* 12)—and *Fab.* 17—with *theios*—it takes on deeper supernatural overtones. *Daimonia, ta daimonia, daimonios, to daimonion* in *Nic.* 4, *Them.* 10, *Aem.* 24, *Cor.* 24, *Fab.* 4, *Rom.* 2, *Sul.* 11 seem to be used as synonyms for portents or portentous. (In *Fab.* 17, *daimonion* and *theion* seem to parallel δαίμονος ἢ θεοῦ ἐμποδὼν στάντος used just before in the chapter.) In *Caes.* 69 *to daimonion* is rather oddly used to designate the vision which appears to Brutus. In the introduction to *Dion-Brutus*—perhaps reflecting Stoic terminology—*ta daimonia* means evil spirits. On two occasions *to daimonion* is that of Socrates which gave him intimations of the future. It warns men through oracles, portents, earthquakes and lightning, eclipses and sacrifices. The passages are interesting enough to be cited here: it warns the Spartans not to elect a lame king,

general principles and emphasis on retribution which one finds in the *Moralia* are adequately represented in the *Lives*. However, the essay devoted entirely to retribution, *De sera numinis vindicta* seems to be more carefully thought out in this regard than those passages in the *Lives* which treat the same theme. This may be partly due to the nature of *De sera*. The essay would naturally subordinate everything to retribution whereas in the *Lives* retribution would be less of a consideration. Yet, it is surprising in view of the opposition between *tyche* and divine retribution in the essay, to find *tyche* responsible for retribution in the *Lives*.

Even in Greek religious literature, literary values are of the greatest importance. When one moves a step farther into something like biography which was regarded by the Greeks as an opportunity for artistic creativity and the projection of an ideal as much as, or rather in preference, to the real, literary values

---

through the Delphic oracle (*Ages.* 30); *t.d.* of Socrates warns him about the Sicilian expedition (*Alc.* 17); there are signs from *t.d.* including the sweating statue of Leibethra as Alexander sets out for Asia (*Alex.* 14); it sends an eclipse (*Alex.* 24); Timaios is criticized for saying *t.d.* signified through the mutilation of the *Hermai* that defeat would come from Hermocrates (*Nic.* 1); *t.d.* of Socrates warns him of the Sicilian disaster (*Nic.* 13); through the death of a ram it signifies the death of 3 kings (*Pyr.* 6); through earthquake and lightning it signifies the Catilinarian conspiracy (*Cic.* 14); it gives signs through statue portents (*Cor.* 38); lightning and thunder prevent Galba from speaking thus signifying *t.d.* did not approve what he was saying (*Galb.* 23); it sends signs of disapproval (through a windstorm) of the founding of Carthage (*G. Grach.* 11); it sends signs to both Lucullus and Cimon warning them on what to do (*Luc.* comp. 3); the sacrifices indicate to a seer that *t.d.* is signifying great things for Marius (*Mar.* 8); through an ass drinking water it signifies that Marius should flee by water (*Mar.* 38); the discovery of the Books of Numa indicates *t.d.* is signifying coming evils (*Num.* 22); there is nothing so sure as what *t.d.* reveals in dreams (*Sul.* 6); it foretells by portents civil war in Rome (*Sul.* 7); by sending rain it signifies its displeasure with Aristion at Athens (*Sul.* 14). One could add to this Alexander's fear after seeing the evil portent at Babylon, that *t.d.* was to devolve his power on an impotent man (a ram with testicles on its head) (*Alex.* 57). *To daimonion* is especially active in retribution. It takes care of the Silver Shields (*Eum.* 19); sends a plague to Athens for the death of Androgeos (*Thes.* 15); takes care of *dike* for Timoleon's mercenaries (*Timol.* 30); of the final stages of Antony's punishment (*Cic.* 49); it sends no more good fortune to Timotheos after he attributes his success to himself (*Sul.* 6). Less easy to categorize is *t.d.* which seems to join his voice in with that of Timoleon in battle (*Timol.* 27); or that which sends down rain after great battles (*Mar.* 21). Otherwise *t.d.* is busy mixing good with evil (*Aem.* 34, *Pomp.* 42). In all cases, even in *Caes.* 69, one should be cautious when translating it by anything suggesting an evil spirit.

come even more to the fore. While apparently taking the idea of retribution with great seriousness, he was also able to use it as the substructure for variety and literary flourish. In many cases we find baroque examples of "beautiful horror" contrasting with the serenity of goodness triumphant, much in accordance with the expressionistic or pathetic styles of art which appeared in the Hellenistic period. There is a certain similarity between the scenes of Hades and Elysion which close the dialogues of the *Moralia* and those of reward and punishment which close the *Lives*.

The scheme of parallel lives from an artistic standpoint also offers the opportunity, much in the form of tableaus, to pick up thematic and other similarities. In this arrangement certain themes can be repeated in almost endless variety, much as in the *carmen perpetuum* style of Ovid's *Metamorphoses*, close to Plutarch's time, but with a more conscious paralleling effect. At the same time the parallel underscores to the reader the basic theme of virtue or vice and permits him to see the details of environment or history as somewhat irrelevant. The total effect is something quite different from that of an individual biography, or of a group of individuals from one country treated in chronological sequence.[14]

Plutarch was at heart a philosopher rather than historian or biographer in the strict sense. He was primarily interested in the many aspects of human life and in particular in the interrelationship between ethical values and human life. He lived most his life in the quiet and reflection of a small town sheltered in its beautiful mountains from the world, yet open to it at a distance. At heart he was not in sympathy with most of his heroes — the great, powerful, and proud creatures who were driven by their passion to conquer the world at the expense of many innocent victims. He resigns himself to the thought that God or providence, working through *tyche* seems to have brought good out of evil.

---

[14] On the development of parallel biography see A. Momigliano, *The Development of Greek Biography*, pp. 96-100. Momigliano sees it as primarily a creation of the circle of Pomponius Atticus and Cornelius Nepos at Villa Tamphiliana, in which new, more international and humane interests in biography emerged. He ends by noting the danger of writing biography under Domitian, and how Tacitus, Suetonius, and Plutarch refused to yield to the 'felicitas temporum' and let biography become an instrument of Imperial propaganda.

Thus his great characters like Alexander and Caesar emerge from his pages as monuments to human folly, in spite of moments of great heroism. It is this concentration on ethical, religious, and basically human values which gives his work, as it did many others of the Imperial writers, a depth going beyond hero worship. He was most sympathetic to failures by the standard of the world of politics: Cicero, Demosthenes, Pompey, Brutus, the Gracchi, Nicias, Philopoimen, Timoleon—who showed greater humanity than those who destroyed them. For this reason there is an intimate *harmonia* between the *Moralia* and the *Lives*, each in a different way expressing a belief in the goodness of the divine and the destiny of man with the divine, the desire of the divine to communicate with men, and the ultimate triumph of good over evil, if not in this life in the opinion of men, then in the next.

BIBLIOGRAPHY

TEXTS: PLUTARCH

1. *Moralia*

a) *Complete works*: Teubner 2nd ed., in the process of publication since 1926: I-VI (C. Hubert, W. Nachstädt, W. R. Paton, M. Pohlenz, W. Sieveking, J. B. Titchener, I. Wegehaupt), Leipzig: 1925-1938; VI fasc. 2 (M. Pohlenz), 1952 (2nd ed. revised by R. Westman, 1959); VI, 3 (K. Ziegler, M. Pohlenz), 1953 (3rd ed. revised by K. Ziegler, 1966); VI, 1 (C. Hubert), 1954 (2nd ed. revised by H. Drexler, 1959); V, 3 (C. Hubert, M. Pohlenz), 1955 (2nd ed. completed by H. Drexler, 1960); V, 1 (C. Hubert, M. Pohlenz), 1957 (2nd ed. revised by H. Drexler, 1960); VII (F. H. Sandbach), 1967; II, 1-3 (rev. W. Nachstädt, W. Sieveking, J. B. Titchener), 1971; IV (rev. C. Hubert), 1971; V, 2, 1 (J. Mau), 1971; I (ed. corr. H. Gärtner), 1974. The texts not yet published in this edition are cited according to the 1st Teubner edition (G. N. Bernardakis, Leipzig: 1888-1896).

Loeb edition with English translation, in the course of publication since 1927: I-V (F. C. Babbitt), London and Cambridge (Mass.): 1927-1936; X (H. N. Fowler), 1927: VI (W. C. Helmbold), 1957; VII (P. De Lacy, B. Einarson), 1959; IX (E. L. Minar, F. H. Sandbach, W. C. Helmbold), 1961; XI (L. Pearson, F. H. Sandbach), 1965; XIV (B. Einarson, P. De Lacy), 1967; XII (H. Cherniss, W. Helmbold), 1968; XV (F. H. Sandbach), 1969; VIII (P. A. Clement, H. B. Hoffleit), 1969; XIII (H. Cherniss), part 1, and part 2 (1976); XVI, Index (E. N. O'Neil) has yet to appear.

Older editions now obsolete: *Opera Moralia*, D. Wyttenbach, ed., with notes (incomplete) and *index graecitatis*, 8 vols. Oxford: 1795-1830 (corr. rep. Leipzig: 1796-1834). *Opera*. T. Doehner and F. Dübner ed., with *index nominum et rerum*, 5 vols. Paris: 1841-1855.

The texts of the *Moralia* are cited according to their traditional Latin titles according to the pagination of the Stephanus edition, adopted by all later editors.

b) *Editions of individual works with text or translation, introduction, and notes*: H. J. Rose, *Plutarch's Roman Questions*, Oxford: 1924; P. Raingeard, *Le "Peri tou Prosopou" de Plutarque*, Paris: 1934; R. Flacelière, *Sur les Oracles de la Pythie*, Paris: 1937 (without transl. 1962), *Sur l'E de Delphes*, Paris: 1941, *Sur la Disparition des Oracles*, Paris: 1947, *Dialogue sur l'Amour*, Paris: 1952); J. Defradas, *Le Banquet des Sept Sages*, Paris: 1954; V. Cilento, *Diatriba Isiaca e Dialoghi Delfici*, Florence: 1962; H. Görgemanns, *Plutarch. Das Mondgesicht*, Paris: 1968; D. Babut, *Plutarque, De la Vertu Éthique*, Paris: 1970; J. G. Griffiths, *Plutarch. De Iside et Osiride*, Swansea: 1970; A. Corlu, *Le Démon de Socrate*, Paris: 1970; J. Hani, *Consolation à Apollonios*, Paris: 1972; F. Fuhrmann, *Oeuvres Morales t. 9, À Propos de Table Livres I-III*, Paris: 1972; R. Flacelière, *Plutarque Oeuvres Morales, t. 6, Dialogues Pythiques*, Paris: 1974; R. Klaerr, Y. Vernière, *Oeuvres Morales, t. 7.2*, Paris: 1974; A. Errico, *Peri Monarchias kai Demokratias kai Oligarchias*, Naples: 1974; J. Dumortier, J. Defradas, *Oeuvres Morales, t. 7.1*, Paris: 1975; E. Valgiglio, *Praecepta Gerendae Reipublicae*, Milan: 1976.

c) *Translations*: Besides the Loeb, in English: *Morals*, translated by several hands, corrected and revised by W. W. Goodwin, 5 vols. Boston: 1870. Some extracts are contained in F. C. Grant, *Hellenistic Religions. The Age of Syncretism*, New York: 1953 (mostly extracts from *De Iside*).

In French; V. Bétolaud. 5 vols., Paris: 1870; M. Meunier, *Sur Isis et Osiris*, Paris: 1924; G. Méautis, *Des Délais de la Justice Divine*, Lausanne: 1935; É. Des Places, *Le Démon de Socrate* (H. Pourrat, *Le Sage et son Démon*, Paris: 1950); É. Bréhier, *Des contradictions des Stoïciens, Des notions communes contre les Stoïciens* (*Les Stoïciens*, Paris: 1962); *De animae procreatione in Timaeo*, partially translated in P. Thévenaz, *L'Âme du Monde, le Devenir et la Matière chez Plutarque*, Neuchâtel: 1938; see also R. Flacelière, *Sagesse de Plutarque*, Paris: 1964 (Partial or complete translations of *De tranquillitate animi, De garrulitate, Septem sapientium convivium, De genio Socratis, De Iside et Osiride, Amatorius, De sera numinis vindicta, De defectu oraculorum, De E apud Delphos, De Pythiae oraculis*).

In German: K. Ziegler, *Plutarch. Über Gott und Vorsehung, Dämonen und Weissagung*, Zurich and Stuttgart: 1952 (Pythian dialogues, *De sera numinis vindicta, De genio Socratis*, the end of the *De facie in orbe lunae*.) B. Snell, *Plutarch. Von der Ruhe des Gemütes und Andere Philosophische Schriften*, Zurich and Stuttgart: 1948 (numerous extracts from the *Moralia*).

2. Lives

a) *Complete editions*: Teubner, Leipzig: 1914-1939 (C. Lindskog, K. Ziegler). Reedited I, fasc. 1, 1957 and 1960; fasc. 2, 1959; II, 1, 1964; II, 2, Ziegler, 1968; III, 1, 1971; III, 2, 1972/1973; II, 2, 1973.

Budé (Collection des Universités de France), with translation, introduction and notes by R. Flacelière, É. Chambry (and I and II, M. Juneaux): I (Thesée-Romulus, Lycurgue-Numa), 1957/1964; II Solon-Publicola, Themistocle-Camille), 1961/1968: III (Périclès-Fabius Maximus, Alcibiade-Coriolan), 1964/1969; IV Timoléon-Paul Émile, Pelopidas-Marcellus), 1966; V (Aristide-Caton l'Ancien, Philopoemen-Flamininus), 1969; VI Pyrrhos-Marius, Lysandre-Sylla), 1971; VII (Cimon-Lucullus, Nicias-Crassus), 1972; VIII (Sertorius-Eumène, Agesilas-Pompée), 1973; IX (Alexandre-César), 1975; X (Phocion-Caton le Jeune), 1976.

Recent editions of individual Lives: *Life of Dion* (W. H. Porter), Dublin: 1952. *Vita di Flaminino* (S. Gerevini) Milan; 1952 (with translation). *Vita Demetri Poliorcetis* (E. Manni), Florence: 1953. *Vita Caesaris* (A. Garzetti), Florence: 1954. *Vita di Bruto* (R. Del Re), 3rd ed., Florence: 1955. *Vita di Mario* (E. Valgiglio), Florence: 1956. *Vita dei Gracchi* (E. Valgiglio), Rome: 1957. *Vita di Sulla* (E. Valgiglio), Turin: 1960. *Vita di Agide e Cleomene* (R. Del Re), Rome: 1960. *Vie d'Alcibiade* (H. Mounard), Liège: 1962. *Vita Ciceronis* (D. Magnino), Florence: 1963. *Vita Aristidis* (I. Calabi Limentani), Florence: 1964. *Vie de Thémistocle* (R. Flacelière), Paris: 1972. There is also a translation and commentary for *Caesar* (K. Atzert), Paderborn: 1968, and translation of the *Parallel Lives* into Rumanian by N. I. Barbu, Bucharest: 1961-68.

The most recent *translations in English* are those in the Penguin series: R. Warner, *Plutarch, Fall of the Roman Republic* (*Marius, Sulla, Crassus, Pompey, Caesar, Cicero*) London: 1958; I. Scott-Kilvert, *The Rise and Fall of Athens* (*Theseus, Solon, Themistocles, Aristides, Cimon, Pericles, Nicias*,

Alcibiades, Lysander), London: 1960; *Plutarch, Makers of Rome* (*Coriolanus, Fabius Maximus, Marcellus, Cato the Elder, Tiberius Gracchus, Gaius Gracchus, Sertorius, Brutus, Mark Antony*), London: 1965 I. Scott-Kilvert, *The Age of Alexander* (Agesilaus, Pelopidas, Dion, Timoleon, Demosthenes, Phocion, Alexander, Demetrius, Pyrrhus), London: 1973. Alexander has been done by K. J. Maidment, *Plutarch, Life of Alexander*. Auckland: 1971.

GENERAL WORKS ON PLUTARCH

Rualdus. *Vita Plutarchi*. Paris: 1624.
Volkmann, R. *Leben, Schriften und Philosophie des Plutarch von Chaeronea*. Berlin: 1869. (rpt. in preparation).
Trench, R. C. *Plutarch*. London: 1873.
Hirzel, R. *Plutarch*. Leipzig: 1912.
Ziegler, K. *Plutarchos von Chaironeia*. Stuttgart: 1964. [2nd ed. of 1949 work with additional notes=*RE* "Plutarchos." XXI, 1 (1951), 636-962].
Barrow, R. H. *Plutarch and his Times*. London: 1967.
Giankaris, C. J. *Plutarch*. New York: 1970.
Jones, C. P. *Plutarch and Rome*. Oxford: 1971.
Russell, D. A. *Plutarch*. London: 1973.

Introductions to many individual editions contain useful information on his life and style, as well as philosophical and religious views. The only lexicon is that by D. A. Wyttenbach, *Lexicon Plutarcheum* (Oxford: 1830 / rpt. 1962), but an unpublished *Index Verborum Plutarcheus*, begun by W. C. Helmbold is being completed by E. N. O'Neil.

OTHER STUDIES ON PLUTARCH

Abernetty, G. *De Plutarchi Qui Fertur de Superstitione Libello*. Regensberg: 1911.
Abramowicz, Z. "Plutarchs Tischgespräche." *Das Altertum*, 8 (1962) 80-88.
Adam, H. *Plutarchs Schrift Non Posse Suaviter Vivi Secundum Epicurum*. Amsterdam: 1974.
Adler, M. *Quibus ex fontibus Plutarchus libellum "De facie in orbe lunae" hauserit*. (Diss. Vienna: 1910).
Almquist, H. *Plutarch und das Neue Testament*. Uppsala: 1946.
Arnim, H. von. *Plutarch über Dämonen und Mantik*. Amsterdam: 1921.
Aulotte, R. "Plutarque et la renaissance du stoicisme en France." *VIIe Budé Congrès*. Paris: 1964, 151-3.
——, *Amyot et Plutarque*. Geneva: 1965.
——. *Plutarque en France au XVIe Siècle*. Paris: 1971.
Averincev, S. S. "Biografičeskie Sočinenija Plutarcha v zarubežnoj Nauke xx veka." *Vestnik Drevnej Istorii*, 3 (1964), 202-212.
——. "Nablyudenija nad compozicionnoj technikoj Plutarcha v 'Parallel'-nych Žizncopisanijach' ('Solon')." *Voprosy Klassičeskoj Filologii*, 1 (1965), 160-180.
——. "Podbor geroev v 'Parallel'nych Žizncopisanijach' Plutarcha i antičnaja biografičeskaja tradicija." *Vestnik Drevnej Istorii*, 2 (1965), 51-67.
——. "Priemy organizacii materiala v biografijach Plutarcha," *Voprosy Antičnoj Literatury i Klassičeskoj Filologii* (Festschrift S. I. Sobolevskij). Moscow: 1966. pp. 234-246.

Babcock, C. L. "Dio and Plutarch on the Damnation of Antony." *CP*, 57 (1962) 30-32.
Babut, D. "La nature de l'âme et les passions chez Plutarque." *Budé Cong.* (1968), 530-532.
——. *Plutarque et le Stoïcisme.* Paris: 1969.
——. *Plutarque. De la Vertu Éthique.* Paris: 1970.
Barbu, N. J. *Les Procédés de la Peinture des Caractères et la Vérité Historique dans les Biographies de Plutarque.* Paris: 1934.
Bargstaedt, H. R. *Untersuchungen in Plutarchs Parallelbiographien.* Hamburg: 1950.
Bassi, P. D. *Il Pensiero Morale, Pedagogico, Religioso di Plutarco.* (*Studi e Testi*). Florence: 1927.
Beaujeu, J. "La religion de Plutarque." *L'Inform. Lit.*, 11 (1959), 207-213.
Becchi, F. "Contributo allo Studio del De Virtute di Plutarco." *Stud. It.*, 46 (1974), 129-147.
Bergen, K. *Charakterbilder bei Tacitus und Plutarch* (Diss. Cologne: 1962).
Bergeron, H. "Le manichéisme de Bayle et Plutarque." *Rev. Philos.*, 156 (1965) 205-210.
Berry, E. G. "Plutarque dans l'Amérique du XIXe siècle." *Budé Cong.*, (1968), 578-587.
Betz, H. D., and E. W. Smith, Jr.,"Plutarch, De E apud Delphos." *Nov. Test.*, 13 (1971), 217-235.
Betz, H. D. "Ein seltsames mysterientheologisches System bei Plutarch." *Ex Orbe Religionum.* (Widengren Festschrift) Leiden: 1972, pp. 347-354.
——. *Plutarch's Theological Writings and Early Christian Literature.* (*Stud. ad Corp. Hell. Nov. Test.*). Leiden: 1972——. (editor).
Bock, F. *Untersuchungen zu Plutarchs Schrift De genio Socratis.* Munich: 1910.
Bolkestein, H. *Adversaria critica et exegetica ad Plutarchi "Quaest. conv." librum primum et secundum.* Amsterdam: 1946.
Borgeaud, W., Roussel, M. "Sur un texte des Contradictions stoïciennes de Plutarque (c. 10: Mor. 1035F-1036A)," *REG*, 82 (1969), 71-75.
Bowersock, C. W. "Some Persons in Plutarch's *Moralia.*" *CQ*, 15 (1965), 267-270.
Braun, H. "Plutarch's Critique of Superstition in the Light of the New Testament." *Occ. Papers of the Inst. for Ant. and Christ.*, 5 (1972), 79-81.
Bravo García, A. "El pensamiento de Plutarco acerca de la paz y la guerra." *CFC*, 5 (1973), 141-191.
Breebaart, A. R. "Plutarch and the Political Development of Pericles." *Mn.*, 24 (1971), 260-272.
Brenk, F. E. "Le songe du Brutus." *Budé Cong.*, (1968), 588-594.
——. *Plutarch's Religion.* (Diss. Cambridge: 1972).
——. "A Most Strange Doctrine: *Daimon* in Plutarch." *CJ*, 69 (1973), 1-11.
——. "The Dreams of Plutarch's Lives." *Latomus*, 34 (1975), 336-349.
——. "From Mysticism to Mysticism, The Religious Development of Plutarch of Chaironeia." *Soc. of Bibl. Lit. Sem. Papers.*, 1 (1975), 193-198.
——. Review of Alan Wardman, *Plutarch's Lives. Gnomon*, 48, (1976), 406-408.
Brozek, M. "Noch über die Selbstzitate als chronologischen Wegweiser in Plutarchs Parallelbiographien." *Eos*, 53 (1963), 68-80.
Bucher-Isler, B. *Norm und Individualität in den Biographien Plutarchs.* Bern: 1972.

Buricks, A. "The Source of Plutarch's *Peri Tyches.*" *Phoenix*, 4 (1950), 59-69.

Canfora, L. "Plutarco su Eforo." *Ann. Fac. Lett. e Filos. Bari*, 12 (1967), 5-8.
Conomis, N. C. "Plutarchea II" in *Philtra* (Kapsomenes Festschrift) Thessalonica: 1975. pp. 73-86.
Constanza, S. "La synkrisis nello schema biografico di Plutarcho." *Messana*, 4 (1955), 127-156.
Carney, T. F. "Plutarch's Style in the Marius." *JHS*, 80 (1960), 24-31.
Clare, L. and F. Jouan. "La plus ancienne traduction occidentale des Vies de Plutarque." *Budé Cong.*, (1968), 567-568.
Codignola, M. "La formazione spirituale di Plutarco e la sua personalita filosofico-religiosa." *Civiltá Moderna*, (1934), 471-490.
Cuvigny, M. "Plutarque et Épictète." *Budé Cong.*, (1968), 560-566.

Danieli, M. L. "Plutarco a Delfi. Note sulla religiosita plutarchea" *Nuovo Didaskaleion*, 15 (1965) 5-23.
DeFradas J. "Les oeuvres morales de Plutarque," *Bull. Budé*, 4 (1972), 219-222.
Deike, H. *De Stoicorum repugnantiis 1-10. Beiträge zu einem kritischen Kommentar.* Diss. Göttingen: 1963.
DeLacy, P. "Biography and Tragedy in Plutarch." *AJP*, 73 (1952), 159-171.
———. "Plutarch and the Academic Sceptics." *CJ*, 49 (1953-4), 79-85.
Del Re, R. "Il Pensiero Metafisico di Plutarcho: Dio, La Natura, Il Male." *Stud. Ital. di Filol. Class.*, 24 (1950), 33-64.
———. "Gli studi plutarchei nell' ultimo cinquantennio." *Atene e Roma*, 3 (1953), 187-196.
———. "De Plutarcho Chaeronensi immortalitatis animorum assertore." *Latinitas*, 13 (1965), 184-192.
Delvaux, G. *Les Sources de Plutarque dans les Vies Parallèles des Romains.* Brussels: 1946.
Dodds, E. R. "The Portrait of a Greek Gentleman." *Greece and Rome*, 5 (1933), 97-107.
Dörrie, H. "Le platonisme de Plutarque." *Budé Cong.*, (1968), 519-529.
———. "Die Stellung Plutarchs im Platonismus seiner Zeit," R. Palmer, ed. *Philomathes* (Merlan Festschrift). The Hague: 1971. pp. 36-56.
Duchemin, J. "Le thème du héros au Labyrinthe dans la Vie de Thésée." *Budé Cong.*, (1968), 533-535.
Dumortier, J. "Le châtiment de Néron dans le mythe de Thespésios." *Budé Cong.*, (1968), 552-559.

Eichhoff. *Über die Religiöse Sittliche Weltansicht des Plutarch von Chaeronea.* Elberfeld: 1833.
Eisele. "Zur Dämonologie des Plutarchs von Chäronea." *Arch. f. Gesch. d. Philos.*, 17 (1904), 29-51.
Erbse, H. "Plutarchs Schrift *Peri Deisidaimonias.*" *Hermes*, 70 (1952), 295-314.
———. "Die Bedeutung der Synkrisis in den Parallelbiographien Plutarchs." *Hermes*, 84 (1956-7), 398-424.
Etherridge, S. G. *Plutarch's De Virtute Morali: A Study in Extra-Peripatetic Aristotelianism* (Diss. Harvard, 1961) summarized in *HSCP*, 56 (1962), 252-254.

Ferro, A. "Le idee religiose di Plutarco." *Archivio della Cultura Italiana,* II fasc. 3-4 (1940), 173-232.
Flacelière, R. "Le functionnement de l'oracle de Delphes au temps de Plutarque." *Annales de l'École des Hautes Études de Gand* II, 82 ff. Ghent: 1938.
——. "Plutarque, Prêtre de Delphes." *REG,* 55 (1942) 50-69.
——. "Plutarque et la Pythie." *REG,* 56 (1943), 72-111.
——. "Plutarque et les Oracles Béotiens." *Bull. de Corr. Hell.,* 70 (1946), 199-207.
——. "Sur quelques passages des vies de Plutarque." *REG,* 61 (1948), 67-103 and 391-429.
——. "Plutarque et les éclipses de la lune." *REG,* 53 (1951), 203-221.
——. "Plutarque, Apologiste de Delphes." *L'Inform. Lit.,* 5 (1953), 97-103.
——. "Plutarque et l'Épicurisme." *Rivist. di Stud. Cl.,* 8 (1960), 197-215.
——. "Rome et ses empereurs vus par Plutarque." *Ant. Class.,* 32 (1963), 28-47.
——. "Plutarque, De Fortuna Romanorum." *Melanges Offerts à Jérome Carcopino.* Paris: 1966. pp. 367-375.
——. "État present des études sur Plutarque." *Budé Cong.,* (1968), 483-505.
——. "Héracles ou Héraclite (Plut. Vita Lysandri 2,5). *Hommages à M. Delcourt.* Paris: 1970 pp. 207-210.
Follet, S. "Flavius Euphanès d'Athènes, ami de Plutarque." *Mélanges Chantraine, ed. A. Ernout,* Paris: 1972, pp. 35-50.
Fornara, C. W. "The Sources of Plutarch's *An seni sit gerenda res publica.*" *Philol.,* 110 (1966), 119-127.
Frejberg, L. A. "The Composition and some Artistic Peculiarities in Plutarch's De audiendis poetis." (in Russian), *VDI,* 3 (1966), 247-253.
Froidefond, C. "Notes critiques sur quelques passages du de Iside et Osiride de Plutarque." *REG,* 85 (1972), 63-71.

Gabba, E. "Studi su Filarco. Le biografie plutarchee di Agide e di Cleomene." *Athenaeum,* 35 (1957), 3-55.
Garzetti, A. "Plutarcho e le sue vite parallele. Rassegni di studi 1934-1952." *Riv. Stor. Ital.,* 65 (1952), 76-104.
Geer, R. M. "Plutarch and Appian on Tiberius Gracchus." *Studies in Honor of E. K. Rand.* New York: 1938.
Geigenmüller, P. "Plutarchs Stellung zur Religion und Philosophie seiner Zeit," *N. Jahr f. d. Kl. Alt.,* 24 (1921), 251-270.
Gil, L. "La semblanza de Nicias en Plutarco." *E. Clas.,* 6 (1962), 404-450.
Goessler, L. *Plutarchs Gedanken über die Ehe.* Basel: 1962.
Goldsmidt, V. "Les Thèmes du *De Defectu Oraculorum* de Plutarque." *REG,* 61 (1948), 298-302.
Görgemanns, H. *Untersuchungen zu Plutarchs Dialog De facie in orbe lunae.* Heidelberg: 1972.
Gossage, A. J. "Plutarch," *Latin Biography,* T. A. Dorey ed., London: 1967.
Gréard, O. *De la Morale de Plutarque.* Paris: 1866.
Groningen, B. A. van. "Plutarque et Apollonios de Tyane." *Bull. de la Fac. des Lettres de Strasbourg,* 30 (1951-2), 107-116.
Guey, J. "Martial VIII,50 (51).7, Plutarque De facie 921c et les 'mers' de la lune." *BSAF* (1966), 114-116.
Gundry, D. W. "The Religion of a Greek Gentleman in the First Century A.D." *Hibbert Journal,* 43 (1945-46), 345-352.

Haan, J. D. Bierens de. *Plutarchus als Godsdienstig Denker*. Nijhoff: 1902.
Hadas, M. "The Religion of Plutarch." *Rev. of Rel.*, 6 (1941-42), 270-282.
——. *On Love, the Family, and the Good Life*: Selected Essays of Plutarch.
    New York: 1957.
Hamilton, J. R. *Plutarch. Alexander*. Oxford: 1969.
Hamilton, W. "The Myth in Plutarch's *De Facie*." *CQ*, 28 (1934), 24-30.
——. "The Myth in Plutarch's *De Genio*." *CQ*, 28 (1934), 176-182.
Hani, J. "Plutarque en Face du Dualisme Iranien." *REG*, 77 (1964), 489-525.
——. "Le mort du Grand Pan." *Budé Cong.*, (1968), 511-518.
——. *La Religion Égyptienne dans la Pensée de Plutarque*. (Diss. Lille: 1972).
Harris, B. F. "The Portrayal of Autocratic Power in Plutarch's Lives,"
    Auckland Class. Essays Presented to Blaiklock. Auckland: 1972. pp.
    185-202.
Hartman, J. *De Plutarcho Scriptore et Philosopho*. Leiden: 1916.
Helmbold, W. C., and O'Neil, E. N. *Plutarch's Quotations*. Baltimore: 1959.
Helmbold, W. C. "Markland's Second Thoughts on the *De Iside et Osiride*."
    Cl. Philol., 52 (1957), 104-106.
Helmer, J. *Zu Plutarchs "De animae procreatione in Timaeo"*. Wurzburg:
    1937.
Herbert, K. "The Identity of Plutarch's Lost Scipio." *AJP*, 78 (1957),
    83-88.
Herschbell, J. "Plutarch as a Source for Empedocles Re-examined." *AJP*,
    92 (1971), 156-184.
Holwerda, D. "Zu Plut. Alex. 52.4." *Mn.*, 20 (1967), 440-41.
Homeyer, H. "Beobachtungen zu den hellenistischen Quellen der Plutarch-
    Viten." *Klio*, 41 (1963), 145-157.
——. "Zu Plutarchs De malignitate Herodoti." *Klio*, 49 (1967), 181-187.
Hood, D. C. *Plutarch and the Persians* (Diss. Univ. of Cal. at Los Angeles:
    1967).
Howard, M. W. *The Influence of Plutarch in the Major European Literature
    of the Eighteenth Century*. Chapel Hill: 1970.

Ingenkamp, H. *Plutarchs Schriften über die Heilung der Seele*. Göttingen:
    1971.

Johnson, J. L. *Plutarch on the Glory of the Athenians, a Reassessment*, (Diss.
    Univ. of Cal. at Los Angeles: 1972)
Johnson, van L. "The Humanism of Plutarch." *CJ*, 66, 1 (1970), 26-37.
Jones, C. P. *Plutarch and His Relations with Rome*. (Thesis, digest in *Harv.
    Stud. in Class. Philol.*, 71 (1966), 322-325).
——. "Towards a Chronology of Plutarch's Works." *JHS*, 85 (1966), 61-74.
——. "The Teacher of Plutarch." *Harvard Studies*, 71 (1966) 205-213.
——. "A Leading Family of Roman Thespiae." *HSCP* 74 (1970), 223-255.
——. "Sura and Senecio." *JRS*, 60 (1970), 98.
——. "Two Friends of Plutarch." *BCH*, 96 (1972), 263-267.
Jones, R. *The Platonism of Plutarch*. Menasha: 1916.

Kapetanopoulos, E. "Klea and Leontis, Two Ladies from Delphi." *Bull.
    de Corr. Hell.*, 90 (1966), 119-130.
Kemper, K. *Die im Corpus der Moralia des Plutarch Überlieferte Schrift,
    Peri Paidôn Agôgês*. (Diss. Münster: 1971).
Kessissoglou, A. "Plutarch. V. Galba. 7.5." *Hermes*, 103 (1975), 127-128.
Klaerr, R. "Quelques remarques sur le style métaphorique de Plutarque."
    Budé Cong., (1968), 536-541.

Klotz, A. "De Plutarchi vitae Caesarinae Fontibus." *Mn.*, 6 (1938), 313-319.
Kokolake, M. *Ploutarcheia.* Athens: 1968.
Konstans, D. "Plutarch, De communibus notitiis 1080c." *CR*, 22 (1972), 217.
Konstantinos, I. *Ploutarchos ho Chairôneus.* Athens: 1968.
Korus, K. "Wokoł genesy traktatu Plutarcha 'De audiendis poetis."
    Meander, 28 (1973), 57-58.
Kraus, F. *Die Rhetorischen Schriften Plutarchs und ihre Stellung im Plutar-
    chischen Schriftenkorpus.* Munich: 1912.
Lassel, E. *De Fortunae in Plutarchi Operibus Notione.* Marburg: 1896.
Latzarus, B. *Les Idées Religieuses de Plutarque.* Paris: 1920.
Levi, M. A. *Plutarco e il V secolo.* Varese-Milan: 1955.
Littman, R. *Plutarch's Use of Thucydides in the Life of Nicias, Life of
    Alcibiades, and Life of Themistocles.* (Diss. Columbia: 1970).
Luppe, W. "Textkritische Bemerkungen zu Plutarchs Vergleich von
    Aristophanes und Menander." *Philol.*, 117 (1973), 127-130.
MacKay, B. "Plutarch and the Miraculous." *Miracles—Studies in their
    Philosophy and History,* C. F. D. Moule, ed. London: 1965, 93-113.

Malingrey, A. M. "Les délais de la justice divine chez Plutarque et dans la
    littérature judéo-chrétienne." *Budé Cong.*, (1968), 542-549.
Marcovich, M. "Textual Criticism of Plutarch." *Emerita*, 40 (1972), 157-165.
——. "Hades as Benefactor, Plutarch De Iside et Osiride 362D." *Cl. Phil.*,
    69 (1974), 287-288.
Martin, H. Jr. "The Concept of *Praôtes* in Plutarch's Lives." *Greek, Roman,
    and Byzantine Studies*, 1-3 (1960), 65-73.
——. "The Character of Plutarch's Themistocles." *TAPA*, 92 (1961),
    326-339.
——. "The Concept of *Philanthropia* in Plutarch's Lives." *AJP*, 326 (1961),
    164-175.
——. "Plutarch's Citation of Empedocles at *Amatorius* 756 D." *Greek,
    Roman, and Byzantine Studies*, 10 (1969), 57-70.
——. "*Amatorius*, 756 E-F: Plutarch's Citation of Parmenides and Hesiod."
    AJP, 358 (1969), 183-200.
——. Review of Griffiths, *Plutarch. De Iside et Osiride, AJP*, 94 (1973),
    98-101.
——. "Plutarch's De facie: The Recapitulations and the Lost Beginning."
    GRBS, 15 (1974), 73-88.
Méautis, G. "Plutarque et l'Orphisme." *Mélanges Glotz*, 1. Paris: 1932.
Meinhardt, E. *Perikles bei Plutarch.* Frankfurt: 1957.
Merentitou, K. *Ploutarchos ho Chairôneus.* Athens: 1968.
Moellering, J. *Plutarch on Superstition.* Boston: 1963.
Mounard, H. *La Psychologie de Plutarque.* (Thesis, digest in *Annales de
    la Université de Paris* (1960), 341-342).
Mühll, P., Von Der. "Antiker Historismus in Plutarchs Biographie des
    Solon." *Klio*, 35 (1942), 89-102.

Nitzche, K. *De Plutarcho Theologo et Philosopho Populari.* 1849.

Oakesmith, J. *The Religion of Plutarch.* London: 1902.
Ogilvie, R. M. "The Date of De Defectu Oraculorum." *Phoenix*, 21 (1967),
    108-119.
O'Sullivan, J. N. "On Plutarch, *De Libidine et Aegritudine* 9." *CQ*, 26,
    (1976), 116.

Panagl, O. "Plutarch." Die Grossen der Weltgeschichte 2 (ed. K. Fassmann). Zürich: 1971. pp. 418-467.
Pelling, C. B. R. "Plutarch, *Alexander and Caesar*. Two New Fragments." *CQ*, 23 (1973), 343-344.
Peter, H. *Die Quellen Plutarchs in den Biographien der Römer*. Halle: 1865.
Philips, E. D. "Plutarque interprète de Zoroastre." *Budé Cong.*, (1968), 506-510.
Pinnoy, M. "De psychologie van Plutarchus van Chaironea." *Handel. der Zuid. Maats. voor Taal-, Letterk. en Geschied.*, 21 (1967), 301-312.
——. "Les rapports entre l'âme et le corps dans les Éthiques de Plutarque." *Antidorum Peremans*. Louvain: 1968 pp. 191-200.
Pizzagalli, A. M. "Plutarco e il Christianismo." *Atene e Roma* (1943), 97-102.
Pohl. *Die Dämonologie des Plutarch*. Breslau: 1859.
Polman, C. "Chronological Biography and *Akme* in Plutarch." *Cl. Phil.*, 69 (1974), 169-174.
Polenz, M. Review of Soury, *La Démonologie de Plutarque*. *Gnom.*, 21 (1949), 347-354.
Powell, J. E. "The Sources of Plutarch's *Alexander*." *JHS*, (59) 1939, 229-240.
Préchac, F. "Du Sénèque dans Plutarque." *Bull. Budé.*, 26 (1967), 408-411.

Rabe, I. *Quellenkritische Untersuchungen zu Plutarchs Alexanderbiographie*. Hamburg: 1964.
Radt, S. L. "Zu Plutarchs *Vita Alexandri*." *Mn.*, 20 (1967), 120-126.
Renoirte, T. *Les Conseils Politiques de Plutarque*. Louvain: 1951.
Romano, F. "Le Questione platoniche di Plutarco di Cheronea." *Sophia*, 33 (1965), 116-131.
Rowland, R. "Plutarch, Romulus 14." *Cl. W.*, 65 (1972), 217.
Russell, D. A. "Notes on Plutarch's *De Genio*." *CQ*, 48 (1954), 61-63.
——. "Plutarch's *Life of Coriolanus*." *JRS*, 83 (1963), 21-29.
——. "On Reading Plutarch's Lives." *Greece and Rome*, 13 (1966), 139-154.
——. "Plutarch's Alcibiades." *Camb. Philol. Soc.*, 192 (1966), 37-47.
——. "On Reading Plutarch's *Moralia*." *Greece and Rome*, 15 (1968), 130-146.
——. "Remarks on Plutarch's *De vitando aere alieno*." *JHS*, 93 (1973), 163-171.

Sandbach, F. H. "The Date of the Eclipse in Plutarch's *De Facie*." *CQ*, 23 (1929), 15-16.
——. Plutarch, *De Sera Numinis Vindicta*. Cambridge Philological Society, (1931).
——. "Rhythm and Authenticity in Plutarque's *Moralia*." *CQ*, 33 (1939), 194-204.
——. "Plutarch and the Stoics." *CQ*, 34 (1940), 20-25.
——. "Three Notes on Plutarch's *Moralia*." *CQ*, 6 (1956), 87-88.
——. "More of the Loeb *Moralia*." *CR*, 18 (1968), 47-48.
——. "Plutarque était-il l'auteur du De Libidine?" *Budé Cong.*, (1968), 550-51.
——. "Plutarque était-il l'auteur du *De libidine et Aegritudine*?" *Rev. de Philol.*, 93,2 (1969), 211-216. (Same as the article in the *Budé Congrès*.)
——. Review of Görgemanns, *Untersuchungen zu Plutarchs Dialog De facie in orbe lunae*. *CR*, 33 (1973), 32-34.
Scardigli, B. "A proposito di due passi su Sertorio." *Atene e Roma*, 15 (1970), 174-181.

—. "Considerazioni sulle fonti della biographia plutarchea di Sertorio." Stud. It., 43 (1971), 35-64.
Scazzoso, P. "Plutarque interprète du baroque ancien," Budé Cong., (1968), 569-575.
Schaefer, W. Der Gottesbegriff Plutarchs im Lichte der Christlichen Weltanschauung. Regensberg: 1908.
Schläpfer, H. Plutarch und die Klassischen Dichter. Zurich: 1950.
Schmertosch, R. De Plutarchi Sententiarum quae ad Divinationem Spectant Origine. Leipzig: 1889.
Schreiter, T. De Doctrina Plutarchi Theologica et Morali. Leipzig: 1838.
Shrimpton, G. S. "Plutarch's Life of Epaminondas." Pac. Coast., Philol. 6 (1971), 55-59.
Schroeter, J. Plutarchs Stellung zur Skepsis. Greifswald: 1911.
Sechan, L. "Plutarque au miroir du Thésée." Annales de la Faculté des Lettres et Sciences Humaines d'Aix, 33 (1959), 95 ff.
Seel, O. "Zu Plutarchs Schrift De latenter vivendo." Antidosis. (Kraus Festschrift). pp. 357-80.
Seillière, E. "La Religion de Plutarque." Séances et Travaux de l'Académie des Sciences Morales, 181 (1921), 422-434.
Sieveking, W. Plutarch über Liebe und Ehe. Munich: 1941.
Smith, G. T. The Importance of Miracle in the Religious Truth of Plutarch of Chaeronea. (Diss. New York University: 1972).
Smith, M. "De Superstitione, Moralia 164E-171F," in H. Betz ed. Plutarch's Theological Writings and Early Christian Literature. I. pp. 1-8.
Smith, R. E. "Plutarch's Biographical Sources in the Roman Lives." CQ, 34 (1940), 1-10.
Soury, G. "Sens de la démonologie de Plutarque." REG, 53 (1940), 51-58.
—. "Plutarque, prêtre de Delphes, l'inspiration prophétique." REG, 55 (1942), 50-69.
—. La Démonologie de Plutarque. Paris: 1942.
—. "Les questions de table et la philosophie religieuse de Plutarque." REG, 62 (1949), 320-327.
Spencer, T. J. B., ed. Shakespeare's Plutarch. London: 1964.
Stadter, P. Plutarch's Historical Methods, an Analysis of Mulierum Virtutes. Harvard: 1965.
—. "Thucydidean Orators in Plutarch." in P. Stadter, ed. The Speeches of Thucydides. Chapel Hill: 1973. pp. 109-123.
Stefano, G. di. "La découverte de Plutarque en France au début du XVe siècle." Romania, 86 (1965), 463-519.
Stoltz, C. Zur Relativen Chronologie der Parallelbiographien Plutarchs. Lund: 1929.
Stiefenhofer, A. "Zur Echtheitsfrage der biographischen Synkriseis Plutarchs." Philol., 73 (1916), 462-503.
Sweet, W. "Sources of Plutarch's Demetrius." Cl. W., 44 (1950-51), 177-181.
Szydelski, S. "The divinity according to Plutarch" (in Polish). Rocz. i. Teol. Kanon., 6 (1960), 93-101.
Tassier, M. "Plutarchus over het leven na de dood, (De anima)." Kleio, 2 (1972), 107-115.
Theander, C. Plutarch und die Geschichte. Lund: 1951.
—. "Plutarchs Forschungen in Rom—Zur mündlichen Überlieferung als Quelle der Biographien." Eranos, 57 (1959), 99-131.
Thévenaz, P. L'Âme du Monde, Le Devenir, et La Matière chez Plutarque. Paris: 1938.

Thompson, W. "The Errors in Plutarch, Nikias 6." *CQ*, 19 (1969), 160-162.
Tracy, H. L. "Notes on Plutarch's Biographical Method." *CJ*, 37 (1942), 213-221.

Uxkull-Gyllenband, W. *Plutarch und die Griechische Biographie.* Stuttgart: 1927.

Valgiglio, E. *Ps. Plutarco "De fato."* Rome: 1964.
———. "Il tema della poesia nel pensiero di Plutarco." *Maia*, 19 (1967), 319 ff.
———. "Postille al testo di Plutarcho." *Stud. It.*, 39 (1967), 232-239.
Valentin, L. "L'Idée du Dieu dans Plutarque." *Rev. Thomiste*, 14 (1914), 313-327.
Van der Valk, M. "Zur Überlieferungsgeschichte der plutarchischen Schriften." *Hermes*, 101 (1973), 343-344.
Vasmanoles, G. "Kritika kai Hermeneutika eis Ploutarchou Themistoklea." *Platon*, 25 (1973), 281-283.
Verbeke, G. "Plutarch and the Development of Aristotle" in I. Düring and G. E. L. Owen, *Aristotle and Plato: the Mid-Fourth Century*. Göteborg: 1960.
Vernière, Y. "Le Léthé de Plutarque." *REA*, 66 (1964), 22-32.

Wagner, G. *Die Quellen zu Plutarchs Gynaikon aretai.* (Diss. Graz: 1968).
Wardman, A. E. "Plutarch and Alexander." *CQ*, 5 (1955), 96-107.
———. "Description of Personal Appearance in Plutarch and Suetonius: The Use of Statues as Evidence." *CQ*, 17 (1967), 414-420.
———. "Plutarch's Methods in the Lives." *CQ*, 21 (1971), 254-261.
Weber, H. *Die Staats- und Rechtslehre Plutarchs von Chaironeia.* Bonn: 1959.
Weizsäcker, A. *Untersuchungen über Plutarchs Biographische Technik.* Berlin: 1931.
Westlake, H. D. "The Sources of Plutarch's *Timoleon*." *CQ*, 32 (1938), 65-74.
———. "The Sources of Plutarch's *Pelopidas*." *CQ*, 33 (1939), 11-22.
Whittaker, J. E. "Ammonius on the Delphic E." *CQ*, 19 (1969), 185-192.
Wilamowitz-Moellendorf, U. von. "Plutarch als Biograph." *Reden und Vorträge* 2⁴ (1926).
Wohlman, H. B. *Plutarch's Views in the Roman Lives.* (Diss. Johns Hopkins: 1966).
Wojcik, A., "De Catonis Maioris fabula ab ipso aliisque antiquitus tradita." *Eos*, 55 (1965), 296-309.
Ziegler, K. "Plutarch's Ahnen." *Hermes*, 82 (1954), 499-
———. "Plutarchstudien XXII. Drei Gedichte bei Plutarch." *Rh. M.*, 110 (1967), 53-64.
Zucchelli, B. "Il *Peri Dysôpias* di Plutarco." *Maia*, 17 (1965), 215-231.

OTHER USEFUL STUDIES

Alföldi, A. *Early Rome and the Latins.* Ann Arbor: 1966.
Altheim, F. *A History of Roman Religion.* London: 1938.
Amandry, P. *La Mantique Apollinienne à Delphes.* Paris: 1950.
Amit, M. *Great and Small Poleis. A Study in the Relationship of Great and Small Cities in Ancient Greece.* Brussels: 1973.
André, J. M. "La philosophie religieuse de Cicéron: dualisme académique et tripartition varronienne." A. Michel, ed. *Ciceroniana* (for Kumaniecki). Leiden: 1975.

Andres. "Daimon." *RE*, Suppl. III (1918), 267-321.

Andrewes, A. *The Greek Tyrants*. London: 1956.

Armstrong, A. H. ed. *The Cambridge History of Later Greek and Early Medieval Philosophy*. Cambridge: 1967.

Babut, D. *La Religion des Philosophes Grecs de Thales aux Stoïciens*. Paris: 1974.

Badian, E. *Foreign Clientelae*. Oxford: 1964.

——. *Roman Imperialism in the late Republic*. Oxford: 1968.

——. "The Administration of the Empire." *Greece and Rome*, 12 (1965), 166-183.

——. *Lucius Sulla, the Deadly Reformer*. Sidney: 1970.

——. "The Family and Early Career of T. Quinctius Flamininus." *JRS*, 61 (1971), 102-111.

——. "Tiberius Gracchus and the Beginning of the Roman Revolution." *ANRW*, I,1 (1972), pp. 668-737.

Ballaira, G. *Il Sogno di Scipione*. Turin: 1970.

Balsdon, J. "Dionysius on Romulus. A Political Pamphlet." *JRS*, 71 (1971), 18-27.

Bayet, J. *Histoire Politique et Psychologique de la Religion Romaine*. Paris: 1957.

——. *Croyances et Rites dans la Rome Antique*. Paris: 1971.

Behr, C. A. *Aelius Aristides and the Sacred Tales*. Amsterdam: 1968.

Bengtson, H. *Griechische Geschichte von den Anfängen bis in die Römische Kaiserzeit*. 2nd ed. Munich: 1960.

——. *Grundriss der Römischen Geschichte*. I. Munich: 1967.

——. *Einführung in die Alte Geschichte*. 7th ed. Munich: 1975.

——. *Herrschergestalten des Hellenismus*. Munich: 1975.

Beranger, J. "Les jugements de Cicéron sur les Gracques." *ANRW*, I,1 (1972), pp. 732-763.

Beujeu, J. *La Religion Romaine à l'Apogée de l'Empire*. Paris: 1955.

Bianchi, U. *The Greek Mysteries*. Leiden: 1976.

——. *La Religione Greca*. Turin: 1975.

Bicknell, P. J. "Lunar Eclipses and Selenites." *Apeiron*, 1 (1967), 16-21.

——. "The Lunar Eclipse of 21 June, 168 B.C." *CR*, 18 (1968), 22.

Bieber, M. *Alexander the Great in Greek and Roman Art*. Chicago: 1964.

——. "The Portraits of Alexander." *Greece and Rome*, 12 (1965), 183-189.

——. "The Development of Portraiture on Roman Republican Coins." *ANRW*, I,4 (1973), pp. 870-898.

Bidez, J. and Cumont, F. *Les Mages Hellénisés*. Paris: 1938.

Bloch, R. *The Etruscans*. London: 1965.

——. "L'état present des recherches sur l'épicurisme grec." *Budé Congrès*. Paris: 1969.

——. "L'état actuel des études étruscologiques." *ANRW*, I,1, (1972), pp. 12-21.

Boer, W. den. "Aspects of Religion in Classical Greece." *Harv. Stud.*, 77 (1973) 1-21.

Boll, F. and Gundel, W. "Sternbilder, Sternglaube, und Sternsymbolik bei Griechen und Römer." in Roscher, 6 (1937), 867-1071.

Bollack, J. and Wismann, H. *Epicurus*. Paris: 1971.

Bolkestein, H. "Theophrastos' Charakter der Deisidaimonia." *Religionswissenschaftliche Versuche und Vorarbeiten*, 21 (1929).

Borgeaud, W. and Roussel, M. "Sur un texte des Contradictions Stoiciennes de Plutarque." *REG*, 82 (1969), 71-75.

Bos, J. *Agesilaus*. Nijmegen: 1949.
Bowersock, G. W. *Greek Sophists in the Roman Empire*. Oxford: 1969.
——. "Greek Intellectuals and the Imperial Cult." *Eos*, 59 (1971), 309-323.
——. *Approaches to the Second Sophistic*. University Park: 1975.
Bowra, C. M. *Periclean Athens*. London: 1971.
Boyancé, P. "Les deux démons personnels dans l'antiquité grecque et latine."
    Rev. de Philol., 79 (1935), 189-202.
——. *Études sur le Songe de Scipion*. Paris: 1936.
——. "La religion astrale de Platon à Cicéron." *REG*, 65 (1952), 109-115.
——. *Études sur la Religion Romaine*. Rome: 1972.
Bradford Wells, C. *Alexander and the Hellenistic World*. Toronto: 1970.
Bram, J. R. *Ancient Astrology, Theory and Practice, the Mathesis of Firmicius
    Maternus*. Park Ridge: 1975.
Breckenridge, J. "Origins of Roman Republican Portraiture. Relations with
    the Hellenistic World." *ANRW*, I,4 (1973), pp. 826-853.
Bréhier, E. *Les Idées Philosophiques et Religieuses d'Philon d'Alexandrie*.
    3rd ed. Paris: 1950.
——. *Chrysippe et l'Ancien Stoïcisme*. Paris: 1951.
Brelich, A. "Le rôle des rêves dans la conception religieuse du monde en
    Grèce," R. Caillois and G. E. von Grunebaum eds., *Le Rêve et les
    Societés Humaines*. Paris: 1967.
Bridoux, A. *Le Stoïcisme et son Influence*. Paris: 1966.
Briscoe, J. *A Commentary on Livy Books XXXI-XXXIII*. Oxford: 1973.
Bröcker, W. *Theologie der Ilias*. Frankfurt: 1975.
Brommer, F. "Pan." *RE*, Suppl. VIII (1956), 1007.
Brown, T. S. "Timaeus and Diodorus' 11th Book." *AJP*, 73 (1952), 337-355.
——. *Timaeus of Tauromenium*. Berkeley: 1958.
Brunt, P. A. "The Aims of Alexander." *Greece and Rome*, 12 (1965), 205-216.
Bruwaene, M. van den. *Cicéron, De natura deorum*, 1. Brussels: 1970.
Büchsenschütz, B. *Traum und Traumdeutung im Altertum*. Berlin: 1868.
Budde, L. "Das römische Historienrelief I." *ANRW*, I,4 (1973), pp. 800 ff
Buffière, F. *Les Mythes d'Homère et la Pensée Grecque*. Paris: 1956.
Buricks, A. *Peri Tychês. De Ontwikkeling van het Begrip Tyche tot aan de
    Romeinse Tijd Hoofdzakelijk in de Philosophie*. Leiden: 1973.
Burkert, W. *Homo Necans. Interpretationen Altgriechischer Opferriten*.
    Berlin: 1972.
——. *Lore and Science in Ancient Pythagoreanism*. Cambridge: 1970.
Burr, V. "Rom und Judäa im 1.Jahrhundert v. Chr." *ANRW*, I,1 (1972),
    pp. 875-886.
Buschor, E. *Das Porträt*. Munich: 1960.
Calderone, W. "Superstitio." *ANRW*, I,2 (1972), pp. 97-420.
Carney, T. F. "The Changing Picture of Marius in Ancient Literature."
    PACA, 10 (1967), 5-22.
Clegg, J. S. "Plato's Vision of Chaos." *CQ*, 26 (1976), 52-62.
Carr, E. H. *What is History*. London: 1961.
Cizak, E. *L'Époque de Néron et ses Controverses Idéologiques*. Leiden: 1972.
Christ-Schmid, W. *Geschichte der Griechischen Literatur*. 6th ed. Munich: 1920.
Clerc, C. *Les Théories Relatives au Culte des Images*. Paris: 1915. Also printed
    as "Plutarque et le culte des images." *Rev. de l'Hist. des Rel.*, 70 (1914),
    8-124.
Cramer, F. H. *Astrology in Roman Law and Politics*. Philadelphia: 1954.
Cornell, T. J. "Aeneas and the Twins: The Development of the Roman
    Foundation Legend." *Proc. Camb. Philol. Soc.*, 21 (1975), 1-33.

Courcelle, P. "La plaine de vérité Platon, Phèdre 248b." *Emerita*, 37 (1969), 119-203.
Crombie, I. M. *An Examination of Plato's Doctrines*. 2 vols. London: 1962.
Cumont, F. *The Mysteries of Mithra* (reprint of translation from 2nd revised ed. of 1902). New York: 1956.

Del Corno, D. *Graecorum de re onirocritica scriptorum reliquiae*. Milan: 1969. (*Test. e Doc. per lo Stud. dell' Ant.* 26).
Des Places, E. *La Religion Grecque*. Paris: 1969.
Detienne, M. "Xénocrate et la démonologie pythagoricienne." *REG*, 60 (1958), 271-279.
———. *La Notion de Daimon dans le Pythagorisme Ancien*. Paris: 1963.
Dicks, D. R. *Early Greek Astronomy to Aristotle*. London: 1970.
Dietrich, B. C. *The Origins of Greek Religion*. Berlin: 1974.
Dihle, A. *Studien zur Griechischen Biographie*. Göttingen: 1956.
Dodds, E. R. *The Greeks and the Irrational*. Berkeley: 1951.
———. *Proclus: The Elements of Theology*. Oxford: 1963.
———. *Christian and Pagan in an Age of Anxiety*. Cambridge: 1964.
Dorey, T. A., ed. *Latin Historians*. London: 1966.
———. *Latin Biography*. London: 1967.
Dörrie, H. "Der Platoniker Eudoros von Alexandreia." *Hermes*, 79 (1944), 25-38.
———. "Zum Ursprung der neuplatonischen Hypostasenlehre." *Hermes*, 82 (1954), 331-343.
———. "Emanation." *Parusia*, ed. K. Flasch, Frankfurt: 1965, 119-141.
———. "Xenokrates." XI, A 2 (1967), 1512-1528.
———. "Die Erneuerung des Platonismus im ersten Jahrhundert vor Christus." *Act. du Coll. Royaumont* (Paris: 1971), 17-33.
———. "Le renouveau du Platonisme à l'époque de Cicéron." *Rev. de Théol. et de Philos.*, 24 (1974), 1-29.
———. "Logos-Religion? Oder Nous-Theologie? Die hauptsächlichen Aspekte des kaiserzeitlichen Platonismus." *Kephalaion* (Vogel Festschrift). Assen: 1975. pp. 115-136.
———. *Platonica Minora. Kleine Schriften zum Platonismus*. Munich: 1976.
Droysen, J. G. *Geschichte des Hellenismus*. 3rd ed. Basle: 1952.
Dugas, C. and R. Flacelière. *Thésée: Images et Récits*. Paris: 1958.
Dumézil, G. *La Religion Romaine Archaïque*. Paris: 1966; trs. as *Archaic Roman Religion*. Chicago: 1970.
———. *Mythe et Épopée*. Paris: 1968.
———. *Idées Romaines*. Paris: 1969.
Dunand, F. *Le Culte d'Isis*. Leiden: 1973.
Dupont-Sommer, A. "Pompée le Grand et les romains dans les manuscrits de la Mer Morte." *MEFRA*, 84 (1972), 879-901.
Düring, I. *Aristoteles*. Heidelberg: 1966.
Dyer, R. R. "The Evidence for Apollinine Purification Ritual at Delphi and Athens." *JHS*, 89 (1969), 38-56.

Earl, D. C. *Tiberius Gracchus*. Brussels: 1963.
Easterling, H. J. "Causation in the Timaeus and Laws X." *Eranos*, 65 (1967), 25-38.
Edelstein, L. *The Meaning of Stoicism*. Cambridge, Mass: 1966.
———. and Kidd, I. *Posidonius of Apamea*. Cambridge: 1972.
Ehrenberg, V. "Sparta: Geschichte." *RE*, II A (1929), 1374-1452.
———. "Nabis." *RE*, XXI (1935), 1471-1482.

——. *The Greek State*. (Transl. of 2nd German ed. Zurich, 1965). London: 1969.

Errington, R. M. *Philopoemen*. Oxford: 1969.

Escudero, C. "Mito y filosofia. El mito platonico y su significado." *Perficit*, 1 (1968), 243-345.

Evans, E. C. "The Study of Physiognomy in the Second Century A.D." *TAPA*, 72 (1941), 96-108.

——. "Physiognomies in the Ancient World." *TAPA*, 59 (1969), 46-58.

Fahr, W. *Theous Nomizein. Zum Problem der Anfänge des Atheismus bei den Griechen*. Hildesheim: 1970.

Ferguson, J. *The Religions of the Roman Empire*. London: 1970.

Festugière, A. J. *L'Idéal Religieux des Grecs et L'Évangile*. Paris: 1932.

——. *La Révélation d'Hermès Trismégiste*: I, *L'astrologie et les sciences occultes* (Paris: 1944); II, *Le dieu cosmique* (1949); III, *Les doctrines de l'âme* (1953); IV, *Le dieu inconnu et la gnose* (1954).

——. *Personal Religion among the Greeks*. Berkeley: 1960.

——. *Études de Religion Grecque et Hellénistique*. Paris: 1972.

Finley, M. I. *A History of Sicily to the Arab Conquest*. London: 1968.

Flacelière, R. *Les Aitoliens à Delphes*. Paris: 1937.

——. with P. Devambez. *Héracles: Images et Récits*. Paris: 1966.

——. "Hadrien et Delphes." *CRAI* (1971), 168-185.

Fontana, M. J. "Fortuna di Timoleonte, Rassegna delle fonti litterarie." *Kokalos*, 4 (1958), 3-23.

Fontenrose, J. A. *Python, A Study of Delphic Myth and its Origins*. Berkeley: 1959.

Forrest, W. G. *The Emergence of Greek Democracy*. London: 1966.

——. *A History of Sparta, 950-192 B.C.* London: 1968.

Forster, W. "Daimon." *Theol. Wörterbuch zum N.T.* G. Kittel, ed., Stuttgart: 1935. II, pp. 1-9.

Forte, B. *Rome and the Romans as the Greeks Saw Them*. Rome: 1972.

Frazer, R. M. "Nero, the Singing Animal." *Arethusa*, 4 (1971), 215-218.

Fritz, K. von. "Philippos." XIX,2 (1938), 2355-2356.

——. *Die Griechische Geschichtsschreibung*. Berlin: 1967- .

——. Review of A. Dihle, *Studien zur Griechischen Biographie. Gnomon*. 28, (1956), 326-332.

Friedländer, P. "Daimon" in *Platon*, I (3rd ed.). Berlin: 1964.

Friedrich, W. H. "Caesar und Sein Glück." *Festschrift J. Kapp*. Munich: 1954, 1-24.

Frisch, Pl. *Die Traüme bei Herodot*. Meisenheim: 1968. (*Beiträge z. Klass. Phil.* 27).

Frösen, J. *Prolegomena to a Study of the Greek Language in the First Century A.D. The Problem of Koiné and Atticism*. Helsinki: 1974.

Frost, F. *Greek Society*. Lexington: 1971.

Fuhrmann, F. *Les Images de Plutarch*. Paris: 1964.

Fuks, A. "Redistribution of Land and Houses in Syracuse in 356 B.C., and its Ideological Aspects." *CQ*, 18 (1968), 207-223.

Gabba, E. "Mario e Silla." *ANRW*, I,1 (1972), pp. 764-805.

Gage, J. *Apollon Romain*. Brussels: 1963.

Gadamer, H. *Kleine Schriften*. Tübingen: 1972.

Gelzer, M. *Caesar: Politician and Statesman* (trs.). Oxford: 1968.

——. *Cicero*. Wiesbaden: 1969.

Gerstinger, H. "Biographie." *Reallexikon für Antike und Christentum*, II (1954), pp. 386-391.

Gigon, O. "Prolegomena to an Edition of the *Eudemus*," in *Aristotle and Plato in the Mid-Fourth Century*, I. Düring, G. E. L. Owen, eds. Goteborg: 1960, 19-33.
——. and C. Andresen. "Biographie." *Lexikon der Alten Welt*. (1965), pp. 469-473.
——. and V. Pöschl. "Autobiographie." *Lexikon der Alten Welt*. (1965), pp. 414-417.
Gomme, A. W. *A Historical Commentary on Thucydides*. Oxford: 1945-1970 (IV with Andrewes and Dover, 4 vols.)
Gomme, A. W. and F. H. Sandbach. *Menander. A Commentary*. Oxford: 1973.
Gould, J. *The Philosophy of Chrysippus*. Leiden: 1970.
Gräser, A. *Probleme der Platonischen Seelenteilungslehre*. Munich: 1969.
Greene, W. C. *Moira. Fate, Good, and Evil in Greek Thought*. Cambridge, Mass.: 1948.
Griffith, G. T. "The Macedonian Background." *Greece and Rome*, 12 (1965), 125-140.
——. *Alexander the Great: the Main Problems* (reprint of various articles). Cambridge (Heffers): 1966.
Griffiths, J. G. "Allegory in Greece and Egypt." *JEA*, 53 (1967), 79-102.
——. *The Divine Tribunal*. Swansea: 1975.
Grillone, A. *Il Sogno nell' Epica Latina Tecnica e Poesia*. Palermo: 1968.
Grimal, P. *Dictionaire de la Mythologie Grecque et Romaine*. Paris: 1951/1969.
——. *Le Siècle des Scipions*. Paris: 1974.
Grodzynski, D. "Superstitio." *REA*, 76 (1974), 36-60.
Gullini, G. "Il santuario della Fortuna Primigenia a Palestrina." *ANRW*, I,4 (1973), pp. 746-799.
Gundel, W. and H. *Astrologumena*. Wiesbaden: 1966.
Guthrie, W. K. C. *The Greeks and Their Gods*. London: 1950.
——. *Orpheus and Greek Religion*. London: 1952.
——. "Plato's View on the Nature of the Soul." *Fondation Hardt*. Geneva: 1955, 3-25.
——. *In the Beginning: some Greeks views on the origins of life and the early state of man*. London: 1957.
——. *A History of Greek Philosophy, I-IV*. (Cambridge: 1962-1975)

Hamilton, J. R. "Alexander's Early Life." *Greece and Rome*, 12 (1965), 117-125.
Hammond, N. G. L. "The Sources of Diodorus Siculus." *CQ*, 32 (1938), 137-151.
——. *A History of Greece*. 2nd ed. Oxford: 1967.
Hani, J. "La consolation antique." *REA*, 75 (1973), 43-81.
Heinze, R. *Untersuchungen*. Berlin: 1872.
——. *Xenokrates*. Leipzig: 1892.
Herter, H. "Theseus." *RE*, Suppl. XIII, (1973), 1046-1238.
——. "Theseus." *Platon*, 25 (1973), 3-13.
Herzog-Hauser, G. "Tyche." *RE*, Hlbd. 14 (1948), 1643-1689.
Heurgon, J. *Rome et la Méditerranée Occidentale jusq'au Guerres Puniques*. Paris: 1969.
Heyob, S. K. *The Cult of Isis among Women in the Graeco-Roman World*. Leiden: 1975.
Hiesinger, U. "Portraiture in the Roman Republic." *ANRW* I,4 (1973) ,pp. 805-825.

Hignett, C. *Xerxes' Invasion of Greece*. Oxford: 1963.
Hinnels, J. *Mithraic Studies*. Manchester: 1973.
Hirzel, R. *Der Dialog*. Leipzig: 1895.
Homeyer, H. *Die Antiken Berichte über den Tod Ciceros und ihre Quellen*. Baden Baden: 1964.
——. "Zu den Anfängen der griechischen Biographie." *Philologus*, 106 (1962), 75-85.
——. "Ciceros Tod im Urteil der Nachwelt." *Altertum*, 17 (1971), 165-174.
Horst, P. C. van der. "*Daimon*" *Mn.*, 3 (1942), 65.
Hornbostel, W. *Sarapis*. Leiden: 1973.
Hundt, J. *Der Traumglaube bei Homer*. Greifswald: 1935.

Janssens, L. "Die Bedeutungsentwicklung von *superstitio/superstes*." *Mn.*, 28 (1975), 135-189.
Jones, R. "Posidonius and Solar Eschatology." *Class. Phil.*, 27 (1932), 113-131.
Jouget, P. *L'Impérialisme Macédonien et l'Hellénisation de l'Orient*. Paris: 1972.

Kagan, D. *Studies in the Greek Historians*. Cambridge: 1975.
Kerényi, C. *The Religion of the Greeks and Romans*. London: 1962.
——. *Humanistische Seelenforschung*. Munich-Vienna: 1966.
Kern, O. *Orphicorum Fragmenta*. Berlin: 1922, 2nd ed., 1963.
Kirk, G. S. and Raven, J. E. *The Presocratic Philosophers*. Cambridge: 1966. (Reprint of 1960 corrected edition of 1957 edition).
Kirk, G. S. *Heraclitus, The Cosmic Fragments*. Cambridge: 1962.
——. *Myth. Its Meaning and Function in Ancient and Other Cultures*. Cambridge: 1970.
——. "Aetiology, Ritual, Charter: Three Equivocal Terms in the Study of Myths." *Yale Cl. Stud.*, 22 (1972), 83-102.
——. *The Nature of Greek Myths*. Hammondsworth: 1974.
Klauser, T. ed. *Reallexikon für Antike und Christentum*, 68-69. Stuttgart: 1974. "Geister-Dämonen": Alter Orient u. Agypten, 553-562 (C. Dolpe); Mesopotamien, Syrien, Kleinasien, 562-585 (J. Maier); Iran, 585-598 (C. Colpe); Vorhellenistische Griechenland, 598-615 (J. ter Vrugt-Lentz), Östliche Mittelmeer seit dem 4/3 Jr. v. C. (J. Maier), Hellenistische u. kaiserzeitliche Philosophie, 640-667 (C. Zintzen); Talmudisches Judentum, 667-688 (J. Maier); Neues Testament, 688-700 (E. Schweizer); Griechische Väter, 700-715 (A. Kollis); Apologeten u. lateinische Väter, 715-761 (P. G. van der Nat); Volksglaube, 761-797 (C. D. G. Müller).
Klees, H. *Die Eigenart des Griechischen Glaubens an Orakel und Seher*. Stuttgart: 1965.
Koch, C. *Religio, Studien zu Kult und Glauben der Römer*. Nurnberg: 1960.
Koets, P. J. *Deisidaimonia*. Utrecht: 1929.
Konstans, K. *Some Aspects of Epicurean Psychology*. Leiden: 1973.
Kosmala, H. "Nachfolge und Nachahmung Gottes. I: Im griechischen Denken." *Annual of the Swedish Theological Institute* 2 (1963), 38-85.
Krämer, H. J. *Der Ursprung der Geistmetaphysik. Untersuchungen zur Geschichte des Platonismus zwischen Platon und Plotin*. Amsterdam: 1964.
——. *Platonismus und Hellenistische Philosophie*. Berlin: 1971.
Krauss, F. B. *An Interpretation of the Omens, Portents and Prodigies Recorded by Livy, Tacitus, and Suetonius*. Philadelphia: 1930.

Kroymann, J. "Phylarchos." *RE*, Suppl. VIII (1956), 484-485.
Kurt, E. *Gnosis und Gnostizismus*. Darmstadt: 1975.
Kurtz, D. and J. Boardman. *Greek Burial Customs*. London: 1970.

Laffranque, M. *Poseidonios d'Apamée*. Paris: 1964.
Laistner, M. L. W. *The Greater Roman Historians*. Berkeley: 1963.
Laqueur, R. "Timaios." *RE*, VI A (1936), 1076-1203.
Latte, K. *Römische Religionsgeschichte*. Munich: 1960.
——. *Kleine Schriften zu Religion, Recht, Literatur und Sprache der Griechen und Römer*. Munich: 1968.
Leach, E. ed. *The Structural Study of Myth and Totemism*. London: 1967.
LeGall, J. *La Religion Romaine de l'Époque de Caton l'Ancient au Règne de l'Empereur Commode*. Paris: 1973.
LeGlay, M. *La Religion Romaine*. Paris: 1971.
Lehmann, G. A. "Dion and Herakleides." *Historia*, 19 (1970), 401-406.
Lemke, D. *Die Theologie Epicurs. Versuch einer Rekonstruktion*. Munich: 1973.
Lennig, R. *Traum und Sinnestäuschung bei Aischylos, Sophokles, Euripides*. Diss. Tübingen: 1969.
Leo, F. *Die Griechisch-Römische Biographie*. Leipzig: 1901.
Levèque, P. *Pyrrhos*. Paris: 1957.
Lévi-Strauss, C. *The Savage Mind*. London: 1966.
——. *From Honey to Ashes* (transl. of *Du Miel aux Cendres*), New York: 1973.
Lewis, N. *The Interpretation of Dreams and Portents*. Toronto: 1975.
Liedmeyer, C. *Aemilius Paulus*. Utrecht: 1935.
Lieshout, R. van. "A Dream on a *kairos* of History. An Analysis of Herodotos, Hist. VII, 12-19; 47. *Mn.*, 23 (1970), 225-249.
Linforth, I. *The Arts of Orpheus*. Berkeley: 1941.
Lloyd, G. E. R. *Polarity and Analogy*. Cambridge: 1966.
——. *Aristotle, the Growth and Structure of his Thought*. Cambridge: 1968.
Lloyd-Jones, H. *The Justice of Zeus*. Berkeley: 1971.
Long, A. A. "Aristotle's Legacy to Stoic Ethics." *BICS*, 15 (1968), 72-85. "The Stoic Concept of Evil." *PQ*, 18 (1968), 329-43.
——. *Hellenistic Philosophy. Stoics, Epicureans, Sceptics*. London: 1974.

Marg, W. Review of Frisch, *Die Traüme bei Herodot. Gnom.*, 42 (1970), 515.
Martin, P. "Deux interprétations grecques d'un rituel de l'Italie protohistorique." *REG*, 85 (1972), 281-292.
Maxwell-Stuart, P. G. "The Dramatic Poets and the Expedition to Sicily." *Historia*, 22 (1973), 397-404.
Martini, "Eudoros." *RE*, VI (1909), 915-916.
Mason, H. J. *Greek Terms for Roman Institutions*. Toronto: 1974.
Meier, C. A. "The Dream in Ancient Greece and Its Use in Temple Cures," in Grünebaum, G. E. von, and Caillois, R. ed., *The Dream in Human Societies*. Los Angeles: 1966, 303-19.
Meiggs, R. *The Athenian Empire*. Oxford: 1972.
Meister, K. *Die Sizilische Geschichte bei Diodor von den Anfängen bis zum Tod des Agathokles. Quellenuntersuchungen zu Buch IV-XXI*. Bonn: 1967.
——. "Die sizilische Expedition der Athener bei Timaios." *Gymnasium*, 77 (1970), 508-517.
Merki, H. *Homoiosis Theôi von der Platonischen Angleichung an Gott bis zur Gottähnlichkeit bei Gregor von Nyssa*. Freiburg: 1952.
Merlan, P. "Monismus und Dualismus bei einigen Platonikern." *Parusia*, ed. K. Flasch. Frankfurt: 1965.

——. "*The Later Academy and Platonism.*" *Cambridge History of Later Greek and Early Medieval Philosophy.* Cambridge: 1967, 53-64.

Mesnil du Buisson, R. *Études sur les Dieux Phéniciens Hérités par L'Empire Romain.* Leiden: 1970.

Mess, A. von. "Die Anfänge der Biographie und der psychologischen Geschichtsschreibung in der griechischen Literatur." *Rh. Mus.*, 70 (1915), 337 ff; 81 (1916), 79 ff.

Michenaud, G. and J. Dierkens. *Les Rêves dans les 'Discours Sacrés' d'Aelius Aristide.* Mons: 1972.

Molé, M. *Culte, Mythe et Cosmologie dans l'Iran Ancien.* Paris: 1963.

Momigliano, A. *The Development of Greek Biography.* Cambridge, Mass.: 1971.

——. *Second Thoughts on Greek Biography.* Amsterdam: 1971.

——. *Alien Wisdom.* Cambridge: 1976.

Mooren, G. *Perikles.* Nijmegen: 1948.

Moreau, J. *L'Âme du Monde de Platon aux Stoïciens.* Paris: 1959.

Morrison, J. S. "Parmenides and Er." *JHS*, 75 (1955), 59-68.

Moulinier, L. *Orphée et l'Orphisme à l'Époque Classique.* Paris: 1955.

Mylonas, G. *Eleusis and the Eleusinian Mysteries.* Princeton: 1961.

Narain, A. K. *The Indo-Greeks.* Oxford: 1959.

——. "Alexander and India." *Greece and Rome*, 12 (1965), 155-166.

Nederlof, A. *Pyrrhus.* Amsterdam: 1940.

Nilsson, M. *Geschichte der Griechischen Religion*, I, Munich: 1940 (3rd ed. 1967); II, 1950, (2nd ed. 1961).

Nock, A. D. *Essays on Relgion and the Ancient World.* Oxford: 1972.

Nowak, H. *Zur Entwicklungsgeschichte des Begriffes Daimon.* (Diss. Bonn: 1960).

O'Brien, D. A. "The Relation of Anaxagoras and Empedocles." *JHS*, 88 (1968), 93-114.

——. "Derived Light and Eclipses in the 4th Century." *JHS*, 88 (1968), 114-128.

——. *Empedocles' Cosmic Cycle.* Cambridge: 1969.

Ogilvie, R. M. *A Commentary on Livy. Books 1-.5* Oxford: 1965.

——. *The Romans and Their Gods.* London: 1969.

Olshausen, E. "Mithridates VI und Rom." *ANRW*, I,1 (1972), pp. 806-815.

Osley, A. S. "Greek Biography before Plutarch." *Greece and Rome*, 15 (1946), 7-20.

Otto, W. F. *The Homeric Gods.* London: 1955.

——. *Die Manen.* (2nd ed.) Darmstadt: 1958.

——. *Aufsätze zur Römischen Religionsgeschichte.* Meisenheim: 1975.

Pack, R. Review of D. Del Corno, *Graecorum de re onirocritica scriptorum reliquiae*, *Gnom.*, 42 (1970), 833-34.

Pallotino, M. "Le origini di Roma: considerazioni critiche sulle scoperte e sulle discussioni più recenti. *ANRW* I,1 (1972), pp. 22-47.

Palmer, R. E. *The Archaic Community of the Romans.* Cambridge: 1970.

——. *Roman Religion and the Roman Empire.* Philadelphia: 1974.

Paratore, L. "La problematica sull' epicureismo a Roma." *ANRW*, I,4 (1973), pp. 116-204.

Parke, H. W. and Wormell, D. E. *The Delphic Oracle*, 2 vols. Oxford: 1956.

Pastorino, A. *La Religione Romana.* Milan: 1973.

Passerini, A. *Caio Mario.* (rev.) Milan: 1971.

Pavan, M. "Due discorsi di Lucio Emilio Paolo." *Stud. Rom.*, 9 (1961), 593-613.
Pépin, J. *Mythe et Allégorie.* Paris: 1958.
——. *Idées Grecques sur L'Homme et sur Dieu.* Paris: 1971.
Peters, F. E. *The Harvest of Hellenism.* New York: 1970.
Petzold, K. E. *Studien zur Methode des Polybios und zu ihrer Historischen Auswertung.* Munich: 1969.
Piatti, C. ed. *DTV Lexikon der Antike: Religion und Mythologie.* Munich: 1970.
Podlecki, A. *The Life of Themistocles, A Critical Survey of the Literary and Archaeological Evidence.* Toronto: 1975.
Pohlenz, M. *Vom Zorne Gottes.* Göttingen: 1909.
——. *Die Stoa.* Göttingen: 1948 (4th ed. 1972).
——. *Kleine Schriften.* H. Dörrie, ed., Hildesheim: 1965.
Pollard, J. *Seers, Shrines, and Sirens. The Greek Revolution in the 6th Cent. B.C.* London: 1965.
Porter, W. H. *The Life of Dion.* Dublin: 1952.
Poucet, J. "Les Sabins aux origines de Rome." *ANRW*, I,1 (1972), 48-135.
Preller, L. and C. Robert. *Griechische Mythologie.* Berlin: 1894-1926/rpt. 1964.

Rademacher, L. *Mythos und Sage bei den Griechen.* (rpt. of 1943 ed.) Darmstadt: 1968.
Raditsa, L. "Bella Macedonica." *ANRW*, I,1 (1972), pp. 564-589.
Rawson, E. "Religion and Politics in the Late Second Century B.C." *Phoenix*, 28 (1974), 193-212.
Rehrenbock, G. : Die orphische Seelenlehre in Platons Kratylos." *Wien. Stud.*, 88 (1975), 18-31.
Reinhardt, K. *Poseidonios.* Munich: 1921.
——. *Kosmos und Sympathie.* Munich: 1926.
Rist, J. *Plotinus, the Road to Reality.* Cambridge: 1968.
——. *Stoic Philosophy.* Cambridge: 1969.
——. *Epicurus, An Introduction.* Cambridge: 1972.
Riverso, E. "Neoplatonismo, neopitagorismo, e magia." *Rassegna di Scienze Fil.*, 18 (1965), 5-26.
Robinson, T. R. *Plato's Psychology.* Toronto: 1970.
Rohde, E. *Psyche.* (Reprint transl. of 8th ed. with intro. by W. K. C. Guthrie). New York: 1966.
Roloff, D. *Gottähnlichkeit, Vergöttlichung und Erhöhung zur Herkunft der Platonischen Angleichung an Gott.* Berlin: 1970.
Roscher, W. *Ausführliches Lexikon der Griechischen und Römischen Mythologie.* Leipzig: 1884-1937/rpt. Hildesheim: 1965.
Rose, H. J. *Religion in Greece and Rome.* New York: 1959 (Reprint of 1946-48 ed. of *Ancient Greek Religion* and *Ancient Roman Religion*).
——. ed *La Notion du Divin depuis Homère jusqu'à Platon*: P. Chantraine, "Le dieu et les dieux chez Homère," B. Snell, "Die Welt der Götter bei Hesiod," O. Gigon, "Die Theologie der Vorsokratiker," H. D. F. Kitto, "The Idea of God in Aeschylus and Socrates," F. Chapouthier, "Euripide et l'accueil du divin," W. J. Verdenius, "Platons Gottesbegriff. Erläuterungen." *Fondation Hardt.* Geneva: 1954.
Rossbach, O. *Fonti su Caio Mario.* Milan: 1971.
Rougemont, G. "La hieroménie des Pythia et les trèves sacrées d'Éleusis, de Delphes et d'Olympie." *BCH*, 97 (1973), 75-106.

Rougier, L. *La Religion Astrale des Pythagoriciens*. Paris: 1959.
Rowe, C. *Introduction to Greek Ethics*. London: 1976.
Sandbach, F. H. *Menandri Reliquiae Selectae*. Oxford: 1972.
——. *The Stoics*. London: 1975.
Sanctis, G. *Storia dei Romani*. Florence: 1970.
Sarkady, J. "Die Theseus-Sage und die sog. theseische Verfassung." *A. Ant. Hung.*, 17 (1969), 1-10.
Scarborough, J. *Greek Medicine*. Ithaca: 1969.
Schachermeyr, F. *Alexander der Große*. Vienna: 1970.
Schadenwaldt, W. "Humanitas Romana." *ANRW*, I,4 (1973), pp. 43-62.
Schaufer, A. *Frühgriechischer Totenglaube*. Hildesheim: 1970.
——. *Perikles*. Stuttgart: 1969.
Schefold, K. *Römische Kunst als Religiöses Phänomen*. Hamburg: 1964.
——. "Caesars Epoche als goldene Zeit römischer Kunst." *ANRW*, I,4 (1973), pp. 944-969.
Schilling, R. "La situation des études relatives à la religion romaine de la république (1950-1970)." *ANRW*, I,2 (1972), pp. 317-347.
——. *La Religion Romaine de Vénus depuis les Origines jusqu'au Temps d'Auguste*. Paris: 1954.
——. "La vision de la religion romaine par Georges Dumézil." *REA*, 70 (1968), 83-91.
——. *The Roman Religion*. Leiden: 1969.
Scholz, U. *Studien zum Altitalischen und Altrömischen Marskult und Marsmythos*. Heidelberg: 1970.
Schneider, C. *Kulturgeschichte des Hellenismus*. I. Munich: 1967; II: 1969.
Schröder, H. O. "Fatum." *Reallexicon f. Antike und Christentum*, fasc. 52 (1967), 533-555.
Scott, R. T. *Religion and Philosophy in the Histories of Tacitus*. Rome: 1968.
Scott, W. *Hermetica*. 4 vols. Oxford: 1924, (rpt. 1968).
Seager, R. *Tiberius*. London: 1972.
Seikert, H. *Alexander der Große*. Darmstadt: 1972.
Sevenster, J. N. *The Roots of Pagan Antisemitism in the Ancient World*. Leiden: 1975.
Sixoo, A. "Autobiographie." *Reallex. f. Antike und Christentum*. I (1950) pp. 1050-1055.
Skovgard, J. S. *Dualism and Demonology, The Function of Demonology in Pythagorean and Platonic Thought*. Copenhagen: 1966.
Smallwood, M. *The Jews under Roman Rule*. Leiden: 1976.
Sokolowski, F. "Propagation of the Cult of Sarapis and Isis in Greece." *GRBS*, 15 (1974), 441-448.
Stallmach, J. *Ate. Zur Frage des Selbst und Weltverständnisses des Frühgriechischen Menschen*. Meisenheim: 1968. (*Beiträge zur klass. Philol.* 18).
Stambaugh, J. E. *Sarapis under the Early Ptolemies*. Leiden: 1972.
Starr, C. G. "The Roman Place in History." *ANRW*, I,1 (1972), pp. 3-11.
Stearns, J. B. *Studies of the Dream as a Technical Device in Latin Epic and Drama*. (Diss. Princeton: 1927).
Ste. Croix, G. E. M. de "The Religion of the Roman World." *Didaskalos*, 4 (1972), 61-74.
——. *Class Struggle in the Ancient World*. London: 1976.
Steidle, W. *Sueton und die Antike Biographie*. Munich: 1951.
Steiner, H. R. *Der Traum in der Aeneis*. *Noctes Romanae*, 5. Bern: 1952.
Strachan, J. C. G. "Who Did Forbid Suicide at *Phaedo* 626?" *CQ*, 20 (1970), 216-220.

Strohm, H. *Tyche. Zur Schicksalsauffassung bei Pindar und den Früh-griechischen Dichtern.* Stuttgart: 1944.
Stuart, D. R. *Epochs of Greek and Roman Biography.* Berkeley: 1928.
Syme, R. *The Roman Revolution.* Oxford: 1939.
Szemler, G. J. *The Priests of the Roman Republic.* Brussels: 1972.

Talbert, R. *Timoleon and the Revival of Greek Sicily, 344-317 B.C.* Cambridge: 1974.
Tcherikover, V. *Hellenistic Civilization and the Jews.* Philadelphia: 1959.
Temporini, H. ed. *Aufstieg und Niedergang der Römischen Welt,* Berlin: 1972- (abbrev. as *ANRW*).
Theiler, W. *Die Vorbereitung des Neuplatonismus.* Berlin: 1934/rpt. Zurich: 1964.
———. "Gott und Seele im Kaiserzeitlichen Denken." Fondation *Hardt.* Geneva: 1955, 65-91.
Thraede, K. "Euhemerismus." *Reallex. f. Antike und Christentum,* VI, (1966), pp. 881-882.
———. "Exorcismus." *Reallex. f. Antike und Christentum,* VII, (1969), pp. 44-117.
Thesleff, H. *An Introduction to the Pythagorean Writings of the Hellenistic Period.* Aabo: 1961.
Thornton, M. K. "Hadrian and his Reign." *ANRW* II,2 (1975), pp. 432-476.
Tram Tam Tinh, V. "*Le Culte des Divinités Orientales à Herculaneum.* Leiden: 1971.
Treu, M. "Biographie und Historie bei Polybios." *Historia,* 3 (1954), 219-228.
Tsekourakis, D. *Studies in the Terminology of Early Stoic Ethics.* Wiesbaden: 1974.
Turcan, R. *Les Sarcophages Romains à Représentations Dionysiaques.* Paris: 1966.
———. *Mithras Platonicus. Recherches sur l'Hellénisation Philosophique de Mithra.* Leiden: 1975.

Ueberweg, F. Revised by K. Praechter. *Grundriss der Geschichte der Philosophie I: Die Philosophie des Altertums.* (12th ed.) Berlin: 1926.

Verbeke, G. *L'Évolution de la Doctrine du Pneuma du Stoïcisme à St. Augustin.* Paris: 1945.
———. "Le stoïcisme, une philosophie sans frontières. *ANRW,* I,4 (1973), pp. 3-42.
Vollenweider, M. L. "Der Traum des Sulla Felix." *SNR,* 39 (1958-9), 22-34.

Weidhorn, M. "Dreams and Guilt," *Harv. Theol. Rev.,* 68 (1965), 69-90.
Westlake, H. D. *Essays on the Greek Historians and Greek History.* Manchester: 1969.
Wetzel, J. G. *Quomodo poetae Graeci et Romani somnia descripserint.* Diss. Berlin: 1931.
White, R. J. *The Interpretation of Dreams. The Oneirocritica of Artemidorus.* Park Ridge: 1975.
Whittaker, C. R. "The Delphic Oracle." *Harv. Theol. Rev.,* 58 (1965), 21-47.
Whittaker, J. *Parmenides.* Oslo: 1971.
Wichmann, O. *Platon.* Darmstadt: 1966.
Wilamowitz-Moellendorff, U. von. *Der Glaube der Hellenen.* 2 vols. Berlin: 1931-32.
Will, E. "Sur la nature du pneuma delphique." *BCH,* 56-57 (1942-3), 161-75.

——. *Histoire Politique du Monde Hellénistique*. I. Nancy: 1966. II, 1967.
——. *Le Monde Grec et l'Orient*. 1. *Le Ve Siècle (510-403)*. Paris: 1972.
Winkes, R. "Physiognomonia, Probleme der Charakterinterpretationen römischer Porträte." *ANRW*, I,4 (1973), pp. 899-926.
Wirth, G. *Alexander der Große in Selbtzeugnissen und Bilddokumenten*. Hamburg: 1973.
Wissowa, G. *Religion und Kultus der Römer*. 2nd ed. Munich: 1912.
Witt, R. E. *Isis in the Graeco-Roman World*. Ithaca: 1971.
Wolbergs, T. *Griechische Religiöse Gedichte der ersten Nachchristlichen Jahrhunderte*. Meisenheim: 1971.
Woods, R. L. and H. B. Greenhouse. *The New World of Dreams. An Anthology*. New York: 1974.

Zaehner, R. C. *The Dawn and Twilight of Zoroastrianism*. London: 1961.
Zeller, E. *Die Philosophie der Griechen* II, 1 (4th ed.) Leipzig: 1889. III, 2 (4th ed.) Leipzig: 1909.
Zintzen, C. "Geister (Dämonen)." *Reallexikon f. Antike und Christentum*, 68-69. Stuttgart: 1974. pp. 640-668.

There have been some works which were seen too late to be included in the bibliography or have been overlooked. It seems worthwhile to mention them here:

Babut, D. "*Historia hoion hyle philosophias*. Histoire et réflexion morale dans l'oeuvre de Plutarque." *REG*, 88 (1975), 206-219.
Baltes, M. *Die Weltentstehung des Platonischen Timaios nach den Antiken Interpreten*. Leiden: 1976.
Conomis, N. C. "Plutarchea II." *Philtra*. (Kapsomenos Festschrift) Thessalonika: 1975, pp. 73-86.
Devereux, G. *Dreams in Greek Tragedy, an Ethno-Psycho-Analytic Study*. Berkeley: 1976.
Ferrarese, P. "Caratteri della tradizione antipericlea nella Vita di Pericle de Plutarco." M. Sordi, ed. *Storiografia e Propaganda*. Milan: 1975, pp. 21-30.
Flacelière, R. "La lune selon Plutarque." P. Ducrey et al., ed. *Melanges à Collart*. Paris: 1976, pp. 193-195.
Fuscagni, S. "Callistene di Olinto e la Vita di Pelopida di Plutarco." *Storiografia e Propaganda*. Milan: 1975, pp. 31-55.
Gärtner, H. *Bibliographie Konrat Ziegler*. 1963-1974. Munich: 1974.
Gianfrancesco, L. "Un frammento sofistico nella Vita di Teseo di Plutarco." *Storiografia e Propaganda*. Milan: 1975, pp. 7-20.
Halliday, R. *The Greek Questions of Plutarch*. Oxford: 1928, rpt. New York: 1975.
Hani, J. "Le mythe de Timarque chez Plutarque et la structure de l'extase." *REG*, 88 (1975), 105-120.
Hengel, M. *Judentum und Hellenismus*. Tübingen: 1968/1973. (transl. as *Judaism and Hellenism*. Philadelphia: 1974).
——, *Juden, Griechen und Barbaren. Aspekte der Hellenisierung des Judentums in Vorchristlicher Zeit*. Stuttgart: 1976.
Jenkinson, E. M. "Cornelius Nepos and Biography at Rome." *ANRW*, I, 3 (1973), pp. 702-719.

Jouanna, J. "Plutarque et la patine des statues à Delphes (Sur les oracles de la Pythie, 395B-396C)." *Rev. Phil.*, 49 (1975), 127-129.

Kessissoglu, A. I. "Plutarch. v. Galbae 7, 5." *Hermes*, 103 (1975), 127-128.

Kragelund, P. *Dream and Prediction in the Aeneid. A Semiotic Interpretation of the Dreams of Aeneas and Turnus.* Copenhagen: 1976.

Krause, J. *Allote allos. Untersuchungen zum Motiv des Schicksalswechsels in der Griechischen Dichtung bis Euripides.* Munich: 1976.

O'Sullivan, J. N. "On Plutarch Moralia 431 E-F (De defectu oraculorum 39)." *AJP*, 96 (1975), 269-270.

Perez-Jimenez, A. "Actitudes del hombre frente a la Tyche en las 'Vidas paralelas' de Plutarco," *Bol. del Inst. de Estud. Helen.*, 7 (1973), 101-110.

Russell, D. A. "Plutarch." *Oxford Classical Dictionary.* Oxford: 1970, pp. 848-850.

Smallwood, M. *The Jews under Roman Rule. From Pompey to Diocletian.* Leiden: 1976.

Solmsen, F. "Beyond the Heavens." *Mus. Helv.*, 33 (1976), 24-32.

Stadter, P. "A Match for Alcestis; Plutarch Mor. 243d." *CQ*, 25 (1976), 157-158.

——, "Plutarch's Comparison of Pericles and Fabius Maximus." *GRBS*, 16 (1975), 77-85.

Vasmanoles, G. E. "*Paratereseis eis Ploutarchou Aristeiden.*" *Platon*, 27 (1975), 153-161.

Wallis, R. T. *Neoplatonism.* New York: 1972.

Ziegler, K. "Plutarchos." *Der Kleine Pauly.* IV. Munich: 1972, pp. 946-954.

The first volume of *Plutarch's Theological Writings and Early Christian Literature*, H. D. Betz, ed. (*Studia ad Corpus Hellenisticum Novi Testamenti* III; series eds. H. D. Betz, G. Delling, W. C. Van Unnik. Leiden: 1975) contains the following individual studies: M. Smith, "De Superstitione (Moralia 164E-171F)," pp. 1-35; H. D. Betz and E. W. Smith, Jr., "De Iside et Osiride (Moralia 351C-384C)," pp. 36-84; H. D. Betz and E. W. Smith, Jr., "De E apud Delphos (Moralia 384C-394C)," pp. 85-102; W. G. Rollins, "De Pythiae oraculis (Moralia 394D-409D)," pp. 103-130; K. O'Brien Wicker, "De defectu oraculorum (Moralia 409E-438E)," pp. 131-181; H. D. Betz, P. A. Dirkse, and E. W. Smith, Jr., "De sera numinis vindicta (Moralia 548A-568A)," pp. 181-235; D. A. Stoike, "De genio Socratis (Moralia 275A-598F)," pp. 236-285; W. A. Beardslee, "De facie quae in orbe lunae apparet (Moralia 920A-945D)," pp. 286-300; D. E. Aune, "De esu carnium orationes I and II (Moralia 993A-999B),"; pp. 301-316; H. D. Betz, "Fragmenta 21-23, 157-158, 176-178," pp. 317-325.

I have been unable to see Y. Vernière, *Mythes et Symboles dans la Pensée de Plutarque.* Paris: 1977.

INDEX OF SUBJECTS AND ANCIENT NAMES

INDEX OF MODERN AUTHORS